D0407831

TAXATION AND TAX POLICIES IN THE MIDDLE EAST

Butterworths Studies in International Political Economy will present new work, from a multinational stable of authors, on major issues, theoretical and practical, in the international political economy.

General Editor

Susan Strange, Professor of International Relations, London School of Economics and Political Science, England

Consulting Editors

Ladd Hollist, Director, Program for International Political Economy Research, University of Southern California, USA

Karl Kaiser, Director, Research Institute of the German Society for Foreign Affairs, Bonn, and Professor of Political Science, University of Cologne, West Germany

William Leohr, Graduate School of International Studies, University of Denver, USA

Joseph Nye, Professor of Government, Harvard University, USA

Published Titles

Economic Issues and Political Conflict: US – Latin American Relations (Domínguez)
The East European Economies in the 1970s (Nove, Höhmann and Seidenstecher)
France in the Troubled World Economy (Cohen and Gourevitch)
The Political Economy of New and Old Industrial Countries (Saunders)

Forthcoming Titles

War, Trade and Regime Formation
Japan and Western Europe: Conflict and Cooperation
Defence, Technology and International Integration
International Political Economy – A Text

Taxation and Tax Policies in the Middle East

Hossein Askari, BS, PhD
George Washington University

John Thomas Cummings, BS, PhD
US–Saudi Arabian Joint Commission
for Economic Cooperation

Michael Glover, BA, MA, MBA
US Department of State

ELMER E. RASMUSON LIBRARY
UNIVERSITY OF Withdrawn
Surplus/Duplicate

HJ
2906
A84
1982

Butterworth Scientific
London Boston Durban Singapore Sydney Toronto Wellington

All rights reserved. No part of this publication may be reproduced
or transmitted in any form or by any means, including
photocopying and recording, without the written permission of the
copyright holder, application for which should be addressed to the
Publishers. Such written permission must also be obtained before
any part of this publication is stored in a retrieval system of any
nature.

This book is sold subject to the Standard Conditions of Sale of Net
Books and may not be re-sold in the UK below the net price given
by the Publishers in their current price list.

First published 1982

© Butterworth & Co (Publishers) Ltd 1982

British Library Cataloguing in Publication Data

Askari, Hossein
   Taxation and tax policies in the Middle East.
   (Butterworths studies in international
   political economy)
   I. Taxation–Near East
   I. Title   II. Cummings, John T.
   III. Glover, Michael
   336.2'00956   HJ 2999.5
   ISBN 0-408-10832-0

Photoset by Butterworths Litho Preparation Department
Printed in England by Whitstable Litho Ltd, Whitstable, Kent
Bound by the Dorsel Press Ltd, Harlow, Essex

Acknowledgements

We wish to thank our families and particularly our wives for their support and understanding during the preparation of this book.

Although, at different times during the writing of the book, the authors were variously associated with the Ministry of Finance and National Economy of the Kingdom of Saudi Arabia, the United States–Saudi Arabian Joint Commission on Economic Cooperation, and the United States Department of State and Department of Treasury, the opinions expressed herein are entirely those of the authors. None of the statements or conclusions contained in this book should be attributed in any fashion to these official agencies.

Contents

Acknowledgements   v
List of Tables   xi
List of Figures   xvii

Part I   *Introduction*   1

   1 Purpose and outline of study   3

Part II   *Types of taxation in developing countries*   9

   2 Direct taxes   14
     2.1 Individual income taxes   14
     2.2 Corporate income taxes   22
     2.3 Property taxes   27

   3 Indirect taxes   37
     3.1 Export taxes   37
     3.2 Marketing boards   40
     3.3 Import duties   41
     3.4 Excise taxes   45
     3.5 Sales taxes   48
     3.6 Value added taxes   51
     3.7 User taxes   54

   4 State enterprises   57

   5 Islam and taxation   60
     5.1 Introduction   60
     5.2 *Zakat*   61
     5.3 Land taxes – *'ushr* and *kharaj* 64
     5.4 *Jizyah*   66
     5.5 Taxes on natural resources   66
     5.6 Summarizing Islamic taxation   67
     5.7 Islam and major sources of fiscal revenue   68
     5.8 Property and responsibility in Islam   74
     5.9 Summarizing Islam and taxation   77

Part III	*Taxation in the Middle East*	85
6	Taxation in the Middle East	87
7	Oil exporting countries	96
	7.1 Bahrain	96
	7.2 Iran	98
	7.3 Iraq	105
	7.4 Kuwait	112
	7.5 Libya	117
	7.6 Oman	123
	7.7 Qatar	126
	7.8 Saudi Arabia	129
	7.9 United Arab Emirates	134
8	Non-oil exporting countries	143
	8.1 Egypt	143
	8.2 Jordan	148
	8.3 Lebanon	152
	8.4 Sudan	158
	8.5 Syria	163
	8.6 Yemen Arab Republic	168
	8.7 People's Democratic Republic of Yemen	172
Part IV	*Analysis of taxation policies*	179
9	Econometric study of Middle East taxation	181
	9.1 General considerations and background	181
	9.2 The Chelliah tax capacity model	183
	9.3 A reconstruction of the model	186
	9.4 The regression results	190
Part V	*Assessment of tax performance in the Middle East*	199
10	General considerations relative to tax policy performance	201
	10.1 Mobilizing the resources of society	201
	10.2 Income distribution in the Middle East	210
	10.3 Progressive and regressive aspects of the tax burden	214
11	Oil exporting countries	226
	11.1 Bahrain	226
	11.2 Iran	231
	11.3 Iraq	237
	11.4 Kuwait	242
	11.5 Libya	246

11.6 Oman   249
11.7 Qatar   251
11.8 Saudi Arabia   253
11.9 United Arab Emirates   258

12 Non-oil exporting countries   266
   12.1 Egypt   266
   12.2 Jordan   272
   12.3 Lebanon   276
   12.4 Sudan   280
   12.5 Syria   283
   12.6 Yemen Arab Republic   289
   12.7 People's Democratic Republic of Yemen   291

13 Regional problems in fiscal policy   297
   13.1 A future regional fiscal policy problem of
       international consequence   297
   13.2 Oil depletion and tax revenues   308

Part VI *Conclusions*   317

14 Review and recapitulation   319

Appendix A Exchange rates and calendars   333

Appendix B Categorical groupings of taxes   337

Index   343

List of tables

Table

2.1	Selected developing countries: direct taxes (1966–1968)	10
2.2	Selected developed countries: direct taxes (1970)	11
2.3	Selected developing countries: individual income taxes (1966–1968)	15
2.4	Selected developed countries: individual income taxes (1961)	18
2.5	Selected underdeveloped and developed countries: burden of income taxes paid by married couple with three children in relation to national per capita income (1957–1960)	19
2.6	Selected developing countries: poll and personal taxes (1966–1968)	21
2.7	Selected developing countries: corporate income tax (1966–1968)	23
2.8	Selected developed countries: corporate income tax (1961)	24
2.9	Selected developing countries: property taxes (1966–1968)	28
2.10	Selected developed countries: property taxes (1961)	29
2.11	Death duties as percentage of total taxes (1969)	33
2.12	Net wealth taxation as percentage of total national tax revenue	34
3.1	Selected developing countries: ratio of export taxes to total tax revenue (1966–1968)	38
3.2	Selected developing countries: ratio of import taxes to total tax revenue (1966–1968)	42
3.3	Selected developing countries: ratios of excise taxes and sales taxes to total tax revenue (1969–1971)	47
3.4	Value-added sales tax as a revenue source in developing countries (1968)	53
4.1	Recent relative contributions of state enterprise profits to Middle East government fiscal receipts	58
5.1	Recent official receipts from religiously-decreed taxes, Middle Eastern countries	79

6.1   Oil production: major Middle Eastern oil producers
      (1915–1978)   88
6.2   Government receipts as a percentage of GNP and per capita;
      GNP per capita, (1950–1977)   90
6.3   Direct and indirect taxes: Middle East countries (1950–1977) 92
6.4   Per capita tax load: Middle Eastern countries (1977)   94
6.5   Oil revenues relative to total revenues: major oil producers 94

7.1   Tax revenues: Bahrain (1950–1977)   97
7.2   Major taxes: Bahrain (1955–1977)   98
7.3   Tax revenues: Iran (1949/50–1977/78)   100
7.4   Major taxes: Iran (1949/50–1977/78)   102
7.5   Iranian overseas investments and returns (1960–1977)   104
7.6   Tax revenues: Iraq (1950/51–1977)   106
7.7   Oil receipts allocations to current and development budgets:
      Iraq (1950/51–1977)   107
7.8   Major taxes: Iraq (1950/51–1977)   109
7.9   Iraqi overseas investments and returns (1960–1976)   111
7.10 Tax revenues: Kuwait (1950–1978/79)   114
7.11 Investment income: Kuwait (1952–1978/79)   116
7.12 Major taxes: Kuwait (1950–1978/79)   116
7.13 Tax revenues: Libya (1952/53–1977)   118
7.14 Major taxes: Libya (1952/53–1977)   119
7.15 Oil revenues relative to total revenues: Libya
      (1961/62–1974/75)   121
7.16 Libyan overseas investments and returns (1960–1977)   122
7.17 Local government revenues: Libya   123
7.18 Tax revenues: Oman (1967–1978)   124
7.19 Oil revenues: Oman (1967–1978)   125
7.20 Tax revenues: Qatar (1950–1978)   127
7.21 Major taxes: Qatar (1973–1978)   128
7.22 Qatari overseas investments and returns (1953–1977)   128
7.23 Tax revenues: Saudi Arabia (1947/48–1977/78)   130
7.24 Major taxes: Saudi Arabia (1947/48–1977/78)   132
7.25 Saudi Arabian overseas investments and returns (1960–1977) 133
7.26 Estimates of Emirate revenues, United Arab Emirates
      (1960–1978)   135
7.27 Oil production in the United Arab Emirates   136
7.28 Tax revenues, Abu Dhabi (1967–1978)   137
7.29 Partial summary of revenues accruing to the government of
      Dubai (1972–1978)   138
7.30 Sources of federal revenues: United Arab Emirates
      (1972–1977)   139
7.31 External investment earnings and internal fiscal receipts:
      United Arab Emirates (1972–1977)   139

8.1 Tax revenues: Egypt (1950/51–1977)   144
8.2 Major taxes: Egypt (1950/51–1977)   145
8.3 Current revenues available to local governments
(1962/63–1977)   147
8.4 Egyptian central and local government shares of property
taxes and service fees (1977)   148
8.5 Tax revenues: Jordan (1951/52–1978)   149
8.6 Foreign economic assistance to Jordan (1951/52–1978)   150
8.7 Major taxes: Jordan (1974 and 1978)   151
8.8 Tax revenues: Lebanon (1950–1975)   153
8.9 Major taxes: Lebanon (1952–1975)   154
8.10 Tax incidence in Lebanon (1968)   156
8.11 Anticipated and actual tax revenues during civil war period:
Lebanon   157
8.12 Anticipated tax revenues during the Lebanese civil war by
major category   158
8.13 Tax revenues: Sudan (1952/53–1977/78)   160
8.14 Major taxes: Sudan (1952/53–1977/78)   162
8.15 Major sources of revenue for local government: Sudan
(1957/58–1973/74)   162
8.16 Local government share of major revenue categories: Sudan   163
8.17 Tax revenues: Syria (1950/51–1977)   164
8.18 Major taxes: Syria (1950/51–1976)   165
8.19 Municipal fiscal revenues: Syria (1955–1976)   167
8.20 Tax revenues: Yemen Arab Republic (1966/67–1977/78)   169
8.21 Major taxes: Yemen Arab Republic (1966/67–1977/78)   170
8.22 Composition of *zakat*, Yemen Arab Republic
(1966/67–1977/78)   171
8.23 Tax revenues: People's Democratic Republic of Yemen
(1951/52–1978)   173
8.24 Tax revenues: Aden Colony and Protectorate   174
8.25 Major taxes: People's Democratic Republic of Yemen
(1951/52–1978)   175

9.1 Regression results: variations of Chelliah tax capacity model   185
9.2 Developing countries included in study   187
9.4 Regression results: revised tax capacity model with mineral
sector as independent variable   191
9.4 Regression results: revised tax capacity model with mineral
exports as independent variable   192
9.5 Comparison of regression results: Chelliah and revised
models   193
9.6 Mean values of regression variables, country sub-groups   195

10.1   Ratios of tax revenue to GNP (1950–1978)   202
10.2   Weighted average tax ratios (1950–1978)   202
10.3   Tax ratios: selected developing countries (1966–1968 and
        1977)   204
10.4   Tax ratios: selected industrialized countries (1977)   206
10.5   Tax buoyancies: Middle Eastern countries (1950–1978)   207
10.6   Oil and non-oil tax buoyancies (1950–1978)   208
10.7   Ratios of oil revenues to total government receipts
        (1950–1978)   209
10.8   Income distribution statistics: selected Middle Eastern
        countries   210
10.9   Measures of income distribution: selected countries   211
10.10   Ratio of income taxes to total government revenues: Middle
        Eastern countries compared to selected developing and
        industrialized countries   215
10.11   Income taxes as a percentage of national income: Middle East
        oil-exporting and selected industrialized countries   216
10.12   Percentage of population in urban areas: Middle Eastern and
        selected developing countries (1960 and 1980)   217
10.13   Percentage of income tax receipts arising from business
        profits   218
10.14   Estimated Muslim percentage of total population: Middle
        Eastern countries   219
10.15   'Religiously appropriate' taxes as a percentage of total tax
        receipts and of national income   220
10.16   Buoyancies of all taxes and 'religiously appropriate' taxes
        (1950–1978)   221
10.17   Ratios of consumer taxes to total government revenues:
        Middle Eastern countries compared to selected developing
        and industrialized countries   223
10.18   Buoyancies of consumer taxes (1950–1978)   224

11.1   Bahrain: selected economic and fiscal statistics (1950–1978)   227
11.2   Gross domestic product by industrial origin: oil exporting
        countries in the Middle East (1962–1978)   230
11.3   Iran: selected economic and fiscal statistics (1950–1978)   232
11.4   Average daily output: Iranian oil fields (1945–1980)   236
11.5   Iraq: selected economic and fiscal statistics (1950–1977)   238
11.6   Annual changes in official consumer price indices: Middle
        East countries (1973–1978)   239
11.7   Average daily output: Iraqi oil fields (1945–1980)   241
11.8   Kuwait: selected economic and fiscal statistics (1950–1978)   242
11.9   Import duties as a percentage of total taxes: Middle Eastern
        countries compared to selected developing and industrialized
        countries   244

11.10 Oil reserve lifetimes (reserves to output ratios): selected oil-
producing developing countries   245
11.11 Average daily output: Kuwaiti oil fields (1947–1980)   246
11.12 Libya: selected economic and fiscal statistics (1952–1977)   247
11.13 Oman: selected economic and fiscal statistics (1962–1978)   250
11.14 Qatar: selected economic and fiscal statistics (1950–1978)   252
11.15 Saudi Arabia: Selected economic and fiscal statistics
(1950–1977)   253
11.16 'Religiously appropriate' taxes as percentage of total tax
receipts: selected Islamic countries   255
11.17 Average daily output: Saudi Arabian oil fields (1946–1980)   257
11.18 United Arab Emirates: selected economic and fiscal statistics
(1964–1978)   258
11.19 United Arab Emirates: federal government revenues
(1973–1979)   259
11.20 Federal budget allocations to major functions (1973–1979)   260
11.21 Average daily output: United Arab Emirates oil fields
(1962–1980)   262

12.1 Egypt: selected economic and fiscal statistics (1950–1977)   267
12.2 Per capita domestically-generated tax revenues: Middle East
countries   268
12.3 Gross domestic product by industrial origin: non-oil
exporting countries in the Middle East (1962–1977)   269
12.4 Jordan: selected economic and fiscal statistics (1952–1978)   273
12.5 Selected measures of official development assistance: Middle
Eastern and other selected developing countries   274
12.6 Projected tax ratios: Jordan (1985 and 1990)   275
12.7 Lebanon: selected economic and fiscal statistics (1950–1978)   277
12.8 Lebanese exports (1953–1973)   278
12.9 Composition of exports: selected Middle East countries
(1973)   278
12.10 Sudan: selected economic and fiscal statistics (1955–1977)   281
12.11 Syria: oil production, exports and export earnings
(1968–1979)   284
12.12 Syria: selected economic and fiscal statistics (1950–1977)   285
12.13 Yemen Arab Republic: selected economic and fiscal statistics
(1962–1977)   290
12.14 Yemen People's Democratic Republic: selected economic
and fiscal statistics (1951–1978)   292

13.1 Oil tax and non-oil tax average annual growth rates
(1950–1977)   298
13.2 Officially-held overseas investments and returns (1960–1978)   299

13.3   Per citizen returns from state-owned overseas investments
       (1960–1978)   301
13.4   Per citizen investment returns in major Middle Eastern oil
       exporters and per capita GNP in selected industrialized and
       developing countries (1978)   302
13.5   Projected per citizen returns from state-owned overseas
       investments: 1985, 1990, and 1995   304
13.6   Future investment returns and current budget expenditures   306
13.7   Non-oil tax revenues and investment earnings (1973–1978)   308
13.8   Estimated petroleum and natural gas reserves and life of
       reserves: Middle East countries   310
13.9   Estimates for petroleum production: 1978–2000   310
13.10 Estimates for domestic petroleum consumption: 1980–2000   311
13.11 Projected ratios of domestic consumption to production:
       1980–2000   312

14.1   'Religiously appropriate' taxes as a percentage of total
       revenues, Middle Eastern and other Muslim countries, by
       per capita GHP   324
14.2   Remitted earnings from emigrant workers (1972–1979)   329

A.1   Annual average exchange rates of Middle Eastern currencies
       versus the US dollar   334
A.2   Islamic, Iranian and Gregorian calendar equivalents   336

List of figures

Figure

2.1 Selected developing countries: relation between share of direct taxes and per capita GNP 1966–1968   12

2.2 Selected developing countries: relation between share of individual income taxes and per capita GNP 1966–1968   16

2.3 Selected developing countries: relation between share of corporate profits taxes and per capita GNP 1966–1968   25

2.4 Selected developing countries: relation between share of property taxes and per capita GNP 1966–1968   30

3.1 Selected developing countries: relation between share of export taxes in total taxation and per capita GNP 1966–1968   39

3.2 Selected developing countries: relation between share of import taxes in total taxation and per capita GNP 1966–1968   43

3.3 Selected developing countries: relation between share of excise and sales taxes in total taxation and per capita GNP 1969–1971   50

10.1 Tax revenue to GNP ratios, 1950–1978   203

10.2 Tax buoyancies, 1950–1978   205

10.3 Lorentz curves for Libya, Egypt, and Iraq   212

14.1 'Religiously appropriate' portion of total tax revenues versus per capita GNP, Middle Eastern and other Muslim countries   325

PART I

Introduction

Purpose and outline of study

Taxes, the adage assures us, are one of life's two certainties. But from the economist's point of view, taxes, and the policies that govern their collection, must be considered with more sophistication than a mere recognition of their inevitability. The importance of taxation to any country, regardless of its level of economic development, is multifaceted.

First, and most obviously, taxes are needed to finance current government spending as well as those capital expenditures that the public sector deems advisable in order to promote economic development. Secondly, taxes can be effectively used to mobilize a society's savings and to direct them toward promising investment prospects. This latter function can be important in any society, but it is particularly so in less developed countries (LDCs) where private capital markets are immature. It is also important, in the case of many developing countries, where the most critical investment needs are for projects which necessitate long payback periods, or in which considerable external factors are involved, such as investments in social and economic infrastructure.

Thirdly, taxes can be an effective and fairly rapidly acting means for altering the distribution of income, especially when the existing pattern favors a rather small wealthy class, while much of the population is on the fringes of subsistence. Though many highly developed societies which adopted the ideal of the social welfare state one or two generations ago are now questioning the effectiveness of current public sector efforts designed to improve income distribution, there is little doubt that previous policies in these countries benefited the lower and middle income classes. Fourthly, carefully designed and monitored tax mechanisms can be used to encourage the private sector of the economy in directions which are deemed to be beneficial, in the long run, to the society as a whole. For example, private investment in industrial or agricultural improvements can be encouraged (or discouraged, in areas such as real estate speculation) by the way in which tax regulations relating to profits are planned. In this way investments leading to greater production, which are often risky or have relatively long payback periods, can be encouraged at the expense of alternative investment opportunities that offer high and quick returns but negligible social gains.

Fifthly, though it may be fashionable today to denigrate the Keynesian fiscal equations, few economists would argue that tax policy has no role in promoting or retarding inflation. Political considerations and the complexity of western capitalist economies in the last 50 years may have blunted the effectiveness of Keynesian remedies and may have impeded their ability to follow the harsh prescriptions for inflationary periods (i.e. government budget surpluses), but that does not mean that in less sophisticated economies fiscal regulation of consumer demand might not still be effective. Finally, if there are doubts as to the usefulness of fiscal policies in slowing existing inflation, there still seems to be general agreement that government spending and tax programs can both initiate and accelerate inflation. Thus, the probablistic linkage between fiscal policy and inflation problems remains strong enough to keep this aspect of taxes firmly in mind.

Our concern here is with the Middle East. Any definition of this region is geographically arbitrary, and the one used here is no exception. Our focus is on the developing economies of southwestern Asia and northeastern Africa – from Libya to Iran and from Syria to the Sudan – a total of 16 countries with a population of about 145 million in the late 1970s. The total GNP of these countries was about \$270 billion, averaging about \$1850 per capita; the GNP per capita in individual countries ranged from less than \$350 to more than \$15 000.

The Islamic heritage of these countries, as we shall see below, has implications for their economies, especially for the role of taxes, that set them apart from the developed capitalist economies in which, and for which, most modern capitalist economic theory has been formulated. In particular, since the beginning of Islam more than 1400 years ago, it has embodied, at the very core of its theology, a fairly complex body of economic legislation and socio-economic guidelines. Taxes, or more properly the individual's financial obligations toward the community at large, are prominent Islamic concerns; more so than in other religions. In a period marked by a strong religious revival within *Dar al-Islam* (literally, the House of Islam) from Senegal to Indonesia and from Iran to Nigeria, serious consideration must be given to how the Quran and other sources of Islamic tradition may influence policymakers in Muslim states.

Obviously not every country of *Dar al-Islam* is showing the new-found theological fervor of Colonel Qaddafi's Libyan Arab People's Jumhuriyyah or Ayatollah Khomeini's Islamic Republic of Iran. Nevertheless, the problem of economic and social dislocation, brought on in some countries by rapidly escalating oil wealth or in others simply by a greater degree of cultural interaction with neighboring non-Muslim areas, has recently prompted many intellectual and political leaders to reexamine their Islamic heritage. (This is so even among those most strongly westernized by education and/or long residence abroad.) Not surprisingly, in the forefront of the concerns of many such Muslims have been economic questions vital to the future development of their countries.

Thus, we must look beyond western economic literature on tax and tax policy concerns: we must explore and summarize the more important aspects of the interaction between Islamic theology and fiscal questions.

Our aim in this book is to evaluate the general role that tax policies have played in the economic development of the Middle East since 1945 and also to advance some recommendations on how fiscal tools could be better used to promote further advancement in this region.

In Part II we will discuss the economic aspects of the major categories of taxes used in most developing countries, including those of the Middle East. Our intention is not to write a textbook on this subject, since many good ones already exist; rather, the first part of this section (Chapters 2, 3 and 4) is for the convenience of the reader whose training is not in economics and who is primarily interested in current government policies in the Middle East, but who would otherwise have to refer regularly to a text on fiscal matters for basic definitions and for explanatory discussion of the questions covered in the later sections of this work. The reader who is already familiar with the basic literature on fiscal questions can proceed directly to Chapter 5 without impeding his understanding of the subsequent discussion.

The fifth chapter discusses specifically Islamic concerns with taxation. The chapters of the Quran contain explicit references to forms of taxation – one of these, *zakat* or almsgiving, can be alternatively defined as a wealth-based tax, and has traditionally been held to be one of the five central beliefs in Islam: in this chapter we will consider *zakat* in some detail. We will also define and discuss other forms of Islamic taxation, such as *'ushr* (or tithe), *kharaj* (levied on land by type of cultivation employed) and *jizyah* (poll tax).

In Part III we undertake, on a comparative basis, an analysis of the recent fiscal history of 16 Middle Eastern countries. The principal concern in this section is with a categorical breakdown of the tax profiles of these countries, on both a cross-sectional basis and with regard to changes that have occurred during the time period and for which data are available.

Thus, in Chapter 7 we will consider as a group the oil-exporting economies of the region: Bahrain, Iran, Iraq, Kuwait, Libya, Oman, Qatar, Saudi Arabia, and the United Arab Emirates (UAE). Oil production varies widely among them: Saudi Arabia, of course, is the world's largest oil exporter, while many counties in the United States produce more oil every day than does Bahrain. During the period covered by this study, the major part of the revenue of the governments of these nine countries has been generated by fiscal returns on oil exports.

On the other hand, among the other seven countries whose tax histories are outlined in Chapter 8 (Egypt, Jordan, Lebanon, Sudan, Syria, the Yemen Arab Republic and the Yemen People's Democratic Republic) are some that are oil producers (Egypt and Syria), but there are none for which oil-generated tax revenues were significant during the approximately 30 years covered here.

Part IV begins with a review in Chapter 9 of the literature on econometric models that endeavour to explain differences among countries in tax effort, and it continues with a discussion of our own model-building attempts using the technique of regression analysis. Like earlier studies, our model relates tax effort to three major factors: the degree to which a country is open to the world economy, the general level of development and income, and the sectoral composition of national income. Several of these earlier efforts encountered problems with which we will attempt to deal: lack of statistical significance for variables given considerable *a priori* weight, lack of stability when a model is applied to different groups of countries, a relatively low degree of explanatory power, and often strong reliance of models on explanatory variables that may not actually reflect the factors which they purport to represent. In addition, of course, we will be trying to identify a model that is successful when applied to a Middle Eastern sample. In this regard, we will also be considering the importance of the presence of a major natural resource export with a highly inelastic demand as a factor affecting the relative tax effort of a country.

In Part V we proceed in Chapter 10 to consider the differences in relative tax efforts across our group of 16 countries, putting these differences into a context that includes Islamic history and culture and natural resource endowment. Two questions are asked: how have tax policies been used as policy instruments and thus as a means of mobilizing the financial resources of these societies, and again, how have they been used in relation to general social principles? In the second case we will be interested in questions of equity and justice, both from general economic and from specifically Islamic viewpoints. In this we will have to consider what data are available regarding income distribution in the region, and the question of tax burdens being progressive or regressive.

In the light of discussions in the two previous chapters, Chapters 11 and 12 will review both the fiscal histories and tax efforts of each of the 16 countries in turn, first the oil exporters and then the non-oil exporters. For the former subgroup we will give foremost consideration to the consequences of their increasing abdication of domestic fiscal policy as a major tool in guiding economic development. Chapter 13 considers two significant problems which will affect future fiscal policies in the region: growing revenues from overseas investments, and the eventual diminishing of oil exports.

Finally, we conclude our efforts in Part VI by summarizing our principal results and by trying to answer three questions. How do Middle Eastern countries compare with other developing countries in regard to tax policies? How do the region's policies compare with the taxation ideals of Islam? How can fiscal policies be improved relative to both economic and social criteria?

Before concluding this introductory chapter, we should again state that our basic approach is focused on the belief that the Islamic heritage of the Middle East sets these 16 countries apart in that economic and fiscal questions must be considered in an Islamic context. In today's world, the Islamic content of the Middle Eastern economy must be of concern to the developed, mostly western, mostly Christian (or post-Christian) world, and not merely because the oil pricing revolution of 1973 accelerated the drive toward economic development throughout the region.

Rather, it must be borne in mind that although this uniquely rich part of the developing world has shown definite signs of discontent with 'established' models of economic development, these models continued through the late 1970s to be the guidelines followed by these countries. Despite the lack of Islamic content in recent regional development policies, or perhaps because of it, the fitful moves in Libya and Iran during the late 1970s and early 1980s toward Islamic economies may be only the harbinger of more significant moves in this direction in the future. Several countries in the Middle East have the potential of evolving models of their own, based on their current resources and on 14 centuries of Islamic philosophy – models which would offer viable alternatives not only to other developing economies, but also to western economies of both the capitalist and Marxist varieties. The richer economic blocs, Euro-American and Soviet, have learned to learn from one another, and yet each faces major, seemingly insoluble, problems: how to achieve the goals of equitable distribution of income and wealth; personal motivation toward greater efficiency in the face of shrinking resource bases; and with worldwide inflation, the halting of the rapid decline of traditional measures of monetary value. Perhaps future generations in these countries may also look to Islamic economics. After all, it was the interaction of Islam and Christianity in medieval Europe that laid the philosophic foundation for the last major economic period – the Industrial Revolution.

Types of taxation in developing countries

Introduction

An attempt to evaluate the numerous forms of taxes in use throughout the world is facilitated by classifying them into a small number of groups. In the literature, various classification schemes have been proposed, but for our purposes it is perhaps best to rely on the distinction that is traditionally made between direct and indirect taxes.

This distinction may be made in various ways, with many commentators relying on the incidence of the tax as the determining factor. Direct taxes are, as the term suggests, those taxes which are borne by the person or institution responsible for paying the tax. Indirect taxes, on the other hand, are taxes which can be shifted, either forward or backward[1]. The ultimate incidence of the tax is not, however, always easily ascertained. The corporate profits tax, for instance, is generally regarded as a direct tax; yet, depending on market elasticities, it may be either shifted forward in product price increases or backward by reducing the prices paid for factor inputs (such as labor). Similarly, if an import duty, commonly categorized as an indirect form of taxation, is paid entirely from the profits of an import merchant, then clearly such a tax should be termed direct[2].

Others maintain that the relevant distinguishing characteristic should be the object of taxation. According to this view, direct taxes are those imposed on persons or corporations, and thus adaptable to the taxpayer's special position and taxable capacity. Indirect taxes are simply defined as all those imposed on commodities, transactions, or services[3].

Perhaps the most satisfactory approach is that suggested by Richard Musgrave in his international comparative study of fiscal systems[4]. Musgrave acknowledges the many difficulties encountered in distinguishing direct and indirect taxation and concludes that the distinction is largely a terminological matter, as most criteria do not provide a definite classification for certain taxes. For our purposes, we will adopt a classification scheme similar to the one proposed by Musgrave[5]:

Direct taxes
Individual income taxes
Poll and other personal taxes
Corporate income taxes
Royalties
Property taxes

Table 2.1 *Selected developing countries: direct taxes (1966–1968)*

	Per capita GNP	Percentage of total taxes	Percentage of GNP
Under $250 per capita GNP (US$)			
Rwanda	48	36.8	3.1
Upper Volta	49	29.1	3.7
Burundi	51	36.3	3.4
Ethiopia	61	23.9	2.0
Tanzania	64	25.5	6.5
Mali	69	34.5	5.2
Chad	70	33.7	4.7
Indonesia	80	30.9	2.4
Nepal	81	30.1	1.0
India	84	29.1	3.4
Somalia	85	8.3	1.2
Congo, Dem. Rep.	86	17.5	3.3
Sudan	104	6.7	0.9
Kenya	117	43.3	6.0
Pakistan	118	21.4	1.8
Togo	131	16.1	1.6
Sri Lanka	144	23.6	3.7
Vietnam	151	13.2	1.8
Thailand	156	15.7	2.0
Bolivia	160	15.3	1.4
Korea	168	42.1	5.0
Egypt	183	28.6	5.2
Philippines	184	32.6	3.2
Morocco	196	35.2	5.8
Tunisia	217	34.9	7.2
Senegal	224	25.1	4.6
Paraguay	225	17.5	1.7
Ecuador	236	21.4	2.8
Honduras	249	29.2	3.1
Average		26.1	3.4
Over $250 per capita GNP (US$)			
Taiwan	262	18.6	2.7
Iran	276	62.4	12.1
Ghana	278	25.9	3.5
Ivory Coast	280	19.6	3.9
Zambia	297	67.2	19.2
Brazil	304	12.8	2.6
Guatemala	305	18.0	1.4
Malaysia	316	39.2	6.6
Guyana	332	38.8	8.1
Turkey	347	41.0	5.8
Peru	368	27.6	3.7
Colombia	391	39.5	4.1
Costa Rica	445	29.4	3.2
Mexico	492	32.4	3.2
Jamaica	493	44.7	7.6
Lebanon	507	28.4	3.0
Chile	623	41.7	8.1

Table 2.1 *(continued)*

	Per capita GNP	Percentage of total taxes	Percentage of GNP
Over $250 per capita GNP (US$)			
Singapore	645	58.2	7.3
Argentina	670	32.2	4.8
Trinidad and Tobago	713	62.9	9.5
Venezuela	871	84.5	18.4
Average		40.3	6.6
Overall average		31.7	4.7

Source: Raja J. Chelliah, Trends in Taxation in Developing Countries, *IMF Staff Papers,* **18**, pp. 278–9, 317–20, 373 (July 1971).

Indirect taxes
Customs duties and fees
Excise and sales taxes
Production taxes
License fees
Charges for government services

On the basis of these criteria, we can now compare the role of direct and indirect taxation in the process of economic development. A comparison of *Tables 2.1* and *2.2* reveals that in LDCs the percentage of total tax revenue

Table 2.2 *Selected developed countries: direct taxes (1970)*

Country	Direct taxes as percentage of total government receipts[a]
Australia[b]	63.2
Denmark[c]	38.1
Federal Republic of Germany	61.7
Italy	22.9
Netherlands	57.3
Sweden[b]	43.2
United Kingdom	57.7
Average	49.2

Notes: [a] Central government only
[b] July 1969–June 1970
[c] April 1969–March 1970

Source: United Nations Statistical Yearbook, 1975.

obtained from direct taxes is significantly less (31.7 percent) than in developed countries (49.2 percent). This suggests that a similar correlation may exist among the LDCs themselves.

If the LDCs are divided into two groups according to per capita gross national product (GNP), it is found that the group of LDCs with a per capita GNP of less than $250 have an average direct tax ratio of 26.1 percent, whereas those LDCs with a per capita GNP greater than $250 have an average ratio of 40.3 percent (*Table 2.1*). The relation between share of direct taxes in total taxes and per capita GNP can readily be seen on a scatter diagram (*Figure 2.1*) which depicts the general tendency for the direct tax share to increase as per capita GNP increases. If a simple regression of direct taxes as a percentage of total taxes on per capita GNP is calculated, we find a slope of +0.0449 and an intercept of +19.97; this regression explains about 32 percent of the variation in the share of direct taxes.

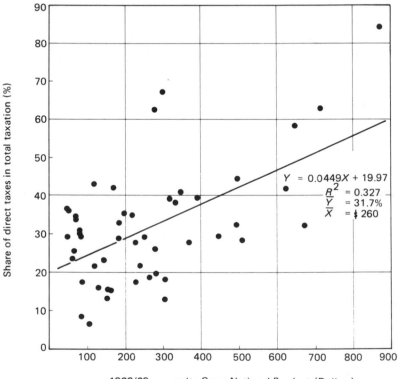

Figure 2.1 *Selected developing countries: relation between share of direct taxes and per capita GNP 1966–1968*

Source: Raja J. Chelliah, Trends in Taxation in Developing Countries, *IMF Staff Papers*, **18**, 283 (July 1971)

If the level of per capita GNP is taken as a rough measure of the level of development, then it is obvious that, with few exceptions, the less economically developed countries tend to rely less on direct taxes. The factors contributing to this relationship include: administrative problems encountered in levying direct taxes, the low degree of monetization of the economy, the importance of the export sector, and the high illiteracy rate. These and other factors will be discussed in greater detail in subsequent sections.

In Chapter 2, we investigate the role of direct taxation in the process of economic development, while Chapter 3 examines the impact of various forms of indirect taxation. Chapter 4 offers a brief examination of state enterprise revenues. Since the present study involves predominately Muslim countries, Chapter 5 surveys the economic aspects of Islam which are relevant to taxation policy.

Notes

1 V. Tan Wai, Taxation Problems & Policies of Underdeveloped Countries, *IMF Staff Papers*, 9 (November 1962), p. 431.
2 Douglas Dosser, Indirect Taxation and Economic Development, in Alan T. Peacock and Gerald Hauser (eds.), *Government Finance and Economic Development* (Paris: Organization for Economic Cooperation and Development, 1964), p. 128. See also John F. Due, *Government Finance: Economics of the Public Sector*, (Homewood, Illinois: Richard D. Irwin, 1968 – Fourth Edition), pp. 87–88.
3 Robert B. Bangs, *Financing Economic Development: Fiscal Policy for Emerging Countries*, (Chicago: University of Chicago Press, 1968), p. 12.
4 Richard A. Musgrave, *Fiscal Systems*, (New Haven: Yale University Press, 1969), pp. 173–175.
5 The major difference between our scheme and the one proposed by Musgrave is our classification of property taxes as a direct tax. Musgrave himself admits that a good case can be made for considering them direct taxes since property value may be viewed as merely the discounted value of imputed incomes. The United Nations' *Yearbook of National Account Statistics* treats real estate and land taxes as indirect taxes unless they are merely administrative devices for the collection of income taxes.

CHAPTER 2

Direct taxes

2.1 Individual income taxes

In *Table 2.3*, we sketch the importance of individual income taxes in the tax structure of a selected group of LDCs[1]. Personal income taxes play a limited role in the tax systems of developing nations as they contribute, on average, only 10.5 percent of total tax receipts. The poorer LDCs (per capita GNP in the late 1960s below $250) derive 9 percent of their tax revenues from personal income taxes, and the less poor LDCs (per capita GNP above $250) only obtain about 13 percent of their revenues from this source. The slope of a simple regression is positive (+0.0120), but only about 16 percent of the variation of the share of individual income taxes in total tax revenue is explained by per capita GNP alone (see *Figure 2.2*).

The importance of individual income taxes is not limited, however, to their relative yield *vis-à-vis* other forms of taxation. The role of individual income taxes (and, indeed, every other type of taxation) must be analyzed with regard to the two major functions of taxation: as a source of revenue for the public sector and as a policy instrument useful in directing the course of development.

The concept of the economic surplus generated in the economy is useful in determining the relationship between taxation and the potential for development. Paul Baran defines the potential economic surplus as 'the difference between the output that could be produced in a given natural and technological environment with the help of employable public resources, and what might be regarded as essential consumption'[2]. Although the precise definition of 'essential consumption' varies according to the particular society and its stage of development, such difficulties do not preclude the use of the concept of economic surplus. The surplus can be used for either productive investment or for unproductive investment (stadiums or palaces) or unproductive consumption (conspicuous consumption). Economic progress requires that the surplus be channeled into productive investment which develops the infrastructure and increases the capital–output ratio, or which improves the existing and future stock of human capital[3].

Effective mobilization of economic surplus is designed to raise the extremely low level of domestic savings which is characteristic of most underdeveloped economies. The ratio of net private savings to national

Table 2.3 *Selected developing countries: individual income taxes (1966–1968)*

	Percentage of total tax revenue[a]
Under $250 per capita GNP (US$)	
Rwanda	6.9
Upper Volta	9.8
Burundi	10.7
Chad	12.0
Indonesia	6.6
India	10.0
Congo, Dem Rep.	5.3
Sudan	0.8
Togo	4.2
Thailand	6.1
Bolivia	6.6
Korea	23.2
Philippines	9.2
Morocco	7.4
Tunisia	15.4
Senegal	9.7
Average	9.0
Over $250 per capita GNP (US$)	
Iran	5.8
Ghana	8.6
Zambia	8.4
Malaysia	8.9
Guyana	15.6
Turkey	26.9
Jamaica	14.1
Chile	11.2
Singapore	14.2
Trinidad and Tobago	15.7
Average	12.9
Overall average	10.5

Notes: [a] Includes only personal income tax (poll and personal taxes not included).

Source: Chelliah (see *Table 2.1*), pp. 317–320.

income is less in LDCs than the level generally found in developed countries (10–15 percent or even higher)[4]. If an increase in voluntary savings is not forthcoming, a system of compulsory savings may be instituted, requiring, for instance, that wage earners and businesses apply a certain percentage of their incomes to the purchase of interest-bearing but non-negotiable government bonds which are redeemable after a certain period[5].

An alternative method that can be employed to raise the level of domestic savings is a system of compulsory collective savings implemented through taxation. Following Chelliah, any tax may be viewed as a compulsory payment to the government in return for which the taxpayer receives no measurable direct benefit[6]. The aim of tax policy for economic development should, therefore, be to raise the ratio of savings to national income. The only alternative to compulsory savings is inflation, which reduces the consumption of the mass of the population by reducing real incomes[7].

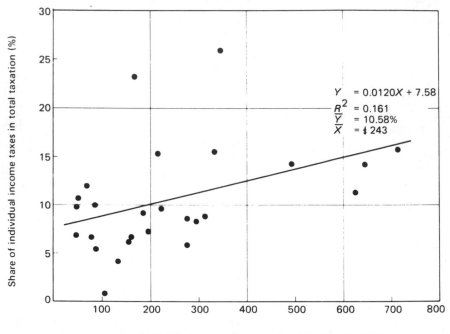

Figure 2.2   *Selected developing countries: relation between share of individual income taxes and per capita GNP, 1966–1968*

Source: See *Table 2.3.*

An increase in private savings may be effected by raising the incentives to save through such schemes as exempting dividends paid in savings accounts, although the potential effect of such policies is extremely limited due to the lack of capital markets and savings institutions in most LDCs. As a result a large proportion of savings is diverted into socially unproductive investment such as real estate or inventory speculation, or the hoarding of precious metals and currency[8]. Upper income groups also tend to engage in an inordinate amount of conspicuous consumption in an attempt to emulate the consumption standards of economically advanced nations. But income taxes can be used to impound income and channel it instead into more productive public investment. This would be in accordance with prevailing political philosophies in which the public sector plays an increasingly important role in the process of social and economic development. Public investment is widely regarded as necessary in developing the infrastructure which is essential to profitable private investment.

Progressive income taxation is often defended by reference to the concept of the diminishing marginal utility of income; that is, the additional 'satisfaction' (utility) derived from an additional unit of income is inversely proportional to the level of income. Equity considerations are also invoked in defense of progressive taxation, particularly with respect to the LDCs where the vast majority of the population may live at subsistence level while, in stark contrast, a small percentage of the population lives in relative opulence.

A highly progressive income tax system is, therefore, often considered desirable in order to reduce income inequalities and raise substantial amounts of revenue, yet care must be taken that the system does not stifle incentives. Although the rates should be highly progressive with respect to that part of the income which is not invested productively, it must be remembered that often extra effort is expended precisely in order to purchase luxury goods.

The experience of developed nations with incentives is not always directly applicable to developing nations with their unique social and economic environment. Rural workers and small businessmen in LDCs are often assumed to have backward-bending supply curves; that is, they work fewer hours at higher wages. In LDCs where incentives to work are not strong and where work is limited to that necessary for subsistance, reducing rural workers' incomes through taxation could result in more rather than less work being performed[9]. It is not sufficient though, to consider only the choice between work and leisure as there is also the option of performing non-taxed work instead of taxed work. Increasing taxation in developed nations may induce many individuals to perform more spare-time jobs (for example, painting one's house) rather than increasing work at the place of employment. In LDCs, however, the choice is largely one between untaxed or partially taxed production in the subsistence sector and production for sale in the monetized sector. Thus, an inappropriate tax system could have the undesirable result of driving farmers back into the subsistence sector and decreasing the rate of growth of the monetized sector[10].

A progressive tax system aids in financing development because, as per capita income is raised by economic development and expansion, this in turn yields larger revenues for the government. As a result, the government is allowed to increase its share in the national income without having to face the politically dangerous prospect of raising the level of taxation.

Another positive aspect of a progressive tax system is the built-in protection (automatic stabilizers) against inflation that is provided to the government. Inflation, characterized by rising prices, often leads to increased money incomes as workers frantically attempt to maintain a constant level of real income. A sufficiently progressive tax system will allow government revenues to increase rapidly in relation to national income and thus help dampen inflationary pressures by reducing aggregate demand, depending on government spending policies. If, on the other hand, a large share of government revenues is comprised of indirect taxes, then revenues will most likely lag behind the increases in money income and prices. Furthermore, if government expenditures increase faster than prices, as is true in most LDCs, then the budget deficit will increase and thereby further stimulate inflationary pressures by adding to the total excess demand[11].

Income tax deductions are effective in providing a flexible measure of an individual's 'taxable capacity', since allowances are made for extraordinary liabilities incurred by the taxpayer. Deductions can, moreover, be employed as a useful policy instrument to direct income into socially desirable areas, such as encouraging education, savings, and investment within the country[12]. Given the rapidly increasing population in virtually all developing areas, it is necessary that deductions for dependents should not be structured so as to encourage still larger families[13].

Table 2.4 *Selected developed countries: individual income taxes (1961)*

	Percentage of total tax revenue
United States	32.3
Canada	19.5
United Kingdom	35.5
Federal Republic of Germany	19.7
Netherlands	27.4
France	14.7
Sweden	52.8
Italy	11.3
Japan	20.3
Average	25.9

Source: R. A. Musgrave, *Fiscal Systems*, p. 172 (New Haven: Yale University Press, 1969).

A comparison of *Tables 2.3* and *2.4* reveals that developing countries, on average, receive 10.5 percent of their total tax revenue from personal income taxes, while the corresponding figure for developed nations is 25.9 percent. An important factor contributing to this disparity in yields is the high exemption level found among the LDCs. *Table 2.5* indicates that the tax base is much smaller in LDCs than in developed nations because the level of exempt income relative to per capita income is much higher in the former. The group of underdeveloped countries has an average exemption limit of close to 11 times the national per capita income, whereas the developed countries have an average exemption limit of slightly less than twice the national per capita income. The high exemption limits prevailing in the underdeveloped countries serve to exempt a sizeable proportion of the middle class[14]. Attempts to tax agricultural income in India and Pakistan have experienced little success, which is partly due to the fact that the exemption limit has been higher than the income of the average farmer[15].

Table 2.5 *Selected underdeveloped and developed countries: burden of income taxes paid by a married couple with three children in relation to national per capita income (1958–1960[a])*

	Level of income up to which no tax is paid (in multiples of national per capita income)	Taxes paid as percentage of earned income (at various multiples of national per capita income)			
		10 times	20 times	50 times	100 times
Underdeveloped countries					
Mexico	1.9	2	4	9	17
Argentina	7.7	3	16	34	43
Malaya	9.8	–	4	12	21
India	11.5	–	2	8	21
Ceylon	12.5	–	2	9	23
Philippines	15.6	–	1	10	19
Burma	19.0	–	–	4	11
Average	11.1	–	4	12	22
Developed countries					
Australia	0.7	30	43	55	59
United States	1.3	23	35	54	69
Canada	1.9	19	32	45	55
United Kingdom	1.9	28	44	67	78
France	2.1	13	23	35	45
Federal Republic of Germany	2.2	20	28	39	46
Japan	3.4	11	19	31	39
Average	1.9	21	32	47	56

Notes: [a] Reference years: for per capita national income – fiscal year 1956 for Burma, 1957 for Federation of Malaya, 1958 for Argentina, Canada, France, Mexico, and the Philippines, 1959 for Ceylon, the Federal Republic of Germany, Japan, India, and the United Kingdom, and 1960 for Australia and the United States; for tax laws – fiscal year 1956 for Burma, 1959 for France, Japan, Federation of Malaya, Mexico, and the Philippines, and 1960 for Argentina, Australia, Canada, Ceylon, the Federal Republic of Germany, India, the United Kingdom, and the United States.

Source: V. Tan Wai, Taxation Problems and Policies of Underdeveloped Countries, *IMF Staff Papers*, 9 (November 1962), p. 433.

The personal income tax yields of the developing nations have also been adversely affected by the relatively low rates charged, especially in the middle ranges of the income scale. Reference to *Table 2.5* reveals that taxes paid as a percentage of earned income, relative to national per capita income, are markedly less in the LDCs. For instance, a married couple with three children living in an LDC and earning some 20 times the national per capita income is taxed only, on the average, about four percent, while a similar family in a developed nation would pay a rate of approximately 32 percent.

A country is able to rely on income taxation as a major revenue source only if it is administratively feasible to collect the taxes. In an excellent study of the structure of foreign tax systems, Richard Goode concludes that the following factors are essential for an efficient system of income taxation:

(1) The existence of a predominantly money economy is the primary condition. Experience has shown that it is virtually impossible to satisfactorily assess the real income of subsistence farmers due to the difficulty of determining the value of home-produced and home-consumed foods which often constitute a major portion of the total real income. Such difficulties encourage the use of other forms of taxation.
(2) A high rate of literacy is helpful, though not essential, in creating a successful tax system. Illiterate, salaried employees may be covered by withholding schemes, yet their inability to read and write may prevent their filing claims for deductions.
(3) The widespread use of accounting records honestly and reliably maintained is another important factor necessary for income taxation, especially when a large segment of the labor force consists of small farmers and businessmen who are not salaried and therefore not easily reached by withholding.
(4) An obvious, but often overlooked, requirement for satisfactory income taxation is the existence of a large degree of voluntary compliance on the part of the taxpayers. Elaborate tax codes and highly-qualified administrators are of little use if tax evasion incurs little or no moral disapproval from the public. Of course, the situation is exacerbated if the wealthy classes have sufficient political leverage to frustrate tax measures which they consider a threat to their position. A highly progressive tax system will invariably fail unless the wealthy political leaders accept the ability-to-pay principle, whether from altruism, a sense of guilt, or fear[16].

The numerous difficulties encountered in levying a personal income tax may be avoided somewhat by also using a combination of poll and personal taxes. Several former British and French colonies in Africa use a simplified form of a direct personal tax which is a hybrid of poll tax and an elementary form of income tax. These taxes contribute significant revenues in several of the nations that employ them. Tanzania receives some 20 percent of its tax

Table 2.6 *Selected developing
countries: poll and personal taxes
(1966–1968)*

	Percentage of total tax revenue
Rwanda	15.1
Upper volta	14.0
Burundi	12.4
Tanzania	20.1
Mali	18.5
Chad	11.8
Togo	3.6
Philippines	3.5
Senegal	3.3
Zambia	0.3
Average	10.0

Source: Chelliah (see *Table 2.1*), pp. 317–320.

receipts from this source, and Rwanda, Mali, Burundi and Chad all rely on poll and personal taxes for between ten and 20 percent of their total revenue (*Table 2.6*).

The administration of the African personal tax differs between countries, but the basic features of the tax may be outlined as follows[17]:

(1) A minimum tax applies to all persons. Persons under 18 are exempted as are those who are ill or destitute. The exemptions rarely apply to more than five percent of the total number of taxpayers.
(2) Rates are fixed amounts per bracket of income rather than percentages of total income. This system provides an incentive to maximize income *within* the bracket, but there is little incentive to increase income beyond the limit of the bracket as the marginal rates are over 100 percent at the end of each bracket.
(3) There are no allowances or deductions.
(4) There is no system of formal returns since assessment of tax liability is usually performed by a local committee of laymen. Assessment of farmers is usually in terms of the estimated typical output of the farmer's acreage, trees, etc. This type of assessment provides an incentive to develop above average production techniques.

The African personal tax is of particular relevance to developing nations in which a large segment of the population is not ready for income taxation. Besides raising revenue, the poll and personal taxes are often considered desirous as they place some tax burden directly on the populace, thus increasing the taxpayers' sense of participation in the political process. In addition, the fact that the payment of the tax requires cash may encourage farmers to enter the market sector of the economy by selling some of their output. Likewise the excessive underemployment commonly found in rural areas may be partially alleviated as people are forced to hire out their services in an effort to earn the cash necessary to pay the tax.

2.2   Corporate income taxes

The corporate income, or profits, tax is often justified on the grounds that a business corporation is a separate legal entity and, as such, has a separate ability to pay, apart from that of its shareholders. Evidence of this can be seen in the fact that in recent years corporate management has become increasingly concerned with the soundness and growth of their firms and has not conducted operations merely in the interests of their shareholders' incomes. Since the corporation is an institution created and nurtured by law in the social interest, it is often contended that the corporation must be subject to some form of social control. A corporate income tax is, furthermore, essential in order to reach the undistributed profits of companies that would otherwise escape taxation[18].

The corporate tax levied in LDCs is often a tax on large scale foreign owned enterprises. The local government does not have jurisdiction to levy personal income taxes which would reach the income distributed to foreign shareholders. The case for corporate taxation is particularly strong when the foreign owned corporations operate in enclaves, contributing little to the development of the country because there are few linkages with the domestic economy, virtually none of their earnings being reinvested within that economy[19].

Taxation of corporations has much political appeal and may therefore be considered absolutely essential in order to obtain general acceptance of the tax structure. Another positive aspect of corporate taxation is its administrative ease (relative to personal taxation). This is because companies are easily identifiable and maintain a reasonably complete set of accounts; hence, it is generally possible to tax the corporate sector long before a personal income tax is feasible[20].

Corporations in a developing economy are often the source of a significant amount of the surplus which can be generated in the economy. Viewed in this context, the role of corporate taxation is to encourage the reinvestment of a portion of that surplus and to collect the remainder for public investment and consumption[21].

The importance of corporate income tax in providing public revenues is evidenced by the fact that this source provides developing countries with an

Table 2.7 *Selected developing countries: corporate income tax (1966–1968)*

	Percentage of total tax revenue
Under $250 per capita GNP	
Rwanda	8.3
Upper Volta	2.9
Burundi	9.3
Chad	5.2
Indonesia	22.2
India	9.8
Congo, Dem. Rep.	8.8
Sudan	5.7
Togo	6.0
Thailand	7.5
Bolivia	8.7
Korea	10.6
Philippines	14.7
Morocco	22.3
Tunisia	14.3
Senegal	7.7
Average	10.3
Over $250 per capita GNP	
Iran	55.2
Ghana	14.6
Zambia	56.0
Malaysia	17.4
Guyana	20.5
Turkey	5.6
Jamaica	22.5
Chile	24.1
Singapore	15.8
Trinidad and Tobago	40.5
Average	27.2
Overall average	16.8

Source: Chelliah (see *Table 2.1*), pp. 317–320.

average of 16.8 percent of their total tax revenue (*Table 2.7*). Those countries with a per capita GNP of less than $250 receive an average 10.3 percent of tax revenue from corporate taxes, while those with a per capita GNP above $250 receive a much larger proportion (27.2 percent). As per capita income increases still further, however, the share of corporate income taxes in total taxes does not increase proportionally. A comparison of *Tables 2.7* and *2.8* indicates that the group of the developed countries receives approximately the same proportion of total tax revenue from corporate taxes as does the group of poorer LDCs (per capita GNP below $250).

While it is beyond the scope of our discussion to examine in detail the relationship between per capita GNP and the share of corporate taxes in total taxes, it is worth noting that many of the less poor LDCs (per capita GNP above $250) included in *Table 2.7* have large scale foreign owned extractive industries. Iran and Trinidad and Tobago, for instance, both have oil reserves that are being exploited by foreign concerns, and Chile is endowed with vast deposits of copper which are mined, processed, and exported by foreign companies. When a simple regression of the share of corporate income taxes in total tax revenue versus per capita GNP is calculated, the estimated slope is only +0.0352 (*see Figure 2.3*); this sample regression explains about 22 percent of the variation in the share of these taxes.

Table 2.8 *Selected developed countries: corporate income tax (1961)*

	Percentage of total tax revenue
United States	16.3
Canada	16.1
United Kingdom	4.0
Federal Republic of Germany	6.9
Netherlands	10.4
France	6.0
Italy	2.1
Japan	26.8
Average	11.1

Source: Musgrave (see *Table 2.4*), p. 172.

The developing countries with large foreign owned extractive industries are exceptional in that corporate taxation in LDCs usually comprises only a small portion of the GNP. The low yield of corporate income taxes in LDCs is explained partly by the fact that the sectors in which the corporations are most numerous (for example, heavy industry) are relatively unimportant. Also, the role of corporations is relatively small in any given sector (for example, many small shops and vendors rather than large department stores)[22].

Company taxation not only makes an important contribution to government revenue but also offers possibilities for directing private investment into those areas considered most essential for development. Additional investment may result from tax policies that lessen the risk of investment. One tax policy that effectively reduces risk is to allow businesses to deduct losses incurred in early years from profits earned in later years ('full loss carry-forward')[23].

Accelerated depreciation is another tax policy that has been widely used in an attempt to lessen risk and thereby indirectly encourage private investment. Risk is reduced as the postponement of tax liabilities into the future means that capital outlay can be recovered in less time. Accelerated depreciation is of particular value under inflationary conditions when the cost of replacing equipment is much greater than the original cost. Another benefit received by the corporation from rapid depreciation is the increase in the liquidity of the firm that occurs soon after an investment is made[24].

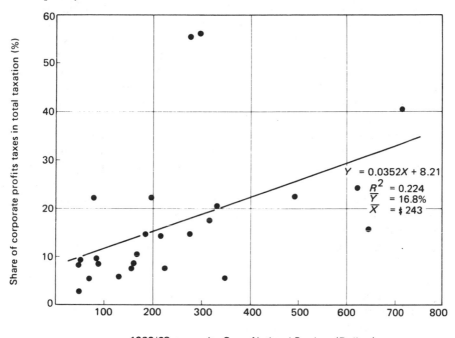

Figure 2.3 *Selected developing countries: relation between share of corporate profits taxes in total taxation and per capita GNP, 1966–1968*
Source: See Table 2.7.

An exemption from income tax for a specified period (a 'tax holiday') is yet another policy that may be used by the government to encourage private investment and channel it into preferred areas. A tax holiday is equivalent to a permanent reduction in the tax rate and, as such, reduces risk and increases the liquidity of the firm. Reducing the risks of investment is of particular importance in developing countries as the generally unstable nature of their economies often prompts investors to use their funds for either short-term investments or land speculation, rather than for long-term projects which are essential for development. If the incentives provided by a tax holiday lead to the establishment of new industries, the government will be able to collect additional revenue, without changing the tax rate since the new industries will increase the size of the tax base after the exemption periods expire. Also, private investment in preferred areas (long term projects, certain geographical areas, etc.) may be stimulated by the use of accelerated depreciation, discussed previously, or tax holidays for specific industries.

Tax holidays differ from accelerated depreciation in the way the base of tax relief is defined. Tax holidays apply to the profits of the firm, whereas accelerated depreciation is dependent upon the level of investment. Thus, the degree of tax relief afforded by either policy depends upon the capital output ratio of each individual firm; for example, firms with high rates of return on fixed capital will benefit more from a tax holiday than will firms in the same industry with lower rates of return[25]. Similarly, accelerated depreciation will provide greater benefits to capital intensive industries than to labor intensive industries. The capital intensive bias of accelerated depreciation means that this tax measure must be used with care so that it does not exacerbate the excessive underemployment of labor found in most developing areas.

Income tax exemption is often allied with relief from other forms of taxation in order to increase incentives to invest; most countries, for instance, waive payment of import duties on materials used by exempted firms. In the early 1960s, Mexico did not require exempted companies to pay export duties, and Puerto Rico waived payment of property taxes and municipal license levies[26]. Some exemption statutes have even gone beyond the corporation by allowing outside equity holders to deduct dividends from exempt firms from their income tax base. As a result, there is a tendency toward less internal financing since outside investors will provide more equity; furthermore, the corporate management will be under increasing pressure from the stockholders to declare dividends. Such a process may also aid the creation of a more efficient capital market which should, in turn, result in an increased mobilization of savings[27].

Tax relief, whether in the form of accelerated depreciation or tax holidays, may not have the desired effect on foreign owned corporations if Double Taxation Agreements are in operation. Basically, these agreements are designed to prevent double taxation of firms operating in more than one country by allowing credit for tax paid to other countries. If a Double Taxation Agreement is in effect between an LDC and a developed nation, then any tax relief given by the LDC is simply a present to the government of the developed nation in the sense that the developed nation will collect the taxes waived by the LDC. In such a case, quite obviously, the original intent of the tax relief – to encourage additional investment activity by the private sector – is frustrated, as the overall tax liability of the corporation is not reduced but merely transferred to another collecting agency. This is not the case, however, for the handful of LDCs which have entered into 'tax-sparing' agreements whereby the developed country reduces the domestic tax liability of the corporation *as if* the corporation had actually paid the amount of tax that was waived by the LDC. The United States has not, at this time, concluded any tax-sparing agreements, yet it is still possible for an American corporation operating under exemption in an LDC to escape US tax liability. The American investor must merely incorporate abroad since no US income tax liability is incurred until the foreign subsidiary pays a dividend to the American firm[28].

The operation of Double Taxation Agreements makes it possible for developing nations to levy corporate income taxes at, or near, the rates prevailing in the developed countries. The relatively high company tax rates found in the US and Great Britain, both major capital exporting countries, allow the LDCs to levy equally high rates on US or UK based companies. Yet, the rates should not be such as to deter new foreign or domestic investment. The impoverished Chilean government, during the 1949–54 period, attempted to increase revenues by levying heavier taxes on copper companies, with the result that it was no longer profitable for the corporations to continue investing[29].

Excessive corporate taxes generally should be avoided in order to encourage the formation of new businesses as corporations, a highly efficient form of business organization. The retarded growth of the corporate sector may quite possibly have the undesirable effect of increasing monopolistic or oligopolistic tendencies among existing companies since few, if any, new firms are added to the competition[30]. Virtually all developing nations tax incorporated businesses much more heavily than unincorporated enterprises or private partnerships. The wisdom of such a policy is questionable, given the fact that developing nations have a great need for efficient capital markets and increased level of investment, both of which may be provided by corporations. In addition, incorporated businesses may well be the only source with sufficient funds to establish industries using modern production methods[31].

2.3 Property taxes

Taxes on various forms of property are often levied on the assumption that the taxable capacity of an individual or business is not determined solely by personal or company income. The possession of property not only yields income to its owner but also confers certain other advantages, such as a reserve of spending power for emergencies (reducing the need to save out of income), security for old age, better access to credit, and increased social status[32]. In terms of administration, wealth taxes are often preferred as wealth is relatively difficult to conceal, and property taxes do not present the myriad problems encountered in levying income taxes; for example, the need for accurate records and a large degree of voluntary compliance on the part of the taxpayer[33].

Property taxes are not a leading source of revenue in most developed or underdeveloped countries (*Tables 2.9* and *2.10*). Taxes on property – land

Table 2.9 *Selected developing countries: property taxes (1966–1968)*[a]

	Percentage of total tax revenue
Under $250 per capita GNP	
Rwanda	6.5
Upper Volta	2.4
Burundi	3.9
Ethiopia	8.3
Tanzania	5.4
Mali	1.5
Chad	4.7
Indonesia	2.1
Nepal	26.3
India	9.3
Somalia	1.1
Congo, Dem. Rep.	0.1
Sudan	0.1
Kenya	0.7
Pakistan	5.7
Togo	2.3
Sri Lanka	2.9
Vietnam	5.6
Thailand	2.1
Bolivia	0.0
Korea	8.3
Egypt	8.2
Philippines	8.2
Morocco	5.5
Tunisia	3.8
Senegal	4.4
Paraguay	5.8
Ecuador	9.9
Honduras	2.0
Average	5.1
Over $250 per capita GNP	
Taiwan	11.3
Iran	1.4
Ghana	2.7
Ivory Coast	4.0
Zambia	2.5
Brazil	1.4
Guatemala	5.6
Malaysia	12.9
Guyana	2.7
Turkey	8.5
Peru	8.7
Colombia	8.9
Costa Rica	6.3
Jamaica	8.1
Lebanon	14.1
Chile	6.4

Table 2.9 *(continued)*

	Percentage of total tax revenue
Over $250 per capita GNP	
Singapore	28.2
Argentina	10.9
Trinidad and Tobago	6.7
Venezuela	0.3
Average	7.6
Overall Average	6.1

Notes: ᵃ Taxes on real estate and net wealth (including land revenue), taxes on property transfer, gift and death taxes, and taxes on motor vehicles.

Source: Chelliah (see *Table 2.1*), pp. 317–321.

taxes, taxes on capital gains, death duties, and net wealth taxes – yield only about six percent of total tax revenue in our sample of developing countries and 6.5 percent for our group of developed countries. The importance of these taxes is not limited, however, to their relatively low revenue yield, as these taxes can be wielded by the government so as to direct the course of development.

There is some slight difference between the lower and middle income LDCs. As can be seen from *Table 2.9*, only 5.1 percent of the former countries' revenues come from property taxes, while the latter receive about half as much again from this source – about 7.6 percent. If a simple

Table 2.10 *Selected developed countries: property taxes (1961)*

	Percentage of total tax revenue
United States	13.2
Canada	14.2
United Kingdom	9.5
Federal Republic of Germany	1.6
Netherlands	0.5
France	1.0
Japan	5.7
Average	6.5

Source: Musgrave (see *Table 2.4*), p. 172.

regression is calculated (see *Figure 2.4*) of the share of property taxes in total tax revenues versus per capita GNP, the slope is positive (estimated value: +0.0077); however, this regression explains only about six percent of the variation in the share of property taxes.

The predominance of the agricultural sector in developing countries and the difficulty of taxing agricultural income make land taxes vitally important. The numerous methods used to tax agricultural land include an annual tax on the capital value of the land (either including or excluding the value of

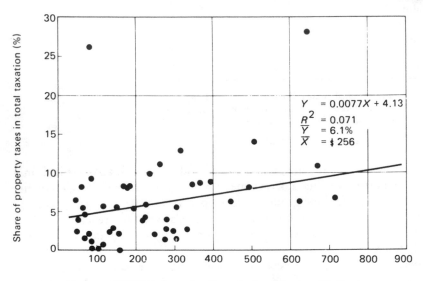

1966/68 per capita Gross National Product (Dollars)

Figure 2.4 *Selected developing countries: relation between share of property taxes in total taxation and per capita GNP, 1966–1968*
Source: See Table 2.9

improvements) or a tax on its rental value. Alternatively, the income from the land may be taxed on the assumption that the value of marketed produce serves as a proxy for the value of the land itself. A tax is sometimes levied on the size of the holding, with increased rates for irrigated land[34].

Considerable difficulty is often encountered in determining the value of the land subject to taxation, but this can be overcome by levying a tax at a constant rate per acre, irrespective of fertility and productivity, although this necessarily results in a rate which even the more unproductive land can pay. As a result, the revenues collected by such a single rate tax tend to be very low[35].

Frequent reassessment of the extent and value of ownership is exceedingly difficult, even in advanced industrial countries and is virtually impossible in developing countries. Consequently, the chronic inflation which characterizes many developing economies has the undesirable effect of reducing the real value of land tax receipts over time, since the value of the land can only be determined every few years. The resulting inelasticity of land taxes (e.g., receipts from land taxes do not increase in proportion to national income) should be of particular concern to LDCs, with their need for increased government revenue as development continues.

The numerous difficulties encountered in accurately assessing the value of agricultural land may be largely avoided by using presumptive methods of assessment. The essence of the presumptive method, according to Bird, 'is to assume that taxable income is related in a relatively fixed way to some factor or factors that can be more easily verified than income itself'. One method of presumptive assessment is to base the presumed income on the yield obtained from 'standard land' using productive methods of average efficiency. The assessed income in each geographical region is thus based on the average yield of various crops on 'standard' farms[36]. Such methods of assessment not only ease the administrative burden but also offer an incentive for the individual landowner to increase his productivity above that found on the representative farm. By penalizing the holding of land for speculative purposes, a common occurrence in developing countries, presumptive assessment may bring into production a large portion of idle land[37].

Taxes on agricultural land may also be useful in attacking an unequal distribution of income as large landowners are usually among the most wealthy in an LDC. The taxes may, of course, fall largely upon the poorer classes, depending upon the shifting of the taxes and the system of landholding. Australia and New Zealand have both successfully used land taxes in an effort to break up large estates into smaller and more productive units[38]. Similarly, the Egyptian land tax of the 1950s placed a heavy interim tax on lands scheduled for subdivision under land reform. The Egyptian government hoped that the increased taxes would force owners to subdivide their holdings, thus precluding government action[39].

The government may also use urban land taxes both as a source of revenue and as a policy instrument with which to shape the course of development. According to Ricardo, taxes on unearned increases in land value, resulting from population growth and higher standards of living, do not have adverse effects on incentives. This argument has particular relevance to urban areas, especially those in developing countries, where the market value of land often increases at astronomical rates.

The tax may apply to either the unimproved ('site') value of the land or to the improved value of the land. If the tax is limited to the site value of the land or if improvements are taxed at a lower rate than the land itself, the urban land tax is, in effect, only taxing increments in value. Such a policy is of particular relevance to those countries, including many LDCs, where land is held primarily as a refuge from inflation[40]. An advantage of site valuation is that the tax is the same whether or not the land is developed; in this way, pressure is exerted upon the owner of vacant or underutilized land to develop it more fruitfully in order to produce the revenue necessary to pay the tax[41]. Critics of such schemes to develop urban land have argued that there is little evidence that such tax incentives have any significant effect. Sydney and Nairobi are often cited as instances where site valuation contributed to development, but such cities as Singapore, Kuala Lumpur, New York, and London developed without the benefit of site valuation[42].

Taxes on urban property can be viewed not only as a traditional tax (i.e., a compulsory payment to the government in return for which the taxpayer receives no directly measurable benefits) but also as a payment to the local government for services rendered (police, fire protection, etc.). Viewed in this context, exempting improvements on urban property may not be equitable, as it most probably fails to allocate the costs of local government in proportion to the direct benefits received. Site valuation may, therefore, favor owners of luxury hotels, condominiums, and other valuable improvements, and place a relatively heavier burden on other land owners[43].

Both urban and rural land taxes may be levied in the form of special assessments or 'land-betterment' taxes. The value of private property is often enhanced by such public projects as the construction of sewers, widening of streets, and installation of irrigation; hence, the payment of the tax may be viewed as simply the payment by the property owner in return for a boost to the value of his property. Legislation in 1960 and 1963 in Tunisia, for instance, required owners of land benefiting from new irrigation facilities to contribute their share of the cost[44].

A system of urban property taxes may be useful, as it allows the public authorities to guide the development of urban and suburban areas. Suitable tax measures may be devised to provide incentives for the construction of socially desirable housing projects, provision of parks and green belts, etc.

Taxes on capital gains differ from the general property taxes discussed above in that they are not levied on the basis of the annual value of the property but rather on the increase in the value of the property which is realized at the time of its sale. Capital gains taxes are usually justified on the grounds of equity, as a large proportion of the increase in value is often attributable to a general increase in the price level. This makes it difficult to separate the real appreciation of the property from either the effects of inflation or of public investment, rather than from improvements provided by the property owner[45]. These taxes have yielded little revenue for LDCs – one estimate places the yield at approximately two to three percent of the personal income tax[46] – since only a small proportion of personal income is typically derived from capital gains realized on the sale of the property. Taxes levied on capital gains received from the sale of real estate may have the undesirable consequence of inhibiting the sale of land and lead to higher reservation prices. George Lent claims that 'if the tax rates are very high, this lock-in effect may result in substantial withholding of property from development[47].

Taxes may also be imposed upon assets, both tangible and intangible, possessed by an individual at the time of his death. Death duties yield comparatively little revenue in both developed and developing countries, with yields of only one to two percent of total tax revenue (*Table 2.11*). But the small yield from death duties is not indicative, however, of their entire role in the tax structure. Death taxes create fewer administrative problems than personal income taxation, since there are fewer returns and a property accounting usually occurs at the time of death, regardless of whether there are death taxes[48]. In addition, the interaction between the administration of

Table 2.11 *Death duties as percentage of total taxes (1969)*

	Percentage
Developed countries	
Australia	3.2
Belgium	1.4
Denmark	0.8
Eire	2.2
France	0.9
Federal Republic of Germany	0.3
Holland	1.0
Italy	1.1
Japan[a]	2.4
Luxembourg	0.1
New Zealand	2.0
Norway	0.2
South Africa	1.2
United Kingdom	2.5
United States	1.8
Average	1.4
Developing countries	
Ceylon	1.5
Malaysia	0.6
Pakistan[b]	0.2
Philippines[c]	0.5
Singapore	1.3
South Africa	0.3
Average	0.7

Notes: [a] Inheritance and gift tax.
  [b] All direct taxes except income tax (1969/1970) and corporation tax.
  [c] Estate, gift, and inheritance tax.

Source: H. W. T. Pepper, Death Duties: With Particular Reference to Developing Countries, *Bulletin for International Fiscal Documentation*, **26**, 231, (June, 1972).

death levies and personal income taxation may aid in the administration of the latter.

The fact that death taxes can be used effectively to attack an unequal distribution of wealth should be of particular importance to the many developing countries which are not yet able to levy progressive individual income taxes. Progressive death duties should not, of course, act as a discouragement to the accumulation of assets during a person's lifetime. There is some evidence to indicate that moderate rates of death duties do not have significantly adverse incentive effects. Kenya, for example, abolished its death duty in the hope of attracting wealthy settlers; yet, the absence of death taxation had such little effect that the tax was soon reintroduced[49].

Table 2.12 *Net wealth taxation as percentage of total national tax revenue*

	Percentage
Developed countries	
Japan (1952/1953)	0.3
Netherlands (1960)	1.5
Sweden (1958/1959)	1.5
Norway (1962/1963)	2.4
Denmark (1958/1959)	2.5
Federal Republic of Germany (1960)[a]	1.6
Developing countries	
Pakistan (1964/1965)	0.8
India (1959/1960)	1.8
Ceylon (1964/1965)	2.0
Uruguay (1965)	2.6
Colombia (1961)	4.4

Notes: [a] Percentage of aggregate government revenue at all levels.

Source: Noboru Tanabe, The Taxation of Net Wealth, *IMF Staff Papers*, **14** (March, 1967), p. 127.

One feature of most death taxation systems does not serve to create a more equitable distribution of wealth; namely, the widespread practice of varying the rates according to the degree of consanguinity to the deceased. In Denmark, for example, the maximum rate for relatives is 13 percent, while the relevant rate for strangers is 60 percent[50]. This discrimination against bequests to distant relations and to strangers (e.g. charitable institutions) prevents an effective redistribution of the assets as the rate structure causes the government to receive the lion's share of assets not left to the immediate family.

The net wealth tax differs from most other property taxes in that it is not imposed on the gross value of the property but on the net value of all assets less liabilities of the particular taxpayer. Thus, the tax takes into account the taxable capacity of the individual or corporation, since allowance is provided for the deduction of liabilities and personal exemptions. Net wealth taxes are usually imposed on an annual basis; hence, they differ from both death duties, which are levied once a generation, and capital levies, which are charged on an irregular basis. The contribution of the net wealth tax to revenue is minimal in most countries, usually accounting for between one and three percent of the total national tax revenue (*Table 2.12*).

The low yield of net wealth taxation is of little significance, however, since the primary purpose of the tax is to increase equity by supplementing income taxes which do not take into account the benefits received from the ownership of property. The implementation of a net wealth tax leads, it is hoped, to greater risk taking and a more productive use of capital, since the tax burden is not affected by the yield of the property. Likewise, a net wealth tax applied to corporations would penalize firms with a low return on their capital and provide an incentive for more efficient utilization of their resources. Another positive aspect of net wealth taxation is that the administration of these taxes provides the tax authorities with valuable information which may serve as a useful cross-check on other forms of taxation; as a result, the actual contribution of net wealth taxes to government revenue may be greater than the receipts alone indicate[51].

Notes

1 The selection of countries was determined primarily by the availability of data.
2 Paul A. Baran, *The Political Economy of Growth*, (New York: Monthly Review Press, 1968), p. 23.
3 Raja J. Chelliah, *Fiscal Policy in Underdeveloped Countries* (London: George Allen & Unwin Ltd., 1960), p. 65.
4 Walter W. Heller, 'Fiscal Policies for Under-developed Countries, in Richard M. Bird and Oliver Oldman (eds.), *Readings on Taxation in Developing Countries*, (Baltimore: Johns Hopkins Press, 1967), p. 5.
5 N. Kaldor, 'The Role of Taxation in Economic Development', in Edward A. G. Robinson (ed.), *Problems in Economic Development*, (London: Macmillan, 1965), pp. 187–188.
6 Chelliah, op. cit. (note 3) p. 62.
7 Kaldor, op. cit. (note 5) pp. 170–171.
8 Heller, op. cit. (note 4) p. 5.
9 Robert B. Bangs, *Financing Economic Development: Fiscal Policy for Emerging Countries*, (Chicago: University of Chicago Press, 1968), p. 23.
10 Alan Richmond Prest, *Public Finance in Underdeveloped Countries*, (New York: Praeger, 1962), pp. 34–35.
11 Tan Wai, Taxation Problems and Policies of Underdeveloped Countries, *IMF Staff Papers*, 9 (November 1962), pp. 433–434.
12 John F. Due, Requirements of a Tax Structure in a Development Economy, in Bird and Oldman (eds.) (note 4), p. 39.
13 John F. Due, *Government Finance: Economics of the Public Sector*, (Irwin: Homewood, Illinois, 1968), p. 463.
14 Alison Martin and W. Arthur Lewis, Patterns of Public Revenue and Expenditure, *Manchester School of Economic and Social Studies*, 24, 203 (September 1956).
15 Wai, op. cit. (note 11) p. 440.

16 Richard Goode, Reconstruction of Foreign Tax Systems, in Bird and Oldman (eds.), (note 4) pp. 122–124.

17 John F. Due, The African Personal Tax, *National Tax Journal*, 15, 385–398 (December 1962).

18 Chelliah, op. cit. (note 3) pp. 76–78.

19 Due. *Government Finance*, pp. 464–465; Richard Goode, 'Reconstruction of Foreign Tax Systems', in Gerald M. Meier (ed.), *Leading Issues in Economic Development* (New York: Oxford University Press, 1964), p. 124.

20 Prest, op. cit. (note 10). p. 40; Bangs, op. cit. (note 9) p. 138.

21 Chelliah, op. cit. (note 3) pp. 78, 85.

22 Prest, op. cit. (note 10) pp. 40–41.

23 Due, op. cit. (note 19) p. 465.

24 Alan Richmond Prest, Taxes, Subsidies, and Investment Incentives, in Alan T. Peacock and Gerald Hauser (eds.), *Government Finance and Economic Development* (Paris: Organization for Economic Cooperation and Development, 1963), pp. 118–119. Chelliah, op. cit. (note 3) p. 78.

25 Prest, Ibid. pp. 20, 120.

26 Kenneth M. Kauffman, Income Tax Exemption and Economic Development, *National Tax Journal*, 13, 158–160 (June, 1960). Kauffman cites Puerto Rico and Israel as examples of where the promise of a tax holiday 'may engender a nonrational response from the potential grantee because it serves as an advertising lure which stimulates interest in the potentialities of an area'.

27 Kauffman, op. cit. (note 26) p. 161.

28 Prest, Taxes, Subsidies, and Investment Incentives, p. 121. Kauffman, op. cit. (note 26) p. 161.

29 Everett E. Hagen, *The Economics of Development* (Homewood, Illinois: Richard D. Irwin, 1975), p. 360.

30 Prest, op. cit. (note 10) p. 41.

31 Wai, op. cit. (note 11) p. 437.

32 Noboru Tanabe, The Taxation of Net Wealth, *IMF Staff Papers*, 14 (March, 1967), p. 127.

33 Bangs, op. cit. (note 9) p. 128.

34 Richard M. Bird, Agricultural Taxation in Developing Countries, *Finance and Development*, 37 (September, 1974).

35 Prest, op. cit. (note 10) p. 45.

36 Bird, op. cit. (note 34) p. 37.

37 Bangs, op. cit. (note 9) p. 128.

38 George E. Lent, The Taxation of Land Value, *IMF Staff Papers*, 14 (March, 1967), p. 92.

39 Haskell P. Wald, *Taxation of Agricultural Land in Underdeveloped Economies* (Cambridge, Massachusetts: Harvard University Press, 1959), pp. 38–39.

40 Lent, op. cit. (note 38) p. 90.

41 H. W. T. Pepper, Taxation of Land and Real Property in Developing Countries: Some Points of Practice and Policy, *Bulletin for International Fiscal Documentation*, 26, 361, (October, 1972).

42 Ibid. p. 367.

43 Lent, op. cit. (note 38) pp. 91, 97.

44 Ibid. pp. 110–116.

45 Wai, op. cit. (note 11) p. 439.

46 Lent, op. cit. (note 38) p. 108.

47 Ibid. p. 109.

48 Bangs, op. cit. (note 9) p. 142.

49 H. W. T. Pepper, Death Duties: With Particular Reference to Developing Countries, *Bulletin for International Fiscal Documentation*, 26 230, (June, 1972).

50 Ibid. p. 235.

51 This section has been drawn largely from Tanabe, op. cit. (note 32) pp. 124–168.

Indirect taxes

Virtually all developing nations rely extensively on indirect taxation because of its ability to yield significantly more revenue than direct taxes. In addition, indirect taxes are often much more effective than direct taxes in reaching the large semisubsistence population and may be politically more acceptable because the distribution of their burden is often unclear. Administrative concerns often favor indirect taxation as the cost of collection may be lower because of the relatively small number of taxpayers (importers, exporters, manufacturers, retail merchants, etc.). We will examine the role of the two most important forms of indirect taxes: taxes on international trade (export taxes and import duties) and taxes levied on internal transactions (excises and sales taxes).

3.1   Export taxes

For centuries various taxes on exports have been levied, yet their importance in recent years is largely a result of the commodity boom that began during the Korean War, the first such boom period following the independence of many Asian countries[1]. It is generally acknowledged that the chief advantage of export taxes for developing nations is that they are so much easier to administer than are other forms of taxation. The levying of taxes on exports may simplify the tax structure as an export tax may serve as a proxy for an agricultural land tax, an income tax, or, in the case of mineral-producing countries, a production or severance tax.

   Table 3.1 sketches the revenue raised by export taxes in a selected group of developing countries. It can be seen that revenue from export taxes is important in many LDCs, but it is also significant that a substantial number of LDCs receive very little or no revenue from this source, despite the fact that they have a large foreign trade sector. In Nicaragua, for example, exports constituted 22.2 percent of the GNP in 1963/1964, yet taxation of these exports yielded only 1.4 percent of total tax revenue. During the same period, the Philippines did not even levy an export tax, yet exports were 14.9 percent of GNP[2].

   For the countries listed in *Table 3.1*, it is clear that export taxes are a more important revenue source for the poorer countries than they are for the middle income countries: the former collect almost twice as much (10.6

Table 3.1 *Selected developing countries: ratio of export taxes to total tax revenue (1966–1968)*

	Percentage of total tax revenue
Less than $250 per capita GNP	
Rwanda	15.1
Upper Volta	3.3
Burundi	17.3
Ethiopia	8.3
Tanzania	1.5
Mali	5.8
Chad	7.3
Indonesia	18.6
Nepal	6.5
India	2.9
Somalia	9.1
Congo, Dem. Rep.	46.4
Sudan	11.0
Kenya	1.2
Togo	7.3
Ceylon	15.2
Vietnam	38.0
Thailand	11.6
Bolivia	12.5
Korea	0.0
Egypt	1.9
Philippines	2.0
Morocco	2.0
Tunisia	3.5
Senegal	8.1
Paraguay	18.3
Ecuador	9.5
Honduras	13.2
Average	10.6
Greater than $250 per capita GNP	
Taiwan	3.2
Iran	2.3
Ghana	16.8
Ivory Coast	20.5
Zambia	17.0
Brazil	0.0
Guatemala	6.6
Malaysia	17.9
Guyana	3.1
Turkey	0.0
Peru	1.9
Colombia	4.8
Costa Rica	2.4
Mexico	4.3
Jamaica	0.0
Lebanon	0.0

Table 3.1 *(continued)*

	Percentage of total tax revenue
Greater than $250 per capita GNP	
Singapore	0.0
Argentina	7.5
Trinidad and Tobago	0.0
Venezuela	0.7
Average	5.45
Overall average	8.5

Source: Chelliah (see *Table 2.1*), pp. 317–320.

percent) in this way than the latter countries (5.45 percent). The negative slope of the relationship between the share of export taxes and per capita GNP can be seen from the scatter diagram (*Figure 3.1*); the estimated regression coefficient was −0.0169, and GNP explained about 12 percent in the observed variation in relative share of export taxes.

The distribution of the export tax burden depends upon both the structure of the domestic economy and the nature of world demand for the commodity being taxed. Under normal conditions in world markets, where a degree of competition generally exists, it is not possible to shift the tax to foreign consumers. If, however, the country is a major world supplier (or if it unites

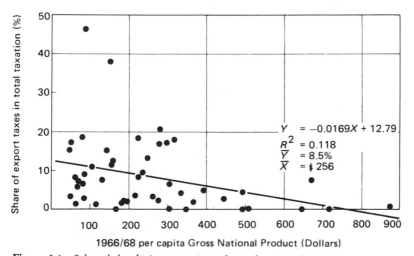

$Y = -0.0169X + 12.79$
$R^2 = 0.118$
$\bar{Y} = 8.5\%$
$\bar{X} = \$256$

Figure 3.1 *Selected developing countries: relation between share of export taxes in total taxation and per capita GNP, 1966–1968*
Source: See *Table 3.1.*

with other producers to form a cartel that dominates the world supply), then the export tax will be largely, or even completely, passed to foreign consumers. Even if such conditions prevail, the exporting country must exercise caution so as not to destroy its market by encouraging production elsewhere or stimulating the development of synthetic substances. The high export taxes that Chile levied on its nitrate monopoly were disastrous in the long run as they encouraged the production of synthetic nitrates.

Under most conditions, the exporting country does not face highly in elastic foreign demand, so much of the burden of the export tax is shifted back to the producers and to the associated factors of production. The shifting of export taxes backward to plantation laborers has been deterred in some countries by the government's establishment of a fixed wage: it was in this way, for instance, that Ceylon's tax on tea exports during the Korean War commodity boom could not be shifted back to the plantation workers[3].

Usually much of the export tax is not passed on to foreigners which has the effect of discriminating between those commodities produced for export and those produced entirely for domestic consumption. As a result, the allocation of resources can be affected, perhaps adversely, as resources are often shifted toward any export goods not subject to taxation or those goods produced for domestic consumption[4].

It is often suggested that developing nations should tax exports at significant rates only when the world price of the commodity rises above the accustomed level. The use of a 'sliding scale' which varies with commodity prices, results in fluctuating government revenues, but even this may be of value since the imposition of the tax tends to stabilize the domestic economy by exerting a counter-inflationary influence (if coupled with appropriate government spending policies). The tax tends to absorb the additional income that results from the increased world price of the commodity[5].

An inability to shift export taxes forward to the foreign buyer may result in less than optimal exploitation of natural resources in the exporting country. Taxation of exports reduces an enterprise's return on each unit produced and may thus result in decreased output as the production of the higher cost units becomes unprofitable. In the case of a mining company, Levin notes that the company 'may decide to bypass lower grade ores, which could thus be permanently lost because of far higher costs involved in returning to work them later on'[6]. A recent United Nations technical assistance mission to Bolivia concluded that the export duties on refined tin induced the mining companies to avoid extracting low grade ore, which is one of Bolivia's most important natural resources[7].

3.2 Marketing boards

During and after World War II several countries established semi-official agencies with a statutory monopoly of the purchases for export of certain agricultural produce. These agencies in some circumstances served to collect export taxes. A state marketing board has the potential to yield a large profit to the government if a positive differential is maintained between the international price and the domestic purchasing price paid by the marketing board[8].

The economic impact of a marketing board depends largely on the extent of its penetration into the domestic economy. A marketing board will have the same effect as an export tax if the board purchases produce at the stage where it reaches the point of export. If, on the other hand, the board sets prices at buying points in the countryside, the effect on production and resource allocation will differ from those of an export tax[9]. In this case the marketing board takes on many or even all of the functions of middlemen in a non-regulated market.

One attractive feature of a marketing board is the possibility of its use for contracyclical operations. The domestic purchasing price that is established and paid by the marketing board is typically kept fairly stable at significantly below the minimum international price likely to occur. This pricing system allows the government to appropriate all the profits arising from an increase in the international price. Similarly, a falling international price will only decrease government profits and will not affect the domestic money incomes of exporters, distributors, and producers[10].

3.3   Import duties

In most developing countries, imports are large in relation to national income, and therefore constitute a substantial tax base. The levying of import duties is usually administratively preferable to direct taxation, as foreign trade is conducted only through a few seaports or points of entry, and the goods arrive in bulk containers (ships or trains) that are easily detected. The evasion of customs duties by smuggling is not easy, except in some island countries like Indonesia and the Philippines, and even if significant smuggling is possible, other tax avoidance is even easier. Another factor contributing to the popularity of import duties with governments is the fact that these levies often do not present any major political problems, because of their hidden nature, unlike various forms of direct taxation[11].

The importance of import duties in the finances of developing countries can readily be seen in *Table 3.2*, which indicates the percentage of total tax revenue provided by import taxes. The group of countries with a per capita GNP of less than $250 receive an average 28.2 percent of their total tax revenue from taxation of imports, while the comparable figure for the less poor LDCs (per capita GNP greater than $250) is 23 percent. The great importance of import duties is obvious as the entire group of developing countries received an average 26 percent of their total tax revenue from this one source. A simple regression of the share of import taxes versus per capita

Table 3.2 *Selected developing countries: ratio of import taxes to total tax revenue (1966–1968)*

	Percentage of total tax revenue
Less than $250 per capita GNP	
Rwanda	29.4
Upper Volta	18.5
Burundi	27.9
Ethiopia	25.0
Tanzania	33.0
Mali	22.6
Chad	27.9
Indonesia	24.7
Nepal	40.0
India	14.9
Somalia	49.0
Congo, Dem. Rep.	15.6
Sudan	41.3
Kenya	33.0
Togo	39.5
Sri Lanka	32.4
Vietnam	23.7
Thailand	29.9
Bolivia	43.2
Korea	16.2
Egypt	19.9
Philippines	19.4
Morocco	17.9
Tunisia	9.8
Senegal	30.1
Paraguay	32.5
Ecuador	47.2
Honduras	25.2
Average	28.2
Greater than $250 per capita GNP	
Taiwan	19.4
Iran	17.7
Ghana	32.3
Ivory Coast	24.4
Zambia	7.8
Brazil	3.5
Guatemala	25.9
Malaysia	28.4
Guyana	42.9
Turkey	27.6
Peru	30.2
Colombia	25.4
Costa Rica	31.8
Mexico	14.9
Jamaica	25.7
Lebanon	38.0

Table 3.2 *(continued)*

	Percentage of total tax revenue
Greater than $250 per capita GNP	
Singapore	26.9
Argentina	9.3
Trinidad and Tobago	22.2
Venezuela	6.1
Average	23.0
Overall average	26.0

Source: Chelliah (see *Table 2.1*), pp. 317–320.

GNP (see *Figure 3.2*) yields an estimated value for the slope of −0.0158; GNP explained less of the observed variation in the share of total taxes of export taxes than it did in most of the instances cited earlier, in fact, only about eight percent.

In addition to being relatively easy to administer, politically desirable and a major source of revenue, import duties may hasten the development process if used in conjunction with other government policies. Accepted standards of equity may be realized if the basic necessities most frequently purchased by the lower income groups are exempted from import taxation. In contrast with more developed countries, such a policy is of particular

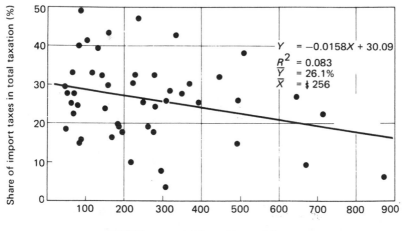

$Y = -0.0158X + 30.09$
$R^2 = 0.083$
$\overline{Y} = 26.1\%$
$\overline{X} = \$256$

1966/68 per capita Gross National Product (Dollars)

Figure 3.2 *Selected developing countries: relation between share of import taxes in total taxation and per capita GNP, 1966–1968*
Source: See *Table 3.2.*

importance to developing countries where there are normally great differences in the consumption patterns of higher and lower income groups[12].

With the proper classification of goods and selection of rates, import taxes can, in effect, be used as a progressive tax on consumption since the income elasticity of demand for imported luxury goods is high. Such a policy may boost the overall savings ratio in the country if individuals save more of their incomes because the price to the consumer of imported luxury goods increases sharply. The domestic production of the luxuries must, of course, be simultaneously curtailed if the full effect is to be felt in savings; otherwise, the import duties may act to promote the domestic production of the formerly imported luxuries. Other leakages are also possible. The money not spent on imported luxury goods may be used by wealthy persons for socially nonproductive uses, such as the purchase of land, gold or jewelry, or for foreign travel, or investments abroad. In such instances, import taxes are not effective policy tools, and must be supplemented by direct taxation of income or wealth[13].

On the other hand care must be taken that the duties on luxuries are not so excessive as to stifle the incentive motive. Incentive goods are of particular importance in developing market economies where they are often essential in encouraging producers to move further into the cash economy[14].

Many countries either eliminate or greatly reduce customs duties on materials, equipment and supplies for new industries they are attempting to encourage. The exemption from import duties on capital equipment serves to reduce the fixed costs of a new business and thus places it in a better competitive position. Also, the resulting reduction in capital requirements eases the financing of the new enterprise[15].

Import duties discourage the importation of the taxed goods, thereby encouraging the development of import substituting industries to produce the high duty goods if the import duty exceeds the cost differential between domestic and foreign production. The establishment of import substituting industries is often aided by duty exemptions for imported inputs. Such a policy should be used with caution, however, as the assembly industry stimulated by the duty exemption often provides little value added or employment in the domestic economy. Indeed, all attempts to levy protective tariffs to shield domestic 'infant industries' should be subjected to close scrutiny, as a protective tariff is justifiable only in those instances where the country has, or will have, a definite comparative advantage in that particular industry. Otherwise, the protective tariff will have adverse long run effects on resource allocation[16].

The use of import duties in the fiscal system of a developing country may contribute to the nation's development goals through several other mechanisms. The use of import taxes to reduce import purchases, unlike taxation on domestically produced goods, does not decrease the market size nor does it interfere with domestic production and investment. Taxation of imports may lessen the need for exchange controls and import licensing, both of which are rather difficult to administer[17]. Finally, import taxes using valuation at FOB prices (i.e., excluding transportation and insurance costs to the port or border) may increase competition by reducing the advantage of nearby suppliers in relation to their more distant competitors[18].

The taxation of imports has several undesirable aspects which must be considered in formulating the optimal tax structure. The greatest defect of import duties is the diminishing level of revenue of a given duty rate schedule as economic development proceeds. Development tends to increase import substitution, so the ratio of luxury imports to national income declines significantly. Also, the goals of a typical developing country inevitably aim at increasing the ratio of domestic value added by manufacture to gross domestic product (GNP). The only exception would be a nation that intended to remain an agricultural producer, exporting agricultural products and importing manufactured goods[19].

Most countries are not totally free in determining their tariff structures; they are subject to certain international constraints. Since World War II, several multilateral agreements have been reached in an effort to further cooperation in matters of international trade. Perhaps the most well known of these agreements is the General Agreement on Tariffs and Trade (GATT) which was signed in 1948 and which has since established a permanent secretariat (equivalent to that of a specialized United Nations agency) to oversee its signatories' obligations[20].

Import duties may be levied on either specific (fixed rate per physical unit) or *ad valorem* (percentage of value) bases. Specific rates are simpler administratively, yet they discriminate against purchasers of cheaper items and their yield does not increase with rising prices. *Ad valorem* duties are not subject to these limitations, but they are much more difficult to administer because of valuation problems[21].

Another difficulty arising from import duties may be an upward movement in retail prices, which may, in turn, help generate demands for higher wages, rents, business profits, etc. The possible inflationary impact of import duties would, of course, depend on the price elasticities of demand for imported goods and the extent to which import substitution occurs[22].

3.4   Excise taxes

The imposition of import duties and the continuing process of economic development generally leads to the establishment of import substituting industries producing commodities for which there is a relatively large and stable domestic market. The resulting change in the composition of imports and increase in domestic value added is usually beneficial to the developing country, but the continued domestic production of the formerly imported goods may be deleterious if the country will lose substantial revenue from import duties unless equivalent taxes are levied on domestic production. A system of excise taxes levied on the commodities produced by import substituting industries is widely used by developing countries because of their ability to generate large revenues[23]. *Table 3.3* shows that the group of developing countries with a per capita income less than $250 received some 21.6 percent of their total tax revenue from excise taxation, while the less poor LDCs (per capita GNP above $250) earned slightly more (22.2 percent). The fact that the average developing country in our sample received more than one-fifth (22 percent) of its total tax revenue from excise taxation indicates the tremendous revenue importance of this form of indirect tax.

In addition to providing substantial revenue to the government, excise taxation may be used as an effective policy instrument to direct the course of development. It is generally agreed that excises on necessities are shifted forward into higher final product prices; hence, the impact of an excise tax must be considered in relation to the price elasticity of demand for the commodity on which the tax is levied[24]. Excises are typically imposed on products with a low price elasticity of demand (i.e., products where sales are little affected by a change of price) such as beer, wine, liquor, tobacco products, matches and motor fuel. Even at low rates, excises on commodities with relatively inelastic demand generate substantial revenue. They also are fairly easy to administer, since the number of domestic manufacturers is usually quite small and/or the commodities are channelled through a few points. The experience of developing nations in recent years indicates that most excise revenue is obtained from taxes levied on alcohol and tobacco products. For example, in 1968, Sierra Leone received 71 percent of its excise tax revenue from tobacco products, while Zambia obtained 56 percent from excises levied on alcoholic beverages[25].

Excises on alcohol and tobacco products are often justified on the grounds that the consumption of such products does not contribute to economic benefit in a socially significant way. Proponents of this view argue that a reduction in the consumption of liquor and tobacco products would not only be socially desirable (decreased drunkenness and lung cancer) but would also increase savings or, alternatively, channel consumption into areas more conducive to the development of the individual and society. Such arguments are suspect, however, as they ignore the fact that products with a low price elasticity of demand will continue to be purchased with little, if any, decrease in quantity, even though the price is increased because of excise taxes. Thus, the excise taxes will be paid out of funds that would otherwise be saved or used for nutritious food. Clearly, under such conditions, the imposition of an excise may not be compatible with the objectives of the development program. On the other hand, there are policies, such as a ban on advertising, that can be used by those governments desiring to reduce the consumption of liquor and tobacco products[26].

Table 3.3 *Selected developing countries: ratios of excise taxes and sales taxes to total tax revenue (1969–1971)*

Less than $250 per capita GNP	Per capita GNP (dollars)	Excise tax ratio (%)	Sales tax ratio (%)	Greater than $250 per capita GNP	Per capita GNP (dollars)	Excise tax ratio (%)	Sales tax ratio (%)
Mali	55	11	24	Syria	252	18	0
Upper Volta	63	12	21	Korea	253	37	7
Somalia	66	31	0	Paraguay	257	20	5
Ethiopia	71	26	16	Ghana	260	21	8
Indonesia	74	19	12	Ecuador	269	16	10
Chad	75	18	14	Honduras	281	28	7
Nepal	76	16	15	Jordan	281	17	0
Zaire	87	6	8	Tunisia	282	17	25
Benin	88	10	4	El Salvador	295	28	0
Tanzania	98	31	11	Columbia	334	15	8
India	98	51	15	Ivory Coast	377	10	26
Nigeria	103	14	0	Iraq	340	5	0
Sudan	110	23	0	Guatemala	349	28	0
Pakistan	113	38	0	Dominican Rep.	364	29	0
Madagascar	130	18	20	Oman	374	0	0
Uganda	132	29	16	Iran	378	10	0
Kenya	138	34	0	Turkey	379	30	20
Mauritania	145	10	25	Taiwan	389	42	6
Sierra Leone	156	26	0	Malaysia	391	35	0
Sri Lanka	166	27	11	Nicaragua	407	41	8
Thailand	181	28	21	Zambia	411	10	0
Bolivia	202	13	6	Saudi Arabia	437	0	0
Egypt	207	12	0	Peru	450	15	0
Philippines	214	16	21	Brazil	494	17	50
Liberia	230	7	0	Costa Rica	561	23	15
Morocco	230	23	26	Lebanon	637	23	0
Mauritius	234	37	0	Mexico	655	17	11
Senegal	234	18	34	Barbados	700	19	0
				Panama	711	28	0
Average	135	21.6	11.6	Jamaica	718	28	0
		(Total 33.2)		Portugal	787	29	12
				Trinidad and Tobago	803	22	0
				Uruguay	847	27	19
				Chile	895	9	32
				Cyprus	906	37	0
				Venezuela	1041	8	0
				Argentina	1065	32	17
				Greece	1141	31	12
				Average	519	22.2	7.8
						(Total 30.1)	
				Overall average	356	22.0	9.5
						(Total 31.4)	

Note: The data presented in this table are not strictly comparable with those shown in earlier tables, which are deriven from the Chelliah studies.

Source: Sjibren Cnossen, 'The Role and Structure of Sales Tax and Excise Systems', *Finance and Development*, March 1975.

Extensive reliance on excise taxation may also be objected to on grounds of equity. Properly administered excises are reasonably equitable horizontally (i.e., among those with similar incomes) but may be quite regressive vertically if the taxed goods are more likely to be consumed heavily by lower income groups. Excises on cigarettes and beer are particularly regressive as these products are price inelastic and are commonly consumed by the poor[27]. A properly structured excise tax system may, however, be neutral or even moderately progressive over a wide range of income groups. Such a system must provide for the great differences in consumption patterns at various income levels; these differences are often much sharper in developing countries than in industrialized nations. Thus, for example, the excise system should provide different rates for the relatively inexpensive package of cigarettes purchased by the poor (and often made from domestic tobacco) as compared to the expensive imported variety more typically purchased by the wealthy. A differentiated rate structure is of particular importance as excises are frequently levied on product specific, rather than on an *ad valorem* basis, due to the administrative difficulties involved in valuation. A rate structure based on brand names would be much more vertically equitable than an undifferentiated excise on all commodities of a certain type, yet it would not encounter the valuation problems of an *ad valorem* excise[28].

As consumption of goods on which excise taxes are typically levied does not increase proportionately (in quantity terms) as incomes rise, excise taxes of a given rate will tend to become a less important source of revenue as development continues. Several countries have attempted to circumvent this problem by extending the coverage of excise taxes to such items as durable consumer goods and various forms of entertainment[29]. Furthermore, the low income elasticity of demand for the goods subject to excises results in a regressive pattern of tax incidence; that is, a relatively heavy burden on the lower income groups[30].

3.5   Sales taxes

A system of excise taxes is 'selective' in the sense that the taxable goods are individually enumerated in the law (beer, wine, cigarettes, etc.). A general sales tax is broader, in that the tax base includes all commodities offered for sale except those specifically excluded. The structure of the sales tax system therefore precludes its use in restricting the consumption of certain goods deemed to have little or no contribution to the development process. The consumption of such goods may be effectively restricted, if desired, by use of other fiscal devices, such as customs duties and excises. Thus, sales taxation restricts overall consumer spending and, in addition, provides revenue to the public sector[31].

Sales taxes are often preferable to excises as development proceeds. At a higher level of economic development, the increasingly complex nature of the economy makes the use of large excise systems exceedingly difficult. The inherently fragmented nature of excise coverage often fails to provide sufficient revenue, while a broadbased sales tax system is potentially capable of generating more revenue. Furthermore, the reliance on an extensive excise system may interfere with domestic business operations as enforcement must depend largely on physical control of the various commodities subject to excises. The use of a general sales tax does not, however, necessarily preclude the use of excises; rather, the excise taxes are often restricted in their coverage to the traditional excise commodities (liquor, cigarettes, motor fuel, etc.) as such goods are typically taxed at a much higher rate than that of the general sales tax[32].

Table 3.3 indicates the contribution of sales tax revenue to 66 developing countries for which data are available. The relatively poorer LDCs (per capita GNP less than $250) received 11.6 percent of their total tax revenues from sales taxation, while the less poor LDCs (per capita GNP greater than $250) obtained some 7.8 percent of their revenues from this source. This may be misleading, however, as the inclusion of nations without sales tax systems obviously distorts the figures. If the countries without sales tax systems are excluded in the averaging process, it is found that the poorer LDCs that do levy sales taxes obtain 16.3 percent of their total tax revenue from sales taxation, while the less poor LDCs obtain some 14.9 percent of their revenue from this source.

If we compare the two groups of countries listed in *Table 3.3* as regards both types of taxes on commodity transactions, we can see that each levies about the same tax burden on these activities (33 percent versus 30 percent) and that each uses specific excises to a much greater extent than general sales taxes (21.6 percent compared to 11.6 percent for the poorer LDCs and 22.2 percent compared to 7.8 percent for the middle income countries). Contrary to what was said above, sales taxes do not gain in relative importance in the more economically developed countries of this sample.

The scatter diagram (*Figure 3.3*) shows the relationship between combined sales and excise tax revenues and per capita GNP. In fact, regression analysis indicates practically no evidence for such a relationship; the slope is only +0.00009, with less than 1 percent of the variation in relative tax share explained by GNP.

It is possible to levy sales taxes at virtually any stage of distribution, but they are most commonly applied at the manufacturing, wholesale, or retail level. A multi-point sales tax, where the commodity is taxed at each level in the distribution network, encourages vertical integration in a business unless the tax is quite small. Such a tax levied at low rates would not usually be desirable, as it would not yield much revenue relative to the effort needed to administer it[33]. These problems can be avoided by the use of a sales tax imposed at only one level (a single-point sales tax), but such levies are often easy to evade. As a result, the performance of the fiscal system may be seriously impaired: one study, for instance, found the evasion of the sales tax in Mexico in 1961 to be almost 50 percent of the legal liability[34].

The simplest form of single-point sales tax is a general levy at the manufacturing level. A manufacturers' sales tax is not often employed in developing countries, however, because the small amount of domestic

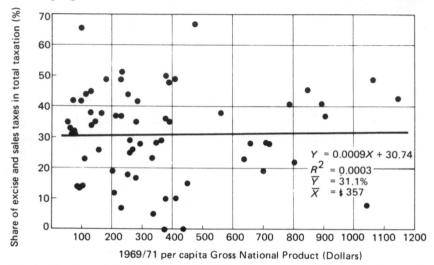

Figure 3.3 *Selected developing countries: relation between share of excise and sales taxes in total taxation and per capita GNP, 1969–1971*

manufacturing compared to imports results in discrimination against domestic goods over and above imported goods. Of course, this problem may be avoided if the sales tax is also levied on imported goods at the time of importation. Such a scheme, however, might present serious administrative difficulties for the comparatively unsophisticated tax authorities found in many developing countries[35].

Another form of single-point sales taxation is the imposition of a levy at the wholesale level. A wholesale sales tax is theoretically inferior to taxation at the retail level (discussed below) as it discriminates against certain distribution channels and makes no allowance for efficiency in retailing, as the amount of tax paid depends solely on the quantity of sales and ignores the retailer's profit margin. Nevertheless, in a low income country where retailing is conducted at roadside stands and by itinerant peddlers, the wholesale sales tax may be the only feasible alternative since taxation of individual retailers would be virtually impossible[36].

Retail sales taxation is generally acknowledged as the most desirable form of taxation if conditions permit its use. In developing nations a retail sales tax is often difficult to administer because of the absence of adequate sales records, the sheer number of retail outlets and the geographical dispersion of retailers in rural areas; consequently, collections are often confined to a few major cities[37]. Some of the difficulties of administering a retail tax may be avoided if a hybrid type of tax is employed. The sales of the large retailer would continue to be taxed, but the small vendor would be exempted and the tax applied to his purchases from a supplier[38].

A major advantage of the retail sales tax is the inclusion of all distribution margins in the tax base. As a result, the base of a typical retail tax is greater than that of 'preretail' taxes (i.e., taxes imposed at an earlier stage in the distribution system). With a larger base, the tax rate necessary to yield a given revenue is lower; a relatively low retail sales tax rate may result in fewer efforts of evasion by vendors and significantly less opposition from consumers[39].

In some low income countries, the sales tax, irrespective of the level on which it is levied, may amount to little more than a supplementary import duty, because there is little domestic manufacturing, domestic manufacturing is exempted, or the sales tax rate on imports is much greater than the rate on domestically produced goods. For example, Bangladesh, Burma, and Nepal collect some 90 percent of their sales tax revenue from taxes levied on imported goods. Countries with such narrow domestic manufacturing sectors probably should postpone imposition of a general sales tax system and use a simpler system of excises[40].

Revenues provided by sales taxes are limited by the exemption of food and other essential items, and although this reduces the revenue potential of sales taxes, it is usually considered socially desirable. Exemption reduces the degree of regressivity since food purchases comprise a significant proportion of the poor's income. Most of the benefits of improved equity may be achieved, however, if only unprocessed foodstuffs are exempted, as they account for the bulk of food purchased by the poorer classes[41].

3.6 Value added taxes

The retail sales tax is usually the most desirable form of single-stage sales taxation, but all single-stage taxes have certain inherent limitations. The use of a tax at only one level requires demarcation of the taxable stage from non-axable stages, but the identification of the taxpaying firms often presents problems in developing countries as businesses are commonly engaged in more than one activity. Another difficulty encountered in the use of a single-stage tax is the high rate required to yield a given revenue. High rates tend to concentrate the impact of the tax on a single stage of distribution (wholesale, retail, etc.) and may provide a greater incentive for tax evasion[42].

A sales tax levied on the value of the good at each stage of production and distribution (also called a turnover tax) does not suffer from these limitations, but it artificially promotes integration of the various production and

distribution stages. Integration of this nature could contribute to misallocation of resources, retarding specialization as each firm is given incentives to
produce its own inputs and to merchandise the finished products. An
additional drawback of the turnover tax is the inherent discrimination
between imported and domestic goods, since imports pass through fewer
taxable stages within the country levying the tax. It is quite difficult to
compensate for this by the use of higher import duties because goods may be
imported at various stages of production[43].

A more suitable form of sales taxation is Value Added Tax (VAT) which is
imposed on the increment in value that is added to goods (and services) by
firms at each stage through production and distribution. The retail price of a
commodity is the sum of the values added; therefore, the total yield of a
VAT must equal the yield of a retail sales price with the same rate, since the
size of the tax bases is identical. Unlike a multistage turnover tax, a VAT
offers no incentive to vertical integration since the total amount of tax paid
on a given good is independent of the number of stages through which the
good has passed. A VAT that does not extend through the retail stage will,
however, contribute to vertical integration as firms will be encouraged to
engage in retailing activities[44].

The VAT was adopted by the member countries of the European
Economic Community (EEC) in 1967 and has seen increasing acceptance by
other nations in recent years. This widespread interest in VAT is explained
partly by its extremely broad base, which enables it to yield substantial
revenue at relatively low rates. For instance, six low income countries which
had adopted VAT by 1975 received almost one quarter of their total tax
revenue from this source (*Table 3.4*)[45]. Another argument frequently heard
in favor of a VAT system is its alleged ability to promote exports of
manufactures. GATT forbids its signatories to subsidize exports by refund-
ing to corporations any part of the profits taxes due as a result of export
activity but does not rule out exempting exports from any sales taxes aimed
at domestic consumption. This has been interpreted as including value added
taxes. Thus, countries (such as those of the EEC) which use VAT in place of
corporate profits taxes may make their manufacturers more competitive,
from a net profit standpoint, as a result of their tax policies[46].

Even though VAT is theoretically superior to other forms of sales
taxation, its use may be precluded in the early stages of development because
of the administrative sophistication required for successful implementation.
Administration is complex because it includes all business enterprises rather
than only those engaged in trade[47]. Value added taxes are, however,
generally easier to administer than corporate income taxes; the latter require
a complete and accurate set of records, while VAT only requires information
on the value of purchases from other companies and the value of the output
sold[48]. Indeed, for this reason alone, it may be desirable to use VAT as a
proxy for an income tax on the producer.

The use of a value added tax may increase the difficulty of evasion, since the VAT system receives much of its receipts from the earlier stages of production and distribution where evasion is more difficult than at the later retail level. Enforcement of VAT is also facilitated by crosschecking which results from the nature of the assessment and collection process. The tax is generally structured so that the tax paid on the firm's purchases is deducted from the tax payable on output sold; consequently, each firm has an interest in requiring that tax is included in the seller's invoices[49].

Table 3.4 *Value-added sales tax as a revenue source in developing countries (1968)*

	Percentage of total tax revenue
Ivory Coast	26
Morocoo	26
Senegal	34
Malagasy Rep.	20
Ecuador	10
Uruguay	19
Average	22.5

Source: Cnossen, p. 32.

Value added taxes are usually shifted forward into final product prices and may therefore be viewed as a generally diffused sales tax[50]. In order to reduce regressivity and thus the burden on lower income groups, VAT systems often exempt unprocessed agricultural products and specific foodstuffs[51]. However, sales taxes levied at the wholesale or retail levels can 'target' fairly easily goods which are specifically recognized as primarily consumed by the poorer classes, and thus effective exemptions can be made which render these taxes less regressive. This is not easily done with broad-based value added taxes.

Not until a product achieves its final form in many cases is it clear for whom it is intended. Sheet steel, for example, goes through many stages from mine to rolling plant (with many value added taxing points); only after this does it become the air conditioning unit of the rich city dweller or the walls of a grain storage unit belonging to the poor farmer. If all steel is taxed at the same rate through fabrication, specificity relative to impact on different economic groups is lost. On the other hand, exemptions granted at the later stages of production are difficult to administer, easy to evade, and probably lead to misallocation of resources.

3.7 User taxes

Another way to classify taxes in addition to the direct-indirect distinction made above has to do with whether a tax is levied generally, and thus is totally separated from resulting government activities, or whether it is levied in such a way that it is specifically linked to some government service, regardless of whether this link relates to the full cost of that service (and to neither more nor less than full cost). All the categories of taxation discussed above are general levies for the most part. Receipts from these taxes go into the treasury's coffer where they are admixed; from this comingling, the government's bills are paid.

But there remain many very specific fiscal levies. Some of them fall within (or very nearly so) the categories discussed above. For example, the excises levied on gasoline in North America are, for the most part, specifically earmarked for highway construction and maintenance or for other very closely related purposes[52].

Others are outside our earlier classifications. For example, nearly all governments levy license fees, stamp duties, and charges for judicial system services. Most of these are charged either on a flat rate basis (that is, so much for each transaction or for each appearance before the agency involved) or are based on sliding scale which reflects either the value to the petitioner of the transaction passing through official purview or the relative difficulty of processing the specific petition. As the fiscal economics literature makes clear, the most important characteristics of these user charges are their correlation to special benefits and the lack of compulsion relative to taxes involved in their use.

Not all the categories which result from taking this viewpoint of classifying taxation fit easily within the direct–indirect tax breakdown discussed earlier. However, most user taxes tend to fall within the guidelines set above for indirect taxes. Furthermore, many of them are clearly identifiable as transaction related taxes (for example, trade related customs fees or excises earmarked for specific purposes)[53], and thus do not require below miscellaneous attribution in our statistical framework. Our framework includes such user taxes as *other* indirect taxes *unless*, in a particular case, a tax fits elsewhere as a direct or indirect tax (see Appendix A).

The effects of such taxes are highly variable. In theory, they are objective: those who seek the service involved, regardless of their incomes, pay the price that is connected with that specific service.

However, at least three important questions must be considered in assessing the effect of such levies:

(1) What sorts of services are rendered only in return for specific fiscal levies?
(2) What absolute levels of fees are imposed relative to the services that are provided?

(3) Are the fees commensurate with the economic value of the services involved?

These questions must be addressed if we are to determine the relative progressivity or regressivity of these miscellaneous taxes. For the most part, the data cited below in Part Three do not have enough sophistication regarding disaggregation to solve satisfactorily the problems posed in the previous paragraph.

The definitions employed in Part Three (see Appendix A) are sometimes arbitrary, and in some cases consistency across countries is absent. With regard to user taxes, we have tried to evaluate, in particular cases, whether a levy is best included in a specific category like excise taxes or whether it can only be lumped under the residual miscellaneous heading.

Notes

1 Edwin P. Reubens, Commodity Trade, Export Taxes, and Economic Development, *Political Science Quarterly*, 71, 47 (1956).

2 Richard Goode, George E. Lent and P. D. Ojha, Role of Export Taxes in Developing Countries, *IMF Staff Papers*, 13 (November 1966), p. 460.

3 Jonathan Levin, The Role of Taxation in the Export Economies, in Richard M. Bird and Oliver Oldman (eds.) *Readings on Taxation in Developing Countries*, (Baltimore: Johns Hopkins Press, 1967), p. 346.

4 Alan Richmond Prest, *Public Finance in Underdeveloped Countries*, (New York: Praeger, 1962), p. 67.

5 Richard M. Bird, *Taxing Agricultural Land in Developing Countries*, (Cambridge: Harvard University Press, 1974), p. 275. John F. Due, *Government Finance: Economics of the Public Sector*, (Homewood, Illinois: Irwin, 1968), p. 467. John Adler, Fiscal Policy in a Developing Country, in Kenneth Berrill (ed.), *Economic Development with Special Reference to East Asia*, (London: Macmillan, 1964), p. 305.

6 Levin, op. cit. (note 3) p. 347.

7 United Nations Fiscal Commission, Special Features of Corporate Taxation in Underdeveloped Countries, in Bird and Oldman, op. cit. (note 3) p. 140.

8 Richard M. Bird, Agricultural Taxation in Developing Countries, *Finance and Development*, 36, (September, 1974). V. Tan Wai, Taxation Problems and Policies of Underdeveloped Countries, *IMF Staff*

Papers, 9 November, 1962), p. 442. Prest, op. cit. (note 4) p. 69.

9 Prest, Ibid. p. 70.

10 Wai, op. cit. (note 8) p. 442.

11 Harley Hinrichs and Richard M. Bird, Government Revenue Shares in Developed and Less Developed Countries, *Canadian Tax Journal*, 11, 435, (September/October, 1963). Wai, op. cit. (note 8) pp. 434–435. Prest, op. cit. (note 4) pp. 62–63.

12 John F. Due, *Indirect Taxation in Developing Countries*, (Baltimore: Johns Hopkins Press, 1970), pp. 29, 34.

13 Robert B. Bangs, *Financing Economic Development*, (Chicago, University of Chicago: Press, 1968), p. 122. John H. Adler, op. cit. (note 5) p. 303. Due, op. cit. (note 12) pp. 16, 29. Raja Chelliah, *Fiscal Policy in Underdeveloped Countries*, (London: George Allen and Unwin, 1960), p. 91.

14 Prest, op. cit. (note 4) p. 65, Due, *Government and Finance*, (note 5) p. 458.

15 Bangs, op. cit. (note 13) pp. 112–113. George E. Lent, Tax Incentives for Investment in Developing Countries, *IMF Staff Papers*, 14, (July, 1967), p. 264. Due, *Indirect Taxation*, (note 12) pp. 21, 35.

16 Charles Fransfield, Tax Structure in Developing Countries: An Introduction, *Finance and Development*, 8, 40, (March, 1971). Due, op. cit. (note 12) pp. 20, 31.

17 John F. Due, Requirements of a Tax Structure in a Development Economy, in Bird and Oldman, op. cit. (note 3) p. 34.

18 Due, *Indirect Taxation*, (note 12) p. 42.

19 Due, *Government Finance*, (note 5) p. 459. Due, *Indirect Taxation*, (note 12) pp. 53–55.

20 Due, *Indirect Taxation*, (note 12) pp. 30–33.

21 Due, *Government Finance*, (note 5) pp. 458–459.

22 Prest, op. cit. (note 4) p. 65. An import duty that is levied in conjunction with a preexisting quota may not increase retail prices if the import duty is less than the amount by which the quota has resulted in higher prices. See World Bank Staff Working Paper No. 222 (Prepared by Charles E. McLure Jr., *Taxation and the Urban Poor in Developing Countries*, (December, 1975), p. 7.

23 Sijbren Cnossen, The Role and Structure of Sales Tax and Excise Systems, *Finance and Development*, 31, (March, 1975). Due, *Indirect Taxation*, (note 12) p. 59.

24 Bangs, op. cit. (note 13) p. 134.

25 Wai, op. cit. (note 8) p. 441. Due, op. cit. (note 12) p. 75.

26 Due, ibid, p. 64. McLure, op. cit. (note 22) p. 18. Due, Requirements of a Tax Structure in a Development Economy, in Bird and Oldman (note 3) p. 33.

27 Due, *Indirect Taxation*, (note 12) p. 64. Bangs, op. cit. (note 13) p. 134.

28 Adler, op. cit. (note 5) p. 302.

29 Richard M. Bird and Oliver Oldman, Sales and Excise Tax, in Bird and Oldman, (note 3) pp. 297–298.

30 McLure, op. cit. (note 22) p. 18.

31 Due, *Government Finance*, (note 5) p. 459.

32 George E. Lent, Milka Casanegra and Michele Guerard, The Value-Added Tax in Developing Countries, *IMF Staff Papers*, 20 (July, 1973), p. 343. Richard S. Thorn, The Evolution of Public Finances During Economic Development, *The Manchester School of Economic and Social Studies*, 35, 31, (January, 1967).

33 Alison Martin and W. Arthur Lewis, Patterns of Public Revenue and Expenditure, in Bird and Oldman (note 3) p. 90.

34 Thorn, op. cit. (note 32) p. 32.

35 Due, *Indirect Taxation*, (note 12) p. 79. Due, *Government Finance* (note 5) p. 460.

36 Prest, op. cit. (note 4) p. 75. Due, *Government Finance*, (note 5) p. 460. Bangs, op. cit. (note 13) p. 135.

37 Adler, op. cit. (note 5) p. 303. Thorn, op. cit. (note 32) p. 32. Wai, op. cit. (note 8) p. 440. Prest, op. cit. (note 4) p. 74.

38 Due, *Government Finance*, (note 5) p. 460. Due, *Indirect Taxation*, (note 12) p. 113.

39 Due, *Indirect Taxation*, (note 12) p. 112.

40 Cnossen, op. cit. (note 23) p. 33.

41 Thorn, op. cit. (note 32) p. 32. Wai, op. cit. (note 8) p. 440. Bangs, op. cit. (note 13) p. 135. McLure, op. cit. (note 22) p. 17

42 Due, *Indirect Taxation*, (note 12) p. 117.

43 Due, ibid. pp. 120–121.

44 Lent, Casanegra and Guerard, op. cit. (note 32) p. 319. Due, ibid. p. 124. Cnossen, op. cit. (note 23) p. 30. George E. Lent, Value-Added Tax in Developing Countries, *Finance and Development*, 35, (December, 1974).

45 Bangs, op. cit. (note 13) p. 136. Lent, ibid. p. 318.

46 Lent, ibid. p. 332. See also Ronald I. McKinnon, The Value-Added Tax and the Liberalization of Foreign Trade in Developing Economies: A Comment, *Journal of Economic Literature*, 11, 520–524, (June, 1973).

47 Bangs, op. cit. (note 13) p. 136.

48 Robert E. Looney, *The Economic Development of Iran*: New York, Praeger, 1973), p. 76.

49 Due, *Government Finance*, (note 5) p. 461. Due, *Indirect Taxation*, (note 12) p. 130. Lent, op. cit. (note 44) p. 368.

50 Bangs, op. cit. (note 13) p. 136.

51 Lent, op. cit. (note 44) p. 332.

52 How closely related such purposes may be can be seen from the strong (and usually successful) opposition voiced by US and Canadian automobile clubs whenever it is seriously suggested that gasoline taxes might be used to subsidize the construction and operation of public rapid transit systems. Even though public transportation obviously saves energy, relieves traffic congestion and reduces wear and tear on highways, the established lobbyists for automobile users resist the transfer of funds traditionally earmarked only for highways to other transportation needs. Defined in typical fashion in Harold Groves, and Robert Bish, *Financing Government* (New York: Holt, Rinehard and Winston, 1973), p. 307.

53 One exception noted below (see Appendix A) are land registration fees which are, for the most part, included among property taxes in this study.

State enterprises

Today, even in the most capitalistic societies, there are economic enterprises reserved to the government, which, at least theoretically, could return a net profit. Even the often maligned United States Postal Administration managed to earn several hundred million dollars during one recent fiscal year. If such an enterprise were profit earning on a regular basis (as, for example, a state oil company might be), it could become an important part of a country's fiscal profile.

Most of the countries included in our study earn important revenues from state-owned business enterprises, though their economies range through the unashamedly *laissez-faire* capitalism of Lebanon and Bahrain, to the mixture of private and public activity that prevails in Syria and Iraq, and on to the forthrightly Marxist-Leninist framework that has been embraced in the People's Democratic Republic of Yemen. As can be seen from *Table 4.1*, the relative importance of state enterprise profits cannot be explained on the grounds of economic ideology. Otherwise, why would capitalist Jordan earn almost three times as much revenue from state enterprises as socialist Libya, or why would Syria's mixed economy generate almost half its state revenues in this way, when thoroughly Marxist South Yemen earns only a quarter of its revenues from state enterprises?

In fact, most of these differences can be explained in bookkeeping terms; that is, in terms of how the profits of state enterprises are entered into the fiscal accounts. For example, nearly all Middle Eastern countries, by the late 1970s, had at least partly nationalized the operating oil companies within their borders. However, all continue to maintain these corporations as quasi-independent enterprises, and most continue (more or less intact) the profits tax and royalty schedules that were in effect before nationalization. Thus, a major part of these state enterprises' *gross* profits enter the state's account books as income taxes or royalties. In fact, since most oil exporting countries use the stateowned oil company as a major focus of development investment, after-tax or net profits are generally kept separate from the fiscal accounts and reinvested in oil related projects. Thus, only a small amount of oil receipts (or none at all) may show up in the form of state enterprise profits[1].

This problem is not readily resolvable. Either a state may choose to tax public enterprises as though they were privately owned, leaving them with net profits to be reinvested or paid out to the stockholders (in this case, the state), or it may put them in a special category.

South Yemen does the former, for example, and thus the returns listed for this country as state enterprise revenues in Part Three are stockholder dividends. Special category situations are by their nature *ad hoc*, and are further complicated by the vagaries of statistical reporting. For example, in some cases, profits of state enterprises may be reported net, if not of profits taxes, at least of depreciation or even of new investment. Thus the intention is indicated of maintaining at least some budgetary independence of the state enterprise sector.

Table 4.1 *Recent relative contributions of state enterprise profits to Middle East government fiscal receipts (percentage of total receipts)*

Country	Percentage	Country	Percentage
Bahrain[a]	1.6	Oman[a]	3.6
Egypt[b]	8.3	Qatar	NA
Iran[c]	2.7	Saudia Arabia	NA
Iraq[b]	2.1	Sudan[c]	13.5
Jordan[a]	13.7	Syria[b]	45.1
Kuwait[c]	1.7	United Arab Emirates	NA
Lebanon[d]	3.5	Yemen Arab Rep.[c]	14.5
Libya[b]	5.0	Yemen People's Dem. Rep.[a]	25.4

Notes: [a] 1978
         [b] 1977
         [c] 1977/1978
         [d] 1974
         NA Data not available

Sources: See country tables in Part Three.

But if gross profits (or even gross revenues) of state enteprises are reported in the fiscal accounts, then the picture becomes quite blurred when cross-sectional comparisons are involved. Fortunately, for the countries involved in this study, we were generally successful in eliminating gross revenues of state enterprises from the reported statistics.

However, yet another problem confronts us in this area – one which is unique in its importance to the major oil exporting countries. Many of these countries, in recent years, have accrued huge trade surpluses since the successful OPEC price action of 1973 and despite their massive increases in imports. This has led to an unprecedented situation in international finance: central banks (and their equivalents) have amassed investment portfolios, containing all manner of financial instruments, that have run into tens of billions of dollars – that is, far more than the few months' equivalent of imports that most countries have officially held in this form in previous situations. By the late 1970s, the *annual* returns on these investments were amounting to billions of dollars; for the most part, these returns were reported under the state enterprise category[2]. However, for some countries[3], only estimates derived from non-governmental sources are available; and, in most cases, this indicated considerable underreporting in the state enterprise category.

In the next chapter we will undertake a discussion of taxation methods which are specifically and historically connected with Islam, and thus with the particular developing countries we are considering.

Notes

1 A major exception in recent years has been Syria. Sales by the state-owned oil marketing agency have been lumped in official statistics in categories which have always included other government activities in the past. Thus, it was not possible in Section Three to distinguish oil sales and to list these revenues under profits taxes or royalties.

2 This problem is discussed in more detail below; see Chapter 13.

3 For example, Kuwait. A major part of the reporting problem arises from the fact that private banks (in which the state has a major interest) may hold many of these assets, especially in countries where central banking is only newly established. Yet, these bank assets are not included in official estimates, even those made independently by agencies such as the International Monetary Fund. The authors are presently preparing another monograph which is a study of the banking systems of most of these countries.

CHAPTER 5

Islam and taxation

5.1 Introduction

The Middle East has been, at various times in its history, one of the commercial centers of the known world; frequently it has been *the* major commercial center. With the birth of the prophet Muhammad in the sixth century of the Christian era and the introduction of Islam in the seventh century, the region embarked on prolonged growth along the path of economic, social and cultural expansion. However, with the onset of the industrial revolution in Europe and later in the New World, the Middle East appeared to lag behind. This divergence in economic performance has prompted many observers to question the compatibility of Islam with the process of economic development. One prominent scholar has expressed the problem thus:

> In the past and in the present, has Islam, or at least, the cultural tradition of the Muslim countries, favored (or does it favor) capitalism, or socialism, or a backward economy of the 'feudal' type? Or does it urge those who are influenced by it in a quite different direction, a new economic system specific to Islam?[1]

In more recent history, since the revenues of the oil exporting countries of the Middle East began to increase in the 1950s, and more dramatically since 1973, casual observers saw little conflict between Islam and contemporary capitalism because of the rapid penetration of western influence into the area. However, in the aftermath of the revolution in Iran during late 1978 and early 1979 and in the face of potential upheavals in Turkey, Pakistan and elsewhere, the question of the compatibility of Islam and modern capitalism has evoked much interest.

On the other hand, the interaction of Islam with the other major western model of economic change, Marxist socialism, has been much more limited. Until the direct confrontation of Soviet expansion and Muslim tradition in Afghanistan in the late 1970s, Marxism in the Islamic world had been mostly a fringe phenomenon[2]. In the past, the possibility of a symbiotic relationship between Islam and Marxism has tended to be dismissed on religious grounds: the basic contradiction between theism and atheism has blocked much discussion of how these philosophies might react on more purely secular (that is, economic) grounds. However, the contemporary Christian leadership of Karol Wojtyla, in Marxist Poland, ought to prompt westerners to ask if other strongly theistic philosophies, such as Islam, could also approach Marxism from a more accessible standpoint.

In fact, Islam, unlike other major religions, has given its followers a detailed description for an economic system; in effect, this could provide a 'third way', economically speaking, for Muslim countries. This basis for society is found in several places: the Quran; the *Sunnah* (utterances of the Prophet Muhammad, excluding the Quran, and his personal acts or sayings, or those of others approved by the prophet); the *Ijma'* (the consensus of the Muslim *mujtahids* – religious scholars); and the *Qiya* (personal opinions based on analogy and on religious doctrines). Specifically, questions of taxation, government expenditure, inheritance, private ownership, social and economic welfare (distribution of income, poverty, etc.), interest, land tenure, natural resources, wage rates, as well as other factors, have received considerable attention, and are thus an integral component of Islam[3].

In our context here, of course, we are specifically interested in what Islamic theology has to say about taxation and related matters. We will discuss in turn the traditional forms of taxation that have been used in *Dar al-Islam* and which have either Quranic or other religious roots. It should first be pointed out that in Islam there are, in effect, two tax structures: one for Muslims, which derives directly from the religious sources mentioned above, and the other for non-Muslims. This distinction will be kept throughout the discussion in this chapter as far as it is relevant and operative.

5.2   Zakat

The principal tax[4] on Muslims is *zakat*. Although the term has been used in many different ways[5] there are three major situations where *zakat* is applicable: the ownership of animals, of gold, silver and articles of trade, and of the produce of the land[6]. While in theory *zakat* is linked to all assets which produce an economic return, in practice it has been applied mostly to commercial and agricultural capital. In short, *zakat* is a rather generalized wealth tax.

As Islam's traditions have evolved, *zakat* has been accorded the central status of being one of the five pillars of Islam. Along with the following obligations:

(1) *shahada*, the profession of faith in the One God and in His Prophet, Muhammad;
(2) *salat*, regular daily prayer;
(3) *sawm*, prescribed fasting during the holy month of *Ramadhan* (when the Quran was revealed);
(4) *hajj*, the making of the pilgrimage to the holy places associated with the prophet Muhammad (Mecca and Medina);

the rendering of *zakat* by poor Muslims is a divinely revealed requirement for those who wish to achieve eternal salvation[7]. As such, it ranks with the Old Testament Decalogue and New Testament Beatitudes in religious significance.

The meanings attributed to the word *zakat* itself go a long way towards indicating the problems of considering it merely as a tax, or as a conventional source of government revenue. Its obligations are founded in Quranic injunctions which praise those who 'expend of that We have provided them, secretly and in public, and who avert evil with good – theirs shall be the ultimate abode'[8], and 'those in whose wealth is a right known for the beggar and the outcast'[9]. Obviously, in theory *zakat* is to be *given* willingly, not to be paid grudgingly, if divine law is to be fulfilled. Its obligations are to the community as a whole: they are to be made specifically and directly to the community's less fortunate members, not to an impersonalized government nor to its revenue collecting agencies.

The etymological derivation of this important word has been traced to verbs that in English translate most closely as 'to be pure' or 'to be pious'[10]. *Zakat* also signifies virtue in general, as well as – in the Quran – giving and the pious gift[11]. Thus *zakat* is seen as an act of purification for one's sins, a means of reducing selfishness and expiation of blame for past selfishness and thus leading to self-improvement[12]. Others have emphasized its link to the verbs 'to grow' and 'to increase'[13], and have interpreted the giving of *zakat* as leading to a significant increase of blessings, both of material property in this world and of spiritual merit for the next.

Whatever interpretation is adopted, *zakat* is primarily a voluntary act of piety, and a far cry from what most modern day taxpayers experience when confronted with increased income levies or complicated regulations. The act of giving to the poor and needy in the form of *zakat* is clearly to guarantee the poor, the orphaned, the elderly, and the needy the necessities of life. It is in a sense intended as a system of social insurance and security for all of those who become destitute in Islamic society, and is supported by a tax on net wealth rather than on income. God might will that even the most fortunate will be destitute tomorrow; thus, those that give today may receive tomorrow.

Muslim-held assets subject to *zakat* were not spelled out specifically in the Quran; therefore they have been much discussed by various scholars of Islamic law. It is generally recognized that only wealth above a certain minimum level and held for 12 months or longer[14] obliges its owner to pay *zakat*. In addition, a large number of items are exempted[15].

The manner in which *zakat* is to be collected has also been a subject of some dispute among legal scholars, the principal point of agreement being what constitutes *apparent* property (on which *zakat* is generally collected by representatives of the state or community) as opposed to *non-apparent* property (on which it is disbursed directly by the owners)[16]. Others have argued that, to ensure proper distribution among the needy, the state should oversee all *zakat*, and should establish the right to collect it by force when Muslims ignore their obligations, or when the needs of one area in *Dar al-Islam* exceeds the ability of that particular region to collect enough *zakat* from those that reside there.

On the other hand, the Quran is specific as to those who are eligible to receive the alms distributed under *zakat* provisions. 'The free will offerings are for the poor and needy, those who work to collect them, those whose hearts are brought together, the ransoming of slaves, debtors, in God's way, and the traveller: so God ordains'[17]. In short, in the time of the Prophet Muhammad, virtually all of those who might experience economic need had a valid claim on the beneficence of the entire Islamic community.

The state was also authorized to collect additional taxes if *zakat* was not sufficient to meet the needs of those with a claim to assistance. For example, the state could always impose other forms of taxation for particular needs and programs. On the one hand, *zakat* was not intended to be used by the state for purposes and recipients other than those stated above, but on the other hand, it was specifically recognized that legitimate claims for community revenues were not limited to *zakat*.

Let us consider specific levies. *Zakat* due from those who owned flocks varied according to what type of animals were involved. For example, the Hanafi lawyers decreed a rate of about 2.5 percent (above a minimum herd size). In the case of camels, this was calculated to be:

For less than five camels, no tax.
For five camels and more up to nine inclusive, one goat (of medium size).
For ten camels and more up to 14 inclusive, two goats.
For 15 camels and more up to 19 inclusive, three goats.
For 20 camels and more up to 24 inclusive, four goats.
For 25 camels and more up to 35 inclusive, one *bint makhad*, i.e., a female camel colt in her second year.
For 36 camels and more up to 45 inclusive, one *bint labun*, i.e., a female camel colt in her third year.
For 46 camels and more up to 60 inclusive, one *hiqqah*, i.e., a female camel in her fourth year.
For 61 camels and more up to 75 inclusive, one *jadha'ah*, i.e., a female camel in her fifth year.
For 76 camels and more up to 90 inclusive, two *bint labuns*.
For 91 camels and more up to 120 inclusive, two *hiqqahs*.
From 120 up to 144 the process is started over again according to the Hanafites, namely, one goat for every five camels after the 120th camel, plus the 2 *hiqqahs* for the 120. Thus 125 up to 129, two *hiqqahs* and one goat, and so on up to 144. And for 145 up to 149, two *hiqqahs* and one *bint makhad*, and for 150, three *hiqqahs*[18].

For sheep and goats (*ghanam*), Hanafi, Shafi, and Maliki lawyers alike agreed there was no levy due on herds with less than 40 head, but above this level, the obligation rose proportionately:

> Upon 40 and more up to 120 head, the *zakat* is one *shat*. (Generic term used interchangeably for sheep and goats)
> Upon 121 and more up to 200, the *zakat* is two *shats*.
> Upon 201 and more up to 399, the *zakat* is three *shats*.
> Upon 400 and more up to 499, the *zakat* is four *shats*.
> Upon 500 and more up to 599, the *zakat* is five *shats*.
> And so on, at the rate of one *shat* for every additional 100 head after 500, fractions being neglected[19].

The lawyers also decreed rates for other common animals. Generally, these rates indicate a 2.5 percent tax on capital tax. In most cases, this resulted in a neutral or proportional tax[20].

While *zakat* due on livestock was defined in specific physical terms, that which was expected on gold, silver and articles of trade was based on commercial value. Again the rate was proportional, at 2.5 percent with an initial exemption, and in these cases (after the exemption), strict neutrality of taxation was likely.

As indicated above, there was serious disagreement among the major schools of law as to whether the agricultural and mineral produce of landholdings, although clearly subject to some form of taxation, fell within the realm of *zakat*. Since almsgiving was an essential obligation for the Muslim who hoped to achieve eternal salvation, this distinction was of considerable theological importance.

Zakat was, of course, not the only fiscal obligation incumbent upon Muslims. During the centuries following the prophet's death, other taxes were employed by secular authorities (the *khalifate*) that had less clear religious antecedents and thus were not agreed upon by all religious authorities at the time of their imposition. However, as has been explained, Islam has historically tolerated diversity in its interpretations of religious laws: the four schools of law differ, in detail often considerably, about *zakat*, an institution with obvious Quranic foundations. One major point of difference relates to land related wealth.

5.3   Land taxes – *'ushr* and *kharaj*

The dues on land, the *'ushr* or tithe, were due when and only when there actually was any output. No minimum exemption was allowed, nor was a year's ownership needed before the obligation fell. Typically, the due depended on the quality of the land (for example, 5 percent on irrigated land, 10 percent on rainfed land). It was applied to gross output, before deduction of most production related costs; however, it was obviously denominated in terms that recognized some production costs.

Dar al-Islam expanded rapidly in the century after the Prophet's death. Large populations of non-Muslims were conquered and incorporated into the *khalifal* empire. Contrary to popular modern belief, conversion by force was forbidden. The faithful soon became a minority within their expanding conquests and the need for secular taxes rapidly became more apparent.

Muslims, under the provisions of *zakat*, were obligated toward their fellow believers and, as believers, they were also required to strive for the expansion and protection of *Dar al-Islam*, undertaking military service if necessary. On the other hand, Christian, Jewish, and Zoroastrian subjects of the Muslim *khalifate* fell under neither obligation. But as citizens of a dynamic state, they could hardly be excused, or expect to be excused, from all fiscal responsibilities.

One tax that hit all citizens regardess of religion was the *kharaj* – literally, the revenue derived from a piece of land. Over the long history of Islam, no universally accepted definition of *kharaj* land has emerged. All commentators agree on the impartial nature of *kharaj*, in that the payment of *kharaj* depends, not upon the religious beliefs of the tax-payers (or upon other such personal categories), but upon the status of the land on which the tax is due.

Unlike *zakat*, *kharaj* is a form of taxation that can be changed by the Islamic state, since it is not ordained in the Quran. Rather, its provisions are based on *ijma'* – the consensus found in the teachings of the religious scholars. As circumstances change, so may *ijma'*. This flexibility regarding *kharaj* found expression in the detail expounded by one esteemed Hanafi source which includes the following comment:

'All lands conquered by force and irrigated by rivers are *kharaj* lands, and if they are not irrigated by rivers, but by springs issuing from them, they are tithe lands'. The author of the *Fath*, however, remarks that the preceding quotation can refer only to waste lands which were conquered by force from infidels and were first developed by Moslems. Indeed the cultivated lands so conquered, if left to their infidel owners, are *kharaj* lands, even if watered by rain (i.e., tithe water); on the other hand, if such lands were divided among the Moslem soldiery, they are tithe lands, even if watered by rivers (i.e., *kharaj* water). For while it is unanimously admitted that in taxing the infidel for his land for the first time, he is always taxed *kharaj*, the Moslem's land is never taxed *kharaj* for the first time unless it be that the Moslem entails upon himself such treatment by his own consent, namely, by developing his land with *kharaj*, instead of with tithe water[21].

The *kharaj* tax can be divided into two parts – fixed and proportional. Fixed *kharaj* rates were collected from all land suitable for cultivation, and were assessed in kind – so much per unit of land or per tree. The rates for several crops were decreed by the second *khalif* 'Umar and were considered thereafter to be immutable. For those cases not covered in this way, rates were set according to the tax-bearing capacity of the land: this depended upon the quality of the soil, the crops grown on it, and the method of irrigation. Rates varied from 20 to 50 percent of the output that could be expected from the land. Whereas many scholars argued fixed *kharaj* was due regardless of actual output, proportional *kharaj* was a percentage of what was actually produced[22].

5.4   *Jizyah*

The *jizyah*, or poll tax, was imposed only on non-Muslims. Its origin is Quranic:

> Fight those who believe not in God and the Last Day and [who] do not forbid what God and His Messenger have forbidden – such men as practice not the religion of truth, being of those who have been given the Book – until they pay the tribute out of hand and have been humbled[23].

In a sense, non-Muslims were liable for this tax because of their disbelief and/or as a payment for sparing their lives, as it guaranteed their security. On the other hand, it was also a levy due instead of military service, to which all Muslim males were at least theoretically liable. Non-Muslims were *ipso facto* exempt and were subjected instead to a payment towards the upkeep and defense of the state. Women and children, who of course did not fight, were exempted from *jizyah*[24].

The amount of the *jizyah* was prescribed in various ways. In some cases, it was fixed by treaty with a tribe as it acceded to Muslim rule, with either a lump sum payment or a regular per capita levy (or both) imposed. Alternatively, the *jizyah* was imposed by Muslim leaders on those who were conquered by force of arms. The tax was somewhat progressive at first glance, recognizing that, as Muslims had varying military obligations depending upon relative wealth (the poor as private soldiers, the rich were required to outfit themselves as horsemen), so non-Muslims were assessed *jizyah* in proportion to their ability to pay. Again as with *kharaj*, *jizyah* was not made explicit in the Quran. Thus, the rates were based on *ijma'* – in particular, on precedents established during the *khalifates* of 'Umar, 'Uthman and 'Ali (the second, third, and fourth deputies of the Prophet). The annual rate for the rich was 48 *dirhams*: 24 *dirhams* were due from the middle class, and 12 *dirhams* from the poor[25].

5.5   Taxes on natural resources

Still another source of revenue was the tax on mines[26]. But basic disagreement on the type of levies on such property being present among the various schools of law meant that the Shafi school included such wealth within the provisions of *zakat*, while the Hanafi did not[27]. According to the latter, no matter who owned the mine, one fifth of the deposit was due as tax to the state. However, only certain types of mineral deposits were subject to taxation. For example, ores which could be refined into pure metals (gold, silver, lead, etc.) were taxable; other deposits (coal, water, etc.) were not.

One tradition attributes to the Prophet the dictum that *all* Muslims are partners in 'grass, water and fire' – these were the only apparent God given natural resources in the Arabia of 1400 years ago; certainly, this exception would explain the exemptions for coal and for well water. At least potentially, this *hadith* could be used to justify an oil policy that exempted from taxation the owners of land on which oil was found (as are the owners of water wells), or conversely, for invoking the guideline of *universal* partnership, in order to keep such land (or at least the mineral rights beneath it) totally within the public domain. In fact, major Muslim oil producers, both in the Middle East and elsewhere (for example, Indonesia, Malaysia, and Brunei), have opted for universal claims over petroleum deposits.

5.6 Summarizing Islamic taxation

This discussion of taxation has been, of necessity, brief; as a consequence, most of the circumstances in which Islamic law has been applied have been neglected. To appreciate fully the implementation and the resulting impact of such taxes, one must interpret them as an integral component of Islam. As we have indicated above, the basic Islamic levy, *zakat*, is far more an obligation imposed by God on the faithful for the general welfare of the community than a tax promoted by the state for the sake of collecting necessary revenues. The levies imposed in this way on Muslims, and in a general fashion the more secular taxes on Muslims and non-Muslims alike, are rooted in a theologically derived premise that those who have received from God ample material blessings are obliged to share, in concrete fashion, with those who are less well off. One contemporary Muslim scholar, in examining Islamic economic doctrines, has made the following points in commenting on what is the most central aspect of Muslim belief – *tawhid*, one-ness or unity:

> *Tawhid* is a coin with two faces: one implies that Allah is the creator, and the other that men are equal partners or that each man is brother to other men. As far as economics is concerned, this means *equality and cooperation*. Thus, divinity in a Muslim society is only for Allah. This means, in economic terms, that natural resources in the universe, such as land, capital, general circumstances such as shortages for reasons of war or disasters as well as laws of nature, *all these belong to the whole of society*, and *all its members have equal shares and right of access to them. No man*

has the right of claiming a *bigger* share since he does not create or generate power independently . . . .

If a man is not going to use certain resources over which he has priority, he should *give it up to another member of society* and should not claim ultimate individual ownership over the income produced by the resource. He should know that he is not the creator. He should give to the weaker members of society *the extra income* which is due to the productivity of those natural resources that are used by him *beyond his equal share* . . . .

Differences in income (in Islamic society) could not be very big and they are limited by *differences in human capacity for work and not by individual claims on natural resource*. Income related to these resources is a collective claim and its fruits should be divided equally. Private ownership here is only a matter of priority[28].

Only a brief outline of the Islamic system of taxation has been conveyed above, and in all likelihood not very much of its spirit or of the ways that it was implemented in Islamic societies. However, at least for the case of *zakat*, the above does present a sketch of what each Muslim must do personally, beyond the immediate needs of the state for operating revenues, to support society and to meet his or her obligations toward the community.

5.7   Islam and major sources of fiscal revenue

Taxation, in the very specific sense, is not alone among the economic matters that claim the attention of the Quran or of Islam's other sources of law. In fact, three major elements of economic discussion with considerable relevance to modern taxation law are clear when we consider Islamic tradition: interest (and its relation to profits), rent, and inheritance. Each of these represents an important form of income or wealth which is subject to taxation in the developed economies and about which much of the economic literature on taxation has been written.

In this section, we will discuss briefly the Islamic attitudes toward these three targets of fiscal legislation and then summarize how the traditional Islamic taxes might or might not be applied. We will begin with the subject that arouses the greatest controversy regarding differences between Islam and the rest of the world – the question of interest and the distinction made between interest and profit.

Islam and interest (usury)

While other religions have looked unfavorably upon moneylending where interest is paid, Islam traditionally has quite forthrightly forbidden it. This attitude toward the taking of interest (*riba*) is derived from the Quran:

Those who devour usury shall not rise again, except as he rises whom Satan of the touch prostrates; that is because they say, 'trafficking is like usury'. God has permitted trafficking and forbidden usury . . . God blots out usury, but freewill offerings he augments with interest[29].

O believers, fear you God, and give up the usury that is outstanding, if you are believers[30].

O believers, devour not usury, doubled and redoubled, and fear you God; haply so you will prosper[31].

And what you give in usury, that it may increase upon the people's wealth, increases not with God[32].

Nevertheless, the Quranic ban on *riba* has still allowed for some differences among Muslims as to precisely what was outlawed, i.e. the taking of interest, or loans that lead to economic exploitation.

The reasons for prohibition of *riba* in Islam are quite clear. First, interest and/or usury increases the tendency to direct wealth into the control of a few; in the process it tends to dehumanize man's concern for his fellow man. Secondly, Islam does not allow gain from economic activity unless there is also the risk of a loss; the legal guarantee of at least nominal interest would be viewed as a sure gain. Thirdly, in Islam wealth should be accumulated through personal activity and hard work, as opposed to the avaricious acquisition of the highest possible interest.

However, one recent commentator, clearly in the minority, emphasized the question of economic exploitation as being the critical element in the ban:

We must dismiss the extreme contention which seeks to reject bank interest on Islamic grounds. If capital has a share in the production of wealth, bank interest must be allowed. What cannot be allowed is economic exploitation[33].

Closer to the Islamic norm, on the other hand, is the following opinion:

Riba is basically a question of ownership and distribution of income – the question of what belongs to whom. Any raising of private or individual claim beyond what Islam considers lawful is *riba*. As far as Muslim societies of today are concerned, the main economic question they face is related to *riba*[34].

Riba goes beyond capital, in that it has a more fundamental meaning in Muslim society . . . *Riba* is a deal to exchange something for nothing[35].

Obviously, the economic implications of this latter view are much more far reaching. It indicates that interest and methods which have the same effect, such as ill-disguised 'service' charges, are outlawed. Thus, the banking system as a profitable enterprise, as it exists in capitalist countries, is impossible in any country that adheres closely to Islamic law.

However, the prohibition of interest need not preclude the useful role played in a dynamic economy by a banking system. In an Islamic society banking could, in our view, still have the same basic role and function as in a Western society – a sink for savings and a source for investment.

The form would, of course, have to be different. As in the west, money would be deposited at a bank either in a demand deposit (checking) or time deposit (savings) account. Service charges could be levied on demand deposits, but no return would be given on such an account if the security of the original deposit was guaranteed. On savings deposits, there would be no contracted positive or negative return. The bank would, as in a capitalist society, decide as an individual institution (possibly under official guidelines) on its desired level of reserves in relation to both savings and demand deposits, by evaluating potential investments. However, unlike capitalist banking practice, it would not loan its funds to its clients but would instead become a partner with the clients in business ventures. In this way, if the venture prospered, the bank's savings depositors (who had thus taken risks) would be rewarded with a share of profit, but there would be no guarantee of this outcome.

Banks constituted in this manner have been operating for some time in several Muslim countries, most notably in Saudi Arabia and Libya. One such bank of international significance is the Islamic Development Bank (IDB), founded in 1973 and which had 40 members by 1980. By early 1978, about $215 million had been pledged to some 32 projects in 19 countries. Some loans are to be repaid without interest but others involve the IDB as an equity partner in industrial projects[36].

Thus, at least in theory, the prohibition of interest need not lead to a reduced level of savings and investment. Certainly a banking system based on equity ownership rather than interest would use somewhat different operating techniques: it would, for example, probably be somewhat more conservative in its 'loan' evaluations and might maintain somewhat higher reserves than western capitalist banks.

Basic questions about interest in Islam remain unclear. Is it the *very concept* of interest that is at the heart of the Quranic injunction, or is it, more precisely, the *exploitative* use of interest that is the true target? For example, when governments (or their affiliated banking institutions) borrow from their citizens under conditions that include some payment of interest, can any element of exploitation be present? Rather, in societies where a degree of inflation seems inevitably present, might not interest rates in line with inflation (the existence of which is largely a government responsibility) merely be seen as maintaining, rather than increasing, the value of capital[37]? Furthermore, whether the borrower is a private individual, a corporation, or a foreign government, the possibility of a loan default is present. Thus, the lender is at some risk, whether holding debt or having some equity. In this way, a banking system could evolve that is based on laws that increase the lenders' risks: for example, one that gave claims against a bankrupt corporation similar to those of equity owners, rather than preferences at the head of the queue of creditors. Though this is a considerable change relative to established western capitalist banking practice, such a system could still provide a conduit between those with surplus capital and those in promising investment situations. In particular, in economic terms, such alterations take the role played by interest in the west – as the price or allocative mechanism for a scarce input (capital) to the production process; the lack of such a mechanism almost inevitably leads to a squandering of the input in question.

Islam and rent

From the discussion of *riba* above, it can be seen that there are some similarities in the Islamic teachings on rent and on interest. To receive rent on virgin land or untapped resources is prohibited. However if the owner has improved the land or resources, through labor and/or capital investment, rent can be levied in proportion to the improvements that have been made.

Rent on land must be paid in money according to prearranged terms, and sharecropping, according to most interpreters, was forbidden. As one scholar has maintained, in stressing the analogy between sharecropping and the charging of interest:

> Sharecropping in such a case would mean *riba* since it is likely that one of the parties will get more or less than he should. Islam has no intention of committing *riba* or injustice toward anyone, worker or owner[38].

In other words, one of the parties would receive a share which is not in proportion to the risk involved. Using similar arguments, the wages of agricultural workers were interpreted as having to be paid in cash according to specific terms arranged in advance, and they were not to be linked to a share in output.

Thus, Muslim land and resource owners incur financial obligations, toward the community, which are based on their wealth. According to Shafi interpretations, *zakat* was due on both agricultural output and mineral produce. Other schools treated the former as subject to the tithe (*'ushr*), in a different category from *zakat*. In any case, landowners and farmers owed some share of their economic return to the community.

Islam and inheritance

Islamic inheritance laws are aimed at achieving a wide distribution of wealth amongst the close relatives of the deceased; at the same time the laws are geared to avoid hoarding and individualistic discrimination and squabbling within the family unit. In essence, the fabric of the family and society are put ahead of the emotional whims of the deceased[39].

Specifically, Islamic inheritance laws can be summarized:

(1) The deceased has the right to transfer one-third of his or her property as desired.
(2) Women are entitled to a share in inheritance along with men.
(3) The share of women, except in a few cases, is half that of male heirs in the same category.
(4) The inheritors include the members of the inner family – the children, parents, and spouse – but other relatives find a place in the share of distribution.
(5) The state inherits the estate of a person without a legal heir and pays the just debts of those who die in poverty.
(6) The general principle of distribution is dispersal of wealth from one to many, rather than its channeling from many to one[40].

Inheritance laws, although complications obviously made them an important subject for lawyers in the specifics of their interpretation, are nevertheless firmly rooted in detailed Quranic guidelines. For example:

> To the men a share of what parents and kinsmen leave, and to the women a share of what parents and kinsmen leave, whether it be little or much, a share apportioned; and the poor, make provision for them out of it[41].

> God charges you, concerning your children: to the male the like of the portion of two females, and if they be female above two, then for them two-thirds of what he leaves, but if she be one, then to her a half; and to his parents, to each one of the two, the sixth of what he leaves, if he has children; but if he has no children, and his heirs are his parents, a third to his mother, or, if he has brothers, to his mother a sixth . . . . And for you half of what your wives leave, if they have no children; but if they have children, then from what they leave a fourth . . . . And for them [wives] a fourth of what you leave if you have no children; but if you have children, then for them of what you leave an eighth . . . . If a man or a woman have no heir direct, but have a brother and a sister, to each of the two a sixth; but if they are more numerous than that, they share equally a third . . . .[42]

Those who cheat the helpless of their just dues or who themselves are not generous out of their own inheritances are strongly condemned:

> Those who devour the property of orphans unjustly, devour fire in their bellies, and shall assuredly roast in a Blaze[43].

> Whoso obeys God and His Messenger [relative to inheritance], He will admit him to gardens, underneath which rivers flow, therein dwelling

forever; that is the mighty triumph. But whoso disobeys God and His Messenger, and transgresses His bounds, him He will admit to a Fire, therein dwelling forever, and for him awaits a humbling chastisement[44].

[he says] 'My Lord has despised me.' No indeed, but you honour not the orphan, and you urge not the feeding of the needy, and you devour the inheritance greedily, and you love wealth with an ardent love[45].

In short, Quranic injunctions had the effect of reducing, if not eliminating, intra-familial strife over the estate of the deceased. Under the law, little was left to chance. On the one hand, the deceased could not disinherit a legitimate heir. On the other hand, the rights of weaker heirs were protected and based on their relationships to the deceased, not on their ability to command the services of probate lawyers for prolonged litigation.

One specific point needs further comment in light of contemporary attitudes. The apparent discrimination against women – daughters inherit half the shares of sons, for example – is deceptive. In fact, in the context of the times when the Quran was revealed, this provision represented a considerable advancement for women's rights. First, it guaranteed a share to a daughter, for example, even though she had left her father's household to join that of her husband. Secondly, other provisions of Islamic law made such inheritances the personal property of Muslim women. Their husbands and brothers had no claim over such property, though wives and sisters had a claim for legitimate support needs on the property of their male relatives. Thus, for nearly 14 centuries Muslim women have had independent property rights that have been denied to women in most Christian countries until very recently.

Islamic taxation and potential revenue sources

If Islam in fact forbids the taking of interest in any form, then there can be no question of any such income accruing to a true Muslim. Thus, Islamic taxation of interest income is ruled out. Why should the community assume the sin of the individual?

However, even in such a clear-cut case, at least two fiscally relevant cases remain. First of all, how should non-Muslim individuals (or institutions) that receive such income be dealt with? And secondly, how should disincentives against Muslims who transgress the Quranic prohibitions be assessed?

The first of these problems can be handled relatively easily. Non-Muslims are outside most provisions of specifically Quranic economic law. In effect, this grants the secular authorities considerable latitude in treating with non-believers. Though the interpretations in this regard of the orthodox schools of law may vary widely, it is clear that such income may well exist within *Dar al-Islam* and thus, by implication, it is a legitimate target of taxation.

Muslims, on the other hand, receiving income in the form of *riba* have sinned grievously. Confiscation of such earnings would be an obvious part of the punishment, and if restitution could not be made to the original borrower, the community would seem justified in adding such funds to the general coffers. However, such a levy is far more in the nature of a judicially-decreed fine, rather than of a tax, and as such it is peripheral to the considerations of this study.

As we have seen, profit is not the same as *riba*; it comes as the reward to the successful risk-taker and is a legitimate form of income for Muslims. No Quranic legislation specifically indicates taxes on any form of income; however, neither does the Quran rule out income taxes. Furthermore, the agricultural tithe *'ushr*, has been levied, by consensus of the community, since the earliest days of Islam. Based as it is on actual output, *'ushr* is an income tax, unlike *zakat* or fixed *kharaj* rates.

Similarly, the flexibility found in traditional Islamic tax legislation can allow for taxation to be levied against other forms of income, such as rental income. The principal criterion for such taxes would be the legitimate needs of the community.

Inheritances are, of course, a form of wealth, and by the nature of the accounting of an estate required at the time of its division among the heirs, they represent wealth likely to be both more readily and more accurately taxed. Thus, the state's responsibilities to oversee the just application of inheritance laws also gives it the opportunity to check on the *zakat* due on the assets of an estate. At the same time, other levies against the state are not ruled out.

5.8   Property and responsibility in Islam

Most forms of taxation originate in ownership (either wealth or income) or transactions associated with ownership. To appreciate Islamic doctrines on private ownership, it may be useful to begin with a brief summary of general Muslim economic principles:

(1) God created the world with natural abundance for people to enjoy and change;
(2) they are, therefore, the owners of all such fruits in the world that result from their endeavours, provided they commit no injustice or wrong-doing;
(3) they must, however, pay attention to the short and long term needs of society at large. As a part of this, the basic needs of the destitute must be met as they also have a claim on the abundance of society at large.

Nearly all interpretations of Islamic economic thinking arrive at the conclusion that the Quran undoubtedly embraces the right of private ownership. One noted scholar has remarked:

Since *tawhid* is made manifest in economics by equality, then man has to have free will, in order to decide what resources to use and develop, and how to divert his material destiny. Therefore, man's freedom of decision should be protected against the tyranny and despotism of capitalists, chairmen and committees. This was done in Islam by reserving for man the right to private ownership.

Private ownership in this sense means that when man puts his hand on resources, it is to help him decide the course of his life. His right to decide for himself is protected by giving him the right of consuming what he produces, and the right of priority in the use of certain resources over which he has priority, he should not claim ultimate individual ownership over the income purchased by that resource. He should know that he is not the Creator[46].

In short, it would be fair to say that in Islam private ownership by legal means (those unharmful to the rest of society) is encouraged and sanctioned, and that the government does not have the authority to curtail *arbitrarily* such a right.

However, private ownership differs from absolute ownership: this is God's alone. Legal ownership is the right of priority, of enjoyment and transfer of such property. Specifically, no man can claim untapped resources if he does not use them productively. Thus, in so far as such a resource exists and it is not being used, then another Muslim can claim it for himself or herself free of charge; this is encouraged to prohibit unproductive hoarding and to increase economic opportunity for all. In the case where an individual has made improvements on such resources, the only price that can be charged must be equivalent to such improvements; to charge a higher price would be illegal, since the owner would be receiving payment for the asset's existence, the due for which is God's alone.

But while Islam encourages private ownership in this sense, it is clear that such rights are not totally unconditional. First, the prophet Muhammad mentioned many individual needs and added that any excess of these overall requirements was not permissible. Secondly, if *zakat* falls short of social needs, then the state is authorized to impose additional taxes, since the poor have additional claims (other than *zakat*) on the wealth of the rich. Thirdly, general redistribution could be applied to productive assets (i.e., on priority of use) and to consumption of (or the right to consume) the output of society. Both forms of redistribution are desirable whenever it is necessary to restore the sense of community, the balance of distribution of resources, social justice and the freedom of individuals[47].

Some aspects of the question of income distribution are discussed above, but it may be useful to summarize them here. Our purpose is to bring out the responsibilities of property owners (that is, those able to afford to pay taxes) to the community.

The Quran makes it clear that God has created the material things of this world in abundance and that He intends that they be shared, in equitable fashion, by all men and women. Not that every Muslim should receive an equal share of society's produce; rather that all have a claim on enough to survive with a decent standard. The faithful are reminded that others will ask them what is a person's obligation to the poor; the answer is clear:

> O believers, expend of the good things you have earned, and of what We have produced for you from the earth; and intend not the corrupt of it for your expending, for you would never take it yourselves . . . God promises you His pardon and His bounty . . . And whatever expenditure you expend, and whatever vow you vow, surely God knows it . . . And whatever good you expend shall be repaid to you in full . . . Those who expend their wealth night and day, secretly and in public, their wage awaits them with their Lord, and no fear shall be on them; neither shall they sorrow[48].

Obviously, what is an individual's from God is not his or hers alone; all Muslims will be judged both on their stewardship of what they have earned or otherwise received, and on how they have in turn treated those who are less economically fortunate.

No burden of judgement is placed on those who have a demand on the better off in Muslim society:

> The freewill offerings are for the poor and needy . . . [for] the ransoming of slaves, debtors, in God's way and the traveller; so God ordains, God is All-knowing, All-wise[49].

That is, God knows who is worthy, and He has made His commandments clear to the Muslim community. We have seen above, in the sections on *zakat*, inheritance and interest, several groups in society specifically singled out as deserving of protection: widows, orphans, travellers, etc. But despite the detail that is provided in the Quran, it is clear that God intends that Muslims be generous and that they must honor the *spirit* as much as the letter of the specific injunctions made.

How can this spirit be defined? The benefit of doubt, on the day of judgement, clearly favors an assumption of the worthiness of the recipient of the faithful Muslim's boon. Merit accrues to the giver, even if the recipient hid behind a cloak of deception.

It is God's abundance in His creation that is the key element in Islamic doctrine. The prophets before Muhammad had preached God's generosity. Moses told the Jews that there would be more than enough for an entire generation to survive in the bleakest of wildernesses. He was not believed, but in Sinai his prophecy was proven. Jesus also preached on God's generosity; even though he fed the poor, his word was doubted. Because of this rejection of God's word that the poor must and will be provided for, He sent another, Muhammad, the last or the seal of the prophets, with the final message in this regard: the fruits of creation are for all men and women. The circumstances of human life in this world may result in a few receiving far more than they need, and in many receiving much less than is necessary for even the barest level of human existence[50]. From the primeval time of Adam, God has sent more than two dozen prophets. With the revelation of the Quran through His last messenger, Muhammad, humankind should learn once and for all. But in the last analysis, the hard-hearted will show their greed despite this final warning:

> Hast though seen him who cries lies to the doom? That is, he who repulses the orphan, and urges not the feeding of the needy. So woe to those that pray and are heedless of their prayers, to those that make display, and refuse charity[51].

5.9   Summarizing Islam and taxation

The basic principles of Islamic taxation, therefore, center on the obligations of those who are most fortunate in economic affairs, toward the community as a whole, the *'umma*. These obligations are imposed by God directly on the faithful and are owed to Him. However, the traditional pragmatism of Islam can be seen in the designation of the state authority as a divine agent in ensuring these obligations are met. Thus, half of the *zakat* dues have been collected by the state, while other religiously endorsed taxes such as *'ushr*, *kharaj* and *jizyah* have been instituted primarily through the prevailing consensus of the *'umma*, acting through the state.

As we have seen above, two factors have been involved in the historical application of the general Quranic principles governing the obligations of the individual to the community of believers. First, assuming that Muslims adhere to the principles of their religion, the needs of the community may exceed the voluntary bounty of the faithful. Thus, the state may have to intercede to assure a reasonable living standard to all Muslims (or to support its own legitimate needs). Secondly, human nature being what it is, individuals may cheat, or adhere only to the letter rather than to the spirit of the Quran. Thus, the state may have to act as the guarantor of at least some minimal standard of compliance with the divine commandment.

A third consideration recommending a secular role in taxation questions might be seen as quasi-Quranic in origin. For the most past, the earliest Muslims – the Prophet and his companions – dealt with Arabs – that is, the people to whom Muhammad was sent by God as the seal of the prophets.

On the one hand, the Quran clearly spells out that the immediate monotheistic neighbors of the Arabs – Jews and Christians – are people to whom God has already spoken. Though both groups were seen as having debased the revelations they had received from great prophets such as Moses, Solomon, John the Baptist and Jesus, they were nonetheless 'people of the book' (*ahl al-kitab*, or popularly, *dhimmi*) and they practiced religions worthy of respect, if inferior to Islam. These points are made many times in the Quran; for example:

> Surely we sent down the Torah, wherein is guidance and light; thereby the Prophets who had surrendered themselves gave judgement to those of Jewry, as did the masters and rabbis, following such portion of God's Book as they were given to keep and were witnesses to[52].

> And we sent, following in their footsteps, Jesus son of Mary, confirming the Torah before him; and We have to him the Gospel, wherein its guidance and light, and confirming the Torah before it, as a guidance and an admonition unto the God-fearing[53].

As mentioned previously, Muhammad preached that mankind had rejected these earlier revelations and distorted them, despite the efforts, suffering and martyrdom of the prophets of God:

> But had the People of the Book believed and been Godfearing, We would have acquitted them of their evil deeds, and admitted them to Gardens of Bliss. Had they performed the Torah and the Gospel, and what was sent down to them from their Lord, they would have eaten both what was above them, and what was beneath their feet. Some of them are a just nation, but many of them – evil are the things they do[54].

The Quran is filled with such warnings about those who had perverted the earlier revelations of God[55], yet their judgement was *to be left to God*, not to men, *even* if the latter were true believers (Muslims). Thus, with very few exceptions, the history of Islam is marked by a degree of tolerance for religious minorities unmatched elsewhere during the period of Arab dominance, roughly 700 to 1300 A.D.

A vital, expanding Islam which during this period came to dominate most of the western, southern and eastern shores of the Mediterranean, plus the entire southwestern quadrant of Asia, incorporated within its borders many non-Muslims[56]. These people soon became a majority within the extended borders of *Dar al-Islam*, and Islamic flexibility found a means of incorporating them within the state's fiscal system while granting them the tolerance that was due to fellow monotheists.

Of course, our interest is primarily in recent times, although historical considerations obviously play a major role in the shaping of current situations. Thus, it might be interesting at this point to preview some of the information examined below that relates to contemporary applications of traditional Islamic taxation principles. Those Islamic taxes that can be specifically identified in contemporary data sources are summarized in *Table 5.1*[57].

As can be seen, official data for such dues are available for few countries – Saudi Arabia, Sudan and the Yemen Arab Republic – only three of the 16 countries we are considering here. In part, the paucity of such information is due to general problems with official data.

Table 5.1 *Recent official receipts from religiously-decreed taxes, Middle Eastern countries*

Country	Period	Amount (millions of national currency)	Total revenue (%)	Total non-oil revenue (%)
Saudi Arabia	1947/48	3.2[a]	1.49	4.71
(*riyals*)	1958/59	1.5[a]	0.11	0.72
	1974/75	16.0[a]	0.02	0.39
	1977/1978	97.5[a]	0.06	0.64
Sudan	1957/58	0.81[b]	4.12	4.12
(pounds)		0.72[c]		
	1969/70	2.11[b]	1.50	1.50
		0[c]		
Yemen Arab Rep.	1966/67	2.64[a]	10.75	10.75
(*rials*)	1977/78	32.5[a]	1.71	1.71

Notes: [a] Includes all officially reported religiously-derived taxes.
  [b] *Zakat.*
  [c] *Jizyah.*

Sources: See below, *Tables 7.24, 8.15* and *8.21.*

The economic researcher, for example, might reasonably assume that the secular authorities have, at least until quite recently, continued to play an officially enforced role in the collection of *zakat* in such religiously dominated countries as Libya, Oman, Qatar, and the United Arab Emirates. On the other hand, some Middle Eastern countries have eliminated such religious levies in this century either because of their multi-communality (Lebanon) or because of their general striving for a degree of secularity (Egypt, Iraq, Jordan and Syria).

In either case, it must be recalled that official data would only reflect, at best, part of the religious levies. Most importantly, information regarding the voluntary *zakat* offerings of faithful Muslims is missing: these range from the countless gifts of a few pennies to beggars, to the usually anonymous multi-million dollar endowments in the wills of wealthy individuals such as the late King Faisal of Saudi Arabia.

Nonetheless, it is clear that traditional Islamic taxes do not play a significant role in the public sectors of the modern Middle East. For example, even if we eliminate the oil revenues of Saudi Arabia (that is, the taxes levied on foreign consumers), *zakat* plays a minor role in the fiscal receipts that are recorded as coming from the kingdom's residents – in fact, less than one percent of Saudi Arabian fiscal receipts during the last generation. Even for Sudan and Yemen, neither of which have enjoyed any sizable mineral royalties, religious taxes have declined to near insignificance in recent years.

It should, of course, be emphasized that, to some considerable extent, official categorization is a factor in this discussion. Some modern taxes similar in intent to religious taxes have been instituted, (for example, land taxes, inheritance taxes, and duties on exports of agricultural produce) and these have come to play a major role in many countries during the third quarter of the twentieth century. Other taxes of western origin that are, arguably, similar to traditional Islamic levies (such as personal and corporate income taxes) have also become important.

On the other hand, it will become clear in the next section that official fiscal policy in all the countries we are considering has paid little or no attention to historical Islamic taxation categories during recent years. We will return later to a discussion of what this trend may mean for the future. The example of the embryonic Islamic Republic of Iran requires that we ask whether this past lack of interest in traditional sources of revenue might now be giving way to very different official attitudes.

Notes

1 Maxime Rodinson (translated by Brian Pearce), *Islam and Capitalism*, (Austin: The University of Texas Press, 1978), p.3.
2 That is, popular in theory (for example in universities or at political rallies), but not in practice – as in contemporary Iraq or Syria, or espoused with greater vigor only in isolated areas like southern Yemen.
3 The authors are currently undertaking a study of the Islamic economic system and its economic implications for such questions as income distribution, efficiency, the operation of factor markets, etc.
4 Tax, as the term is used today, is not altogether an appropriate term, since it implies a payment made under duress of legal penalty to a government entity; still, the word tax serves as a convenient term where no other modern English word might be an improvement. As we shall indicate below, *zakat* includes alms given privately by one individual to another.
5 The specific interpretation of this and other taxes varies among the various orthodox legal schools – Hanafi, Shafi, Maliki, and Hanbali. For more detail, refer to Nicholas P. Aghnides, *Mohammedan Theories of Finance*, (New York: Columbia University Press, 1916).
6 Against the latter came to be levied the *'ushr*, or tithe, and many commentators then distinguished this as basically different from *zakat*.

7 *Zakat*, plus the first three pillars listed above are *sine qua non*, absolutely required of all true Muslims. The obligation of the *hajj* is qualified; one must be financially able to undertake the pilgrimage.

8 Sura XIII, v. 22; a similar phrasing is found in Sura XXXV, v. 29. This and all following Quranic quotations are taken from the translation of A. J. Arberry, *The Koran Interpreted*, (London: George Allen and Unwin Ltd., 1955). This translation follows the traditional Quranic ordering of the chapters, or *suras*.

9 Sura LXX, v. 24.

10 For example, this is the interpretation cited as primary by Joseph Schacht in the article on *zakat* in the *Encyclopedia of Islam*, (Leyden: E. J. Brill Ltd., 1934).

11 According to Schacht in Sura XXIX, v. 31 and 55, and in Sura VII, v. 156, Sura XXI, v. 73, etc.

12 As, for example, in Sura XCII, v. 14 ff., 'Now I have warned you of a fire that flames . . . from which the most Godfearing shall be removed, . . . he who gives his wealth to purify himself'. The expiation connected with the payment of *zakat* is clearly connected with sins of economic origin; thus, it is particularly recommended to the rich.

13 Cf. Aghnides, op. cit. (note 5) p. 203.

14 However, transactions undertaken specifically to avoid the 12 month requirement do not qualify for exemption.

15 For example, Aghnides, op. cit. (note 5) pp. 216–17, lists several items that are either nonproductive or primary necessities: dwelling-houses; wearing apparel; household utensils; slaves employed as servants; riding animals; arms kept for use; food used by one's self and family; articles of adornment, if not made of gold and silver; gems, pearls, rubies, hyacinths, emeralds, and the like; coins of other than gold and silver, if intended for personal expenditure; books and tools. All the preceding articles are exempt from *zakat* even when they are not destined for primary necessities, and are not actually used – for instance, even when the tools are not owned by people who use them, provided, however, they are not intended for trade. It must be remarked that the tools (*alat*) referred to above are the tools which render a use without

leaving a trace in the thing on which they have been used. If, however, they do leave a trace in the thing, as is the case with yellow dye or saffron bought by a dyer in order to be used for the dyeing of people's clothing in consideration of a price (*ajr*), they are then subject to *zakat*, provided their value amounts to a *nisab* and a year has passed from the time of their purchase. Likewise subject to *zakat* is every article ('*ayn*) brought for use in the process of work, if a trace of it remains in the object worked upon. Gallnut and grease used for the dressing of leather are of this category. No *zakat* is due on instruments, however, if, as in the case of soap and potash, no trace of them is left.

16 Cf. Aghnides, op. cit. (note 5) Ch. III, p. 296 ff. For example, the *Hanafi* school held that gold, silver, and articles of trade were non-apparent property, while livestock and any otherwise non-apparent property taken outside of the city were apparent property, with the obligations on agricultural produce (the tithe) held to be an obligation distinct from *zakat*. On the other hand, the Shafi school included agricultural produce and the output of mines along with livestock as apparent property.

17 Sura IX, v. 60. However, there was some dispute among the various schools as to whether religious authorities had the right to make exceptions, deleting or adding specific recipients, or to transfer *zakat* revenues from one region to another.

18 As quoted from Aghnides, op. cit. (note 5) pp. 249–50.

19 Aghnides, op. cit. (note 5) p. 254.

20 Economists term neutral or proportional a tax that strikes all tax payers with the same impact; a progressive tax is one whose relative burden rises with income or wealth (that is, with the ability to pay), while a regressive tax hits the poor harder, less severely the rich. The levy on the smallest and most common livestock, sheep and goats, as indicated above, was actually somewhat regressive, above minimum flock sizes. A Muslim with 40 sheep, for example, owed *zakat* of 2.5 percent, while another with 121 sheep owed about 1.66 percent, and one with 400 sheep one percent.

21 The *al-Hikayah*, Vol. V, as quoted in Aghnides, op. cit. (note 5) pp. 367–68.

22 The proportional *kharaj* was thus similar to the tithe. The difference was largely one of location, with land subject to the tithe being for the most part in Arabia proper or land granted to members of the Arab army after its conquest.

23 Sura IX, v. 29. The word *jizyah* is derived from *jaza*, meaning compensation or requital for good or evil.

24 Over time, the imposition of *jizyah*, depending as it did upon the specific terms agreed upon by treaties negotiated by various Muslim political and military leaders with the peoples swept up in the expansion of *Dar al-Islam*, led to many anomalies. For example, some tribes originally agreed to payment of the poll-tax and later converted to Islam; without forgiveness of their tax obligations, they assumed the Muslim duty of military service in defense of the community. Other tribes might agree to serve in a military capacity, with no reference to religious conversion, and thus earned exemption from *jizyah*.

25 Various definitions have been given to these general economic classifications; among those cited in Aghnides, op. cit. (note 5) p. 403, a typical one is that the poor are those who must work, the middle class includes those with some wealth (for example, more than 200 *dirhams*) but who still work, while the rich have enough wealth (above 10 000 *dirhams*) to be idle. The apparent progressivity of *jizyah* thus clearly is deceptive. For example, under these guidelines, the rich never pay an annual tax exceeding about one-half percent of their wealth, while those in the middle class could pay as much as 12 percent of wealth annually, and the poor even more.

26 Which also included levies against discoveries of secreted treasure.

27 The Hanbali school held views similar to the Shafi, and the Maliki school seems to have straddled the issue. Under *zakat* provisions, as indicated above, the levy due would be 2.5 percent; by Shafi interpretations, at least, mines belonging to non-Muslims were exempt from taxation.

28 Abdul-Hamid Ahmad Abu-Sulayman, The Theory of the Economics of Islam, *Contemporary Aspects of Economic Thinking in Islam*, (Proceedings of the Third East Coast Regional conference of the Muslim Students Association of the USA and Canada, American Trust Publications, April, 1968); emphasis added discretionally.

29 Sura II, v. 275–76.

30 Sura II, v. 279.

31 Sura III, v. 125.

32 Sura XXX, v. 38.

33 Fazlurrchman, Economic Principles of Islam, *Islamic Studies* 8, 7, (March, 1969).

34 Abdul-Hamid Ahmad Abu-Sulayman, op. cit. (note 28) p. 17.

35 Ibid., p. 24.

36 The Islamic Development Bank is discussed by the authors, in the context of other Middle Eastern economic assistance programs, in *Oil, OECD and the Third World: A Vicious Triangle?* (Austin: University of Texas Press, 1978). This sort of equity situation may well be easier for international institutions that have only a small number of projects to evaluate or where largely political considerations are involved in the lending procedure. Also, over the long run, a society might find itself with a few financial institutions owning huge amounts of equity.

37 In fact, private borrowers in times of inflation do not repay the true value of their loans if the Quranic injunctions are strictly adhered to; thus, the borrower of anything would be exploiting the lender.

38 Abdul-Hamid Ahmad Abu-Sulayman, op. cit. (note 28) p. 24.

39 For example, see Zianddin Ahmed, Socio-Economic Values of Islam, *Islamic Studies* 10, 351, (December 1971).

40 See M. Najatullah Siddiqi, Moral Bases of Islamic Personal Law, *Islam and the Modern Age* 5, 85 ff, (November 1979).

41 Sura IV, v. 8.

42 Sura IV, vv. 12–15.

43 Sura IV, v. 11.

44 Sura V, vv. 17–18.

45 Sura LXXXIX, vv. 17–20.

46 Abdul-Hamid Ahmad Abu-Sulayman, op. cit. (note 28) p. 48.

47 Ibid., p. 27.

48 Sura II, vv. 269 ff.

49 Sura IX, v. 60.

50 It has been indicated above (cf. Abdul-Hamidf Ahmad Abu-Sulayman, op. cit. (note 28) p. 30) that shortages and the resulting hardships must be shared among the faithful. This interpretation clearly emphasizes the importance of the problem of income distribution to Islam's theology of economic morality.

51 Sura CVII, vv. 2–7.

52 Sura V, v. 48; similar points are made in many other places – for example, Sura VI, vv. 92 and 155; Sura XXIII, v. 48; Sura XXVIII, v. 43; Sura XL, v. 56; Sura LXI, v. 5.

53 Sura V, v. 50; similar language is found in Sura LXI, v. 6.

54 Sura V, v. 70.

55 These perversions, as seen by Muslims, centered on racial pride and exclusivism on the part of Jews and on identification of the non-divine (the human prophet, Jesus) with God on the part of Christians, and references to them are scattered throughout the Quran, especially in Suras II through V.

56 Mostly monotheists at first – Jews and Christians – but also the dualistic Zoroastrians of Persia. Islamic tolerance in some respects tended to grow – eventually to allow some degree of freedom of religion even to the polytheism of popular Hinduism. However, the toleration we are referring to herein is principally a phenomenon of the period when the Islamic *khalifate* was still an Arab institution.

57 Obviously from what has been said above, it must be kept in mind that such payments by Muslims that are voluntary will not be included as *zakat* in official tax statistics.

PART III

Taxation in the Middle East

Taxation in the Middle East

Following on from the description contained in Part II of the operation and effect of most major types of taxation, Part III will concentrate on the region with which we are specifically concerned: the Middle East, which we will define as more or less the northeastern corner of Africa and the southwestern part of Asia[1]. This definition is arbitrary, but it includes the heart of the Arabic speaking world (the Arabian peninsula, the historic Fertile Crescent and the Nile Valley) plus Iran.

In this way, we encompass some 16 countries, which can be divided into two groups. First are those countries where oil production and exports are so large, relative to the rest of the economy, that oil based taxes tend to dominate the fiscal accounts. Most of these countries are members of OPEC: Iran, Iraq, Kuwait, Libya, Qatar, Saudi Arabia and the United Arab Emirates[2]. In addition, Oman (which still remains somewhat aloof from OPEC as well as from the parallel regional group, the Organization of Arab Petroleum Exporting Countries (OAPEC)) is for the most part dependent on oil, as will be demonstrated below. Bahrain too, (an OAPEC member) depends mostly on oil production, even though its annual output is quite small.

The second group consists of non-oil economies. These include two countries, Egypt and Syria, with some oil, and several with little or no oil production so far: Jordan, Lebanon, Sudan and both Yemens. We will find many distinctions between this second group, the members of which have rather diverse tax bases, and the first group, some of whose members have only negligible taxes outside the oil sector.

Several basic statistical series are set forth in *Tables 6.1* and *6.2*. The first indicates how the oil industry has grown in the region and which countries are now the largest producers. Though regional oil production precedes World War I, it was not until after World War II that these countries became a major part of the world's oil industry. Since then, production in the Middle East has grown much faster than in the world as a whole, and today we realise that these countries are vital to the world economy. For example, in 1945, the 11 countries listed in *Table 6.1* produced about 7.9 percent of the world's oil. Over the next 33 years, world output grew at an annual average rate of more than 6.8 percent, but the total production of this group climbed almost twice as rapidly – at an average of about 12 percent. Thus by 1978, they supplied almost 38 percent of the world's oil.

Table 6.1 *Oil production: major Middle Eastern producers (1915–1978)* *(millions of barrels annually)*

Year	Bahrain	Egypt[a]	Iran	Iraq	Kuwait	Libya	Oman
1915	–	0.2	3.7	–	–	–	–
1920	–	1.0	12.2	–	–	–	–
1925	–	1.2	35.0	–	–	–	–
1930	–	2.0	45.8	0.7	–	–	–
1935	1.3	1.3	57.3	28.5	–	–	–
1939	7.6	4.7	78.2	31.2	–	–	–
1942	6.2	8.3	72.3	20.3	–	–	–
1945	7.3	9.4	130.5	36.6	–	–	–
1947	9.4	8.6	155.0	37.6	16.2	–	–
1950	11.0	16.3	242.5	51.0	125.7	–	–
1952	11.0	16.5	10.1	142.4	273.4	–	–
1954	11.0	13.8	22.4	232.2	350.3	–	–
1956	11.0	11.9	198.3	234.6	405.7	–	–
1958	14.8	22.0	301.5	266.9	524.1	–	–
1960	16.5	24.0	390.8	355.8	619.2	–	–
1962	16.4	32.3	487.0	368.4	714.6	66.5	–
1964	18.0	42.9	626.1	459.4	842.2	315.7	–
1966	22.5	44.0	771.2	507.4	906.8	550.2	–
1968	27.5	67.1	1042.2	551.2	956.6	951.5	87.9
1970	28.1	119.5	1403.6	571.6	1090.6	1212.0	121.3
1972	25.6	77.6	1849.3	536.4	1201.6	805.3	103.1
1973	24.8	93.4	2152.2	717.7	1103.2	796.4	106.9
1974	24.5	85.8	2210.6	680.9	903.1	550.8	106.0
1975	22.2	111.3	1965.4	820.5	760.9	551.3	124.2
1976	21.2	119.9	2166.4	874.4	786.9	699.5	133.8
1977	20.8	150.5	2080.0	909.9	720.2	758.0	124.8
1978	20.0	197.5	1910.4	959.6	765.5	721.5	114.7

Notes: [a] Beginning in 1968, oil production figures include estimated removals from the Sinai oil fields by Israeli occupation authorities; official Sinai production figures are not available inasmuch as these Israeli operations have generally been held to be contrary to international law.

Over this same period, there were several shifts within the group as to relative importance. In 1945, Saudi Arabia was well behind Iran and Iraq, producing little more than two minor producers, Bahrain and Egypt, together. Saudi Arabia today, of course, is the Middle East's largest (and, after the USSR and the USA, the world's largest) producer. Kuwait did not begin to produce until 1946, while Qatar followed in 1949, Libya in 1961, and the United Arab Emirates in 1962. Each of these produces far more than either Bahrain or Egypt now.

The role of oil generated tax receipts depends, of course, as much on the relative size of the non-oil sector of an economy as it does on oil production. For example, as we will see below, a minor exporter, such as Bahrain, may be much more dependent on oil taxes than a much larger supplier such as

Table 6.1 *(continued)*

Year	Qatar	Saudi Arabia	Syria	United Arab Emirates	Total Middle East	World total
1915	–	–	–	–	3.9	432.0
1920	–	–	–	–	13.2	688.9
1925	–	–	–	–	36.2	1 067.9
1930	–	–	–	–	48.5	1 411.9
1935	–	–	–	–	88.4	1 654.9
1939	–	3.9	–	–	125.6	2 086.2
1942	–	4.5	–	–	111.6	2 093.1
1945	–	21.3	–	–	205.1	2 594.7
1947	–	89.9	–	–	316.7	3 022.1
1950	12.3	199.5	–	–	658.3	3 803.0
1952	25.3	301.9	–	–	780.6	4 531.1
1954	36.5	351.0	–	–	1017.2	5 016.8
1956	45.3	367.0	–	–	1273.8	6 124.2
1958	63.9	386.3	–	–	1579.5	6 616.9
1960	63.9	480.7	–	–	1950.9	7 674.5
1962	68.0	599.7	–	6.0	2358.9	8 881.9
1964	78.9	694.1	10.0	67.5	3154.7	10 309.6
1966	105.9	949.7	17.5	131.3	4006.4	12 021.8
1968	124.4	1113.7	30.3	182.6	5135.0	14 084.2
1970	131.4	1386.7	37.6	284.0	6386.4	16 398.4
1972	176.8	2202.0	43.9	441.8	7463.4	18 744.0
1973	207.9	2773.6	36.1	555.2	8567.4	21 113.4
1974	189.2	3096.2	48.2	615.0	8537.3	21 127.7
1975	160.3	2583.2	66.9	619.0	7785.3	20 174.2
1976	178.1	3140.1	70.2	712.6	8903.1	21 831.2
1977	159.2	3359.0	74.8	724.8	9082.0	22 672.0
1978	175.9	3023.3	73.9	660.5	8622.8	22 904.7

Source: *Twentieth Century Petroleum Statistics* (Dallas, De Golyer and MacNaughton); *International Petroleum Encyclopedia* (Tulsa, The Petroleum Publishing Co.). Various editions.

Iran. Generally, the more oil exported by a country, the larger the government revenues that oil generates loom, relative to the economy as a whole, as can be seen in *Table 6.2*[3]. But again the non-oil sector is a factor. For example, in Saudi Arabia, Kuwait and Qatar, where non-oil economic activity is still relatively undeveloped, government receipts are as much as 80 percent of GNP. But in Iran, despite the 1973 increase in oil prices and the country's position as the second largest oil producer in the Middle East, government receipts were still less than 40 percent of GNP in 1977. Of course, this share is still well above the levels prevailing in the non-oil exporting countries, which as *Table 6.2* shows, were less than 30 percent of GNP in most cases.

Table 6.2 *Government receipts as a percentage of GNP and per capita; GNP per capita (1950–1977)*

Country	Year	Government receipts: as a percentage of GNP	per capita	GNP per capita
Bahrain	1968	67.7	126	186
(*dinars*)	1977	45.0	674	1 500
Egypt	1950	20.0	9.0	45
(pounds)	1960	25.5	14.4	56
	1968	27.9	18.7	82
	1977	40.3	49	122
Iran	1950	10.2	938	9 211
(*rials*)	1960	16.1	2 333	14 421
	1968	19.1	4 390	22 964
	1977	38.4	58 967	153 734
Iraq	1950	10.2	6.4	36
(*dinars*)	1960	30.2	22	73
	1968	33.9	35	102
	1977	52.1	236	453
Jordan	1960	13.3	8.3	62
(*dinars*)	1968	13.4	12.6	94
	1977	21.7	40	233
Kuwait	1960	44.0	612	1 390
(*dinars*)	1968	41.1	419	1 259
	1977	62.6	2 280	3 969
Lebanon	1950	4.4	45	1 021
(pounds)	1960	11.4	150	1 320
	1968	12.9	245	1 892
	1974[a]	13.4	364	2 723

Notes: [a] 1974 was the last complete year before the outbreak of the Lebanese Civil War.
         [b] Estimated.

The overall growth of tax revenues in these 16 countries is shown in *Table 6.3* for the 1950–1977 period; this table also reduces revenues to the common denomination of US dollars. All have seen considerable increases in this regard, but of course the fastest growth has been among the oil producers. For example, in Egypt tax revenue multiplied at an average of about nine percent, but in Libya at about 30.7 percent. In Syria, the rate of growth of revenues averaged more than eight percent, but in Iraq it was more than 19 percent. (Even in abutting oil producers, contrasts are notable with Bahrain, Saudi Arabia, and Qatar having annual average growth rates of 20.7, 24.5 and 31.1 percent respectively.)[4] The relative tax loads, on a per capita basis, also reflect this oil/non-oil dichotomy as can be seen in *Table*

Table 6.2 *(continued)*

Country	Year	Government receipts: as a percentage of GNP	per capita	GNP per capita
Libya	1962	15.1	17	115
(*dinars*)	1968	40.5	194	489
	1977	59.5	1 180	1 979
Oman	1960[a]	2.6	1	33
(*rials*)	1968	42.3	48	114
	1977	72.8	635	870
Qatar	1960[b]	90.3	5 580	6 145
(*riyals*)	1968	59.3	5 000	8 432
	1977	80.4	14 125	17 554
Saudi Arabia	1960	35.6	298	836
(*riyals*)	1968	42.8	688	1 608
	1977	80.4	14 125	17 554
Sudan	1955	10.2	3.0	29
(pounds)	1960	17.8	6.0	32
	1968	18.3	7.7	42
	1977	29.0	30	103
Syria	1960	22.4	132	586
(pounds)	1968	29.5	268	907
	1977	21.6	774	3 582
United Arab Emirates	1968	48.5	3 275	6 746
(*dirhams*)	1977	79.6	44 740	56 286
Yemen Arab Rep.	1968	4.4	9.5	215
(*rials*)	1977	19.6	345	1 780
Yemen People's Dem. Rep.	1968	10.7	5.3	50
(*dinars*)	1977	17.4	19.4	111

Sources: World Bank Atlas and *International Financial Statistics*, various issues; *World Tables 1976*; various government documents.

6.4 (though most of the burden of oil taxes falls upon foreign consumers, not local tax payers).

In most oil exporting countries revenue has been derived from two types of oil industry taxes, and sometimes from a mixture of both: one is an income or profits tax on the producing companies and the other is in the form of royalties paid to the government on the basis of physical output measures. In this chapter both types are treated as direct taxes. Thus, in their overall fiscal receipts, oil producers do not resemble most other developing countries with respect to the relative importance of direct and indirect taxes. As indicated in *Table 6.3*, direct taxes in the major oil producing countries

Table 6.3 *Direct and indirect taxes: Middle East countries (1950–1977)* *($ millions)*

Country	Tax category	1950	1958	1965	1970	1977
Bahrain	Direct	2.0	11.8	12.4	20.2	456.7
	Indirect	1.6	2.3	5.2	8.3	118.0
	Total	3.6	14.1	17.6	28.5	574.7
Egypt	Direct	93.0	174.1	285.4	374.4	1 051.4
	Indirect	350.4	520.4	881.6	1127.9	3 473.1
	Total	443.4[b]	694.5[g]	1167.0[i]	1502.3[m]	4 524.5
Iran	Direct	71.7	311.6	772.2	1480.8	24 469.9
	Indirect	79.2	163.9	400.1	662.5	3 552.7
	Total	150.9[b]	475.5[g]	1172.3[i]	2143.3[m]	28 022.6[o]
Iraq	Direct	26.4	259.2	420.3	666.3	8 342.9
	Indirect	57.0	100.9	248.9	355.7	968.8
	Total	83.4[c]	350.1[g]	669.2[i]	1022.0[m]	9 311.7
Jordan	Direct	2.8	2.8	10.5	9.8	58.9
	Indirect	11.0	11.1	55.3	58.3	363.8
	Total	13.8[d]	13.9[f]	65.8[i]	68.1	422.7
Kuwait	Direct	13.7	356.7	631.5	848.1	8 388.4
	Indirect	NA	10.8	15.7	37.0	283.4
	Total	NA	367.5	647.2[i]	885.1[m]	8 671.8[o]
Lebanon	Direct	4.4	11.5	30.9	46.6	90.9
	Indirect	17.1	55.7	111.0	134.7	296.2
	Total	21.5	67.2	141.9	181.3	397.1[n]
Libya	Direct	2.2	3.1	345.0	1326.1	9 034.6
	Indirect	10.1	25.8	83.0	154.0	930.2
	Total	12.3[e]	28.9[g]	428.0	1480.1	9 964.8
Oman	Direct	NA	NA	0	106.5	1 413.1
	Indirect	NA	NA	2.5	2.4	60.2
	Total	NA	NA	2.5	108.9	1 473.3

have always contributed the greatest share of all tax revenues; this tendency was strengthened after the price increases of 1973. In 1977, for example, direct taxes ranged from about 90 percent of total tax revenues in Iran and Libya to more than 97 percent in Kuwait and Qatar (*Table 6.5*). In contrast they constituted about a fifth of all taxes among the non-oil exporters; with contributions ranging from about eight percent in North Yemen to about 28 percent in Syria.

The discussion in this section will commence with the countries which are heavily reliant on oil-based taxes, although we do not intend to outline in historical detail the tax structures of the 16 countries under consideration.

Table 6.3 *(continued)*

Country	Tax category	1950	1958	1965	1970	1977
Qatar	Direct	1.1	54.6	69.1	108.1	1 888.8
	Indirect	0.2*	1.7*	5.9*	13.5	57.3
	Total	1.3	56.3	75.0	121.6	1 946.1
Saudi Arabia	Direct	36.9	305.8	707.2	1231.7	32 742.4
	Indirect	13.9	39.0	57.3	131.3	3 860.5
	Total	50.8^a	344.8	764.8	1373.0	36 602.9
Sudan	Direct	6.0	5.6	11.6	54.3	146.5
	Indirect	33.9	72.4	140.1	241.9	1 087.2
	Total	39.9^e	78.0^g	151.7^i	296.2^m	1 233.7^o
Syria	Direct	13.4	41.6	68.7	110.5	231.6
	Indirect	81.8	64.9	89.8	114.4	610.5
	Total	105.2^c	106.5^g	158.5	224.9	842.1
United Arab Emirates†	Direct	NA	0.2	99.7	230.0	7 808.9
	Indirect	NA	1.2	0.8	8.0	454.5
	Total	NA	1.4^b	100.5^j	238.0	8 263.4
Yemen Arab Rep.	Direct	NA	NA	0.5	1.6	29.2
	Indirect	NA	NA	3.9	15.4	327.0
	Total	NA	NA	4.4^k	17.0	356.2^o
Yemen People's Dem. Rep.	Direct	1.9	2.6	2.8	7.0	26.1
	Indirect	2.9	5.4	10.9	9.6	65.7
	Total	4.8^d	8.0	13.7	17.6	91.8

Notes: NA Data not available.   * Data estimated.   † Pre-independence data aggregates more than one fiscal jurisdiction.

^{a} 1947/48	^{e} 1952/53	^{i} 1965/66	^{m} 1970/71
^{b} 1949/50	^{f} 1955/56	^{j} 1966	^{n} 1974
^{c} 1950/51	^{g} 1958/59	^{k} 1966/67	^{o} 1977/78
^{d} 1951/52	^{h} 1960	^{l} 1967/68	

Our task is to determine more general movements in the fiscal profiles of the Middle Eastern countries that we are examining.

In many cases below, we have cited, by way of illustration, specific tax rates or tax schedules; in other cases, we discuss changes in this regard. However, we do not represent this data in the same fashion as the more general information – for example, as regards direct and indirect taxation, or when broad categories, such as income, profits or excise taxes are cited. The latter, we hope, are shown below more or less completely for the chosen time period, generally 1950 to 1978, though country to country variations are necessary, depending upon data availability.

Table 6.4 *Per capita tax load: Middle
Eastern countries (1977) (dollars)*

Country	Tax revenues per capita
Bahrain	1 675
Egypt	115
Iran	812
Iraq	782
Jordan	147
Kuwait	8 240
Lebanon	130[a]
Libya	3 780
Oman	1 797
Qatar	9 052
Saudi Arabia	3 957
Sudan	75
Syria	107
United Arab Emirates	11 018
Yemen Arab Rep.	65
Yemen People's Dem. Rep.	51

Notes: Figures derived from *Table 3.3.*
          [a] 1974.

Table 6.5 *Oil revenues relative to total revenues: major oil producers (%)*

Country	1950	1962	1970	1973	1977
Bahrain	55.2	72.0	66.2	65.2	78.1
Iran	11.6	40.1	49.7	67.0	73.6
Iraq	17.3	64.1	53.7	80.9	85.5
Kuwait	81.7	94.6	91.2	92.7	96.6
Libya	0.0	7.6	83.1	75.1	83.2
Oman	0.0	0.0	98.0	94.3	92.6
Qatar	84.1	94.0[a]	88.9	92.5	97.0
Saudi Arabia	68.0[a]	86.4	86.9	93.3	88.3
United Arab Emirates	0.0	25.0[a]	96.6	89.2[a]	94.5[a]

Notes: Total revenues excludes borrowing.
          [a] Estimated.

   In Chapter 7 we will discuss the nine oil exporting countries of the region:
Bahrain, Iran, Iraq, Kuwait, Libya, Oman, Qatar, Saudi Arabia and the
United Arab Emirates, whilst Chapter 8 will focus on the other seven
countries: Egypt, Jordan, Lebanon, Sudan, Syria, Yemen Arab Republic
and Yemen Democratic People's Republic.

Notes

1 The Middle East is generally a vague
geographic term. Some definitions omit all
African states, others extend all the way
from Mauritania to Pakistan.
2 OPEC members not included in this study
are Algeria, Ecuador, Gabon, Indonesia,
Nigeria and Venezuela.
3 *Table 6.2* and several subsequent tables
present data in terms of national currencies.

Historic time series of exchange rates
relative to the dollar are presented in
Appendix A.
4 These growth rates are derived from *Table
6.3* and are not strictly comparable with
those used in later sections. These figures
are in dollars, not national currencies, and
exclude non-tax revenues from state
enterprises.

CHAPTER 7

Oil exporting countries

7.1 Bahrain

The smallest of the Middle East countries we are considering in this section, Bahrain is in many ways more economically developed and socially modernized than any of its neighbors in the Gulf region. Though it has long been an oil producer and exporter, Bahrain has never enjoyed such high revenues as the nearby states of Qatar and Abu Dhabi. Thus, oil production *per se* has not overwhelmingly dominated the Bahraini economy. The island's traditional pursuits, especially those related to *entrepôt* trade, have remained strong, and its people have searched for other promising economic activities over recent years. At an early point Bahrain added a refinery, that handles both Arabian and Bahraini crude oil, to its longtime commercial activity. In the last decade, a major aluminium smelting plant and a growing banking sector have employed thousands of Bahraini residents. Unlike the situation in most of the other states along the Gulf's southern littoral from Kuwait to Oman, the majority of those who work in these newer industries are actually Bahraini citizens. This is largely a result of Bahrain's efforts to provide mass education which now go back almost two generations – to the 1930s.

Despite the diversification of its economy, Bahrain still remains heavily dependent on oil to generate the bulk of its tax revenues. As can be seen in *Table 7.1*[1], in 1950 oil royalties were responsible for about 53 percent of the state's modest revenues of less than $4 million. By 1975, oil accounted for a much higher percentage (84 percent) of total revenues that had climbed, by then, to more than $160 million. Since 1975, these changes in oil revenues have pushed up both customs receipts and fees for government services and licenses. The fiscal picture has thus shifted slightly in favor of non-oil sources.

Total revenues over the 1950 to 1978 period increased at an annual rate of about 19.4 percent. However, most of this growth occurred in the 1970s, when both the formula for computing the government's take from oil production and oil prices themselves changed drastically. For example, growth in revenues averaged about 11.3 percent a year from 1950 to 1970, and more than 42 percent a year from 1970 to 1978. Oil royalties multiplied somewhat faster than other taxes over the entire period – at an average of about 21.1 percent a year.

Table 7.1 *Tax revenues: Bahrain (1960–1977)*

	1950	1954	1958	1962	1966	1968	1970	1971	1972	1973	1974	1975	1976	1977	1978
Direct taxes															
Total (millions of *dinars*)	0.9	5.3	5.6	5.4	7.9	8.1	9.6	21.5	26.0	29.4	103.4	110.9	156.4	180.7	191.8
Percentage of revenues	55.2	84.1	82.4	72.0	69.3	67.5	66.2	78.2	79.3	62.8	83.5	84.2	80.7	78.1	77.9
Royalties	0.9	5.3	5.6	5.4	7.9	8.1	9.6	21.5	26.0	29.4	103.4	110.9	156.4	180.7	191.8
Indirect taxes															
Total (millions of *rials*)	0.8	1.0	1.1	2.0	3.3	3.4	4.1	6.0	6.8	15.7	18.1	18.2	34.5	46.7	50.5
Percentage of revenues	44.8	15.9	16.13	26.7	28.9	28.3	28.3	21.8	20.7	33.5	14.6	13.8	17.8	20.2	20.5
Customs	0.6	1.0	1.0	1.8	2.3	2.6	3.2	NA	NA	5.2	6.7	7.5	18.5	24.9	26.1
Excise, sales and production taxes	0	0	0	0	0	*a*	0.2	0.2	0.3	0.3	0.3	0.2	0.3	0.4	0.5
Other indirect taxes	0.2	0.3	0.1	0.2	1.0	0.7	0.6	NA	NA	10.2	8.9	10.5	15.7	21.4	23.9
State enterprises															
Total (millions of *dinars*)	*a*	*a*	*a*	0.1	0.1	0.5	0.7	*b*	*b*	1.7	2.2	2.5	3.0	3.9	4.0
Percentage of revenues	–	–	–	1.3	0.9	4.2	4.8	–	–	3.6	1.8	1.9	1.5	1.7	1.6
Total revenues	1.7	6.7	6.8	7.5	11.4	12.0	14.5	27.5	32.8	46.8	123.7	131.6	193.9	231.3	216.3

Notes: NA indicates separate data not available.
  a Less than 50 000 *dinars.*
  b Included in total indirect taxes.

Source: Bahrain Ministry of Finance and National Economy, *Statistical Abstract*

Although Bahrain's economy has become quite diversified in recent years, while its oil production necessarily remains at a modest level, there has so far been little tendency for the country's fiscal profile to change to a non-oil direction. It has not only been the rise in oil prices that has obviated any greater relative reliance on other existing taxes (see *Table 7.2*) such as customs duties, the gasoline excise, or the adoption of new levies, for example, income or property taxes. During this same period, Bahrain has been the recipient of considerable largesse in the form of grants and low interest loans from its more affluent neighbors, particularly Saudi Arabia. In fact, much of the island's current development plans are based on foreign funding sources.

Table 7.2 *Major taxes: Bahrain (1955–1977)*
(thousands of dinars)

	1955	1966	1977
Oil company payments	5250	7851	180 700
Customs duties	1222	2269	24 900
Excises on gasoline	–	–	400
Fees and licenses	355	644	751
Land sales and rentals	92	20	NA
Profits from government enterprises	58	130	3 859

Note: NA indicates data not separately available.

Source: See *Table 7.1.*

It is not difficult to appreciate why Bahrain might be wary of discouraging the development of its newer economic sectors by imposing higher taxes on them. Still, the modest and rapidly dwindling oil reserves[2] point out the need to seek domestic income sources to replace gradually falling oil receipts. Not only is foreign economic assistance no long-run substitute for a locally generated fiscal revenue, but there is also danger of encouraging the development of industries which can survive only with subsidies, including those implicit in tax exemptions. Bahrain should be seeking economic diversification in preparation for its post-petroleum era. However, these newer sectors must eventually be able to 'pull their own weight' in the national economy, which includes increasing their contributions to the tax base.

7.2   Iran

At the beginning of 1979 Iran had a population of more than 36 million, making it the second largest nation in the Middle East. With an estimated GNP of more than $75 billion in 1977, it was by far the region's largest economy (at least until the devastating effects of the revolution in 1978 –1979). While the majority of the labor force is still employed in the agricultural sector, it is, of course, petroleum that dominates the economy (in value added terms).

As *Table 6.1* shows, Iran is a mature oil economy, producing since 1913; in fact, Iran was a major part of the world oil industry before its neighbors, Saudi Arabia and Kuwait, even started to export. It was in Iran that the first major political confrontation over oil policies in the Middle East occurred in the early 1950s: this was between British corporate interests and Iranian nationalism in the person of Prime Minister Mussadeq. At that time oil exports (and of course revenues) all but ceased for nearly three years; government receipts fell from about $45 million in 1950[3] to less than $20 million in 1951 and then to nil in 1952 and 1953. 1954 saw a recovery to $21 million and receipts rose further to $90 million in 1955. The production level of 1950 was not surpassed however, until 1957; by then oil receipts were nearly $213 million – an amount five times greater than the earnings from an almost identical volume of exports in 1950.

From the Iranian viewpoint the political and economic effects of the crisis were mixed. The new arrangements with the multinational producers, agreed on at the settlement of the crisis, resulted in a considerable improvement in Iranian oil revenues: but nevertheless, production effectively remained under the control of the multinationals – hardly the outcome hoped for by Mussadeq. If after the settlement, Iran realized a much larger share of the final value of its petroleum than before, the prolonged crisis quickly took from the country its predominant position among Middle Eastern producers. The proliferation of oil discoveries south of the Gulf before and after World War II would, of course, have eventually lessened Iran's relative importance as a regional producer; but nevertheless, Iran felt the consequences of Mussadeq's policies in its oil exports (and tax revenues) for a full decade.

Most of the effects of this crisis, on the fiscal side, are lost if we look only at the entire time span shown in *Table 7.3*. Over 28 years, total government revenues grew from about 8 thousand million *rials* to about 2035 thousand million *rials* – at an annual average rate of growth of about 22 percent. This gain was clearly paced by oil revenues, which grew at an annual rate of more than 30 percent. Over this period, oil went from directly accounting for only about 11.6 percent of total government revenues in 1949/50 to almost 74 percent in 1977/78.

However, this growth in both total and oil-derived revenues has not been consistent over the entire time span. Not surprisingly, the OPEC price action of 1973/74 contributed a major spurt to Iran's fiscal profile. During the 1973/74 period, oil revenues grew by more than 48 percent a year on average, while total revenues were up at almost the same annual rate – 45 percent.

ELMER E. RASMUSON LIBRARY
UNIVERSITY OF ALASKA

Table 7.3 *Tax revenues: Iran (1949/50–1977/78)*

	1949/50	1954/55	1959/60	1962/63	1966/67	1968/69
Direct taxes						
Total (millions of *rials*)	2311	4477	23603	29974	56676	76651
Percentage of revenues	29.7	39.6	58.2	46.8	58.2	63.7
Income taxes	1160	1114	3476	4311	8144	13064
Royalties	901	3113	19877	25650	47093	61822
Property taxes	250	250	250	403	1439	1765
Indirect taxes						
Total (millions of *rials*)	2555	6317	12418	26805	30309	36867
Percentage of revenues	32.8	55.9	30.6	41.9	31.1	30.6
Customs	1697	4231	7742	9067	19177	21600
Excise, sales and production taxes	550 ⎫	} 2086 {	1878	2829	7948	8085
Miscellaneous indirect taxes	326 ⎭		2798	14909	6993	7182
State enterprises						
Total (millions of *rials*)	2919	500	4572	7205	6506	6793
Percentage of revenues	37.4	4.4	11.3	11.3	6.7	5.6
Total revenues						
(millions of *rials*)	7785	11294	40593	63984	97300	120311

Source: Bank Markazi Iran, *Annual Report and Balance Sheet*

Other direct taxes also surged during the few years preceding the Ayatollah Khomeini's successful campaign against the Pahlavi dynasty. However, given the broad dissatisfaction shown during the last year of the Shah's reign, the tax situation that prevailed may seem somewhat surprising. For example, profits taxes showed the fastest climb (at about 54 percent a year) from 28.8 thousand million *rials* in 1973/74 to 160.2 thousand million *rials* in 1977/78. Personal income taxes, on the other hand, went from 17.9 thousand million to 51.8 thousand million *rials* – at an annual average growth rate of 30 percent, well below that for taxes in general. Of course, this indicates a tax benefit to the generally richer elements of Iranian society. However, the country's income tax structure hit hardest at those on a salary, especially those who were enployed by government agencies or large corporations; that is the middle class, rather than the very rich. (Presumably, the latter were more affected by higher profits taxes; however, though the increases in the latter were quite sizable in percentage terms, they remained small relative to the total size of the economy – profits taxes on privately held corporations amounted to only 2.6 percent of total government revenues in 1977/78.) The middle class figure prominently in the rebellion that replaced 25 centuries of monarchy with an anti-western theocracy.

Table 7.3 *(continued)*

1970/71	1971/72	1972/73	1973/74	1974/75	1975/76	1976/77	1977/78
113 040	186 600	217 400	364 150	1 267 200	1 383 800	1 609 300	1 728 100
65.6	72.2	72.0	78.3	90.9	87.5	87.6	84.9
24 442	27 100	33 700	45 400	52 600	124 400	170 800	212 000
85 562	155 300	178 290	311 250	1 205 200	1 246 800	1 421 500	1 497 800
3 036	4 200	5 500	7 500	9 400	12 600	17 000	18 300
50 575	60 600	74 100	89 550	111 000	156 500	185 600	250 900
29.4	32.5	24.5	19.3	8.0	9.9	10.1	12.3
32 052	37 300	45 700	60 700	63 600	92 600	122 600	167 400
11 574	13 100	14 500	17 600	22 000	26 300	32 500	44 100
6 947	10 200	13 900	11 250	25 400	37 600	30 500	39 400
8 685	11 100	10 600	11 100	16 200	41 800	41 500	55 300
5.0	4.3	3.5	2.4	1.2	2.6	2.3	2.7
172 300	258 300	302 100	464 800	1 394 400	1 582 100	1 836 400	2 034 300

In theory, income taxes were quite progressive in rate structure during the early and mid 1970s. Wage, salary and personal income derived from business activities were subject to levies beginning at the eight percent level on income between 144 000 and 240 000 *rials*; the rate increased to ten percent between 240 000 and 400 000 *rials*; it went up to 12 percent for incomes between 400 000 and 700 000 *rials*, and so on to a maximum rate of 60 percent on income increments above 50 million *rials*. Effective rates ranged from about 2.2 percent on 200 000 *rials* a year to about 8.5 percent on 700 000 *rials* to about 45.6 percent on 50 million *rials*. Agricultural incomes were liable to rates progressing from ten to 45 percent, depending upon the value of annual production as assessed at harvest time. Merchants and craftsmen were subject to surtaxes on their gross incomes for the benefit of the municipality governments. Of course, accurate collections were difficult from self-employed individuals, whether they were rural or urban residents.

Under the Pahlavi régime corporate profits were also taxed according to progressive schedules, the structures of which varied according to whether the company was foreign or domestically owned. For the former, rates were as high as 60 percent. A number of exemptions designed to promote various economic development goals were in effect in the early 1970s. For example, plants located away from the major cities could have their profits exempted from 20 to 100 percent of tax liabilities for as long as ten years, depending on the location. Companies engaged in mining or the processing of mineral ores were entitled to exempt half their profits from taxation. Hotels in major business and tourist areas benefited from tax exemptions as high as 75 percent.

Another category of taxes hitting hard at Iran's growing middle class during the last years of the Pahlavi era was made up of customs duties, which were levied on nearly all imports. *Ad valorem* rates ranged from a low of 5–10 percent on many capital goods to as high as 150 percent on certain luxury goods. Duties on common consumer goods (except for food-stuffs) were generally in the middle or upper end of this range. In recent years, the burden of many tariffs has become heavier. As Iran proceeded to diversify its economy, an increasing number of consumer goods were produced

Table 7.4 *Major taxes: Iran (1949/50–1977/78) (millions of rials)*

	1949/50	1958/59	1965/66	1971/72	1977/78
Inheritance taxes	NA	66	204	610	51 500
Income taxes	1160	3476	7168	10 800	
Profits taxes				15 200	160 200
Oil royalties	901	19 877	50 965	155 300	1 497 800
Property taxes:					
Real estate	250	350	490	1 100	5 700
Property transfer fees	0	0	323	2 100	9 400
Customs:					
Import duties				13 400	94 600
Import profits assessments	1679	7435	13 028	9 700	51 500
Import registration fees				–	
Excises:					
Petroleum products	NA	1376	4462	9 500	32 000
Beverages	NA	501	1 021	1 700	4 200
Automobiles	–	–	–	1 600	13 700
Government service fees	NA	399	2430	5 200	20 000
Stamp duties	NA	307	581	1 700	
Government monopoly profits	NA	3 365	11 990	11 100	34 900

Note: NA indicates data not separately available.

Source: See *Table 7.3*

domestically; thus, the local constituency for higher protective tariffs grew apace. However, as *Table 7.4* shows, customs receipts increased on the average less than 18 percent a year over the 28 year period, as opposed to about 22 percent a year for total revenues. After the beginning of the oil boom in 1973/74, the average annual gain for customs revenues jumped to about 29 percent, but again this was well below the average growth rate for total revenues – about 44.7 percent. Not only is the rate of growth for customs revenues slower than for both total tax revenues and income and profits taxes, but it is also well below the growth of import *values* over this period – which was almost 43 percent a year.

After the successful OPEC price action in late 1973, Iranian imports surged in direct relation to the country's heightened development ambitions, and therefore overall import growth is not directly a reflection of increased consumption. However, preliminary figures from the Bank Markazi Iran[4] (the central bank) indicate that consumer goods import values actually grew *faster* during this period than did capital goods import values. If this difference was also borne out in quantity terms[5], then the consumer burden from customs duties (which are levied almost entirely on consumer goods[6]) rose slower than both imports and total taxes.

The other category of consumption taxes – excises levied mostly on petroleum products, automobiles, and soft and hard beverages of both domestic and foreign origin – saw an increase from 17.6 thousand million to 44.1 thousand million *rials* during these four years, or at an average increase of slightly less than 26 percent, which is below the growth rate for total revenues. Again this is an example of a tax mostly aimed at the middle class, that did not become more onerous during recent years.

The point here, however, is not that the economic groups in the forefront of anti-Pahlavi revolt (the urban middle and working classes) had few real fiscal complaints, at least relative to other groups. And, of course, we are only examining here taxes *explicitly* levied, and not the *implicit* tax so prevalent recently in Iran, as in many other countries, both in the Middle East and elsewhere – *inflation*. According to official price data, the overall consumer price index rose nearly 106 percent between 1973/74 and 1977/78, or by about 20 percent a year. Other estimates, less subject to the restraints imposed by Pahlavi officialdom, placed the annual rate of inflation during this period at between 40 and 60 percent. Particularly hard hit was the housing sector; even official figures showed annual price increases for this item to be, on average, in excess of 33 percent.

The basic fact remains that in Iran, as in most other oil exporting economies, explicitly levied taxes which actually affect Iranians (as opposed to those that mostly hit foreigners, such as oil taxes), remain a relatively minor part of the overall fiscal picture. For example, though recent and disaggregated national income data for individual sectors are not available, the IMF has estimated that private consumption or spending power in Iran amounted to about 2160 thousand million *rials* in 1976/77. In the same year, non-oil taxes amounted to about 370 thousand million *rials* – or about 17 percent of domestic spending power at most. In contrast to this, federal taxes alone in the US (very little of this burden falls on non-US residents) came to almost 30 percent of consumer spending power; state and local taxes probably would increase this to between 38 and 42 percent. Whatever economic problems urged Iran's middle class to the barricades in Tehran during the winter of 1978/79, they were not primarily of a fiscal nature.

Nevertheless, tax relief has evidently received priority in the Islamic Republic of Iran. Only a few weeks after the Ayatollah's régime was installed in 1979, a revised income tax law was published. The individual exemption jumped 150 percent to 360 000 *rials*, with a ten percent levy then due on income up to 480 000 *rials*, 12 percent on the excess up to 720 000, and from this point the previous rates continue to apply. This change is most beneficial to the urban working class, where income had been badly eroded by inflation. Effective tax rates after the promulgation of this new legislation dropped to one percent on 400 000 *rials* a year from 5.9 percent, and to 5.5 percent on 700 000 *rials* from 8,5 percent. At the other end of the income scale, salaries exceeding 2.4 million *rials* are subject to a ten percent surtax. Thus, an annual income of four million *rials* is now subject to an effective tax of about 29.5 percent instead of the previous rate of about 26.1 percent.

Table 7.5 *Iranian overseas investments and returns (1960–1977) (millions of rials)*

	Investments	Returns
1960	4 015	100
1962	4 850	167
1964	3 790	227
1966	9 165	455
1968	9 990	600
1970	5 800	755
1971	36 500	760
1972	58 050	1 150
1973	67 070	3 450
1974	548 400	26 760
1975	583 200	47 470
1976	598 800	49 290
1977	843 200	47 240

Source: International Financial Statistics and
Balance of Payments Yearbook.

One last point about Iran remains to be made in order to facilitate comparisons among the oil exporters. Particularly in recent years, several of these countries have begun to realize another major type of government earnings – the returns on overseas investments. As we shall see below, this item is most important in the oil exporting nations with smaller populations. Even the most populous exporters like Iran and Iraq have seen a surge since 1973 in officially held foreign investments. *Table 7.5* indicates that these investments have jumped sharply and in two distinct stages – during 1974 and again in 1977. However, though Iranian returns from this source by 1977 represented a considerable sum, it remained rather insignificant in relation to total government revenues. Returns on foreign investments amounted to about 2.3 percent of government revenues in 1977 – a major advance over 1973, (the year of increased oil prices) when it came to only about 0.75 percent of total revenues. The revolution and the Iran–Iraq war have, however, reduced the size of Iran's external assets to an insignifcant level.

7.3 Iraq

Another of the countries in the region which became a significant oil exporter fairly early, Iraq began earning oil royalties in 1927 which rose slowly to about 5.3 million *dinars* by 1950. During this period, oil royalties were treated as extra-budgetary receipts, to be used only for capital spending. Partly because of increasing demands on the current expenditures portion of the budget, and partly because spending on capital projects tended to lag well behind available funds, in 1950 oil revenues were incorporated into the budgetary procedure. A government agency, the Development Board, was created and given the responsibility of systematizing the capital spending process. Oil revenues began to be divided specifically between current spending needs and development projects. At about the same time, Iraqi production grew sharply as a result of Iran's dispute with its oil concessionaire; in addition, the formula determining Iraq's revenues from oil was altered significantly in its favor. Oil royalties thus climbed almost nine-fold between 1950/51 and 1954/55 (*Table 7.6*).

Though the division of oil revenues initially allocated 70 percent to the Development Board, the current budget has generally secured, over most of the period considered, a larger share than the remaining 30 percent[7]. For example, if we examine *Table 7.7*, the current budget's actual share of oil revenues began to run ahead of that of the development budget as early as 1959/60, the first fiscal year under the republican régime. Only in recent years, as development plans have been geared up after the rise in oil prices, has Iraq's development budget again claimed the larger share of oil receipts.

As the accompanying tables indicate, oil related revenues have grown much faster than total revenues. For instance, over the entire 1950–1977 period oil related revenues grew at an average rate of about 25 percent a year for the former, while the latter was multiplying at about 17.8 percent a year. However, for readily identifiable historical reasons, Iraqi oil receipts have not grown evenly during this period. First, as mentioned above, oil output increased rapidly in the early 1950s as Iraq became a major alternative source of supply when Iranian exports temporarily ceased. As can be seen in *Table 6.1*, Iraqi production went from 51 million barrels in 1950 to more than 232 million barrels by 1954. At the same time, the change in the payments formula pushed earnings up even faster – from 6.7 million to 57.7 million *dinars* for the same calendar years.

Table 7.6 *Tax revenues: Iraq (1950/1951–1977)*

	1950/51	1954/55	1958/59	1962/63	1966/67	1968/69	1970/71	1971/72	1972/73	1973/74	1974/75	1975	1976	1977
Direct taxes														
Total (millions of *dinars*)	9.4	55.3	92.6	110.3	137.8	195.0	239.3	387.0	254.7	859.6	1755.2	1761.2	2376.5	2463.8
Percentage of revenues	28.1	63.5	67.4	65.6	61.7	63.8	60.8	73.5	65.8	84.4	86.6	86.0	85.9	87.6
Income taxes	1.9	2.3	3.8	7.6	12.2	16.2	21.4	24.4	27.9	28.8	23.8	35.0	94.1	50.5
Royalties	5.8	51.5	86.9	99.0	122.4	174.7	211.7	356.3	218.6	823.2	1724.1	1719.7	2273.0	2403.5
Property taxes	1.7	1.6	1.9	3.8	3.2	4.0	6.2	6.3	8.2	7.6	7.3	6.5	9.4	9.8
Indirect taxes														
Total (millions of *dinars*)	21.4	28.4	36.0	50.4	68.8	93.2	127.7	115.1	109.9	130.7	181.5	183.5	269.5	286.1
Percentage of revenues	63.8	32.6	26.2	30.0	30.8	30.5	34.4	21.9	28.4	12.8	9.0	9.0	9.7	10.2
Customs	10.0	16.5	18.7	23.0	33.1	31.2	40.3	41.5	36.7	44.1	80.6	120.4	184.5	179.3
Excise, sales and production taxes	7.7	8.4	11.6	13.3	17.2	16.6	21.5	27.3	26.6	29.6	34.3	35.1	54.2	58.2
Other indirect taxes	3.7	3.5	5.8	14.1	18.6	45.4	66.9	46.3	46.6	57.0	66.6	28.0	30.8	48.6
State enterprises														
Total (millions of *dinars*)	2.7	3.4	8.7	7.5	16.6	17.3	26.7	24.4	22.4	27.7	90.5	102.6	121.0	60.3
Percentage of revenues	8.0	3.9	6.3	4.5	7.4	5.7	6.8	4.6	5.8	2.7	4.5	5.0	4.4	2.1
Total revenues (millions of *dinars*)	33.5	87.1	137.3	168.2	223.3	305.4	393.7	526.5	387.0	1018.0	2027.2	2047.3	2767.0	2810.2

Note: Tax year is 1 April to 31 March 1950/51 to 1974/75; 1 April to 31 December, 1975; 1 January to 31 December, 1976 and 1977.

Source: Central Bank of Iraq, *Annual Report*; Ministry of Planning, *Statistical Abstract of Iraq*.

But a few years later, Iraq itself became locked in a dispute with its major concessionaire, the British-Dutch-French-USA-owned Iraq Petroleum Company (IPC). After the revolution of July 1958, the republican régime reflected the country's general xenophobia in its hostility toward IPC. In December 1961, the government seized the part of the concession that was not being exploited at that time. This was not nationalization of the entire concession, as Mussadeq had tried, but only of about 99 percent of the IPC holding, which had originally covered nearly the whole country. IPC was not prevented from continuing to produce from (or even further developing) its existing 'working area', but it did lose several important and promising oil reserves which had already been discovered but not opened – most notably, the huge North Rumaila field near Basrah.

Table 7.7 *Oil receipts allocations to current and development budgets: Iraq (1950/1951–1977) (millions of dinars)*

Year	Total oil receipts	Allocation to development budget	Total development budget[a]	Allocation to current budget	Total current budget
1950/51	5.8	5.3[a]	5.3[b]	0.5	28.2
1953/54	47.9	32.9	35.3	15.0	47.7
1956/57	68.7	48.2	51.1	20.7	62.7
1959/60	75.1	31.8	31.9	43.3	89.7
1962/63	99.0	50.5	70.0	48.5	114.7
1965/66	135.4	67.7	75.0	67.7	179.1
1968/69	174.7	83.1	88.5	91.6	220.4
1970/71	211.7	97.3	101.1	114.4	292.6
1972/73	218.6	109.3	135.9	109.3	270.5
1973/74	823.2	411.6	441.8	411.6	597.9
1974/75	1724.1	600.8	661.8	1123.3	1400.2
1975[c]	1719.7	1135.7	1165.2	584.0	896.3
1976	2273.0	1239.2	1259.0	1033.8	1522.1
1977	2403.5	1502.7	1511.4	900.8	1310.0

Notes: [a] For most years the largest non-oil source of development revenues was foreign and domestic borrowing.
[b] The first formal development budget was for 1951/52; this amount represents the oil royalties set aside for development expenditures in 1950/51.
[c] Nine months only.

Source: See Table 7.6

Unlike Anglo-Iranian after Mussadeq's 1951 action, IPC did not withdraw completely from the scene. A long series of discussions with the Iraqi government was initiated which continued into the 1970s, with no real resolution of the basic issues. As a result, Iraqi oil production tended to stagnate during a period when worldwide demand was booming. IPC showed its displeasure by generally neglecting its Iraqi holdings[8]. For example, Iraqi oil production went from about 368 million to 565 million barrels a year between 1962 and 1970, a climb averaging 5.5 percent a year.

But during this same period, world demand for oil grew by about 8 percent a year and world trade in oil by about 11.1 percent a year and neighboring producers shared in this boom: Iran's production was up by about 14.1 percent a year during this period, Saudi Arabia's by 11.1 percent a year, and Qatar's by 21.3 percent. Libya and the United Arab Emirates were only beginning to produce a significant oil output in the early 1960s: thus, their outputs grew even faster between 1962 and 1970; 43.7 and 65.9 percent a year respectively. Only in Kuwait was there a rate of increase in output – about 5.4 percent a year – as low as in Iraq, and this was because oil revenues had surpassed domestic needs by the mid-1960s and beginning conservation of known reserves was to affect government production decisions.

Iraq's dispute with IPC was only resolved during the period of increased worldwide confrontation between producers and companies in the early 1970s; and then it was through the drastic mechanism of nationalization, a move that Iraqi governments of differing ideological principles had avoided for over a decade. This, plus the OPEC price actions of 1973, finally freed Iraqi oil revenues from the doldrums which they had experienced throughout this period of confrontation.

With oil receipts showing relatively slow gains during the 1960s, their relative importance in Iraq's fiscal profile did not change greatly. As *Table 7.6* indicates, oil revenues in 1958/59 accounted for a larger share (about 63.3 percent) of total revenues than they did in 1972/73 (about 56.5 percent). During this period, both income and property taxes grew much faster (15.3 and 11 percent annually, respectively) than did oil receipts (6.8 percent a year).

However, since the OPEC price action of 1973, Iraq's fiscal profile has become much more like neighboring major oil producers. Oil revenues have assumed a much larger role relative to total tax receipts – almost 86 percent in 1977, as opposed to the 56.5 percent share they had in 1972/73. Direct and indirect taxes falling on Iraqi taxpayers have, with one exception (customs duty receipts), changed very little, even in absolute terms, during the first few years of higher oil prices. Income, property, and excise, sales and production tax categories showed little absolute change (and considerable relative decline) from 1970 to 1976, though both income and excise taxes jumped sharply in 1977 (see *Table 7.8*).

Income taxes have been levied both against personal incomes and the profits of corporate and non-corporate forms of business entities; however, except for oil company profits taxes, data below the level of disaggregation shown in *Table 7.8* are not available. In theory, rates levied against all forms of income are steeply progressive. For example, in the mid-1970s personal income, up to an annual level of 500 *dinars*, after allowed exemptions, was subject to a five percent levy. Income between 500 and 1000 *dinars* was taxed at ten percent, and rate brackets were at five percent increments until income above 15 000 *dinars* was taxed at 75 percent. In addition, a 20 percent surcharge on the tax is earmarked for national defense. Effective rates for a family of four, for example, range from 1.2 percent on annual incomes of 1000 *dinars*, to about 10.6 percent on 3000 *dinars*, about 21 percent on 6000 *dinars*, about 33 percent on 10 000 *dinars*, about 48 percent on 15 000 *dinars*, and about 69 percent on 30 000 *dinars*. However, in practice, these taxes were collected almost entirely from salaried employees of the state and of state owned enterprises. Agricultural incomes (except for land rentals) were specifically exempted, and collections from those in the private sector, which continued to thrive even under socialist regimes, were, at best, haphazard. Thus, personal income taxes were almost entirely the burden of only a portion of the middle class[9].

Table 7.8 *Major taxes: Iraq (1950/51–1977) (millions of dinars)*

	1950/51	1958/59	1966/67	1970/71	1977
Income and inheritance taxes	1.70	3.76	12.98	21.4	50.5
Oil receipts	5.80	86.87	122.43	211.7	2403.5
Property taxes on:					
Agricultural land	0.62	0.21	0.67	1.3	} 9.8
Real estate	0.87	0.98	2.56	4.9	
Excises on:					
Fuel	1.29	4.14	8.63	10.2	
Tobacco	1.19	2.94	4.99	5.7	} 58.2
Alcohol	0.57	1.33	1.68	2.0	
Cement	–	0.32	0.65	0.9	
Customs duties	9.00	18.68	32.04	40.3	179.3
Agricultural production taxes [a]	4.38	2.03	1.06	–	–
Stamp duties	0.57	0.97	2.52	4.3	14.0
Land registration taxes	0.25	0.75	1.13		
Court fees	0.30	0.59	0.88	} 42.8	45.6
Other government service fees	1.94	2.54	4.33		
Profits of government corporations	2.72	8.66	16.62	26.7	60.3

Note: [a] Including export taxes.

Sources: See Table 7.6

Sliding scales were similarly applied to the profits of business partnerships and corporations. Most of the former were in the retail trade sector, a sector very hard to hold to the strict accounting procedures needed for reasonably accurate tax assessments; most of the latter, of any size, had long since passed into the public sector by the early 1970s. Non-oil business taxes (as opposed to the earnings of public enterprises) have continued to play only a minor role in Iraq's fiscal profile.

In the mid 1970s inheritance taxes ran from 5 percent on net legacies of less than 10 000 *dinars*, up to 35 percent on the net value above 100 000 *dinars*. Relatively generous exemptions included family housing, life insurance, and death benefits from employers.

In addition, municipal governments have subjected businesses and individual professional people to a series of license fees and other charges which, though levied in relation to the place of business, have been aimed at taxing a share of the income received by the business. Rates have generally been lower for so-called essential activities, like pharmacies, garages and basic manufactures; somewhat higher for professional individuals, such as physicians and lawyers; and higher still for such enterprises as banks and insurance agencies. By its very nature, being assessed on a sliding scale against the rental value of the premises, this tax has been reasonably easy to collect.

In the mid 1970s, real estate was taxed relative to its rental value at a flat rate of 10 percent for urban properties (subject to certain minimum income exemptions allowed to owners) and on a sliding scale running from 5 to 15 percent on agricultural land. Transfer taxes were also levied on the sale of real estate, depending upon its rental value.

While no general sales tax had been levied during this period, several sumptuary excises have been utilized. As *Table 7.8* shows, these have fallen on largely locally produced fuel, tobacco and alcohol products. But despite the recent oil boom these have not increased drastically, going from about 16 million *dinars* in 1966/77 to about 18.8 million *dinars* in 1970/71 and then to 27 million *dinars* in 1976 – indicating an annual average growth rate of only about 5.4 percent over the decade.

Customs duties have historically been the most onerous levy faced by most Iraqis, regardless of class. They are computed on an *ad valorem* basis and hit nearly all imports, especially consumption goods, at rates which have ranged in recent years from five to 100 percent or even higher. After the 1973 oil price increases, they escalated more than three-fold over five years (or an average increase of about 42 percent a year). In relative terms, however, customs receipts fell from about 9.5 percent of total revenues in 1972/73 to about 6.4 percent in 1977. During approximately the same period, Iraq imports actually increased somewhat faster than customs duties – from 320 million *dinars* in (calendar) 1973 to 1660 million *dinars* in 1977 (averaging an increase of 51 percent a year).

Like other major oil producers of the area, Iraq has also become an international creditor. This has meant profits for the government (through the central bank) resulting from increased international reserves. Unlike some of its neighbors which have relatively limited internal development prospects (like Qatar, Abu Dhabi and even Kuwait), or which have oil incomes so high that they outrun their ambitious development schemes (like Saudi Arabia), Iraq has not found itself (since 1973) with any dearth of projects: and these projects have a claim on the increased earnings. Still, the Iraqi trade balance has seen a broadening surplus: about 135 million *dinars* in 1972; 320 million *dinars* in 1973; more than 1200 million *dinars* in both 1974 and 1975; more than 1700 million *dinars* in 1976; and finally levelling off at aout 1600 million *dinars* in 1977 and 1978. Officially held overseas assets climbed sharply as a result of higher oil revenues, as have, of course, the earnings generated by these assets (see *Table 7.9*). However, these earnings remained a relatively minor item relative to total government revenues – about 4 percent in 1976, though this was a sharp increase from the previous decade, when such earnings were barely 1 percent.

Table 7.9 *Iraqi overseas investments and returns (1960–1976) (millions of dinars)*

	Investments	Returns
1960	92.5	2.6
1962	69.5	2.7
1964	89.6	5.7
1966	116.5	4.6
1968	161.7	8.2
1970	165.1	8.2
1971	197.5	8.5
1972	260.1	9.0
1973	462.1	18.8
1974	993.9	78.5
1975	805.7	53.1
1976	1356.8	NA

Sources: International Financial Statistics and Balance of Payments Yearbook.

In the late 1970s there were many indications that this source of revenue will soon become much more important in government accounts. The sharp rise in oil prices since 1978, of course, had a major impact on the export earnings of most oil producers. Iraq has been no exception. Iraq also moved quickly into the void in world oil markets, created by the Iranian Revolution, by sharply boosting production – from an average of about 2.49 million barrels a day in 1977 to 2.63 million in 1978, 3.43 million in 1979, and 3.53 million by early 1980. While import spending also climbed, there still was a considerable surge in net Iraqi earnings – for example, a 1980 study by the First National Bank of Chicago estimated a current account surplus of about 3360 million *dinars* in 1979 rising to about 4370 million *dinars* in 1980. In addition, as for other Middle Eastern countries, there are reasons for official Iraqi statistics to understate foreign assets and earnings.

All of these considerations led the First National Bank to estimate recent Iraqi foreign holdings and earnings well above the levels shown in *Table 7.9*; for example, it suggests total net foreign assets of more than 7650 million *dinars* in 1979, 12 100 million *dinars* in 1980, and more than 15 350 million *dinars* by the end of 1981. Earnings levels are projected at almost 600 million *dinars* in 1979, then peaking (along with record OECD country interest rates) in 1980 at almost 1120 million *dinars* before falling slightly to about 1090 million *dinars* in 1981. Even so, this 1981 estimate amounts to about 45 percent of 1977 oil revenues and about 39 percent of total government revenues that year, which is the most recent for which detailed budget figures are available (see *Table 7.6*). Undoubtedly, the disastrous Iran–Iraq border has sorely eroded Iraq's portfolio. However, a few years of peace and normal oil production would restore it to pre-war levels. The future implications for fiscal policy of such growing nontax revenues is discussed in greater detail in Chapter 13.

7.4   Kuwait

Although oil production in Kuwait began later (1946) than in neighboring Iran, Iraq and Saudi Arabia, it was the first country in the Middle East to see its society and economy totally transformed by oil. There were two major reasons for this, the first simply being incredibly rapid expansion in oil production from 5.9 million barrels in 1946 to 125.7 million in 1950 and to 402.8 million by 1955. Revenues climbed even faster, from less than 200 thousand *dinars* a year, when production began, to 4.9 million *dinars* in 1950 and then to 100.5 million *dinars* by 1955. Factors contributing to this rapid acceleration were the almost total disruption in Iran's oil exports, making Kuwait an excellent alternative supplier and the change in oil company payment methods to the 50/50 profit sharing formula that prevailed until the early 1970s.

The second reason for Kuwait's transformation was its small population. For example, with approximately 175 000 people in 1955[10], oil revenues on per capita basis came to about 575 *dinars* or about $1610.

Total tax revenues have mostly reflected activity in the oil sector. Using an estimated base of 6 million *dinars* in receipts in 1950, the total (*Table 7.10*) grew by an annual average rate of about 25 percent over the following 28 years[11]. This was almost the same rate at which oil revenues multiplied (25.8 percent).

If we look at other tax categories, the overwhelming dominance of oil becomes clearer. Income taxes, after oil royalties (the second largest source of fiscal revenue), are corporate profits taxes, since no individual income tax has yet been levied on Kuwait residents. To the present, almost all this tax is paid by oil companies; in fact, it was the major oil based tax until very recently. As can be seen from *Table 7.11*, non-oil company profits taxes have generally amounted to considerably less than 1 percent of this category. This tax, in theory, has been steeply progressive, ranging, in the early 1970s, from 5 percent of net profits between 5250 and 18 750 *dinars* in 5 percent incremental steps to 55 percent of net profits above 375 000 *dinars*. Given the growing level of business activity in Kuwait, one might expect greater receipts under this category than the approximately 100 000 *dinars* shown for recent years in *Table 7.12*. (For example, even one company with net profits as low as 331 000 *dinars* would owe a tax of 100 000 *dinars*.) However, businesses are subject to this tax only if they are corporations; such entities as partnerships treat net profits as the personal income of the partners and, therefore, are not subject to tax. In this way Kuwait's fiscal legislation encourages noncorporate forms of organization. This is particularly true in wholesale and retail commerce, which continues to dominate the private sector of the national economy.

In addition to these loopholes, foreign corporations are only subject to profits taxes if they are actually registered as a corporation in Kuwait. Even firms which register can qualify for generous exemptions under the provisions of the Industrial Encouragement Law; a ten-year tax holiday is available if 51 percent of the enterprise's capital is Kuwaiti supplied.

Until the economically revolutionary year of 1973/74 in the world oil industry, oil companies paid Kuwait about two or three times as much in profits taxes as they did in royalties. Kuwait then made two changes that have affected its fiscal accounting. First, when OPEC took control of prices, the extra revenues accruing to the state were entered on the books as royalties[12] – this accounts for the 22 fold increase in royalties seen in *Table 7.9* from 1973/74 to 1978/79. Secondly, Kuwait began the process of nationalizing the oil companies operating within the borders. This changed the companies' tax base, and profits taxes dropped sharply, to only 79 million *dinars* by 1978/79.

The only wealth based tax has a rather indirect link: a real estate tax levied as a percentage of net realized rental income. The tax is graduated, using the same schedule as that applied to corporate taxes. Devout Kuwaitis are conscience-bound to the obligations of *zakat*; however, the Kuwaiti Government has not yet chosen to add the weight of state authority to that of religion to enforce the Quranic dictums on almsgiving.

Customs levies have brought in increasing receipts since higher oil prices went into effect; they climbed from 11.8 million *dinars* in 1973/74 to 46.7 million *dinars* by 1978/79, or at about 32 percent a year. However, this only reflected the growth in imports, which went from 270 million *dinars* in 1973 (calendar year) to 1100 million *dinars* in 1978, also an annual average increase of about 32 percent. The basic customs duty remains unchanged – a flat *ad valorem* levy of four percent on nearly all items. This tax in the past has mostly paid the expenditures of the customs department and the costs of other state involvement in the foreign trade process; it has not really been regarded as a general revenue raising mechanism.

The returns from investment of past oil surpluses have rapidly become the Kuwaiti Government's most important source of income after oil related taxes (see *Table 7.11*). As long as 20 years ago, these earnings were an

Table 7.10 *Tax revenues: Kuwait (1950–1978/79)*

	1950	1954	1958	1962/63	1966/67	1968/69	1970/71
Direct taxes							
Total (millions of *dinars*)	NA	NA	127.4	173.0	231.9	244.2	298.4
Percentage of revenue	–	–	95.2	94.6	94.2	92.6	91.4
Income taxes	} 4.9	} 69.3	127.4	{ 118.4	164.3	171.2	215.7
Royalties				{ 54.6	67.6	72.3	82.4
Property taxes	NA	NA	[b]	[b]	[b]	0.7	0.4
Indirect taxes							
Total (millions of *dinars*)	NA	NA	3.9	5.8	9.0	10.7	12.9
Percentage of revenues	–	–	2.9	3.2	3.7	4.1	4.0
Customs	NA	NA	2.1	5.0	5.4	7.0	8.3
Other indirect taxes	NA	NA	1.8	0.8	3.6	3.8	4.6
State enterprises							
Total (millions of *dinars*)	NA	NA	2.5	4.1	5.2	8.8	15.0
Percentage of revenues	–	–	1.9	2.2	2.1	3.3	4.6
Total revenue[c]	6.0[d]	72.0[d]	133.8	182.9	246.1	263.7	326.3

Notes: NA indicates data not separately available.
    [a] 15 month fiscal year.
    [b] Figures for this type of tax are included with other indirect taxes; all indications are that
      such receipts were very small.
    [c] Does not include revenue for investment income.
    [d] Estimated.

Source: Central Statistical Office, *Statistical Abstract of Kuwait.*

important element in the overall government accounts. For example, in 1958, investment earnings of some 9.2 million *dinars* were equal to about seven percent of the total revenue from all other sources. In recent years they have gained in importance, and by 1978/79, official figures indicated that they were over 15.9 percent of all tax revenues. In the 1970s alone, investment earnings have climbed more than 16 fold – at an annual rate of almost 42 percent between 1970/71 and 1978/79. This growth seems likely to continue as the Kuwaiti government has made it clear that one of its fundamental economic policies is to provide now for the post-petroleum era and to this end a major share of current and future budget surpluses is to be invested abroad. It is anticipated that the Fund for Tomorrow, as it has been called, could earn Kuwait almost as much as oil exports by the mid-1980s, particularly since current needs do not require drawing any earnings from the Fund's portfolio.

As indicated in our discussion of Iraq, there are reasons to believe that official statistics understate both the foreign assets and the annual earnings

Table 7.10 *(continued)*

1971/72	1972/73	1973/74	1974/75	1975/76[a]	1976/77	1977/78	1978/79
354.6	506.8	545.0	2058.2	3531.0	2602.6	2578.6	3040.6
92.6	92.8	93.0	97.6	97.8	96.5	95.3	92.8
240.5	386.9	412.3	450.1	767.8	109.1	257.7	79.4
113.6	119.3	131.7	1606.4	2760.2	2489.3	2317.9	2957.4
0.5	0.8	1.0	1.7	3.9	4.2	3.0	3.8
13.1	14.9	17.3	23.9	39.0	49.5	73.7	172.8
3.4	2.7	3.0	1.1	1.0	1.8	2.7	5.3
8.9	10.0	11.8	17.7	31.9	41.2	45.6	46.7
4.2	4.9	5.4	6.2	7.1	8.3	28.1	126.1
15.1	24.7	23.9	26.0	41.8	46.0	52.2	64.4
3.9	4.5	4.1	1.2	1.2	1.7	1.9	2.0
382.8	546.4	586.2	2108.1	3612.7	2698.1	2704.5	3277.8

from these investments in many Middle East countries. In part, this results from difficulties in distinguishing official and nonofficial holdings; a problem exacerbated by the quasi-official status of many large institutional investors such as partly government owned banks and insurance companies. The First National Bank of Chicago report, mentioned earlier, puts total Kuwaiti investments above previous official estimates. Though this report obviously includes some private holdings, it is interesting nonetheless to consider how massive foreign investment earnings have become in relation to the Kuwaiti economy. It estimates total returns during 1979 to have been more than 1090 million *dinars*, rising along with record interest rates in the industrialized countries to a projected 1820 million *dinars* during 1980, before falling slightly (again with interest rates) in 1981 to about 1740 million *dinars*. (In fact, average interest rates did not decline in 1981.)

Total Kuwaiti overseas investments are portrayed as multiplying rapidly in the face of the 1978/80 oil price increases and, as a result of Kuwait's gains in world oil market shares in the wake of the Iranian Revolution, Kuwait's production rose from 1975 thousand barrels a day in 1977 to 2100 thousand

Table 7.11 *Investment income: Kuwait (1952–1978/79) (millions of dinars)*

Year	State reserve fund	Investment income
1952	4.4	0.1
1956	175.0	4.8
1960/61	293.5	9.5
1964/65	460.3	22.8
1966/67	528.3	25.2
1968/69	506.2	24.1
1970/71	583.4	31.8
1972/73	NA	50.8
1973/74	NA	89.0
1974/75	NA	152.0
1975/76	NA	328.1
1976/77	NA	329.4
1977/78	NA	384.0
1978/79	NA	522.0

Note: *NA indicates data not separately available.*

Source: See *Table 7.10*

barrels a day in 1978 and to 2510 thousand barrels a day in 1979 – the highest level since 1974. Net foreign assets are estimated to have been 12 430 million *dinars* at the end of 1979, and climbing to 17 670 million and 23 190 million by the end of 1980 and 1981, respectively. This increase results from both reinvestments of earlier earnings and higher oil induced surpluses. For

Table 7.12 *Major taxes: Kuwait (1950–1978/79)*

	1950	1957	1964/65	1970/71	1973/74	1978/79
Income taxes:						
Non-oil companies	–	–	0.2	0.3	0.1	0.7
Oil companies	} 4.9	} 110.2	{ 114.2	215.3	412.2	78.7
Oil royalties			{ 62.0	82.4	131.7	18.7
Sales of crude oil	–	–	–	–	–	2938.7
Property taxes	[a]	[a]	[a]	0.4	1.0	3.8
Customs duties	NA	1.8	5.2	8.3	11.8	46.7
Government department fees	NA	1.1	1.9	4.6	5.4	NA
Government enterprise profits	–	1.8	3.9	15.0	23.9	64.9
Investment revenue	–	7.1	14.0[b]	31.8	89.1	521.4

Notes: [a] Less than 50 000 *dinars*.
           [b] Estimated.
           NA. Indicates data not separately available.

Source: See *Table 7.10*.

example, a favorable trade balance of 1600 million *dinars* in 1978 more than doubled to almost 3450 million *dinars* in 1979.

In the face of such accumulating investments, over and above continued high levels of oil revenues, the Kuwaiti government has not felt pressured to search for alternative fiscal bases or to increase its reliance on those tax alternatives already used in a minor fashion. A generation ago, a much poorer Kuwait – though already a major oil producer – was slightly less reliant on oil as a revenue source than it is now. For example, in 1950 about 82 percent of the government's receipts came from oil. By 1978/79 oil profits taxes, royalties, and sales brought in nearly 3030 million *dinars*, and oil financed foreign investments added another 520 million *dinars* – all together coming to about 93.6 percent of 3800 million *dinars* in total government revenues.

7.5 Libya

Libya has only quite recently made the transition from being among the world's poorest states to being one of the richest. Though oil now dominates the economy, export only began in 1961, bringing in a paltry 700 000 *dinars* (see *Table 7.13*) or about $2 million to the government.

Nevertheless, this was a welcome addition to the fiscal climate of a country whose total domestic tax revenues, in the fiscal year prior to oil production (1960/61), were then only about $40 million although this was an all-time high. About two-thirds of this revenue was derived from customs duties.

In the pre-oil period, as has often been pointed out, Libyan exports were dominated by scrap metal recovered from the battlefields of World War II and by a desert grass preferred by British paper makers for certain high quality grades for which there was a limited demand. The year 1960 saw total Libyan exports of less than $25 million. A major source of additional foreign exchange came from the ground rents paid by Britain and the United States for two airbases left over from the anti-Nazi campaigns, generally only of marginal defense value to the North Atlantic Treaty Organization even at the height of cold war tensions in the 1950s.

Oil had been sought since the early days of the Italian colonial era but, fortunately from the Allied viewpoint, its discovery came after victory in World War II. Although the monarchical government of Libya in the 1960s signed several agreements with international oil companies that can only be described as out of step with the increasing militancy of those oil exporters who founded OPEC in 1960[13], oil revenues climbed rapidly and soon rivaled and then completely dwarfed other Libyan government revenues (see *Tables 7.13* and *7.14*).

Table 7.13 *Tax revenues: Libya (1952/53–1977)*

	1952/53	1954/55	1958/59	1962/63	1966	1968	1970	1971	1972	1973	1974	1975	1976	1977
Direct taxes														
Total (millions of *dinars*)	0.8	0.8	1.1	5.2	148.0	297.3	473.6	678.6	665.6	657.6	1480.8	1339.5	2096.7	2674.7
Percentage of revenues	16.3	14.3	10.7	20.7	78.7	83.3	86.8	83.6	82.1	80.1	79.5	76.9	81.2	86.1
Income taxes	0.8	0.8	1.1	3.3	8.0	16.0	16.2	25.0	31.9	39.8	37.0	55.4	71.9	89.4
Royalties[a]	– [b]	– [b]	– [b]	1.9 [b]	138.8	279.8	453.2	652.3	632.2	616.5	1442.9	1283.2	2023.6	2584.3
Property taxes	[b]	[b]	[b]	[b]	1.2	1.5	4.2	1.3	1.5	1.3	0.9	0.9	1.2	1.0
Indirect taxes														
Total (millions of *dinars*)	3.6	4.8	9.2	20.0	36.3	50.2	55.0	65.8	77.8	109.0	178.3	230.0	240.6[e]	275.4
Percentage of revenues	73.5	85.7	89.3	79.7	19.3	14.1	10.1	8.1	9.6	13.2	9.6	13.2	9.3	8.9
Customs	1.6	2.9	5.7	11.7	24.7	34.8	35.5	43.0	57.4	77.7	118.8	156.5	157.2	190.0
Excise, sales and production taxes	1.0	0.9	1.5	2.4	3.2	5.0	3.9	[c]	[c]	[c]	6.7	3.1	10.0	11.1
Other indirect taxes	1.0	1.0	2.0	5.9	8.5	10.4	15.6	22.7	20.4	31.3	52.8	70.4	73.4[e]	74.3
State enterprises														
Total (millions of *dinars*)	0.3	[d]	[d]	[d]	8.9	9.4	16.9	67.8	67.0	54.1	204.7	171.7	246.3[e]	155.0
Percentage of revenues	6.1	0	0	0	4.7	2.6	3.1	8.4	8.3	6.6	11.0	9.8	9.5	5.0
Total revenues														
(millions of *dinars*)	4.9	5.6	10.3	25.1	187.9	356.9	545.5	812.2	810.5	820.6	1863.8	1741.2	2583.6	3105.1

Notes:
[a] Includes all payments by oil companies.
[b] Included in income taxes.
[c] Included in state enterprise.
[d] Less than 500 000 *dinars*.
[e] Estimated.

Source: Ministry of Planning, *Statistical Abstract.*

With oil production, Libya's GNP has climbed concomitantly, from some 164 million *dinars* in 1962 to about 5700 million *dinars* in 1977, at an annual average rate of about 26.7 percent over this 15 year period. As *Table 7.13* demonstrates, non-oil derived tax categories have also shown sharp gains as oil revenues have pumped income and purchasing power into the economy as a whole. For example, income taxes (outside the oil sector) in 1960/61 amounted to less than 1.7 million *dinars*[14]. These grew to more than 89.4 million *dinars* by 1970 – an annual growth rate of more than 26 percent. Total government revenues grew much faster during this period – from about 15.5 million *dinars* to about 3105 million *dinars*, or at an annual rate in excess of 36 percent.

Table 7.14 *Major taxes: Libya (1952/53–1977) (millions of dinars)*

	1952/53	1961/62	1968	1974	1977
Income taxes	0.8	2.4	16.0	37.0	89.4
Property taxes			1.5	0.9	1.0
Oil royalties	–	0.7	279.8	1442.9	2584.3
Customs duties	1.6	10.9	34.8	118.8	173.1
Excise taxes[a]	1.0	2.7	5.0	6.7	11.1
Licenses and fees	0.8[b]	1.4[b]	5.5	7.5	6.5
Government department surpluses	0.2[b]	1.8[b]	7.3	9.6	37.0

Notes: [a] Collected through government monopolies.
   [b] Estimated.

Source: See *Table 7.13*.

During the mid-1970s Libya has used several distinctions among types of income in determining tax liabilities. For example, wages and salaries are subject to a levy of 8 percent on the first 1800 *dinars* of taxable income, 10 percent on the next 1200 *dinars*, 15, 20 and 25 percent respectively on each of the next three 1800 *dinar* brackets, and then 35 percent on all remaining income (that is, above 8400 *dinars*). The income of professional persons is subject to the same maximum rate (35 percent) with a larger levy at the lowest levels (15 percent on the first 4000 *dinars*). However, so-called unearned income is less heavily taxed; for example, income earned from real assets is subject to a maximum rate of 25 percent above 10 000 *dinars*, while all interest earnings are taxed at a flat rate of 15 percent. In addition to these specific income taxes, there is a steeply progressive general income surtax imposed equally on all types of income. This obligation exempts the first 4000 *dinars*, then asses a 15 percent levy on the next 3000 *dinars*, 25 percent against the next 5000 *dinars*, and so on until all income above 100 000 *dinars* is subject to a 90 percent levy.

Corporate profits are also subject to a sharply progressive schedule. Taxable profits up to 10 000 *dinars* are assessed at the rate of 20 percent; the next 20 000 *dinars* is liable to a 25 percent rate; and so on until all taxable profits in excess of 150 000 *dinars* are subject to levy of 60 percent.

These tax schedules have pushed income tax receipts up rapidly. Nevertheless, this growth has been less rapid than that seen in the Libyan economy as a whole and in the oil sector in particular. Therefore, it must be concluded that direct non-oil related tax receipts have probably lagged behind government intentions, at least as far as the latter are indicated by the official tax schedules. Income taxes more than doubled between 1973 and 1977, but this meant an annual average increase of only about 22.5 percent, while total revenues climbed at an annual rate twice as high – 39.5 percent. Thus, socialist Libya's economic intentions of relative income and welfare equality do not seem to be receiving much assistance from a major policy tool in this area – direct taxation[15].

Property tax receipts have all but faded into insignificance in Libya during the 1970s. Most of the revenues listed under this category in *Table 7.13* come from a relatively oblique wealth tax levied on rental property using rental value as the evaluative basis. There is a capital tax levied on the shares of corporations, but its valuation is determined by a rather generous system from the stockholders' viewpoint.

Libya is renowned throughout the whole world for its Islamic orthodoxy, and from a fiscal viewpoint this can be examined in terms of *zakat*. In theory, Libya follows established practice in levying a 2.5 percent duty on the net value of all goods, monies, corporate shares, minerals, livestock, farm produce and other divine bounties owned by adult Muslims. In practice, there has yet to be much in the way of a serious institutionalized effort to enforce the collection of *zakat*. Such action (or rather lack of action) remains entirely within the rather wide boundaries of established Islamic teaching.

The Quran imposes the obligation of *zakat* on believers as a condition of salvation but leaves the question of enforcement uncertain. The state may step in, according to most teachers of Islamic law, to ensure that in fact the general principles of *zakat* are followed. Though Libya recognizes *zakat* as a legal obligation, there is little evidence that the state has imposed its authority to enforce the obligations existing on the consciences of individual Muslim citizens. In particular, there are no data whatsoever on *zakat* receipts.

Customs receipts serve as a reasonable indicator of consumption-based tax revenues in a country like Libya which is extremely dependent on foreign sources for much of its consumption goods, including food. This dependence has tended to approach nearly absolute levels since the late 1960s, as average personal incomes have soared. In 1960/61, as oil production began, some 9.7 percent of the government's 15.5 million *dinars* in revenue came from customs levies – about two-thirds of all fiscal receipts. By 1977, customs receipts were up to 190 million *dinars*, but their relative importance has slipped to about 6.1 percent of total revenues. Nevertheless, customs receipts grew by the fairly high annual average rate of about 15.9 percent. Excise taxes have also shown considerable growth during this period, growing by an annual average of about 10.6 percent between 1960/61 and 1977 to more than 11 million *dinars*. Nonetheless, consumption taxes remain very low relative to both GNP and total tax revenues.

Together with what has been mentioned above about non-oil direct taxes, it seems that oil revenues continue to dominate the country's tax profile. Although Libya strongly professes devotion to a socialist orientation, from a strictly fiscal viewpoint there is little indication that taxes were being used to any great extent to forward this philosophy – at least through the mid-1970s or outside the easily nationalized oil sector. Income taxes have actually declined as a percentage of GNP during this period. It is not clear exactly what have been the effects of the country's economic changes, acting through the fiscal mechanism, on most Libyans. As is indicated below[16], the only data on Libyan income distribution seem quite unreliable for current policy purposes – at best indicating a lowest common denominator of working-class urban poverty before oil became a major factor in the Libyan economy.

Table 7.15 *Oil revenues relative to total revenues: Libya (1961/62–1974/75)*

Year	Total revenues (millions of dinars)	Percentage derived from oil
1961/62	18.9	3.7
1963/64	53.5	44.9
1965/66	127.8	65.4
1967/68	249.5	76.5
1969/70	447.1	81.3
1971/72	812.2	80.3
1973/74	820.6	75.1
1974/75	1855.3	79.8

Source: See *Table 7.13*.

Like other major oil exporters, whether socialist or capitalist in orientation, Libya has clearly determined that the easiest course, through the mid 1970s, has been to impose most of its fiscal burden on foreign customers. As already mentioned, such policies, by their nature, tend to forego the possibilities of using domestic taxes as a means of guiding internal development policies.

Along with many of the Middle East's major oil producers with small populations, Libya has been running a sizeable trade surplus, especially since higher oil prices came into being in 1973. According to the Internatinal Monetary Fund, Libyan exports of about 815 million *dinars* in 1972 were accompanied by imports of about 345 million *dinars*, indicating a surplus of about 470 million *dinars*. By 1977, exports were over 2955 million *dinars* and imports about 1415 million *dinars* – a trade surplus of some 1540 million *dinars*. However, unlike other similar countries (cf. Kuwait and Saudi Arabia), Libya's officially held overseas investment assets did not grow substantially in the first five years after the 1973 oil price increase – only by about two-thirds from 960 million to 1620 million *dinars* between 1972 and 1977. Thus, an important source of government revenue in some neighboring states – the return on overseas investments – had not yet become a major factor in Libya during the period shown in *Table 7.16*. These returns reached a peak in 1974 when they came to about 4.6 percent of total

Table 7.16 *Libyan overseas investments and returns (1960–1977) (millions of dinars)*

	Investments	Returns
1960	29.4	0
1962	34.3	1.6
1964	61.4	2.4
1966	121.1	5.0
1968	192.4	11.4
1970	567.9	34.6
1971	876.8	45.9
1972	962.3	42.1
1973	629.6	34.2
1974	1200.4	86.1
1975	753.0	63.6
1976	1064.2	53.7
1977	1623.6	71.5

Sources: International Financial Statistics and Balance of Payments Yearbook.

revenues and then declining along with overseas assets afterwards. Clearly, the role that such investments might play in providing income to future generations was not, at least during the mid 1970s, credited with as much importance by the Libyan government as it was in Kuwait or other low population oil exporting states.

More recently, however, there have been signs of change in this regard, whether as a result of shifts in government policy or of movements in world oil markets. Since the Iranian Revolution, Libyan oil revenues have climbed; the current account surplus in 1979 has been estimated to have been about

1250 million *dinars*, but in 1980 it was projected to reach as much as 4200 million *dinars*. The First National Bank of Chicago report referred to above concluded that these larger oil revenues brought considerable increases in Libya's net foreign assets. The latter were estimated to have been more than 3550 million at the end of 1979 and then to rise to about 7700 million *dinars* and to 10 360 million *dinars* by the end of 1980 and 1981, respectively. This, of course, meant much higher investment income as well, and the report included projection for receipts of about 300 million *dinars* in 1979, 680 million *dinars* in 1980 and more than 710 million *dinars* in 1981. Whatever the reasons are for the growth of Libyan reserves and other overseas investments, if they continue to grow, then their returns will figure very prominently in the government's fiscal accounts.

Table 7.17 *Local government revenues: Libya (millions of dinars)*

	1952/53	*1962/63*	*1974*
Income and property taxes	0.8	3.3	6.2
Import excises	0.2	1.7	3.2
Government enterprises	1.0	2.4	0.7
Other indirect taxes	1.0	5.2	1.6

Source: See *Table 7.13.*

Libya began its independence as a federal state, and considerable revenue raising power was delegated to the provincial governments. Through the early 1960s, all income and property taxes as well as a portion of customs revenues were collected by the provinces. As late as the fiscal year 1962/63, half of all government revenues were being collected below the federal level (see *Table 7.17*). Though local governments still retain some taxing authority, their receipts are now a tiny fraction of total government revenues.

7.6 Oman

Though Oman is still one of the Middle East's most economically primitive states, it is one of the oldest on the Arabian peninsula to be internationally recognized as separate and independent[17] within (approximately) its present borders. A major trading center for the Indian Ocean region for many centuries, the Omani Sultanate remained a traditional economy based on trade, fishing, and agriculture, until oil was discovered in 1964. Exports began in 1967 when pipelines and an oil shipping terminal were completed. At that same time, as *Table 7.18* shows, the modern era of Omani fiscal revenues began.

Table 7.18 *Tax revenues: Oman (1967–1978)*

	1967	1968	1969	1970	1971	1972	1973	1974	1975	1976	1977	1978
Direct taxes												
Total (millions of rials)	1.9	25.5	38.6	44.4	47.9	50.1	62.0	292.0	375.2	459.3	488.1	447.2
Percentage of revenues	67.9	95.9	97.5	97.8	95.6	94.5	95.4	96.3	96.7	94.3	93.8	92.7
Income taxes	–	–	–	–	–	0.5	0.7	0.5	2.1	4.6	5.9	7.0
Royalties	1.9	25.5	38.6	44.4	47.9	49.6	61.3	291.5	373.1	454.7	482.2	440.2
Indirect taxes												
Total (millions of rials)	0.9	1.1	1.0	1.0	2.2	2.8	2.6	5.8	7.3	19.2	20.8	17.8
Percentage of revenues	32.1	4.1	2.5	2.2	4.4	5.3	4.0	1.9	1.9	3.8	4.0	3.7
Customs	0.9	1.1	1.0	1.0	2.2	1.6	1.7	2.3	0.5	4.5	4.6	4.6
Other indirect taxes	–	–	–	–	–	1.2	0.9	3.5	6.8	14.7	16.2	13.2
State enterprises												
Total (millions of rials)	–	–	–	–	–	0.1	0.4	5.4	5.6	8.8	11.7	17.2
Percentage of revenues	–	–	–	–	–	0.2	0.6	1.8	1.4	1.8	2.2	3.6
Total revenues (millions of rials)	2.8	26.6	39.6	45.4	50.1	53.0	65.0	303.2	388.1	487.3	520.6	482.2

Source: General Development Organization, *Statistical Yearbook*; Central Bank of Oman, *Annual Report*.

Before 1967, all tax receipts amounted to less than one million *rials* (about $2.4 million)[18]. During the next decade, Omani revenues increased almost two hundred fold – at an annual average rate of about 69 percent over the 1967–1978 period. This was almost entirely due to oil, the earnings from which rose at an average rate of about 59.6 percent during this period. At the same time the almost entirely oil-dominated direct tax category rose from about two thirds of government revenues to about 93 percent of revenues[19]. Non-oil companies have been subject to a modest profits levy since 1972. However, as can be seen from *Table 7.18*, by 1978 Oman still had not begun to use this tax at even the modest levels of realization found in neighboring Gulf oil exporters.

Unlike nearly all other Middle Eastern oil exporters, Oman has not shown much growth in customs receipts – its major consumption based levy – despite a rapid jump in per capita GNP (and, eventually, in consumer spending power) since the oil price increases of 1973/74. For example, Omani GNP per capita rose from $515 to $2720 between 1973 and 1977 (that is at an annual average of more than 39 percent), while imports climbed from $116 million to $987 million (at an average of about 82 percent). At the same time custom receipts (*Table 7.18*), rose much more slowly – at an average of only about 32 percent. Dutiable imports (aside from alcohol) are subject to only a flat 2 percent levy, and many items are exempt from even this nominal charge. In addition, in recent years the mix of Omani imports has shifted in favor of capital goods, many of which are exempted from duties.

Table 7.19 *Oil revenues, Oman (1967–1978) (millions of rials)*

	1967	1970	1972	1974	1976	1977	1978
Royalties and oil Company income taxes	1.9	44.4	49.3	159.3	178.8	158.9	142.1
'Buy-back' sales receipts	–	–	–	116.4	190.4	197.5	132.7
Third-party sales receipts	–	–	–	15.3	76.1	125.4	165.0
Oil port fees	–	–	0.3	0.5	0.4	0.4	0.4
Total oil revenues	1.9	44.4	49.6	291.5	454.7	482.2	440.2

Source: See *Table 7.18.*

The composition of oil revenues themselves has become more complex since the changes during 1973/74 in the international oil industry (*Table 7.19*). Royalties and income taxes levied against operating company profits comprised nearly all oil related revenues until 1973. Since then the Omani government has acquired a participation share in the production of oil within its borders. Unlike many of its neighbors, this participation has remained at a rather passive level, with much of the gain in revenues reflected in the exercise of buy-back agreements – that is, oil which the government technically owns and may sell as it chooses, but which the original concessionnaire companies then buy from the government. Some independently arranged third party sales by Oman have taken place since 1974, and as *Table 7.19* demonstrates, these became very important in 1977 and 1978. By the latter year, they accounted for about three eighths of oil related revenues.

Oman in the late 1970s remains one of the states most fiscally dependent on oil exports in this region. Though this is probably in large part due to the fact that oil exports have yet to lead to much internal economic diversity (which could then be taxed), still the data cited above relative to customs receipts indicate a governmental unwillingness to transfer much of the fiscal burden from the export sector to Omani residents.

7.7 Qatar

Qatar is demographically the smallest country among the oil producers and exporters along the Gulf littoral. It has not yet conducted an official census; at best, we have only rough estimates of its total population. These range between 100 000 and 215 000, with most of the uncertainty related to the number of non-Qataris that have been attracted by the country's prosperity[20]. The best available estimates as to the number of Qatari citizens in the late 1970s range between 40 000 and 80 000. Obviously, a greater degree of exactness is necessary for a reliable evaluation of the country's GNP in per capita terms. Most of the input to this statistic can be traced to the oil sector. This employs rather few workers, many of whom are foreigners. A per capita GNP figure for 1977 ranges from $11 670 (if all residents at the high estimate of 215 000 are included) to $62 750 (if only, at the low estimate, the 40 000 citizens with a legal claim on Qatar's wealth are included).

No matter how wide this range actually is, two basic facts are quite clear. First, Qatar is one of the world's richest independent states; second, almost all of this wealth is tied to oil.

Qatar began to export oil in 1949, almost ten years after commercially exploitable quantities were discovered. For most of this intervening decade, the Qatari government received a basic payment from the concessionaire companies of about £100 000 a year. Data regarding non-oil tax receipts are not available in detail until the late 1960s, though as can be seen from *Table 7.20*, oil-based revenues have comprised nearly all of the government's intake throughout the last generation. Total receipts climbed at an annual average rate of about 29.7 percent between 1950 and 1978. Most of the absolute gain was oil related, as oil revenues climbed slightly faster – at about 30 percent a year. Oil revenues are realized both as royalties and as oil company income taxes. Oil revenues are almost identical with direct taxes, as no personal income taxes exist and there is only a small levy on business profits. Theoretically, all firms except those engaged in joint ventures with the Qatari government are subject to the profits tax. The schedule used in the mid-1970s was graduated, and the first 70 000 *riyals* of net profits were tax free. Between 70 000 and 250 000 *riyals*, the levy was 5 percent, rising to 10 percent between 250 000 and 500 000 *riyals*, 15 percent on 500 000 to

Table 7.20 *Tax revenues: Qatar (1950–1978) (millions of rials)*

	1950	*1960*	*1967*	*1970*	*1972*	*1974^b*	*1975^b*	*1976^b*	*1977^b*	*1978^b*
Oil revenues	5.3	260.0	402.0	515.2	1147	7053	6623	8020	7451	8143
Non-oil revenues	1.0^a	8.0	36.0	64.2	117	266	512	567	704	916
Total revenues	6.3^a	268.0^a	438.0	579.4	1264	7319	7135	8587	8154	9059

Notes: ^{a} Estimated.
  ^{b} Based on *Hijral* (or lunar) fiscal years (1394–98), ending respectively on 14 January 1975, 3 January 1976, 21 December 1976, 10 December 1977 and 29 November 1978.

Sources: Qatar Monetary Agency, *Annual Report*; *Studies on Development Problems in Countries of Western Asia*; *OPEC Annual Statistical Bulletin*.

750 000 *riyals*, and so on up to a maximum rate of 50 percent on net profits above 5 million *riyals*. As part of the government's program to attract foreign investment, corporations have been offered 5 year exemptions from the profits tax since 1976. As a result of these tax holidays and the fact that many private investors are partners of the government in joint ventures, the profits tax remained quite minor in the late 1970s. Though revenues from this source increased about twelve-fold between 1973 and 1978, they accounted for less than 0.3 percent of all government revenues in 1978.

Customs duties comprise the bulk of the indirect taxes. During most of the period shown in *Table 7.20*, an *ad valorem* tariff of 2.5 percent on most items prevailed, with higher levies on alcohol (50 percent) and tobacco products (10 percent). Many basic items (for example, rice, sugar, fruits and vegetables, and animal feed) have been exempted from even these nominal levels. All tariffs were recently removed from goods in transit in an effort to improve the prospects of Doha Port an an *entrepôt*. Recent figures for major revenue sources are shown in *Table 7.21*. Adding to government revenue in the last few years are two categories for which only some disaggregated data are available. First are the several industrial enterprises within Qatar of which the government is the major stockholder. For example, the Qatar Fertilizer Company and the Qatar Flour Mills Company, each founded in 1969 and fully operating by the mid 1970s, presaged the much more intensive program of industrial diversification undertaken after the OPEC price action of 1973. No data on the profitability of these enterprises has yet been published.

Second is the investment policy undertaken by the Qatar government using its excess oil revenues. As in Kuwait and Abu Dhabi, oil revenues were generating for Qatar excess funds, relative to its import needs, even

Table 7.21 *Major taxes: Qatar (1973–1978)*
(millions of riyals)

	1973	1976	1978
Oil revenues	1559.4	8020.0	8143.4
Business and profits taxes	2.1	18.2	25.0
Customs duties	14.2	49.1	126.3
Public utilities fees	NA	24.1	NA
Investment income	69.6	434.5	618.0

Note: NA indicates data not separately available.

Table 7.22 *Qatari overseas investments and returns (1953–1977)*
(millions of rials)

Year	Investments	Returns
1953	8.0	0.24
1955	NA	1.6
1966	NA	17.0
1968	NA	27.0
1970	NA	33.8
1971	729.7	NA
1972	1133.5	NA
1973	1146.6	69.9
1974	5142.0	206.9
1975	6991.9	408.8
1976	8692.8	434.5
1977	8200.1	449.8

Note: NA indicates data not available.

Source: 1953–1971 – *Oil Revenues in the Gulf Emirates;* later years – *International Financial Statistics* and *Balance of Payments Yearbook.*

before 1973. The relatively modest internal development prospects of a country with well less than 100 000 citizens and few non-oil resources have given the government, before and after 1973, a major interest in promising overseas investments. Qatar's goal is to provide for its citizens, from both overseas and domestic investment, the standard of living to which they have become accustomed – even as oil production declines.

As a long time oil producer under British tutelage before independence in 1971, Qatar's practice of investing part of its oil revenues was well established before the price increases of the 1970s. By 1973, the country's foreign holdings of 1150 million *rials* were enough to cover about 16 months' worth of imports – a reserves to import ratio about the same as Kuwait's and Abu Dhabi's at that time, but well ahead of the ratios then found in other Middle East oil exporters. Since 1973, both investments and returns have grown rapidly (more rapidly, in fact, than is shown in *Table 7.22*, since these official figures are not believed to be complete). Foreign investment earnings grew by nearly 55 percent a year over the five year period shown. Significantly, by 1978 they amounted to more than all Qatari government revenues in 1970.

7.8 Saudi Arabia

Not only is Saudi Arabia the leading oil producing and exporting country in the Middle East, but its only rivals in production on a worldwide basis, the Soviet Union and the United States, are themselves major consumers. Saudi Arabia, with a small population and a still mostly nonindustrial economy (outside the oil sector), ranks first among the world's oil exporters, and the importance of oil-based taxes is reflected in Saudi Arabian receipts.

Major oil discoveries within the Kingdom occurred during the 1930s, but both the worldwide depression of that decade and then the wartime disruption of trade patterns postponed Saudi Arabian realization of its oil wealth until the postwar period. As can be seen from *Table 6.1*, oil production then climbed rapidly – an almost ten-fold increase from 21.3 million barrels in 1945 to 199.5 million barrels in 1950, and then to more than 480 million barrels by 1960. As *Tables 7.23* and *7.24* show, oil revenues climbed along with production. In 1947/48[21], royalties yielded about 147 million *riyals*; by 1960/61 they were up more than nine-fold to about 1376 million *riyals* – that is, at an annual average rate of about 18.8 percent. During the same period, they moved to the overwhelming position in the Saudi Arabian fiscal profile that they have occupied ever since. By 1960/61, oil brought in nearly 5 out of every 6 *riyals* received by the treasury.

Generally, oil revenues grew much faster than total revenues through most of the period shown in *Table 7.23*. For example, from 1947/48 to

Table 7.23 *Tax revenues: Saudi Arabia (1947/48–1977/78)*

	1947/48	1954/55	1958/59	1962/63	1966/67	1968/69
Direct taxes						
Total (millions of *riyals*)	149.9	972.1	1146.6	1933.3	3991.8	4251.0
Percentage of revenues	69.9	85.1	84.3	86.5	90.0	86.8
Income tax	} 146.7 {	692.3	850.3	1276.3	2826.1	3068.0
Royalties		274.4	294.8	674.5	1160.7	1177.0
Property tax	3.2	5.4	1.5	2.5	5.0	6.0
Indirect taxes						
Total (millions of *riyals*)	58.1	170.9	147.8	204.1	399.8	594.3
Percentage of revenues	27.1	14.9	10.9	9.0	9.0	12.1
Customs	25.0	80.0	120.0	132.2	170.0	247.5
Excise, sales and production taxes	0	0	0	0	20.0	23.5
Other indirect taxes	33.1	90.9	27.8	71.9	209.8	323.2
State enterprises						
Total (millions of *riyals*)	6.6	a	65.0	100.5	44.5	50.6
Percentage of revenues	3.1	a	4.7	4.5	1.0	1.0
Total revenues (millions of riyals)	214.6	1143.0	1359.4	2257.9	4436.1	4895.9

Note: ᵃ Included in other indirect taxes.
Source: Ministry of Finance and National Economy, *Statistical Yearbook.*

1960/61, when oil revenues grew at an annual average of 18.8 percent, total revenues climbed at a 17.3 percent average annual rate. From 1960/61 to 1974/75, the first full tax year after the OPEC oil price action, oil revenues were up more than 35.2 percent a year. More recently, it seems oil revenues have to some extent receded in importance, dropping off to less than 90 percent by 1977/78. However, it would be quite premature to conclude that a diversifying trend in Saudi Arabian taxes has set in. For one thing, most of the shift between 1974/75 and 1977/78 is lumped under the heading 'other indirect taxes'. During this period, this category has increasingly been dominated by returns from government investments, rather than from taxes.

Several non-oil taxes have shown considerable growth in the last few years, but both relatively and absolutely they remain quite small in overall fiscal accounts. Customs revenues increased as higher oil prices began an important boom. However, trade activity expanded much more rapidly than the levies on it. For example, while customs duties went from 325 million *riyals* to 1008 million *riyals* between 1972/73 and 1977/78, imports over the period actually were up more than 12 fold. The only other historically sizable consumption tax, an exercise on gasoline and other petroleum products, was sharply reduced in 1975/76, while a small excise on cigarettes was introduced in 1977/78.

Table 7.23 *(continued)*

1970/71	1971/72	1972/73	1973/74	1974/75	1975/76	1976/77	1977/78
5542.5	9963.4	12213.7	21278.7	94448.0	87186.6	99890.9	131251.7
87.0	92.5	92.6	93.5	96.1	91.0	90.1	89.6
3963.0	7728.7	9673.8	15929.9	56871.0	65701.9	76854.0	99336.8
1573.0	2226.7	2528.9	5336.0	37561.0	21457.7	23002.4	31817.4
6.5	8.0	11.0	12.8	16.0	27.0	34.5	97.5
741.0	724.0	811.6	1330.5	3543.8	8344.4	10609.7	14687.7
11.6	6.7	6.2	5.8	3.6	8.7	9.6	10.0
300.5	322.0	325.0	340.0	412.0	375.0	500.0	1008.2
89.0	49.0	52.0	68.0	93.0	3.0	3.0	16.9
351.5	353.0	434.6	922.5	3038.8	7966.4	10106.7	13662.6
84.5	81.6	157.9	191.3	243.2	302.0	417.9	531.8
1.3	0.8	1.2	0.8	0.2	0.3	0.4	0.4
6368.0	10769.0	13183.2	22800.5	98235.0	95833.0	110918.5	146171.2

The major form of income tax is levied against business profits, though one long-time tax, *zakat*, has come to realize considerable revenue (relatively speaking) during the 1970s. As was indicated above in Chapter 5, *zakat* has traditionally been the levy in *Dar al-Islam* against individuals, and it has been the responsibility only of Muslims. When the nascent Saudi state found that oil activity would attract a sizable number of non-Muslim foreigners to its territory, it initiated a personal income tax. In recent years, this tax on non-Saudi citizens was both progressive and relatively mild in its impact. Those with incomes less than 6000 *riyals* were exempt, with a 5 percent levy on earnings between 6000 and 16 000 *riyals*; over the base of 16 000 *riyals*, the rate shifted to 10 percent up to 36 000 *riyals*, to 20 percent up to 66 000 *riyals*, and then to 30 percent on earnings above 66 000 *riyals*[22]. The tax was collected through withholdings by corporate employers on their non-Saudi employees. In 1975 as oil revenues began to swell, the individual income tax was all but abolished when wage and salary income was totally exempted[23].

Corporations are subject to a progressive levy on their net profits ranging from 25 percent (on the first 100 000 *riyals*) to 45 percent (on the excess over one million *riyals*) if they are foreign owned. Some exemptions are allowed if they are at least 25 percent owned by Saudi Arabian citizens, and the distributed profits of companies subject to profit taxes are not again subject to personal income levies. As profits have boomed in recent years, so have the tax revenues they generate. However, as can be seen from *Table 7.24*, the vast majority of profits taxes still come from oil company operations.

According to the Saudi Arabian Monetary Agency, the formula for determining property tax levies on Saudi citizens is derived from the traditional *zakat* provisions. Specific revenues from the latter are also shown in *Table 7.24*, relative to assessments on wealth. However, even with the broadest inclusions of profits taxes within the *zakat* category, it is obvious that these receipts of the state represent only a tiny fraction of the wealth that is in fact likely to be subject to *zakat* provisions in today's Saudi Arabia. The administration of this tax specifically applies to the capital assets of

Table 7.24 *Major taxes: Saudi Arabia (1947/48–1977/78) (millions of riyals)*

	1947/48	1958/59	1966/67	1974/75	1977/78
Income taxes	–	850	43	216	672
Oil receipts:					
Oil company income taxes	145		2792[a]	56 655	98 665
Royalties		295	1161	37 561	31 817
Zakat	3	1.5	5	16	98
Excise taxes on fuel	–	–	20	93	7
Automobile excises and fees	–	10	39	75	1
Excise tax on cigarettes	–	–	–	–	10
Customs duties	25	120	170	412	1008
Pilgrimage taxes[b]	18	7	–	–	–
Stamp duties	–	5	8	30	49
Government service fees	11	64	82	309	540
Sale and rental of government property	7	7	8	18	40

Notes: [a] Includes Trans-Arabian Pipeline (Tapline) transit fees.
        [b] Includes health and quarantine fees.

Source: See *Table 7.23.*

individuals, merchants, and Saudi Arabian owned companies as well as to agricultural products and livestock, at the rate of 2.5 percent a year. In keeping with Islamic tradition, the government has never tried to collect directly more than half (1.25 percent) of what is theoretically due, leaving it up to the individual to pay the rest voluntarily. Since the reporting process itself is voluntary, it seems likely that human nature contributes doubly to the resulting underpayment of *zakat* dues – by undervaluing the assets on which it is due and by paying little more than the state demands. Thus, the government has experimented in recent years with several methods of enhancing the role of *zakat*, as an institutional representation of one of the major pillars of Islam. So far, its success has obviously not been great, as

Table 7.24 indicates. Beyond *zakat*, no tax, religious or secular, is directly levied on land or buildings; however, rental income has been subject to a 5 percent tax.

Like some of its neighbors (for example, Kuwait), Saudi Arabia is beginning to see another source of income rivalling tax revenues: returns on the country's overseas investments. As can be seen from *Table 7.25*, these have grown far more rapidly than total revenues – by an average of some 48 percent a year over the period shown. Their relative importance has also increased sharply, and by 1977, they came to about 10 percent of total

Table 7.25 *Saudi Arabia overseas investments and returns (1960–1977) (millions of riyals)*

	Investments	Returns
1960	830	18[a]
1962	1 200	28[a]
1964	2 680	67
1966	3 660	121
1968	3 920	225
1970	4 020	275
1971	6 950	306
1972	11 990	437
1973	16 990	775
1974	70 710	4 325
1975	136 980	6 500
1976	180 840	10 200
1977	208 270	14 200

Note: [a] Estimated.

Sources: *International Financial Statistics;*
            Balance of Payments Yearbook.

revenues. Though Saudi Arabian imports continued to climb, the trade surplus was close to 100 billion *riyals* in both 1976 and 1977, further fueling the expansion in overseas investments and of returns on these investments. It is probable that this source of revenue will outstrip all non-oil tax receipts for the indefinite future. As is indicated by *Tables 7.23* and *7.25*, overseas investment returns by 1977 already exceeded total Saudi Arabian fiscal receipts in a year as recent as 1972.

Since 1977, not only have oil prices risen still further, but Saudi Arabia has been responsible for supplying much of the oil needed in world markets to make up for the shortfalls caused by the chaotic conditions in Iran. Saudi Arabian production went from about 8.28 million barrels a day in 1978 to

9.53 million barrels a day during 1979. As a result, the additional revenues have magnified the balances in Saudi Arabian international accounts. The recent study by the First National Bank of Chicago estimated that the country's current account surplus climbed to more than 52 000 million *riyals* in 1979, and projected a level of more than 135 000 million *riyals* for 1980.

Along with this, the report included estimates of net foreign assets that indicated levels of 258 000, 393 000, and 500 000 million *riyals* would be reached by the end of 1979, 1980, and 1981, respectively. Such a situation would be consistent with a continuation of similar rates of growth enjoyed by overseas investments from 1974 (see *Table 7.25*). The report estimated that Saudi Arabia received more than 23 100 million *riyals* in earnings from its overseas investments in 1979 and projected that higher interest rates in the industrialized countries would raise their receipts to more than 38 700 million *riyals* in 1980, before they fell slightly (along with interest rates) to 35 700 million *riyals* in 1981. Should these estimates be reasonably accurate, then a glance at *Table 7.25* reveals that investment earnings will have multiplied more than 100-fold during the 1970s.

7.9   United Arab Emirates

Near the vital Straits of Hormuz are grouped seven small states, very different from one another, which as a matter of expedience sought and agreed upon an outward form of national unity after Great Britain's long announced retreat from 'East of Suez'. Prior to 1972 these sheikhdoms – Abu Dhabi, Ajman, Dubai, Fujairah, Ras al-Khaimah, Sharjah and Umm al-Quwain – historically had little in common other than their physical contiguity and a history of association with Britain's 'Indian connection' in Arabia and its periphery; but in that year protracted negotiations[24] led to the formation of an independent federation known as the United Arab Emirates (UAE).

Until oil was discovered along this stretch of Gulf littoral, the seven sheikhdoms were amongst the poorest of the third world's states, as the 1960 data in *Table 7.26* demonstrates. Barely $1.5 million then accrued to all seven, even including the financial subsidies customarily extended by Britain to these tributaries. Little of this revenue went beyond support for the members and retainers of the sheikhly families, and even they were hardly living in luxury.

All of the sheikhdoms have experienced a considerable surge in population as oil production has increased – first, in Abu Dhabi, the major exporter so far, and later in Dubai and Sharjah (*Table 7.27*). Oil revenues rose from a humble $2 million during 1962, the first year of operation, to about $230 million by 1970, to an estimated $8000 million in 1978.

It is inherent in the UAE's constitutional and economic structure that these oil revenues have accrued neither to the federal government nor directly, in any sort of across-the-board fashion, to most of the individual emirates. As *Table 7.27* shows, Abu Dhabi is the major oil producer (around 82 percent of federation output in recent years), with Dubai supplying most (16 percent) of the rest. Most UAE revenues go to these two emirates directly, in about the same proportion as oil production would indicate. Individual emirates in turn make grants to the federal government to cover its current expenditures and to finance national development projects.

Table 7.26 *Estimates of Emirate revenues: United Arab Emirates (1960–1978) (millions of dirhams)*

Emirate	1960	1964	1968	1971	1974	1976	1978
Abu Dhabi	3.49	66.65	554.4	1651.0	14 131.0	19 663.3	19 200.0
Ajman	0.15	0.32	0.8	1.3	1.6	NA	NA
Dubai	2.51	14.00	37.3	164.3	2 498.0	4 275.0	5 433.0
Fujairah	0.07	0.33	2.4	2.7	3.0	NA	NA
Ras al-Khaimah	0.16	0.59	3.0	3.6	4.1	NA	NA
Sharjah	0.40	1.47	7.2	9.8	120.0	180.0	200.0
Umm al-Quwain	0.15	0.43	0.8	1.5	1.8	NA	NA
Total	6.92	83.78	605.9	1834.2	16 759.5	24 118.3	24 833.0
Abu Dhabi percentage	50.4	79.6	91.5	90.0	84.3	81.5	77.3
Dubai percentage	36.3	16.7	6.2	9.0	14.8	17.7	21.9

Note: NA indicates data not separately available.

Sources: For 1960, K. G. Fenelon, *The Trucial States: A Brief Economic Survey*, 2nd edition (Beirut, Khayats, 1967); for 1964, Donald Hawley, *The Trucial States* (London, Allen & Unwin, 1970); since 1964, various government and international sources.

Because of the federation's complex political structure and of the very personal way in which some of the emirate rulers have continued to regard the revenues accruing to their states, drawing a complete picture of UAE finances requires making a number of estimates and educated guesses[25]. For the period in question, Abu Dhabi has consistently led the others because of its larger oil revenues. Even in 1960, before any exports, this emirate's promising petroleum prospecting reports brought it in a third more than neighboring Dubai, still dependent almost entirely on the customs revenues earned from its role as a major Gulf *entrepôt*. Since 1960, these two states have earned all but 2 or 3 percent of total UAE revenues, and nearly all of this has come from oil.

For Abu Dhabi we have somewhat more complete fiscal data than for Dubai; but for the other emirates, data are even sparser. A breakdown for Abu Dhabi is shown in *Table 7.28*. All income taxes are derived from oil companies; other business endeavors and individuals have continued to remain exempt from any such levies. Thus, all but about four percent of government revenues have been oil derived in recent years. Throughout 1977 Abu Dhabi earned little from its vastly increasing imports as much of this trade was still going through Dubai's more developed port. In any case, customs levies have remained low – 2.5 percent on most dutiable goods until the early 1970s when even these low levels were reduced – and many items, particularly foodstuffs, are exempt. Duties on goods coming from other members of the UAE have now been abolished.

Table 7.27 *Oil production in the United Arab Emirates (millions of barrels annually)*

Year	Abu Dhabi	Dubai	Sharjah	Total
1962	6	–	–	6
1963	18	–	–	18
1964	69	–	–	69
1965	103	–	–	103
1966	132	–	–	132
1967	138	–	–	138
1968	181	–	–	181
1969	219	4	–	223
1970	253	31	–	284
1971	341	46	–	387
1972	384	56	–	440
1973	472	81	–	553
1974	512	88	8	608
1975	514	92	14	620
1976	577	116	13	706
1977	596	114	10	721

Source: Petroleum Economist.

For other emirates, as indicated, we must be satisfied with less disaggregation as well as with less current data. In Dubai, the second richest emirate, about 75 percent of its revenues came from custom duties until 1969 when oil exports began. By the mid 1970s, the share of oil revenues had probably risen to the same 95 percent plus level that prevails in Abu Dhabi, as the partial summary shown in *Table 7.29* indicates. The same is probably now also true in Sharjah.

Dubai has encouraged its *entrepôt* role by keeping its customs levies low, thus relying on trade volume to generate high receipts. Through the early 1970s, nearly all dutiable goods were subject to a duty of 4.625 percent; rice, wheat, flour and sugar were subject to only 2 percent. Goods in transit to nearby emirates were also charged at the latter rate. As the volume of trade increased after 1973, the general levy was reduced to 3 percent. While

Table 7.28 *Tax revenues: Abu Dhabi (1967–1978)*

	1967	1970	1972	1973	1974	1975	1976	1977	1978
Direct taxes									
Total (millions of *dirhams*)	371.9	827.0	2075.2	3043.3	13702.5	14390.4	18953.6	20794.0	18460.0
Percentage of total revenues	90.6	96.6	95.1	94.8	97.0	95.8	96.4	96.3	96.1
Income taxes	371.9	827.0	2075.2	3043.3	13702.5	14390.4	18953.6	20794.0	18460.0
Indirect taxes									
Total (millions of *dirhams*)	32.1	23.2	74.2	97.6	215.8	624.9	709.4	808.0	740.0
Percentage of total revenues	7.8	2.7	3.4	3.0	1.5	4.2	3.6	3.7	3.9
Customs	1.8	6.4	11.3	13.1	28.6	21.8	25.8	44.2	} 740.0
Other indirect taxes	30.3	16.8	62.9	84.5	187.2	603.1[a]	683.6[a]	763.8	
State enterprises									
Total (millions of *dirhams*)	6.5	6.0	31.4	80.9	212.8	..	..	..	..
Percentage of total revenues	1.6	0.7	1.4	2.5	1.5	..	..	..	..
Total revenues (millions of *dirhams*)	410.6	856.1	2180.8	3211.8	14131.1	15015.3	19663.3	21602.0	19200.0

Note: [a] Included in other indirect taxes.

Source: UAE *Currency Board Bulletin*; Directorate-General of Planning and Coordination, *Statistical Abstract – Abu Dhabi*.

customs receipts were up sharply between 1972 and 1978 (*Table 7.29*), the average annual growth rate, about 28.4 percent, was still only half that realized for Dubai by oil – more than 59 percent.

Among the other emirates, only Sharjah and Ras al-Khaimah see much import activity directly through their own ports. The former has levied a 2.5 *ad valorem* duty on most entering goods. The latter charges 4 percent, but offers a reduction to 1 percent if the goods enter its territory directly on cargo ships. Ras al-Khaimah has followed suit in an attempt to reestablish itself as a major port.

Table 7.29 *Partial summary of revenues accruing to the government of Dubai (1972–1978) (millions of dirhams)*

	1972	1974	1976	1978
Oil revenues	311	2376	4028	5094
Customs duties	49	86	172	220
Municipality fees and taxes	–	21	50	77
Other fees and taxes	a	15	25	52
Total	360	2498	4275	5443

Note: [a] Less than 50 000 *dirhams.*

Source: Statistics Office, *Statistics Report – Dubai.*

The northern emirates, before the independence of the UAE, earned most of their income from the prolific printing and distribution of postage stamps in their names by New York and London entrepreneurs. Such dealings probably never earned all of them together as much as $500 thousand in any year, though their official agents netted much more. Ironically, these poorest Gulf emirates became notorious among the world's philatelists for blatant exploitation of a venerable hobby, while the agents, masked behind corporate forms of anonymity, continued to be respected as prominent stamp dealers[26].

As was mentioned above, the revenues of the federation are almost completely derived from the contributions of the still sovereign emirates (see *Table 7.30*). Although institutional shifts had boosted federal sources to about 3.7 percent of the total revenue by 1977, the federal regime remained essentially dependent upon the politically determined largesse of Abu Dhabi. For example, in 1977 Abu Dhabi contributed an estimated 5368.1 million *dirhams* of the total shown in *Table 7.30*, or about 92.6 percent. Dubai was the only other identifiable source of federal revenues, rather begrudgingly providing only an estimated 426 million *dirhams*[27]. Unless some sizeable federal tax base, independent of the emirates (for example, customs duties or a tax on personal incomes and business activity), is

Table 7.30 *Sources of federal
revenues: United Arab Emirates
(1972–1977) (millions of dirhams)*

Year	Contributions of emirates	Other payments	Total
1972	196.1	4.8	200.9
1973	402.7	17.1	419.8
1974	779.5	21.0	800.5
1975	1722.4	52.4	1774.8
1976	3010.9	102.7	3113.6
1977	5794.3	220.8	6015.1

Source: Currency Board Bulletin.

developed, it is difficult to see how the federation can proceed in the direction of greater political unification.

We indicated above the paucity of fiscal data available on earnings from foreign investments, even for the statistically more open emirate of Abu Dhabi. Nevertheless, knowledgeable observers can supply us with some estimates, and these indicate the rapidly expanding importance of these earnings (see *Table 7.31*). It is obvious that the overseas investments of the UAE (that is, mostly those of Abu Dhabi) will continue to follow an

Table 7.31 *External investment earnings and internal
fiscal receipts: United Arab Emirates (1972–1977)*

Year	Investment earnings	All internal fiscal receipts	Investment earnings as a percentage of receipts
1972	30	2 799	1.1
1973	80	4 330	1.8
1974	400	20 904	1.9
1975	600	23 165	2.6
1976	700	29 710	2.4
1977	1300	32 255	4.0

upward path, reflecting the country's massive export surpluses. Though it is unlikely that the annual average rate of growth in these earnings indicated in *Table 7.31* will continue at such an extraordinarily high level (125 percent), it is clear, nevertheless, that these investment earnings will grow rapidly over the next few years. No little significance should be attached to the fact that in 1977 the official overseas investments of the UAE constituent governments had earned more than all their 1970 fiscal earnings.

Along with some of its neighbors along the Gulf, the UAE has benefited from the chaotic conditions in the world oil market which followed Iran's Islamic revolution. Oil production has not changed much, but the country has, of course, received significantly higher prices for all its oil. As a result, the surpluses in its international accounts have swollen. For example, the UAE's current account surplus in 1979 reached an estimated 18 700 million *dirhams*, and the 1980 level was projected to be close to 31 300 million *dirhams*.

Most of these funds have been added to the UAE foreign assets, which according to the recent study by the First National Bank of Chicago, amounted to a net total of nearly 68 700 million *dirhams* by the end of 1979. The study also projected rapid growth in these investments – to more than 97 100 million *dirhams* by the end of 1980 and to more than 127 000 million *dirhams* by the end of 1981. Furthermore, the returns on this accumulated capital in 1979 were estimated to have been more than 6100 million *dirhams* (not all of which would fall into the official category, since no distinction is made in the study between public and private investment funds). This income, mostly deriving from capital held in western industrialized countries, was projected to rise sharply in 1980, along with the higher interest rates prevailing in those countries, to about 9700 million *dirhams*, before dropping slightly to about 9000 million *dirhams* in 1981.

It is clear that the large current account surpluses enjoyed by the UAE (and other highly populated major oil exporters like Kuwait, Libya, Qatar and Saudi Arabia) will continue in the early 1980s. It is also clear that, given the volatile state of world oil and capital markets, both net foreign assets and investment income will continue to climb, though prediction of the amounts of these gains is, of course, fraught with difficulty. However, the earnings from past investments will become an increasingly larger part of total government revenue over the next several years. The implications of this for tax policy in the UAE and in other oil producers will be discussed in some detail in Chapter 13.

These summaries emphasize the dependence of these nine countries on consumers outside their own borders, who effectively pay most of their government's current receipts. Chapter 8 will cover the countries that do not have this particular option, and therefore rely instead on domestic fiscal resources.

Notes

1 Detailed descriptions of what taxes are included in the categories of *Table 7.1*, and other tables in this section can be found in Appendix B.

2 At current production levels and given current estimates of oil reserves, oil production will be sustained only until the early 1990s.

3 According to the Gregorian calendar, rather than the Iranian calendar which is used in the tables accompanying this section.

4 *Annual Report 1356*, p. 153.

5 Unfortunately, preliminary trade data do not allow any firm conclusions in this regard.

6 And in particular on so-called 'luxuries' – that is, the consumables of the middle class.

7 In the early 1960s, the law was altered to authorize a 50/50 split, but for most of the period, actual development expenditures simply lagged behind authorized levels, leaving a surplus to be transferred to current uses, whatever the theoretical shares were supposed to be.

8 The same companies that owned IPC were also partners in concessions in nearby Qatar and Abu Dhabi; in addition, the British, Dutch and US interests all had extensive holdings elsewhere in the Middle East. In short, all the IPC partners were able to satisfy the increased demand they encountered during the 1960s by increasing production outside Iraq.

9 As one author, Siham Kamil Sharif, writing in December 1968 (Income Tax in Iraq, in the *Bulletin for International Fiscal Documentation*) pointed out, in the mid 1960s, an individual had to earn nearly 7 times the per capita income before being subject to any personal income tax; for a married man with dependents under age 18, earnings would have to exceed fourteen times per capita income before tax assessments would have been a factor. Sharif also pointed out that in the late 1960s, almost 91 percent of all personal income taxes came from residents of Baghdad liwa (for all practical purposes, the capital city, where only about 26 percent of Iraq's residents were enumerated during the census of 1965). The concentration of income tax payers in 1966 was such that only about two-thirds of one percent of the population paid any income tax.

10 By the mid 1950s, Kuwait's population was already made up largely of noncitizens, attracted by the jobs in its booming economy; e.g. in 1957, census takers found that 45 percent of the 206 000 residents enumerated were non-Kuwaitis.

11 Or if government investment returns are included (see *Table 7.11*), the total revenues for 1976/77 were 2.872 million *dinars*, and the 1950–77 growth rate

averages about 25.7 percent. Since investment earnings are growing rapidly, they should be kept in mind when government revenues are considered.

12 Or more properly as sales of crude oil. These came to 1308 million *dinars* in 1974/75; 2511 million *dinars* in 1975/76; 2457 million *dinars* in 1976/77; 2291 million *dinars* in 1977/78; and 2939 million *dinars* in 1978/79.

13 The authors have elsewhere discussed the Libyan situation *vis-à-vis* other oil exporters, in *Middle East Economies in the 1970s: A Comparative Approach* (New York, Praeger, 1976).

14 This amount apparently includes 100 000 to 200 000 *dinars* of property taxes not separately identifiable.

15 Which of course in this case means non-oil taxation.

16 See below, Chapter 10, p. 210.

17 Though like most other states lining the southern and western littoral of the Gulf, Oman was *de facto* a British protectorate until quite recently.

18 Earlier fiscal data for Oman are almost non-existent. In *Oman: The Making of the Modern State*, the author, John Townsend, includes a brief memoir of Sultan Sa'id bin Iaimur (r. 1932–1970) which indicates revenues of only £50 000 in 1931, just before he succeeded his father as sultan (p. 193).

19 Actually, before oil payments began in 1967, direct taxes were nil in Oman; thus the decline in relative importance of indirect taxes is even sharper than is indicated in *Table 7.18*.

20 A discussion of Qatar's overwhelming dependence on foreign workers can be found in H. Askari and J. T. Cummings, op. cit., pp. 289–91. Prior to the initiation of oil exports in 1949, Qatar's population was estimated to be 17 000 to 20 000; of these probably 85 percent were native born Arab Qataris.

21 Saudi Arabia uses a fiscal year based on the lunar calendar used by Muslims in other countries only for religious purposes. This calendar results in a year averaging 354 days. Thus, during the data period considered in this section, there was about one full additional lunar year relative to the solar years indicated in the tables. See *Table A.2* in the Appendix for further information.

22 The tax schedule was revised upward in the 1960s; previously, five percent was charged for income between 5000 and

20 000 *riyals*, 10 percent between 20 000 and 50 000, etc.

23 Also abolished at about the same time was an income-based tax assessed for the purpose of constructing highways. All salaried individuals, whether citizens or not, paid two percent of income in excess of 4800 *riyals* a year. This tax was based on the theory that this group represented the major highway users.

24 These negotiations, in their earlier forms, also included Bahrain and Qatar, two sheikhdoms with similar histories of links to the Indian Empire, but both states eventually opted for separate independence. Two other nearby entities, Kuwait and Oman, were also erstwhile British-Indian protectorates, and have maintained a certain feeling of kinship with their neighbors, though without, as yet, direct discussions to enlarge the existing federal arrangements. Only Aden and its bordering states remained completely outside even informal discussions which possibly might have led to a single British-oriented federation stretching almost uninterruptedly from the Bab al-Mandab to the mouth of the Shatt al-Arab.

25 Among the statistical problems confronting the researcher in the UAE are that fiscal data are published only for the federal government, Abu Dhabi and some government departments and entities in Dubai. Even for Abu Dhabi, no reliable figures are available for the receipts of the increasingly important Abu Dhabi Investment Authority (ADIA) which manages the overseas holdings of the Abu Dhabi government. By the end of 1977, these were estimated to amount to some 28 billion *dirhams* (about $7.2 billion). However, since it is believed nearly all of ADIA's earnings are reinvested outside Abu Dhabi, these receipts do not, as yet, directly affect the fiscal situation in either Abu Dhabi or the UAE.

26 One consequence of this situation was the assumption by the federal government of all post office operations immediately upon the UAE's independence. This action, insisted upon by Abu Dhabi, was aimed at restoring the federation's reputation in this regard.

27 Though available estimates indicate that Abu Dhabi and Dubai together accounted for 5794.1 million *dirhams* of the total federal receipts shown in *Table 7.27* for 1977 as coming from emirate grants of 5794.3 million *dirhams*, it is not clear that any of the remaining 0.2 million *dirhams* (about $50 000) came from the other emirates or whether this miniscule amount is merely a rounding error.

Non-oil exporting countries

8.1 Egypt

The Middle East's most populous nation, Egypt has long been a modest oil producer, and recently output has allowed some exports. But as oil does not yet figure prominently in Egyptian tax receipts, we will include it among our non-exporting group of countries. Though the exact extent of oil related taxes cannot be determined from government sources (they are included, in recent years, in *Table 8.1* under the income tax and government enterprise categories), the increases in output of late have affected the revenue breakdown only marginally. As *Table 8.2* shows, indirect taxes have slightly increased their relative share over the past quarter century or so, expanding by about 9.3 percent a year during this period. Direct taxes have also grown slightly faster than total revenues, by a slightly larger average of about 9.8 percent a year. Most of this has been due to the increased importance of profits taxes; as can be seen from *Table 8.2*, personal income taxes still contribute very little to total revenues – only about 2.5 percent in 1975, for example.

However, using the broad categories of *Tables 8.1* and *8.2*, there seems to have been general stability over a momentous period in Egypt's economic history. In 1952, the monarchy was overthrown and with it much of the country's landowning power structure. One of the first major programs of the new republic was land reform. The first land reform legislation decreed a statutory maximum of 200 *feddans* (about 84 hectares per landholding). Land owned in excess of this (and later the limits were sharply lowered) was to be purchased by the government and resold to smallholders[1]. The compensation paid to landlords was based on a formula incorporating the annual rents derived from the land. However, the officially sanctioned sources for such information were the declarations made by landlords themselves – before the revolutionary government's program was announced – as to the payments they were receiving. These declarations had served as the basis for determining the taxes due on agricultural land (see *Table 8.2*). Before the revolution, these declarations were widely known to notoriously underestimate rents and, hence, land values. Before the revolution, landlords avoided much of their tax burden in this way; after the revolution, the same landlords were compensated for their expropriated

Table 8.1 *Tax revenues: Egypt (1950/51–1977)*

	1950/51[a]	1954/55[b]	1958/59[b]	1962/63[b]	1966/67[b]	1968/69[b]	1970/71[b]	1971/72[c]	1973	1974	1975	1976	1977
Direct taxes													
Total (£E millions)	32.4	45.3	61.1	75.8	112.3	132.4	162.8	173.2	197.1	207.8	253.7	330.0	411.4
Percentage of revenues	17.7	20.8	20.2	16.0	15.0	20.5	22.8	23.1	22.1	21.5	21.8	21.9	21.3
Income taxes	17.4	21.6	30.2	41.7	74.1	96.0	124.2	131.3	157.1	172.5	181.8	253.8	328.2
Royalties	1.9	6.6	3.0	8.1	10.7								
Property taxes	13.1	17.1	27.9	26.0	27.5	36.4	38.6	41.9	40.0	35.3	71.9	76.2	83.2
Indirect taxes													
Total (£E millions)	122.1	132.0	182.6	313.8	512.9	460.5	490.4	492.5	611.4	664.7	816.7	1049.1	1359.0
Percentage of revenues	66.6	60.7	60.4	66.1	68.6	71.4	68.6	65.6	68.5	68.8	70.0	69.5	70.4
Customs duties	17.2	41.3	31.2	113.6	168.1								
Excise, sales and production taxes	48.9	63.9	73.6	70.5	90.8	248.2	258.0	269.4	301.0	363.4	594.6	510.6	712.0
Miscellaneous indirect taxes	26.0	26.8	72.1	129.7	254.0	212.3	232.4	223.1	310.4	310.3	222.1	538.5	647.0
State enterprises													
Total (£E millions)	28.7	40.3	58.4	85.2	122.8	52.4	61.7	85.6	84.0	92.9	95.5	130.0	159.0
Percentage of revenues	15.7	18.5	19.3	17.9	16.4	8.1	8.6	11.4	9.4	9.6	8.1	8.6	8.3
Total revenues (£E millions)	183.2	217.6	302.2	474.8	748.0	645.3	714.9	715.3	892.5	965.4	1165.9	1509.1	1930.0

Notes: [a] 1 March to 28 February.
  [b] 1 July to 30 June.
  [c] 18 month fiscal year, 1 July 1971 to 31 December 1972.

Source: Ministry of Finance, *Annuaire Statistique*; National Bank of Egypt, *Economic Bulletin*.

holdings at only a fraction of their true worth[2]. Significantly, tax receipts from agricultural land rose sharply during the early and mid 1950s; as *Table 8.2* shows, they went from about £E5.8 million in 1950/51 to £E18.2 million by 1957/58. This represents an average annual growth rate of almost 18 percent a year, when total revenues were increasing at only about 7.5 percent a year.

Income taxes were first introduced to Egypt in 1939, but after the 1952 revolution they became much more important, as both the rates and the range of income covered were increased. Wages and salaries are subject to

Table 8.2 *Major taxes: Egypt (1950/51–1977) (millions of pounds)*

	1950/51	1957/58	1964/65	1970/71	1977
Income taxes:					
Earned income	} 13.6	26.3	{ 15.6	24.8	44.4
Dividend income[a]			{ 10.6		
Business profits	3.1	0.1	20.3	} 97.1	281.0
Royalties	1.9	1.7	15.4		
Inheritance taxes	0.8	2.0	3.0	2.3	2.8[d]
Wealth taxes:					
Agricultural land[b]	5.8	18.2	} 8.9	38.6	83.2
Urban land and buildings	2.4	1.1			
Defense surtax	–	4.5			
Automobiles	2.0	2.0	NA	NA	NA
Customs duties	47.2	41.2	168.2	} 227.5	712.0
Excise taxes	45.9	66.9	56.4		
Price differential receipts	–	–	22.5	111.1	183.0
Stamp duties	2.5	8.0	12.6	30.5	72.0
Government service fees	5.9	18.2	24.5	18.5	34.1
Government enterprise profits	28.7	68.7	108.1	61.7	159.6
Total revenues	183.2	300.5	567.9	714.9	1930.0

Notes: NA Indicates data not separately available.
 [a] Includes other unearned income such as interest.
 [b] Land tax assessed on basis of rents.
 [c] Includes taxes on motorized river boats.
 [d] Estimated.

Source: See *Table 8.1.*

withholding on the part of employers, and the taxes on interest payments and dividends are usually subtracted before these are paid out. Profits taxes have generally been the largest revenue earner in the income tax category.

Though income tax rates have been progressive, they have not been, at first glance, very onerous in the higher income brackets. For example, salaries in the mid 1970s were subject to a 2 percent levy on the first £E100 of taxable income, 3 percent on the next £E150, and so on up to a maximum rate of only 22 percent on taxable income in excess of £E4850. For a married taxpayer with two children, this structure means effective levies of about 0.7 percent on an annual income of £E500, for example, of about 2.4 percent on £E1000, of about 10.5 percent on £E5000, and of about 17.1 percent on £E10 000.

To increase the progressiveness of this structure (as well as of similar ones for other types of income) a somewhat complex series of surtaxes have come into service. The most important of these is the general revenue tax. Though the burden of this on middle and upper income brackets was eased in a 1979 tax reform, it is still sharply progressive. After allowances for income taxes that have been paid and for family status, a tax of 8 percent on net income between £E1200 and £E2000 is levied; the rates then climb to 9 percent on the next £E1000, 10 percent on the next thousand, and so on to a maximum rate of 80 percent on net income over £E100 000.

The high priority that has been assigned in Egypt to national preparedness against external military threats has had the fiscal result of creating several small taxes earmarked for defense. While these are fairly progressive, maximum tax rates take effect at only £E1200 in taxable income.

The overall effect of all these income related taxes is to increase the theoretical burden considerably. In the case cited above, to take as an example, a married taxpayer with two children, the total effective rate on an annual income of £E500 is about 6 percent, on £E1000 – about 9.5 percent, on £E5000 – about 29.5 percent, and about 36.6 percent on £E10 000. Of course, as we have said, few taxpayers are likely to pay the full income tax that is theoretically due.

Profits taxes were computed at a flat rate of about 26.5 percent during the 1960s, but in the early 1970s as part of his campaign to attract foreign investment, President Sadat offered several exemptions. These included profits tax holidays of up to eight years depending upon the type of enterprise as well as partial exemptions from the general income surtax on distributed dividends.

But, even in the mid 1970s, direct taxes on income and wealth continued to play a relatively minor fiscal role in Egypt. The principal taxes continued to be those levelled on consumption. In 1950/51, customs duties brought in £E47.2 million and excise taxes another £E48.9 million, or a total of about 52.5 percent of total revenues. The most important excise during the entire period shown in *Tables 8.1* and *8.2* was that on tobacco products; in 1950/51, this alone raised nearly £E27.5 million. By 1966/67 customs receipts had climbed to £E158.1 million, a much more rapid climb than excises which brought in £E55.8 million; the average growth rates for each category over this period were 8.3 and 3.9 percent respectively (or averaging both categories, about 6.8 percent). However, the government had by that time begun to subsidize the prices of several basic staples, a program financed by the profits from the sales of certain items controlled through government monopolies – especially those for cottonseed, coffee, tea, and sugar. Some of these revenues are clearly consumption excise taxes (which accounted, along with customs duties, for about 52.5 percent of receipts at the beginning of this period in 1950/51), though in recent years they have been reported (see *Table 8.2*) under the categorical heading 'price differential receipts'.

If we combine these revenues with customs duties and excise taxes, then the total comes to about 46.1 percent of total revenues in 1966/7 and to about 46.3 percent in 1975. Altogether, over the entire period of 27 years, consumption related taxes climbed slightly more slowly than total revenues – at an average rate of about 8.7 percent for the former versus 9.1 percent for the latter.

Table 8.3 *Current revenues available to local governments (1962/63–1977)* *(millions of pounds)*

	1962/63	*1964/65*	*1968/69*	*1971/72*	*1975*	*1977*
Property taxes	14.0	14.9	17.5	19.0	53.4	65.0
Service fees	23.2	20.8	} 50.6	39.1	34.4	33.3
Other taxes	14.2	15.2				
Total	51.4	57.8	68.1	58.1	87.8	98.3

Note: Total does not include borrowing by local municipal councils.

Source: See *Table 8.2.*

Egyptian provinces and municipalities have limited revenue raising powers: these are primarily levies on real estate and buildings and from charges made for local government services, *(Table 8.3)*. Various levies, collected either by the local governments or by the central authorities in their names, are categorized as 'other taxes'. Among the former have been excises on automobiles and entertainment, and the latter have mostly been surcharges on central government taxes. For example, before the closing of the Suez Canal in June 1967, the central government collected a 10 percent surcharge on travel dues on behalf of the three municipalities along the Canal – Port Said, Ismailia and Suez.

Local revenues have tended to fall gradually in importance in the overall fiscal picture; for example, local council revenues amounted to about 10.8 percent of total government receipts in 1962/63, about 9.8 percent in 1968/69, and only about 5.1 percent in 1977. Local councils continued to collect the bulk of the real estate taxes in 1977 (see *Table 8.4*), while local service fees seemed on the decline in absolute as well as relative terms. The local share of the real estate taxes has actually risen during the last decade: in

Table 8.4 *Egyptian central and local government shares of property taxes and service fees (1977)*

	Property taxes	Service fees
Total collected (millions of pounds)	83.2	67.4
Central government share (%)	21.9	50.6
Local government share (%)	78.1	49.4

Source: See *Table 8.1.*

1967/68, the central government collected £E17.7 million from this source, while the local share was only £E16.5 million, or about 48.2 percent of such taxes.

8.2   Jordan

Jordan has been one of the Middle East's poorest countries in both natural and financial resources. As *Table 8.5* indicates, total tax revenues of the kingdom in the first years of its independence came to only about $15 million or less a year, with another $1 million or so being collected by local government bodies. Total government spending during the early 1950s was in fact more than double the revenue levels, thanks to fo. eign assistance (see *Table 8.6*), mostly from Great Britain.

Tax revenues rose gradually during the 1950s and 1960s, at an annual average rate of about 10.3 percent during the first decade and of about 8.4 percent during the second. But the 1970s saw a sharp acceleration in the growth of tax receipts, reaching about 23 percent in 1978. Despite the increased capabilities of the Jordanian economy to generate local support for government activities, foreign economic assistance (*Table 8.6*) has grown quickly, and through 1978, such funding continued at least to match tax revenues, as it has throughout the period of Jordan's political independence. However, aid from Arab countries (primarily Saudi Arabia, Kuwait and the United Arab Emirates) is now dominant (about 74 percent of the aid Jordan received in 1977), with the US a distant second donor (about 14 percent).

The figures in *Table 8.5* show that despite the more than 28 fold increase in revenues from 1951 to 1978, the composition of these taxes has hardly varied. Indirect taxes still account for about 3 of every 4 *dinars* collected by the government, with customs duties and other consumption excises together accounting for about half of all revenues during 1978. Income tax levies have grown slightly more rapidly than customs duties and excises – by about 16.3 percent a year for the former as opposed to about 14.4 percent a

Table 8.5 *Tax revenues: Jordan (1951/52–1978)*

	1951/52	1954/55	1962/63	1966	1968	1970	1971	1972	1973	1974	1975	1976	1977	1978
Direct taxes														
Total (millions of *dinars*)	1.0	1.6	4.8	2.9	3.1	3.5	6.4	5.8	6.3	8.0	15.7	19.8	19.4	21.9
Percentage of revenues	18.2	21.3	25.4	12.4	11.8	11.6	17.9	13.6	13.6	12.7	18.6	17.9	13.3	13.5
Income taxes	0.3	0.4	3.1	1.8	1.8	2.5	2.9	3.2	3.9	5.5	9.2	11.5	13.4	19.5
Royalties	0.4	0.8	1.7[a]	1.0[a]	1.3	1.0	3.5	2.6	2.4	2.4	5.3	5.0	4.0	0.0
Property taxes	0.3	0.4	[b]	0.1	0.1	[c]	0.1	0.1	0.1	0.1	1.2	3.3	2.0	2.4
Indirect taxes														
Total (millions of *dinars*)	3.9	5.3	12.0[a]	17.4[a]	19.3	20.8	23.1	31.8	33.3	45.5	55.3	75.5	110.0	118.6
Percentage of revenues	70.9	70.7	63.5	74.7	73.4	68.7	64.5	74.6	72.1	72.0	65.9	68.3	75.7	72.9
Customs	2.0	2.9	6.4	11.8	8.9	9.1	7.7	9.5	12.2	15.2	19.9	32.5	64.8	67.8
Excise, sales and production taxes	0.2	0.2			5.5	5.1	6.9	7.8	7.8	9.1	10.3	9.3	9.1	10.2
Miscellaneous indirect taxes	1.8	2.2	5.6[a]	5.6[a]	5.0	6.6	8.5	14.5	13.3	21.2	25.3	33.8	36.1	40.6
State enterprises														
Total (millions of *dinars*)	0.5	0.6	2.2	3.0	3.9	5.8	6.3	4.9	6.6	9.7	13.1	15.2	16.0	22.3
Percentage of revenues	9.1	8.0	11.7	12.9	14.8	19.2	17.6	11.5	14.3	15.3	15.6	13.8	11.0	13.7
Total revenues (millions of *dinars*)	5.5	7.5	18.9	23.3	26.3	30.3	35.8	42.6	46.2	63.2	84.2	110.5	145.4	162.8

Notes: [a] Estimated.
[b] Included in income taxes.
[c] Less than 50 000 *dinars*.

Sources: Central Bank of Jordan, *Annual Report*; Ministry of National Economy, *Statistical Abstract*.

year for the latter – but they still only account for about 12 percent of government revenues.

For the sake of comparison with its neighbors, Jordanian royalty receipts shown in *Table 8.5* include *all* oil related income (except petroleum consumption taxes), which means, for all practical purposes, the transit duties that are generated by that portion of the Trans-Arabian Pipeline (Tapline) that crosses northeastern Jordan. Several companies have surveyed parts of Jordan for oil and have paid for these survey rights, but this revenue has never been great. As no oil or gas in commercially exploitable quantities has ever been found, tax revenues have never benefited from oil royalties. Tapline receipts have been moderate in size and, in the last decade, rather irregular, as the line has been closed much of this time. This is a result of the June 1967 war and subsequent sabotage, and also economic considerations that often make tanker transportation cheaper than a pipeline for Gulf crude which is heading for Europe.

Table 8.6 *Foreign economic assistance to Jordan (1951/52–1978)*

Year	Amount (JD millions)
1951/52	7.2
1955/56	8.7
1964	21.9
1967	44.9
1970	42.5
1972	58.9
1974	74.0
1975	116.8
1976	86.1
1977	168.9
1978	149.1

Source: See *Table 8.5.*

A more important royalty generating natural resource in Jordan has been phosphate, the mining output of which has more than doubled since 1967. However, while phosphate now accounts for about a third of Jordanian exports, it still does not contribute very much to the country's tax revenues. Phosphate exports were subject to an export levy of 11 *dinars* a ton until 1976, but this was then reduced to 6 *dinars* a ton until 1978 when the tax was eliminated. Of course, the phosphate company continues to have corporate profits tax obligations.

For Jordan, we do not have as much disaggregated tax data as for other larger Middle Eastern countries. Recent figures for a few major categories are shown in *Table 8.7*. Individual income and corporate profits taxes have shown considerably larger returns for 1977 and 1978, mostly as a result of improved collection techniques. In addition, the maximum profits tax rate was raised from 38.5 to 45 percent in 1977. Still, these major direct taxes only accounted for an eighth of Jordanian tax revenues in 1978, while import related levies continued to provide more than 42 percent.

Individual income tax levies in the late 1970s were sharply progressive: the first 400 *dinars* of taxable income was subject to a tax of 5 percent, with these rates rising on an incremental basis to a maximum of 50 percent on all taxable income in excess of 8000 *dinars*. However, despite recently improved collection methods, only employees of the government and of major

Table 8.7 *Major taxes: Jordan (1974 and 1978)*
(millions of dinars)

	1974	1978
Individual and business income tax	5.4	18.5
Income tax surcharge	0.3	1.0
Land taxes	0.1	–
Customs duties	15.2	60.8
Export taxes	5.3	3.0
Other foreign trade-related fees	3.3	5.7
Excise taxes	8.7	10.2
Licenses and government service fees	9.1	24.0

Source: See *Table 8.5.*

foreign and domestic corporations pay anything approaching the tax theoretically due on personal incomes. It continues to be particularly difficult to collect anything but the most nominal taxes from selfemployed individuals for example.

Profits taxes are levied on all corporations, whether privately or state-owned, domestic or foreign. After 1977, the tax rates on both distributed and undistributed profits ranged from 38.5 percent for state owned companies to 40 percent for privately held industrial institutions to 45 percent for banks, insurance companies and other financial institutions. Several exemptions were allowed by the Encouragement of Investment Law, which also lifted from eligible enterprises certain customs and property tax levies. These exemptions are tied to the type of investment project and its location (that is, outside the immediate area of Amman).

Property taxes, which as we can see from *Table 8.5*, continue to be quite a minor source of revenue, are assessed according to the location and use of the land in question. There is a distinction as to whether farm land is planted in tree crops or field crops; if the latter, higher levies apply to irrigated than to unirrigated acreage. Buildings on rural land are assessed at five percent of their rental value, while those in urban areas are liable to a rate of about five times higher, which is in addition to an urban land tax equal to ten percent of its value.

8.3   Lebanon

The most prosperous of the Middle East non-oil producers (at least until the onset of the current civil war), Lebanon has been in many ways the most economically developed country in the group we are considering. However, as *Table 8.8* shows, direct taxes have continued to play a relatively minor role in Lebanon's fiscal situation, amounting to only about a fifth of all taxes in 1974 (the last tax year before the outbreak of civil war), a share similar to that in 1950.

Total revenues grew at an annual rate of about 12.3 percent over the 1950 to 1974 period, but growth varied widely – averaging more than 15 percent a year in the 1950s, dropping to about half this level during the 1960s, then climbing back to about 17 percent a year in the early 1970s. Income taxes actually grew somewhat more slowly than revenues in general, and thus fell from about 12.5 percent of receipts in 1950 to close to 11 percent by 1974. On the other hand, customs levies have continued their dominant position, increasing from about 27 percent of all government revenues in 1950 to about 38 percent in 1974.

Oil and mineral royalty data are not available for Lebanon, and thus direct comparisons cannot be made with the other countries under consideration. However, no commercially exploitable oil or natural gas has ever been found in the country, and other mining activity is slight. Like Jordan, Lebanon does receive transit duties for oil shipped in pipelines across its territory. One of these is the Trans-Arabian Pipeline (Tapline) which terminates in the southern Lebanese port of Sidon, and the second is a branch of the line from Kirkuk, in Iraq, that crosses northern Lebanon on its way to Tripoli. It is not possible, using published sources, to distinguish pipeline payments from taxes levied on refinery activities and therefore all such payments were combined under state enterprises.

A breakdown of tax revenue sources more disaggregated than that used in the general format (*Table 8.8*) is seen in *Table 8.9* for 1952, 1962, and 1975. It is generally conceded that collecting income taxes is particularly difficult, especially from the selfemployed middle class. Thus, it is not surprising that direct taxes have remained relatively minor throughout the period shown in this table.

Income taxes imposed in recent years have been progressive, though both rate increments and maximum applicable rates have been less severe in effect than those found in neighboring countries. For example, net salary income in the early 1970s was subject to only a two percent levy up to £L4800, three percent from £L4800 to £L8400, and so on up to a maximum of 31 percent on income above £L90 000. Effective tax rates ran from 1.2 percent on £L4800, 2.9 percent on £L12 000, 4.6 percent on £L36 000, 7 percent on £L60 000 to 16.1 percent on £L200 000. (Referring to *Table A.1* we can see that in the early 1970s, the latter income level was more than $60 000.) In

Table 8.8 *Tax revenues: Lebanon (1950–1975)*

	1950	1954	1958	1962	1966	1968	1970	1971	1972	1973	1974	1975
Direct taxes												
Total (£L millions)	14.0	26.7	36.5	62.9	104.3	123.2	152.4	165.4	172.0	196.1	258.8	114.2
Percentage of revenues	18.5	17.0	16.2	17.5	19.9	21.5	23.0	21.3	19.2	20.3	20.8	14.7
Income taxes	14.0	18.1	22.8	33.8	61.1	66.2	86.4	87.8	93.9	107.0	148.8	52.5
Property taxes		8.6	13.7	29.1	43.2	57.0	66.0	77.6	78.1	89.1	110.0	61.7
Indirect taxes												
Total (£L millions)	54.5	122.4	177.2	243.1	368.6	397.9	440.3	524.3	616.9	701.4	944.9	661.0
Percentage of revenues	72.1	77.7	78.6	67.5	70.2	69.4	66.4	67.6	68.8	72.8	75.8	85.0
Customs	20.5	55.5	66.0	114.6	176.3	177.6	189.3	250.1	305.7	363.2	476.9	335.1
Excise, sales and production taxes	34.0	37.5	39.4	64.1	95.0	100.6	92.3	98.5	124.1	107.3	197.0	114.4
Other indirect taxes		29.4	71.8	64.4	97.3	119.7	158.7	175.7	187.1	230.9	271.0	211.5
State enterprises												
Total (£L millions)	7.1	8.3	11.7	54.1	51.5	52.0	70.6	86.3	108.2	66.4	43.1	1.8
Percentage of revenues	9.4	5.3	5.2	15.0	9.8	9.1	10.6	11.1	12.1	6.8	3.5	0.3
Total revenues (£L millions)	75.6	157.6	225.4	360.1	524.4	573.1	663.3	776.0	897.1	963.9	1246.8	777.3

Source: Ministry of Planning, *Requiel des Statistiques Libanaises.*

addition, Lebanon allowed deductions depending upon the taxpayer's marital and childsupporting status. These meant that in 1971, for example, a Lebanese couple with children and a gross salary of, say, £L30 000 (about $9 000), a very high income by national standards, were legally obliged to pay a maximum income tax of about £L1125 – that is, less than 3.8 percent of gross salary income, a low rate by either developed or developing country standards.

Table 8.9 *Major taxes: Lebanon (1952–1975) (millions of pounds)*

	1952	1962	1975
Income tax	13.5	31.7	48.2
Inheritance tax	0.1	2.1	4.3
Property taxes on:			
Buildings	3.7	20.9	30.7
Land	0.7	0.4	0.1
Automobiles	1.3	6.9	30.9
Customs duties	36.7	114.6	335.1
Excises on:			
Petroleum products	17.5	31.5	63.4
Tobacco	16.8	26.2	43.4
Cement	1.2	4.3	5.0
Alcohol	0.9	2.0	2.4
Stamp duties and notary fees	4.1	12.2	} 118.7
Registration fees	5.1	14.5	
Payments from petroleum companies	5.5	47.2	0.1
Total revenues	124.9	360.1	777.3

Note: Categories shown are not exhaustive and therefore do not add to totals.

Source: See *Table 8.8.*

Business profits are also subject to progressive rates, which in the late 1960s and early 1970s ascended somewhat more steeply than personal income tax levies; profits were subjected to a maximum rate of 42 percent, double that applying to salary incomes. The net profit brackets depended upon the type of business concerned, the size of the enterprise and its payroll, and the location of its major activities.

In the early 1970s, partly as a result of Lebanon's export boom in the wake of the Israeli invasion of Egypt in 1967 and the subsequent closure of the Suez Canal, the Lebanese government undertook to use fiscal incentives to promote industrial exports[3]. New enterprises established between 1971 and 1975 were granted a total exemption from profits levies for six years if they were either engaged in producing new products of a semi-finished nature from raw materials or in assembling finished goods from semi-finished inputs. To encourage large scale foreign investors, minimum investment and employment standards were also applied. Tax holidays were extended when local raw materials were used or when the degree of technical precision of the final good exceeded defined levels. Unfortunately, this very liberal tax legislation (considering preexisting corporate taxes and Lebanon's emerging role as a regional supplier) came into effect shortly before the country's fragile social and economic structure disintegrated into civil war. Thus, we have no good indications as to the effects, if any, of these tax concessions on industrial investment.

Lebanon, in keeping with its *laissez-faire* traditions, has avoided taxes on invested capital and on the dividends returned on it, apart from minor fees on securities transactions. Deductions applicable to capital gains have been generous. Real estate, the most prominent source of capital appreciation in Lebanon during the last decade, has been subject to a modest sliding scale of 3 to 15 percent on net gains.

Given the obvious and long existing problem in Lebanon, regarding collection of income and profits based taxes due especially from the selfemployed, it is not surprising that taxes on tangible wealth or consumption are widely used. As is true in many developing countries, automobiles are a popular target for Lebanese tax authorities, and annual assessments on vehicles plus gasoline taxes[4] have recently raised even more than the income tax.

Less explicable, from the point of economic equity, is the small role played by real estate taxes in relation to taxes on both income and automobiles. Prior to the outbreak of civil war in 1975, Lebanon in general (and Beirut in particular) had seen more than a decade of booming conditions in the real estate sector, with many Lebanese and foreign property owners realizing considerable gains in both annual rental income and capital appreciation from rising property values. Yet real estate holders continued to pay less than half the taxes that were imposed on automobile owners.

Real estate taxes were assessed both nationally and locally: with profits from turnovers being theoretically assessed according to a sliding scale. Obviously this levy was difficult to collect in amounts anywhere close to those legislatively determined. Taxes on incomes generated by property were, again in theory, based on actual rental value, or imputed value if the property was occupied by the owner; however, actual or imputed rents were subject to a flat rate tax – one-twelfth of the rental value in the early 1970s. Municipalities imposed other charges and in addition, both real estate sales and the subsequent registration of the property in the name of the new owner, were subject to national tax levies based on declared property values.

Customs duties, one of the easiest taxes to administer and to collect in developing countries, remained the major revenue source for Lebanon through the onset of the civil war. They actually increased in relative importance from about 27 percent of total revenues in 1950 to about 33 percent in 1966 and then to about 38 percent by 1974. Customs receipts climbed, therefore, at an annual average rate of about 14 percent from 1950 to 1974, while total Lebanese revenues rose at an average rate of about 12.3 percent.

The other major category of consumption taxes, excises assessed mostly against petroleum, tobacco and alcohol products, and cement, have also shown gains, through these have been slower (averaging about 8.5 percent a year) than those shown for total revenues.

Import levies in the early 1970s averaged about 25 percent *ad valorem* on imports, including customs duties, port fees and municipal excises on imports. Sales and excise taxes, as indicated above, were levied mostly on domestically produced (or at least refined) products, such as fuel, tobacco and alcohol.

If we assume that the marginal propensity to consume declines in the Lebanon with rising income and that income tax collections tend to hit the salaried middle class harder than either the poor or the selfemployed and/or property owning rich, we can see the origin of the situation described in a recent study of Lebanon by De Wulf[5]. He found virtually no difference in tax incidence across middle income (beginning at annual expenditures of £L12 000, or about $3800 per family) and upper income groups (see *Table 8.10*). A marginal reliance on income taxes together with heavy customs

Table 8.10 *Tax incidence in Lebanon (1968)*

Family expenditure class (thousands of £L)	Taxes as percentage of expenditure	Taxes as percentage of computed income
Under 6	8.00	8.44
6 to 12	12.52	12.40
12 to 18	17.42	17.36
18 to 24	19.93	20.19
24 to 30	22.41	21.73
Over 30	23.32	20.33

Source: Luc De Wulf.

duties and excises on imported goods and/or luxuries can lead to some progressiveness in the fiscal structure, at least as far as the poorest income groups are concerned, but to a neutral or even regressive structure beginning at middle income levels.

Since 1975, of course, Lebanon has been the scene of a prolonged and devastating civil war. The consequences, from a fiscal point of view, have been an inability of the central government to exercise effective control over either the collection of taxes or budgetary expenditures. For some periods this inability has been nearly total, while at other times, the situation has approached, if not normalcy, at least manageability. Some taxes (for example, those on income) have proved harder to collect in wartime than in peace, while the administration of others (for example, customs duties) has suffered less. The variability of the overall situation can be seen from *Table 8.11* if we compare the anticipated revenues indicated in the budget with those estimated to have been actually collected. Actual receipts were about 63 percent of those anticipated in 1975, and this ratio fell to only 11.5 percent during 1976. Greater realism on the part of budget planners and a general respite in the fighting brought expectation and realization more or less into line in 1977, but the situation worsened again in 1978.

Table 8.11 *Anticipated and actual tax revenues during civil war period: Lebanon (millions of pounds)*

Year	Budget anticipation of tax revenues	Estimated actual tax revenues
1975	1228.9	777.3
1976	1424.8	163.3
1977	1084.0	1050.0
1978	1605.1	1000.0

Sources: Various unpublished sources available to the authors.

Detailed data relative to the categories of taxation shown in *Table 8.8* are not available after 1975, the first year of civil war, for actual collections. As can be seen from *Table 8.8*, direct taxes fell much more drastically in 1975 than did indirect taxes, so that the share of the former was less than 15 percent in 1975. Income tax receipts in 1975 were barely a third of what they had been in 1974, while total receipts fell by only about 38 percent. Property tax payments dropped 44 percent, and thus kept direct taxes from showing an even greater decline than the problems with income tax collections might have indicated[6]. Since property tax collections have been partly in the hands of local authorities, they have suffered less, as a result of the fighting which is concentrated in the capital, Beirut.

Customs duty receipts dropped by less than 30 percent between 1974 and 1975. Some of this decline was undoubtedly due to evasion, but imports also fell. Official figures indicate imports of £L5077 million in 1974 and of £L4379 million in 1975, though obviously some imports went unreported after the outbreak of war[7].

As has been indicated above, there have been considerable discrepancies between the anticipations of budget planners and actual tax receipts since 1974. Nevertheless, a brief look at the former can indicate whether civil war wrought any changes, at least through 1978, in the relative importance that

fiscal authorities have given to various types of taxes[8]. *Table 8.12* indicates
the sources, by major tax category, of the revenues anticipated in 1975,
1976, 1977, and 1978: the general breakdown of tax revenues budgeted for
1978 shows few differences when compared with the actual revenues of the
years immediately preceding the civil war. Customs receipts remain the
major tax – almost 44 percent of the 1978 budget, a sharp increase from the

Table 8.12 *Anticipated tax revenues during the Lebanese civil war by major category*

	1975	1976	1977	1978
Direct taxes				
Total (£L millions)	243.0	299.0	175.0	300.0
Percentage of revenues	19.4	21.3	16.5	18.6
Income taxes	133.0	169.0	85.0	135.0
Property taxes	110.0	130.0	90.0	165.0
Indirect taxes				
Total (£L millions)	NA	1027.4	867.0	1274.3
Percentage of revenues	NA	73.4	81.9	79.4
Customs	490.0	520.0	425.0	700.0
Excise, sales and production taxes	154.5	168.0	112.0	130.8
Other indirect taxes	NA	339.4	330.0	443.5
State enterprises				
Total (£L millions)	NA	73.4	17.0	22.8
Percentage of revenues	NA	5.2	1.6	1.4
Total revenues (£L millions)	1253.9	1399.8	1059.0	1605.1

Note: NA indicates data not separately available.
Source: See *Table 8.11*

38 percent they provided in 1974. Income and inheritance taxes were to
bring in less than 8.5 percent in 1978, while they realized almost 12 percent
in 1974. Generally, no shift between direct and indirect sources has been
indicated, despite considerable discussion of tax reform during the war
period.

8.4   Sudan

The Sudan, despite its current poverty, is in many ways the crucial Middle
Eastern economy. Geographically, it is the biggest country that we are
considering: in population, only Egypt and Iran exceed it. But it is natural
resources that gives the Sudan its importance. The largest country on the
African continent, it also has one of the world's few remaining major stores

of un- and underutilized arable land (given available agricultural technology)[9].

However, this considerable potential has yet to distinguish the Sudan, from a fiscal point of view, from its neighbors. Despite oft-expressed official optimism, significant petroleum production remains a dream, along with the revenues such an eventuality would generate. Thus the traditional sources of tax returns in a largely subsistence level agricultural economy still dominate the country's fiscal profile.

From *Table 8.13*, we can see a fairly steady growth in government revenues; the annual average increase over the 1952/53 to 1977/78 period was about 12.6 percent. According to the major taxation categories used in this study, indirect taxes have become notably more important during this period. Leading this fiscal growth have been both customs receipts, up by an annual average of about 14.4 percent, and excise taxes, increasing at about 14.7 percent a year.

Direct taxes maintained their relatively minor position, providing about one pound in ten of total revenues over the 25 year data period. Income and profits taxes were responsible for all the growth in this category; central government collections of property taxes hardly varied during most of this time.

State enterprises, on the other hand, showed relatively slower growth in their returns to the government – about 8.8 percent a year. The profits of that uniquely Sudanese institution the agricultural schemes (that is agricultural development companies found mostly in the Jezirah region south of the confluence of the Blue and White Niles) have become relatively less important in the government's fiscal profile. This is not because the schemes themselves have lost prominence in the Sudanese economy: on the contrary, they have grown both in number and extent and are in the forefront of current plans to expand the agricultural and export sectors. The profits of the schemes (see *Table 8.14*) are subject both to the vagaries of international markets (e.g. cotton), and to internal political considerations. The agricultural development committees act as middlemen to some extent; since they are also quasi-cooperative in nature, their profits (unless reinvested) are at the expense of the participating farmers. Thus politics may dictate how agricultural produce is to be taxed – either through the schemes or by the imposition of levies that affect *all* peasants whether in or out of the schemes.

Table 8.14 indicates that one somewhat broadly based agricultural tax, on exports, has become more important than the profits of the schemes in recent years. This category covers production taxes placed on the Sudan's major agricultural exports. In 1967, for example, some £S6.1 million were collected from this tax: about 45 percent from cotton; 25 percent from gum arabic; five percent from groundnuts; and 2.2 percent from cottonseed[10]. Much of the profit from the schemes is also related to exports – cotton in particular. Generally speaking, the role of these levies in the export sector

Table 8.13 *Tax revenues: Sudan (1952/53–1977/78)*

	1952/53	*1954/55*	*1958/59*	*1962/63*	*1966/67*	*1968/69*
Direct taxes						
Total (£S millions)	2.1	1.7	1.9	2.3	4.1	5.8
Percentage of revenues	9.1	5.4	5.1	3.1	5.3	5.5
Income taxes	1.7	1.3	1.6	2.2	4.0	5.7
Property taxes	0.4	0.4	0.3	0.1	0.1	0.1
Indirect taxes						
Total (£S millions)	11.8	19.3	25.2	48.6	52.7	71.5
Percentage of revenues	51.1	62.2	67.9	65.3	68.4	67.5
Customs	5.2	8.2	10.3	29.8	26.2	39.0
Excise, sales and production taxes	3.6[a] } 11.1		{ 7.6 } 18.8		{ 16.2	19.7
Other indirect taxes	3.0[a]		7.3		10.3	9.4
State enterprises						
Total (£S millions)	9.2[a]	10.0[a]	9.9	23.5	20.3	32.0
Percentage of revenues	39.8	32.3	26.7	31.6	26.4	30.2
Total revenues (£S millions)	23.1	31.0	37.1	79.4	77.0	105.9

Notes: NA indicates data not separately available.
         [a] Estimated.
Source: Department of Statistics, *Internal Statistics* and *Statistical Yearbook.*

has declined during the period being considered. *Tables 8.13* and *8.14* show that nearly 60 percent of total revenues came from export taxes and scheme profits in 1952/53, but by 1976/77 this portion had fallen to only about 4 percent. By contrast, import related taxes (customs duties and sugar monopoly profits[11]) moved from about 28 percent to 40 percent of total revenues during the same period. Recent rapid growth has made excise taxes on locally produced items such as beer, cigarettes, petroleum products and cement, the second most important group after customs duties. In part, this represents the changes since the mid 1960s in the Sudan's burgeoning, if still small, industrial sector. These excises rose from only £S5.2 million in 1964/65 to £S40.4 million by 1974/75, and then more than doubled during the next two years. However, industrial production fell in 1977/78, dropping excises back to £S48.2 million.

Partly as a result of its ethnically-varied population, the Sudan has stressed since independence, at least on paper, governmental decentralization. This has left some tax raising authority in provincial and other local government hands. Some data for the 1950s and 1960s are available and are summarized in *Tables 8.15* and *8.16*[12]. As can be seen, local governments collect most of the property taxes levied in the Sudan, but their receipts have not amounted to much – some £S2.1 million in 1957/58 and about £S5.35

Table 8.13 *(continued)*

1970/71	1971/72	1972/73	1973/74	1974/75	1975/76	1976/77	1977/78
15.1	17.8	20.3	21.6	31.0	32.4	40.8	50.2
9.9	11.4	12.0	10.8	11.3	10.1	10.9	11.1
14.9	17.7	19.9	21.4	30.6	31.9	40.1	48.2
0.2	0.1	0.4	0.2	0.4	0.5	1.7	2.0
98.1	106.0	116.8	140.4	198.3	223.3	244.8	323.8
64.6	68.0	69.3	70.4	72.3	69.8	65.6	71.8
51.3	52.7	56.7	66.1	116.3	138.3	122.7	150.1
34.5	36.3	37.6	53.1	67.3	72.8	98.0	110.3
12.3	17.0	22.5	21.2	14.7	12.2	24.1	63.4
38.6	28.3	31.6	37.6	45.1	64.1	87.1	77.0
25.4	18.2	18.7	18.8	16.4	20.9	23.5	17.1
151.8	155.8	168.7	199.6	274.4	319.8	373.3	451.0

million in 1969/70. While the national property tax is assessed against the income of rental property, the local taxes are mostly the traditional Islamic *zakat* or *'ushr* (tithe) dues (discussed in Chapter 5) paid only by Muslims. Unlike the Yemen Arab Republic, for which we also have some relatively detailed *zakat* data, the more religiously diverse Sudan has not relied much on these Quranic levies[13]. From the limited official figures available, it seems that the central government has been looking for other means to finance local government[14]. In a short experiment in the early 1960s, 85 percent of the profits of the important sugar monopoly were directly earmarked for local government. Later in the 1960s, fees charged for locally provided services and taxes on houses became more important.

The Sudan employs a fairly steeply progressive schedule in determining both income and profits tax obligations. The large exemption, £S400 on individual income leaves most Sudanese without obligations in this regard. On the next £S200 of wages and salaries, the rate charged is only 5 percent, then 10 percent on the next £S400, 15 percent on the next £S1000, and so on until the maximum rate of 60 percent is applied to income in excess of £S10 000. Income from business profits and rents is subject to the same initial exemption and maximum rate, but the incremental structure of the schedule is slightly different. In theory, this results in lower tax obligations

Table 8.14 *Major taxes: Sudan (1952/53–1977/78) (millions of pounds)*

	1952/53	*1958/59*	*1964/65*	*1970/71*	*1977/78*
Income taxes	–	–	0.2	5.4	48.2
Profits taxes	1.7	1.6	3.7	9.5	
Property taxes	0.4	0.3	0.1	0.2	2.0
Import duties	5.2	10.3	25.9	51.3	150.1
Export taxes	5.9	2.6	5.1	8.2	12.3
Excise taxes	0.5	2.6	5.1	26.3	48.2
Stamp duties	–	–	–	1.2	2.7
Government service fees	NA	5.3	5.7	8.6	11.5
Government enterprises:					
Sugar monopoly	1.4	7.8	11.0	18.7	26.3
Agricultural schemes	7.8	1.9	3.4	9.0	35.8
Nationalized companies	–	–	–	9.9	

Note: NA indicates data not available.

Source: See *Table 8.13.*

on wage and salary earners as opposed to businessmen and landlords. For example, the effective tax rate on £S500 of wages or salary is 1 percent, but if the income derives from business activity, it is levied at 3 percent; at the £S1000 level the effective rates are 5 and 11.5 percent respectively, and on £S5000 they are 20 and 28.3 percent respectively. Of course, in practice, it is much easier to tax wage and salary earners than merchants for example, and

Table 8.15 *Major sources of revenue for local government: Sudan (1957/58–1973/74) (millions of pounds)*

	1957/58	*1962/63*	*1969/70*	*1973/74*
'Ushr (tithe)	0.38	0.70	1.31	
Zakat				
Land	0.34	0.62	0.93	
Date palms	0.07	0.08		4.90
Animals	0.40	0.69	1.18	
Tribute	0.72	0.39	0	
Housing taxes	0.17	0.31	1.94	
Entertainment excises	0	0.7	0.13	
Local government fees	0	0	3.79	5.80
Sugar monopoly profits[a]	0	8.20	0	0
Total revenues	2.10	11.44	9.28	10.70

Note: [a] 85 percent of the government sugar monopoly's profits went to local government during the period 1961/62 to 1963/64 only.

Source: See *Table 8.13.*

undoubtedly the theoretical disadvantages on business and landowning taxpayers do not weigh heavily in reality.

Corporate profits are also subject to progressive taxes. The first £S1000 is assessed at 25 percent, the next £S9000 at 40 percent, the next £S10 000 at 45 percent, the next £S30 000 at 50 percent, and all profits in excess of £S50 000 at the maximum rate of 60 percent. Like many other developing countries, the Sudan has offered exemptions from profits tax obligations, which can extend for as long as 10 years, to corporations undertaking certain types of enterprises deemed to promote economic development. Tax holidays, also covering some import duties and domestic production excises, have been

Table 8.16 *Local government share of major revenue categories: Sudan (%)*

	1957/58	1962/63	1969/70	1973/74
Property taxes	92.0	96.8	90.6	NA
Excise taxes	0	0.6	0.5	NA
Service fees	0	0	29.2	31.0
Monopoly profits	0	85.0	0	0

Source: See *Table 8.13.*

granted in the industrial, agricultural, transport and tourism sectors, and are particularly aimed at enterprises promoting the use of local resources and the production of commodities which either add to the Sudanese export potential or reduce import requirements.

The performance of the tax structure in supplying the Sudan's fiscal needs can be evaluated, of course, only in conjunction with a full assessment of those needs, which is not possible in this context. However, in the early 1970s, the buoyancy of the structure (that is, the ratio of changes in total tax revenue to changes in gross domestic product) was well under one in value. During this time, many tax rates were increased; thus the elasticity of the tax system as a whole was probably even lower.

8.5 Syria

A minor oil producer and a member of OAPEC but not of OPEC, Syria has until recently been almost entirely dependent on non-oil sources for government revenues, as a comparison between royalty payments and total revenues shown in *Table 8.17* would indicate.

During the 1950 to 1977 period, total revenues grew at an annual average rate of about 13.2 percent, but they mounted more rapidly after oil prices were increased in 1973. From 1973 to 1977, the average rate of growth was nearly 32.5 percent a year, while from 1950 to 1962, it was about 12.3 percent, and from 1962 to 1973 only about 7.7 percent.

Table 8.17 *Tax revenues: Syria (1950/51–1977)*

	1950/51	1954	1958/59	1962/63	1966	1968	1970	1971	1972	1973	1974	1975	1976	1977
Direct taxes														
Total (£S millions)	29.4	38.0	156.2	304.6	263.5	406.1	422.0	430.3	649.9	616.3	917.3	937.5	1295.0	915.0
Percentage of revenues	13.6	15.7	38.7	35.1	25.5	25.8	24.9	26.8	36.1	31.3	23.5	16.7	21.7	15.1
Income taxes	13.0	16.7	32.1	74.9	56.3	91.2	117.5	118.0	149.5	161.0	187.0	217.0	490.0	600.0
Royalties	4.1	7.6	85.7	150.9	125.0	230.0	212.0	220.0	400.0	350.0	608.0	575.0	500.0	–
Property taxes	12.3	13.7	38.4	78.8	82.2	84.9	92.5	92.3	100.4	105.3	122.3	145.5	305.0	315.0
Indirect taxes														
Total (£S millions)	179.2	196.3	239.4	435.6	552.3	689.4	570.1	585.0	628.4	794.0	1296.6	1512.1	1867.7	2411.1
Percentage of revenues	83.1	80.9	59.3	50.2	53.5	43.8	33.7	36.6	34.9	40.3	33.2	26.9	31.3	39.7
Customs duties	45.5	58.0	72.7	176.1	110.3	118.5	135.0	148.0	160.0	195.5	343.0	410.0	735.0	1100.0
Excise, sales and production taxes	93.7	96.7	144.6	221.4	206.9	201.0	252.3	274.4	280.8	313.3	397.5	439.5	678.3	701.5
Miscellaneous indirect taxes	40.0	41.6	22.1	38.1	235.1	369.9	182.8	162.6	187.6	285.2	556.1	662.6	454.4	609.6
State enterprises														
Total (£S millions)	7.1	8.2	7.9	127.1	216.6	479.5	700.1	585.2	521.2	558.5	1688.1	3167.9	2813.8	2741.2
Percentage of revenues	3.2	3.4	2.0	14.7	21.0	30.4	41.3	36.6	29.0	28.4	43.3	56.4	47.2	45.1
Total revenues (£S millions)	215.7	242.5	403.5	867.3	1032.4	1575.0	1692.2	1600.5	1799.5	1968.8	3902.0	5617.5	5976.5	6067.3

Source: Central Bureau of Statistics, *Statistical Abstract.*

As can be seen from both *Tables 8.17* and *8.18*, the returns of state enterprises led this growth. This was partly because of increased government involvement in the oil sector, especially since 1973, and partly a result of the gradual socialization of the economy during the period of Ba'th party dominance since 1963. Before Syria first forsook its capitalist background in 1958, (merging briefly into the United Arab Republic led by Egyptian President Gamal Abd al-Nasr) government enterprises were quite marginal, and their net returns were responsible for only a tiny fraction of government returns. However, during the 1960s, this source quickly climbed to about 25 percent of total revenues, and by the mid 1970s, their share moved to about half of budget receipts, largely as a result of increasing Syrian oil production (see *Table 6.1*).

Table 8.18 *Major taxes: Syria (1950/51–1976) (millions of pounds)*

	1950/51	1956	1964	1970	1976
Income taxes:					
Wages and salaries	3.5	6.4	10.8	18.0	75.0
Business-related	9.5	19.9	36.2	99.5	415.0
Inheritance and gift taxes	–	–	–	3.7	25.0
Oil company taxes and royalties	4.1	56.8	122.0	210.0	500.0
Property taxes:					
Real estate	6.2	9.0	17.8	45.5	100.0
Livestock	6.0	11.3	12.7	15.0	15.0
Capital funds	0.1	0.5	1.1	1.3	5.0
Automobiles	1.8	8.9	23.3	23.0	100.0
Television sets	–	–	1.6	3.7	25.0
Excise taxes:					
Fuel	18.8	20.7	13.3	25.0	100.0
Tobacco	22.5	21.1	37.6	51.8	125.0
Cement	1.8	5.3	12.1	16.0	50.0
Sugar	15.0	7.9	4.9	22.0	35.0
Electricity	1.0	1.6	3.5	5.0	25.0
Alcohol	1.2	1.4	4.2	5.0	10.0
Customs duties	45.5	62.0	82.0	95.0	550.0
Other trade taxes and fees	0.4	0.6	36.1	40.0	185.0
Land transfer and registration fees	4.1	6.7	11.6	15.3	50.0
Agricultural production taxes	21.4	30.6	67.1	73.4	200.0
Stamp duties	6.4	14.5	23.9	33.0	110.0
Court and notary fees	2.4	3.8	6.1	8.5	16.5
Profits of government corporations	–	0.9	7.4	680.0	2790.0

Source: See Table 8.17.

Meanwhile, non-oil related direct taxes have shown fairly strong growth. As a result, unlike many developing countries both in the Middle East and elsewhere, Syria has actually tended to boost its reliance on these levies[15]. Income taxes over 27 years went from £S13 million to £S600 million, climbing at about 15.2 percent a year. Property-related taxes, of which the most important now are those on land, automobiles and television sets, grew by about 12.8 percent a year, and non-oil derived direct taxes as a whole saw an annual average increase of about 14.2 percent. Thus, whereas non-oil direct taxes contributed less than 12 percent in 1950, they showed a relative gain, to about 15 percent, by 1977.

Available income tax data disaggregates levies on wages and salaries from the total, but does not distinguish among the various forms of business related forms of income; whether a merchant's income from a retail shop or a corporation's profits. Business income is by far the most heavily taxed type of income, as *Table 8.18* indicates. However, both wage/salary and business related income tax receipts grew by almost identical rates during the 1970s – at an average of about 26.8 percent a year.

Tax schedules on all types of income have been progressive throughout the period in question. However, for wage and salary income the degree of progressivity has been milder; for example, at least through the mid 1970s, rates began at 4 percent on £S1200 to £S12 000 a year, then rose at 2 percent increments on £S12 000 brackets to a maximum of 12 percent on annual income above £S48 000. The effective tax rates on £S3000, £S20 000 and £S50 000, for example, were about 2.4, 4.6, and 7.1 percent respectively.

For business income and profits, schedule rates rose somewhat more sharply. Again during the mid 1970s, they began at 6 percent of income between £S1500 and £S10 000 and eventually reached a maximum of 36 percent on income over £S750 000. In addition, business establishments were subject to *temettu*, a flat-rate tax assessed on the rental value of the premises that they occupied.

If we look at indirect taxes, on the other hand, we find they underwent a sharp drop in relative importance over the period shown in *Table 8.17*. This is in the face of much enlarged state enterprise returns and came as a result of the fact that indirect taxes grew considerably slower than total revenues, at about 10.1 percent a year. Customs duties, the largest source of indirect taxes in the mid 1970s, climbed at a somewhat faster rate, at about 12.5 percent a year, but excise and production taxes were increasing at only about 7.7 percent a year. Among the excises, those likely to have been hitting hardest at the poorest classes (tobacco, sugar and salt), became relatively less important over time. Tobacco excise revenues grew at only about 6.5 percent over this period, and those on sugar showed annual increases averaging only about 3.2 percent. Salt excises, first imposed in the early 1960s, at slightly less than half the rate on sugar, were withdrawn within five years and have never been reimposed.

One indirect tax, that on agricultural production, is rather similar in intent to a direct tax – that on income – which is particularly difficult to collect in the agricultural sector of most developing countries. This tax grew more rapidly (about 9 percent a year) than other major Syrian indirect taxes, but still quite a bit less quickly than the income taxes aimed mostly at urban dwellers. In 1950 agricultural production taxes raised about 50 percent more revenue than income taxes, but by the late 1970s they were responsible for only about a third of the amount of money brought in by income taxes. Another shift tending to favor the agricultural sector can be seen in the property taxes on urban real estate and livestock, each of which brought in about £6 million in 1950 (*Table 8.18*). But the former grew by about 11.3 percent a year over the period in question, while the latter increased by only about 3.6 percent annually, and had become quite minor in Syria's fiscal picture by the late 1970s.

A clarification concerning oil revenues is necessary. The figures shown for royalties in *Table 8.17* comprise mostly pipeline transit dues through the late 1960s. As Syrian oil production increased (see *Table 6.1*) and especially after the increase in world prices, then the sale of domestic oil became a more important money earner than the transit of Iraqi or Saudi Arabian oil. However, by the mid 1970s, these revenues were mostly reported as the earnings of state enterprises, prominent among which is a publicly owned oil company. This should be kept in mind when comparisons are made between Syria and any of the other oil exporters for which oil revenues are still reported under the category of royalties.

Table 8.19 *Municipal fiscal revenues: Syria (1955–1976) (millions of Syrian pounds)*

	1955	1963	1971	1976
Taxes collected through central government	8.2	28.7	48.4	169.2
Taxes collected by municipalities	14.7	12.2	24.2	
Municipal department fees	4.9	3.7	21.0	178.5
Miscellaneous revenues	13.0	5.6	24.6	43.8
Total revenues	40.8	50.2	118.2	391.5

Source: See *Table 8.17.*

In addition to the central government, Syrian municipalities have limited taxing authority, as well as the revenues deriving from locally provided services. As can be seen from *Table 8.19*, their total revenues rose from about £S40.8 million in 1955 to more than £S391 million by 1976, slightly more slowly than central government revenues did during the same period. However, a significant share of municipal revenues were actually transfers from the central government; about 20 percent had this origin in the mid 1950s, and this fraction climbed to more than 50 percent over the next decade, before slipping back somewhat in the early 1970s. Though disaggregated data as to the origin of municipal taxes by collecting agency (local or central governments) are not available for recent years, it seems that municipalities were probably collecting about £S300 million of what is shown in *Table 8.19* during the mid 1970s.

8.6   Yemen Arab Republic

Until very recently, the Yemen Arab Republic (North Yemen) has been almost at the very bottom of the world list of countries as far as per capita income was concerned. Clearly the Middle East's poorest country, North Yemen's bare subsistence economy, even as recently as the early 1970s, could yield very little in tax receipts to support even the current budget of the government, to say nothing of modest economic development efforts.

Nevertheless, largely by virtue of its proximity to Saudi Arabia, since 1973 North Yemen has undergone an economic boom unprecedented in its history. Though estimates vary widely, as many as 1.25 million of the country's 5.5 million inhabitants have sought and found employment in nearby oil producing countries. These emigrants have sent much of their earnings back home to their families, and this had pushed North Yemen's GNP from about $550 million in 1972 to $2130 million by 1977, or, in per capita terms, from about $90 to about $390. This represents a growth (per capita) of more than 34 percent, on average, per annum over this 5 year period.

Of course, remittances by themselves, even to this extent, will do little to alter the basic structure of an economy[16]. North Yemen, shorn of a large part of its adult male labor force, probably produces even less now in its still predominantly agricultural economy than it did in the early 1970s. But still, as the country's fiscal structure has been traditionally dependent on trade-related taxes (see *Table 8.20*), government revenues have grown apace with GNP. Increased remittances have added to the purchasing power of the emigrants' families, which has mostly increased Yemeni demands for imported goods. For example, imports went from $80 million in 1972 to $1040 million by 1977; on the other hand, the country's meagre exports barely changed, going from $4 million to $11 million.

On the fiscal side, import duties and other consumption excises have moved up with purchasing power and imports. These two categories accounted for about 71.9 percent of North Yemen's less than 25 million *rials* in tax receipts in 1966/67 and for about 71.7 percent 11 years later, when total receipts had grown more than 75 fold. Customs duties grew at an annual average rate of about 49.6 percent during this period, while excises multiplied somewhat more slowly – by about 38.2 percent a year. Not only did the amount raised in this manner grow, but the variety of excises imposed (some of which are listed in *Table 8.21*) proliferated during this decade. In 1966/67, even the major excise tax, which was levied on motor vehicles, brought in well under one million *rials*; by 1977/78, though, the same levy was responsible for almost 26 million *rials*, and the new excise on petroleum raised even more.

Table 8.20 shows that indirect taxes have continued to dominate the Yemen Arab Republic's fiscal profile, rarely failing to be responsible for

Table 8.20 Tax revenues: Yemen Arab Republic (1966/67–1977/78)

	1966/67	1968/69	1970/71	1971/72	1972/73	1973/74	1974/75	1975/76	1976/77	1977/78
Direct taxes										
Total (millions of *rials*)	2.66	6.1	9.1	13.5	15.8	33.1	31.0	44.3	47.0	133.3
Percentage of revenues	10.8	11.8	9.3	8.9	7.9	12.0	8.2	7.8	6.0	7.0
Income taxes	0.02	0.1	1.8	2.6	2.9	16.1	15.0	21.2	21.0	96.4
Property taxes	2.64	6.0	7.3	10.9	12.9	17.0	16.0	23.1	26.0	36.9
Indirect taxes										
Total (millions of *rials*)	21.35	41.4	84.8	130.3	170.5	225.5	309.7	480.9	677.5	1492.1
Percentage of revenues	86.9	79.8	87.0	86.1	85.6	81.9	81.6	85.2	86.7	78.5
Customs duties	15.48	25.6	52.7	80.3	113.0	155.4	222.2	394.0	492.4	1303.4
Excise, sales and production taxes	2.17	5.2	11.5	19.6	26.5	37.3	47.2	59.3	94.2	66.1
Other indirect taxes	3.70	10.6	20.6	30.4	31.0	32.8	40.3	27.6	90.9	122.6[a]
State enterprises										
Total (millions of *rials*)	0.55	4.5	3.6	7.5	12.7	16.6	38.9	39.3	56.7	276.3[a]
Percentage of revenues	2.2	8.7	3.7	5.0	6.4	6.0	10.2	7.0	7.3	14.5
Total revenues (millions of *rials*)	24.56	51.9	97.5	151.3	199.0	275.2	379.6	564.5	781.2	1901.7

Note: [a] Certain government returns included in other indirect taxes through 1976/77 are included in state enterprises in 1977/78.

Sources: Central Bank of Yemen, *Annual Report*; Planning Board, *Statistical Yearbook*.

about 5 of every 6 *rials* in tax receipts during the last decade. Direct taxes have actually declined in relative importance, growing somewhat more slowly (about 42.7 percent a year) than total revenues (about 48.7 percent a year).

Despite the obviously minor role played by direct taxes, data available for North Yemen offer an opportunity to examine some traditional Islamic forms of taxation. If *Tables 8.20* and *8.21* are compared, it can be seen than most of the property taxes are actually *zakat*. In fact, until quite recently

Table 8.21 *Major taxes: Yemen Arab Republic (1966/67–1977/78) (millions of rials)*

	1966/67	*1971/72*	*1977/78*
Income tax	0.02	2.6	39.6
Profits tax	–	–	56.8
Zakat	2.64	10.86	32.5
Rental property tax	–	0.2	4.4
Import duties and surtaxes	13.96	72.6	950.2
Foreign trade fees	1.52	7.8	353.5
Excise taxes:			
Fuel	–	12.9	39.3
Automobiles	0.88	2.6	25.9
Tobacco	–	–	4.6
Services	–	–	0.7
Stamp duties	–	–	61.3
Government service fees	3.70	22.3	61.3

Source: See *Table 8.21.*

(after commercial and industrial profits tax was imposed in 1973/74), *zakat* accounted for almost all the receipts categorized as direct taxes. Though the importance of *zakat* has declined from about 10.7 percent of all receipts in 1966/67 to about 1.7 percent by 1977/78, its own composition has not changed much during this period (see *Table 8.22*).

The three major categories of wealth subject to *zakat* under the broadest Islamic interpretations – livestock, gold, and silver (i.e., wealth) and agricultural produce – are all represented in North Yemeni receipts[17]. As previously indicated, assessments on livestock depend upon both the number and type of animals. *Zakat* on wealth under Yemeni practice exempts the first 20 *dinars* in gold and the first 200 ounces of silver; the remainder is subject to a 2.5 percent annual levy. Agricultural produce is subject to *zakat* at the rate of 10 percent if it is from rainfed land, but at only 5 percent if it is grown on irrigated land. In other words, the more the crop is dependent upon the bounty of God rather than on the labor of man, then the greater amount that must be returned to the common weal. It is believed that much of the *zakat* collected by local officials is in kind, rather than cash, and that the true amount reported in national fiscal accounts may, therefore, represent considerable underreporting.

The last major category of fiscal receipts shown in *Table 8.20*, state enterprises, shows more than a 100 fold increase over the decade in question, and a significant leap in relative importance from 3.2 to 7.3 percent of total revenues. However, this is not a result of major structural changes within

Table 8.22 *Composition of zakat: Yemen Arab Republic (1966/67–1977/78) (millions of rials)*

	1966/67		1977/78	
	(m. rials)	*(%)*	*(m. rials)*	*(%)*
Agricultural produce	1.65	62.5	23.2	71.4
Livestock	0.18	6.8	3.6	11.0
Wealth	0.24	9.1	2.2	6.8
Poll tax	0.58	22.0	3.5	10.8

Source: See *Table 8.21.*

the North Yemeni economy (for instance, in the direction of increased government ownership) as nearly all these revenues represent rents from government properties, and these earnings have grown particularly rapidly as emigrant remittances have vitalised the domestic economy.

Though North Yemen is a poor country, its tax effort must be rated as being rather low. As *Table 6.4* shows, its citizens bear the lightest tax burden in the region – only about five sixths that of the Sudanese, whose per capita GNP is below Yemeni levels. Only about 20 percent of Yemeni GNP went to the government in the form of taxes (*Table 6.2*), despite the relative boom in the nation's economy in recent years[18]. The rather desultory efforts of Yemeni officials to raise this share significantly probably results from the ample foreign economic assistance the country has been receiving – since 1974, this funding has matched or exceeded internal tax collections.

This low level of tax effort can be seen if we look at the tax schedules for assessing personal income and corporate profits taxes. Though in both cases the rate structures are progressive, the maximum tax levels are well below those employed in neighboring countries. For example, the first 1800 *rials* of taxable annual wage or salary income is assessed at 3 percent, the next 1800 at 6 percent, the next 1800 at 9 percent, the next 1800 at 12 percent, and all such income in excess of 7200 *rials* is taxed at a 15 percent rate. Most business corporations pay 7 percent of the first 7500 *rials* of taxable profits, then 10, 15 and 20 percent of successive 7500 *rial* increments, until a maximum rate of 25 percent is levied on all profits in excess of 30 000 *rials* a year[19].

The argument can be made with some validity that, given the general difficulty that developing countries have in collecting anything even close to the amounts theoretically due under income and profits tax laws, North Yemen, in its first efforts to use such taxes, might as well impose low rates and thus encourage less tax avoidance. However, as most income taxes are paid by wage and salary employees who mostly work for the government or larger corporations, these taxpayers have only a limited ability to avoid paying what is due. Similarly, most profits tax receipts come from a few large and middle sized firms, often state or foreign owned: again, therefore, they are not likely to be able to avoid what is due on their taxable profits.

Thus, while the low tax rates used in North Yemen may result in less inequity being imposed on those individual and corporate taxpayers who cannot easily avoid income and profits levies, it also means less revenue accruing to the state. The difficulty in collecting these taxes in developing countries is not such a good argument for low tax rates. Rather the need is for better enforcement over the long run of tax legislation or for the imposition of taxes which are designed to fall on those who escape the burden of income taxes (for example, licence fees for merchants or production excises for agricultural land owners).

It is also probably naive to assume that relatively less tax avoidance occurs in North Yemen because of the low rates which are imposed. In the absence of specific evidence to the contrary, it seems more reasonable to assume that a North Yemeni merchant, for example, will manage to avoid a similar share of his theoretical tax bill whether the applicable effective rate is 10 percent or 30 percent.

8.7 People's Democratic Republic of Yemen

Until a few years ago, only the relative prosperity of the port of Aden kept the present People's Democratic Republic of Yemen (PDRY or South Yemen) from being the poorest state in the Middle East, slightly ahead of the neighboring Yemen Arab Republic. But the construction of bigger tankers and the closure of the Suez Canal after the Israeli invasion of Egypt in 1967 sorely diminished activities in Aden's harbour and refinery, while North Yemen has enjoyed something of an economic boom since the early 1970s. Despite major adversities, the PDRY had expanded from an estimated GNP of $152 million in 1967 to about $580 million by 1977, or, in per capita terms, from about $130 to some $320. But much of this growth has been more apparent than real. Since gaining independence in 1967, South Yemen has undergone major economic turmoil and is now generally regarded as the Arab world's only Marxist economy. These changes, coupled with external effects, have caused considerable inflation. According to recent World Bank estimates[20], real GNP per capita declined by about 5.2 percent a year over the 1960–1976 period, and by even more, 6.6 percent, from 1970 to 1976.

Table 8.23 *Tax revenues: Yemen People's Democratic Republic (1951/1952–1978)*

	1951/52	1957/58	1962/63	1968/69	1970/71	1971/72	1972/73	1973/74	1974/75	1975[c]	1976	1977	1978
Direct taxes													
Total (millions of *dinars*)	0.68	0.94	1.51	2.00	2.90	3.76	2.47	3.17	4.87	4.14	7.59	9.03	9.74
Percentage of revenues	31.7	23.3	27.8	25.7	27.8	23.5	20.5	20.7	26.4	29.9	29.5	25.9	22.4
Income taxes	0.66	0.90	1.46	2.00	2.90	3.76	2.47	3.17	4.87	4.14	7.59	9.03	9.74
Property taxes	0.02	0.04	0.05	NA	NA	NA	NA	NA	NA	NA	NA	NA	NA
Indirect taxes													
Total (millions of *dinars*)	1.04	1.93	3.92	3.13	3.99	7.77	6.57	8.55	9.84	7.11	12.09	19.75	22.71
Percentage of revenues	48.6	47.8	72.2	40.2	38.4	48.6	54.5	55.7	53.3	51.3	47.0	55.2	55.2
Customs duties				2.07	2.40	5.87	4.40	5.28	5.69	3.85	6.35	11.37	13.41
Excise, sales and production taxes	0.30	0.71	1.62	0.71	0.90	1.07	1.40	2.31	3.07	2.78	4.81	6.57	7.83
Other indirect taxes	0.74[c]	1.22[b]	2.30	0.35	0.69	0.83	0.77	0.96	1.08	0.48	0.93	1.31	1.47
State enterprises													
Total (millions of *dinars*)	0.40	1.13	—[a]	2.65	3.50	4.46	3.01	3.62	3.76	2.61	6.03	6.61	11.03
Percentage of revenues	18.7	28.0	—[a]	34.1	33.6	27.9	25.0	23.6	20.4	18.8	23.5	18.9	25.4
Total revenues (millions of *dinars*)	2.16[b]	4.04[b]	5.43	7.78	10.40	15.99	12.06	15.34	18.47	13.86	25.71	34.89	43.48

Notes: NA indicates data not separately available.
[a] Included in other indirect taxes.
[b] Includes estimates of Aden Protectorate revenues.
[c] April to December only.

Sources: PDRY Central Bank, *Annual Report*; Aden Colony, *Aden Report*.

As can be seen from *Table 8.23*, South Yemen tax revenues have grown at a much more modest rate than those of its neighbors, even when compared to its northern twin which is also not an oil producer. Total revenues increased annually by about 19.3 percent on average over the period from 1951/52 to 1978. Most of this growth, however, came after 1974/75, as revenues more than doubled over the four subsequent years. In addition, until the end of 1975, South Yemen's tax revenues tended to oscillate back and forth, showing no clear upward trend over several years. This together with the low level of receipts prevailing during the period (an average of 15.1 million *dinars* or about $42 million annually from 1970/71 to 1975) provided few resources for the South Yemeni government to devote to economic development.

South Yemen's basic fiscal problem has been its general lack of a tax base. In the fiscal year 1966/67, the last before its independence, total internal revenues were some 9.7 million *dinars*, but this was more than matched by a British subsidy of 12.3 million *dinars*. After independence, the subsidy ceased, and, as indicated above, the closing of the Suez Canal cut sharply into domestic taxes.

Table 8.24 *Tax revenues: Aden Colony and Protectorate (thousands of pounds)*

	1951/52	1957/58
Aden Colony[a]	1703.8	3304.1
Western Aden Protectorate	117.0	111.4
Eastern Aden Protectorate	337.6	623.2

Note: [a] Exclusive of British subsidies.

Source: Aden Colony, *Aden Report.*

As *Table 8.23* shows, indirect taxes have generally accounted for more than half of South Yemen's total fiscal receipts, but the country's relative reliance on taxes of this sort has been less overwhelming than that of many of its neighbors. The reporting systems employed before and after independence cause certain problems in making comparisons. For example, only the city of Aden and its immediate surroundings comprised Aden Colony, for which rather detailed fiscal data are available prior to the mid 1960s. The rest of the country consisted of technically independent sheikhdoms (with a status like that of the erstwhile Trucial Coast), which were British protectorates. Though each sheikhdom had its influential British resident, the metropole's impact did not extend to such matters as tax collection and accounting procedures and reports. Thus, a detailed breakdown of the categories under which the protectorates revenues were collected is not available[21]; and as *Table 8.24* indicates, they received much less revenue in the 1950s than did Aden Colony. With the end of British rule, tax receipts and accounts were merged, and post-independence data are national in scope by major tax category.

If we examine South Yemen's fiscal situation on a somewhat more disaggregated basis (*Table 8.25*), it is clear that most major individual taxes have been subject to oscillations similar to those seen for total revenues. One exception during the mid 1970s has been the profits tax – that is, the levies on the increasingly publicly owned business sector. This has come to rival excise taxes as second in importance only to import duties, accounting for about one sixth of all government revenues. In addition, the after tax profits of publicly owned business also accrue to the state, but most of those have been reinvested.

Table 8.25 *Major taxes: People's Democratic Republic of Yemen (1951/52–1978) (millions of dinars)*

	1951/52	1962/63	1968/69	1974/75	1978
Income taxes	0.66	1.46	1.00	1.09	2.54
Profits taxes	–	–	1.00	3.79	7.21
Import duties	{ 0.30	1.62	{ 2.07	5.69	13.41
Excise taxes: total	}		{ 0.71	3.07	7.83
(Tobacco)	(NA)	(0.40)	(NA)	(1.22)	(4.35)
(Gasoline)	(0.07)	(0.45)	(NA)	(0.96)	(1.10)
(Alcohol)	(NA)	(0.30)	(NA)	(NA)	(NA)
(Qat)	(0.03)	(0.28)	(NA)	(0.47)	(0.91)
Stamp duties	–	–	–	0.53	1.47

Note: NA indicates data not available.

Source: See *Table 8.23.*

Before independence, no profits taxes were levied, most locally consumed items entered the country duty free, and excises were generally quite low. After independence, South Yemen was thrown on its own meagre resources, and taxes in each of these categories had to be introduced or raised. Direct taxes on incomes however have fallen sharply in relative importance, from about 20 percent of total revenues just before independence to less than 5 percent in 1975. The major payers of incomes taxes a decade ago were foreigners and the wealthier local residents, mainly merchants; the former have emigrated and the latter have been coopted into South Yemen's socialist economy. Most Yemenis, especially those in agriculture, remain outside the reach of effective income tax collections.

Profits taxes, at a flat rate of 37.5 percent are levied on the net profits of both private and state corporations. The Encouragement of Investment Law of 1971 allowed certain enterprises exemptions from the profits tax of 3 to 8 years, but the increasingly socialistic orientation of the government has generally halted private investment in most sectors eligible for benefits under this law.

Personal income taxes are steeply progressive. After exemptions, taxable income from private business activity, for example, is subject to a 10 percent levy on the first 200 *dinars* of annual income, 12 percent on the next 200 *dinars*, 20 percent on the next 400 *dinars*, and so on until 75 percent of all income in excess of 10 000 *dinars* is due the government. Wage and salary taxable income is exempt up to 282 *dinars* a year, then 5 percent of that between 283 and 300 *dinars*, 7.5 percent of that between 301 and 361 *dinars*, and so on through 47.5 percent of that above 2400 *dinars* must be paid. Though business derived income is, in theory, taxed more heavily (for example, the effective tax rate on 500 *dinars* a year is 14 percent if the income is business derived and only 4.4 percent if it is from wages), it is of course much easier for the government to collect income taxes from wage and salary workers.

Agriculture and fishing are subject to production excises, which spread some of the tax load to these two traditional sectors where it would be nearly impossible to collect income taxes from the labor force. Levies of 10 to 15 percent are placed on agricultural products and of 10 percent on fish catches.

Notes

1 For a discussion of Egyptian land reform, see H. Askari and J. T. Cummings, *Middle East Economies in the 1970s: A Comparative Approach*, Chapter 4.

2 The authors, along with James Toth, have discussed this situation in some detail in Agrarian Reform: A Model and the Middle Eastern Experience, *L'Egypte Contemporaine*, (July 1978).

3 This phenomenon has been elsewhere discussed by the authors in some detail; cf op. cit. (note. 1) Chapter 6.

4 In addition, duties on automobiles are a major portion of customs receipts.

5 Luc DeWulf, First-Order Effect of the Tax Payments by Income Class, the Case of Lebanon 1968, *Proche Orient, Etudes Economiques*, No. 74 (September–December 1972), p. 533, and Taxation and Income Distribution in Lebanon, *Bulletin for International Fiscal Documentation*, Vol. 28 (April 1974), p. 151.

6 It should be kept in mind that civil war has not only restricted government ability to collect income taxes, it has also obviously reduced personal incomes and corporate profits, and thus even if the fiscal

authorities were able to operate normally, they would be assessing a shrinking tax base.

7 The Lebanese Parliament has continued to meet during the civil war and has made numerous legislative changes, some of them (on paper at least) representing major social and economic reforms. Thus, major shifts in official tax policies could well have occurred since 1974 and these changes would effect budget planners in their estimates of tax receipts.

8 International Monetary Fund figures published in the *International Financial Statistics* indicate estimates of imports of £L1646 million in 1976, £L4373 million in 1977 and £L4640 million in 1978. Since these estimates are derived in part from the export reports of Lebanon's trading partners, they account at least partially for the evasion problems that have plagued official Lebanese data sources since 1975.

9 See Askari and Cummings, op. cit. (note. 1). The authors are also preparing a more detailed monograph on the future of the Middle Eastern food supply, in which the Sudan plays an obviously central role.

10 Taken from Adel Amin Beshai, *Export Performance and Economic Development in Sudan 1900–1967*, (London: Ithaca Press, 1976), p. 250.

11 Until the early 1970s nearly all sugar was imported, and the sugar monopoly was the sole authorized importer and distributor.

12 Since the conclusion of the Sudan's long and bitter civil war between the Arabized (and Isamicized) north and the black and more tribalized south in the early 1970s, decentralization has become even greater. However, the available disaggregated data do not refer to this recent period.

13 The 'tribute' tax shown in *Table 8.4*, which in 1957/58 was the most important local tax, was apparently phased out during the 1960s, dropping from £S392 000 in 1961/62 to £S218 000 in 1963/64, £S246 000 in 1964/65, £S51 000 in 1966/67 and £S18 000 in 1967/68. This tax (in Arabic, *al-jizyah*) was codified into modern Sudanese tax law in 1901, shortly after the Anglo-Egyptian reconquest of the Sudan. It was a combination of several other religiously based taxes (*'ushr, zakat* on land and animals, and the poll tax) and was assessed on a *tribal* rather than an individual basis, on all *bedouin* within the national borders. The condominium era also saw a poll tax (begun in 1925) levied almost exclusively upon the non-Muslim southern provinces. Its basic purpose, while not religious, did parallel existing traditional levies on Muslim-owned land and livestock, (subject to *'ushr* and *zakat*); in addition, it had the intention of drawing tribal populations into the cash economy. After Sudanese independence, this poll tax was rapidly phased out of existence. The housing taxes shown in *Table 8.15* have no particularly religious basis but were levied against most *urban* structures (mostly to pay for *urban* services) after 1899, at a rate approximating 8.5 percent of a structure's rental value. For further details, see A. A. Beshai, *Export Performance and Economic Development in Sudan 1900–1967* (London: Middle East Centre, St. Anthony's College, Ithaca Press, 1976).

14 Additional revenues are transferred to the local governments from the national budget; these are not shown in any tables.

15 Note when comparing Syria with other minor and major oil producers, we have included the bulk of oil generated revenues under direct taxes (royalties and oil company profits taxes) rather than under state enterprises. Published Syrian statistical series make it difficult to group all oil revenues together for recent years.

16 See John C. Swanson, Some Consequences of Emigration for Rural Economic Development in the Yemen Arab Republic, *Middle East Journal* (Winter 1979).

17 The poll tax, listed under *zakat*, is not *jizyah*, mentioned above as the levy on non-Muslims, very few of which live in the Yemen Arab Republic. Rather, it has been a general custom in Islamic countries not to remove the levies represented by *jizyah* just because an individual converts to Islam, lest conversion be tainted by pecuniary motives (incidentally, to the detriment of the state). A poll or head tax, similar in amount to the *jizyah* initially imposed at the time of a region's conquest or accession to Islam, has frequently continued to be used after the Islamicization of the region.

18 The sharp rise in government revenues in 1977/78 resulted in an increase in the government revenues to GNP ratio from about 10.5 percent to about 20 percent. Most of this was due to increased customs receipts on imports, which rose more than 150 percent from 1976 to 1977.

19 Companies granted some type of government concession, such as a monopoly, are subject to slightly higher tax rates across the board and to a maximum rate of 35 percent. Furthermore, like other neighboring countries, North Yemen encourages business investment by offering certain exemptions from taxation. The Investment of Foreign and National Capital Law of 1975, in order to promote the use of locally available resources and the production of import substitutes, grants qualifying enterprises in industry, agriculture, mining and tourism, holidays for up to 5 years from profits taxes and production excises and for up to 8 years from certain import duties.

20 *World Bank Atlas 1978*.

21 All protectorates revenues are included in *Table 8.23* under the heading 'other indirect taxes'.

PART IV

Analysis of taxation policies

Econometric study of Middle East taxation

We have reviewed in the earlier chapters both the recent fiscal history of the Middle East and the basic structure of fiscal systems as they operate in developing countries. If we are to determine how this group of countries uses the tax mechanism, both as a means of raising revenue and as a tool of economic policy, we must now examine matters further. Chapter 9 will, therefore, discuss briefly the recent literature concerning the determinants of the ratio of taxes to gross national product. This is done in preparation for developing and applying an econometric model to a sample of developing countries which includes the 16 countries examined in the last two chapters. The model will relate the tax ratio to three independent variables: general level of economic development; degree of 'openness' of the national economy to the world at large; and the sectoral composition of the national economy.

9.1   General considerations and background

The amount of taxes collected in a developing country depends not only upon the structure of the tax system and the degree to which fiscal legislation is enforced, but also upon various characteristics of the economy which may influence both the level and the type of taxes which may be collected. A country with an insignificant foreign trade sector, for instance, could hardly expect to generate substantial revenue from customs duties even if high rates were imposed, because of the small size of the tax base. Such considerations are of particular interest when examining the Middle East countries included in the present study as nine of the 16 countries export petroleum. These oil exporting countries, as discussed in Chapter 7, tend to rely on oil-based taxes for a significant portion of government revenues. Of course, the average developing country does not enjoy such bountiful reserves of a mineral resource so vital to the world economy. Under these circumstances, much of the development literature dealing with fiscal policy may not be of particular relevance to the Middle East.

In recent years, several cross-sectional studies of national tax ratios (defined as the ratio of tax revenue to GNP) have been published. These studies have tried to relate the tax ratio to a number of measurable economic factors that may affect the ability of the population to pay taxes on the one hand, and on the other, to the ease with which public authorities can collect taxes. Economic variables are not the sole determinants of tax ratios, but the contribution of other elements (such as the degree of tax evasion, competence of assessors, forms of government and various sociopolitical characteristics) has not been considered generally because of the difficulty in obtaining satisfactory data. We will not provide a detailed review of these studies[1], but a brief discussion is necessary in order to provide a basis for describing our model.

The statistical studies have generally used simple or multiple regression on a sample of countries: this is in order to measure the degree of variation in the tax ratios that can be explained by the economic factors contained in a particular model. The studies differ in the number of countries included and the years of coverage, yet all attempt to obtain the best statistical fit by including as many explanatory factors as possible in order to increase the explained variance in the tax ratios (as measured by the value of the statistic R^2). The models contain many different combinations of explanatory variables, but virtually all include some measure of per capita income as an indicator of the level of economic development.

In one of the earliest attempts to determine the relationship between the tax ratio and the stage of development, Williamson fitted an exponential function to data from 33 developed and developing countries. He found a significant positive relationship between the tax ratio and the level of per capita income which served as a proxy measure for the level of development[2]. The positive direction of the relationship (i.e., the tax ratio increases as per capita income increases) is not surprising given the argument, advanced in Chapter 2, that a higher level of development generally provides a greater taxable surplus.

Later studies which have replaced Williamson's exponential function with linear multiple regression models have generally increased the size of the samples, and have been limited to developing countries. These later studies have also attempted to increase the explained variance by adding as explanatory variables a number of economic factors which could reasonably be expected, on *a priori* grounds, to affect the tax ratio of a country.

For example, in his study of 20 developing countries, Plasschert included two independent variables: per capita income as a proxy for the level of development, and the ratio of imports to GNP as a measure of the foreign trade tax base. His results indicated a significant relationship between the tax ratio and the import ratio, but the per capita income variable lost its statistical significance (at the standard 0.05 level) when used in conjunction with the import ratio[3]. Similarly, Hinrichs, in his study of 40 developing countries (all with per capita incomes below \$400 in the early 1960s), found that the import ratio rather than per capita income was the significant determinant in explaining the variations in the ratio of government tax revenue to gross national product[4]. On the other hand, a study by Thorn of

32 countries differs, in that he found per capita income to be a significant determinant of the tax ratio while the import ratio was insignificant[5]. Thorn's results suggest that a model which incorporates only per capita income and the import ratio as independent variables is not very useful; the statistical properties of the model seem to be unduly dependent upon the particular group of countries selected.

In their first paper on tax ratio analysis, Lotz and Morss used the ratio of the sum of imports and exports to GNP to measure the potential foreign trade tax base. For a sample of 52 developing countries, they found both this ratio and per capita income to be significant, but the degree of explained variance (that is, R^2) was fairly low[6]. In a later paper[7], the same authors attempted to increase the explained variance by including aditional explanatory variables. The addition of the monetization ratio (that is, per capita money supply) resulted in a substantial increase in the explained variance, but reduced the role of per capita income to a point of insignificance; a highly collinear relationship between per capita income and the monetarization ratio was indicated for their sample. Lotz and Morss also tried measures of export composition and the degree of government centralization as explanatory variables, but they were unable to increase substantially the explained variance.

Most studies of the determinants of the tax ratio have included only those factors that would influence the tax ratio through their effects on the capacity of the populace to pay the tax levies or the ability of the government to collect them. On the other hand, those factors which determine the demand for tax revenue, such as the preferences of the people or government for public or private services, are not generally taken into account. Among the industrialized countries, for instance, there exists considerable variation in tax ratio due, in part, to differences in the extent to which transfer payments are used for redistributive purposes and in the scope of welfare services provided by governmental institutions. Although such differences on the demand side are not explicitly included in any of the models discussed herein, they must nevertheless be taken into consideration when evaluating the tax system of a particular country.

9.2   The Chelliah tax capacity model

Pursuant to the Lotz–Morss and other statistical studies, Chelliah developed an econometric model relating the tax ratio to several variables which were hypothesized, on *a priori* grounds, to affect the tax capacity of a developing country. Chelliah incorporated three major economic factors which could be expected to influence the tax ratio via their effect on the supply of funds:

(1) the degree of 'openness' of a national economy to the world at large;
(2) the general level of development and income;
(3) the sectoral composition of national income.

Proxy measures for these factors were chosen on the basis of economic theory and the simple correlation between the tax ratio and the various proxy variables. The degree of openness could be expressed in terms of the import ratio, the export ratio, or the total foreign trade ratio (the ratio of imports plus exports to GNP). The export ratio was chosen by Chelliah as the most appropriate measure since large imports of consumer goods, which contribute a substantial portion of revenue for many LDCs, are usually financed through export earnings. In addition, correlation analysis revealed that the tax ratio was more highly correlated with the export ratio than either the import or foreign trade variables.

The tax ratio may be influenced by the level of development since any income above the subsistence level may be viewed as a surplus which is subject to taxation. A high level of per capita income is usually associated with a more advanced degree of development and, therefore, a greater taxable capacity, in line with a higher literacy rate, better organization, and more efficient tax administration. Another possible indicator of the stage of development is the share of national income generated in the agricultural sector. A large agricultural share in gross domestic product is typically associated with lower per capita income, an extensive subsistence sector that has not yet entered into the market economy, and only a small industrial sector. Such conditions are usually indicative of a low tax capacity, particularly as in developing countries it is generally quite difficult to tax the agricultural sector because of relatively inefficient tax administration. Chelliah maintained that, in constructing a tax capacity model, the agricultural sector of the economy should be excluded. He argued that the relative size of the agricultural sector may indicate not only capacity (or ability) to tax, but also the willingness to tax; in this regard, he refers to the fact that many developing countries have found it difficult for political reasons to tax agriculture.

After an examination of the data for a sample 50 countries indicated that mineral production was of major importance in at least six of the ten countries having the highest tax ratio during the 1969–71 period[9], Chelliah contended that the composition of national income affects the tax ratio. He hypothesized that the heavy fixed investment involved in extractive industries and the existence of a few large firms in the mineral sector provides a large tax base that is administratively easy to tax. Correlation analysis also showed that the mining share had a stronger relationship with the tax ratio than did any other variable used in the model. The share of income generated in the domestic manufacturing sector also appeared to affect the tax ratio. Such domestic production generates a tax base and, moreover, the existence of large industrial concerns tends to facilitate the collection of taxes. Correlation analysis, however, indicated there was little measurable relationship between the tax ratio and the share of manufacturing in the national income.

Chelliah's reasoning indicated that an econometric model incorporating tax capacity factors would include: per capita income as a measure of the level of development; the export ratio as an indicator of the degree of openness of the economy; and the share of mining in the economy as a measure of the sectoral composition of national income. The fact that there is an overlap between exports and income caused Chelliah to use per capita nonexport income instead of per capita income. Similarly, he considered the use of export ratio excluding mineral exports to be preferable to the overall export ratio, as minerals often constitute a substantial portion of a country's total exports. Thus, the model tested was represented by the equation:

$$\frac{T}{Y} = a_0 + a_1(Y_p - X_p) + a_2N_y + a_3X_y' \tag{9.1}$$

where T = tax revenue; Y = gross national product; Y_p = per capita GNP; X_p = per capita exports; N_y = share of mining sector in GNP; and X_y' = non-mineral export ratio.

Using least squares regression techniques, Chelliah applied his model with slightly different samples, using in one case 1966–68 data and in another 1969–71 data[10]. The resulting estimates are shown in columns (A) and (B) in *Table 9.1*. As can be seen, only the coefficient of mining's share in GNP had statistical significance (at the 0.05 level), with slightly less than 40 percent of the variance in the tax ratio explained in each case.

Despite the apparently disappointing explanatory performance of his income and export measures (especially for the 1969–71 period), Chelliah nevertheless argued for the retention of these variables in the model on *a priori* grounds. This was despite the fact that versions of his model without

Table 9.1 *Regression results: variations of Chelliah tax capacity model*

Estimated coefficient	Formulation				
	(A)	(B)	(C)	(D)	(E)
$Y_p - X_p$	+0.003 (0.77)	+0.001 (0.38)	−0.001 (0.34)	+0.002 (0.94)	+0.0025 (0.73)
N_y	+0.397 (5.55)	+0.44 (5.45)	+0.407 (5.41)	+0.570 (9.31)	+0.540 (11.30)
X_y'	+0.088 (1.89)	+0.05 (1.17)	+0.194 (3.12)	+0.222 (4.17)	+0.052 (0.86)
Constant	+10.05	+11.47	+9.99	+7.11	+11.32
$\bar{R}^2$	0.393	0.376	0.413	0.581	0.708
n	49	47	47	63	67

Note: Numbers in parentheses are t-statistics.

an income variable gave marginally better statistical results. These variants included the share of agriculture in GNP, which Chelliah felt probably affected the willingness rather than the capacity to tax.

A further updating of Chelliah's survey was carried out in another International Monetary Fund survey[11]. Tait, Gritz, and Eichengreen used 1972–76 data for the same 47 countries; their regression estimates are shown in column (C) of *Table 9.1*. The major difference relative to the earlier periods is the statistical significance found for exports. The proportion of explained variance in tax capacity remains close to 40 percent. The results for all three time periods tested indicated considerable stability for the Chelliah model.

However, neither the regressions shown in *Table 9.1* nor those done with variants of the Chelliah model in these studies yielded any attribution of particularly high explanatory powers of the model for cross-sectional variation in tax capacity. As can be seen, the formulation favored by Chelliah has R^2 values of about 0.40 associated with it. Other regressions had about the same R^2 values; some indicated that as little as 11 percent of variation in the dependent variable was explained. Thus, in this effort, we were concerned first of all with trying to identify a formulation with greater explanatory powers.

Another major consideration related to our basic geographic interest in the Middle East: we wished to test the Chelliah model (and its close variants) as predictors of tax capacity variance in this region. In the earlier studies cited above, only four Middle Eastern countries (Iran, Egypt, Lebanon and Sudan) were included.

Finally, the Tait study also included some regressions run on an expanded sample of 63 countries (see column (D), *Table 9.1*). There results indicated that, if stability was found across time for the same sample it was not necessarily present when the sample was changed.

9.3   A reconstruction of the model

Thus, while we began with Chelliah's basic hypothesis (tax capacity is a function of an economy's openness, level of development, and sectoral composition), we examined specific variables relating to these three factors that differed from Chelliah's variables. We also introduced considerations deemed pertinent to the Middle East, as our expanded sample of 67 countries (see *Table 9.2*) included 19 countries from the region: Algeria, Bahrain, Egypt, Iran, Iraq, Jordan, Kuwait, Lebanon, Libya, Morocco, Oman, Qatar, Saudi Arabia, Sudan, Syria, Tunisia, United Arab Emirates, Yemen Arab Republic and Yemen People's Democratic Republic.

As indicated above, the stability found in the Chelliah regressions on the same sample over time did not seem to hold up when the sample was changed. Before testing any other models, we used equation (9.1) and our sample of 67 countries, with the results shown in column (E) of *Table 9.1*. As can be seen, for this sample, the explanatory power of the Chelliah model is nearly twice what it was in some of the earlier studies. However, most of the model's success continues to depend upon one independent variable, the share of mining in Gross Domestic Product (GDP) (N_y). In fact, when the even simpler equation:

$$\frac{T}{Y} = a_0 + a_1 N_y \tag{9.2}$$

was applied for the 67 country sample, an even higher adjusted value of R^2 was obtained (0.712). Thus, though Chelliah had *a priori* arguments for retaining the income and export variables, the predictive value of his model does not seem to depend upon them to any great extent.

Table 9.2 *Developing countries included in study*

Algeria	Jamaica	Senegal
Argentina	Jordan	Sierra Leone
Bahrain	Kenya	Singapore
Bolivia	Korea	Sri Lanka
Brazil	Kuwait	Sudan
Brunei	Lebanon	Surinam
Burundi	Libya	Syria
Chile	Malaysia	Taiwan
Colombia	Mali	Tanzania
Costa Rica	Mauritania	Thailand
Ecuador	Mexico	Togo
Egypt	Morocco	Trinidad & Tobago
Ethiopia	Nepal	Tunisia
Gabon	Nigeria	Turkey
Ghana	Oman	Uganda
Guatemala	Pakistan	United Arab Emirates
Guyana	Paraguay	Upper Volta
Honduras	Peru	Venezuela
India	Philippines	Yemen Arab Rep.
Indonesia	Qatar	Yemen People's Dem. Rep.
Iran	Rwanda	Zaire
Iraq	Saudi Arabia	Zambia
Ivory Coast		

This sensitivity of the Chelliah model to changes in the size and composition of the sample seems in fact to be explained to a large degree by the fact that the share of mining is the only significant variable. This presents a particular problem relative to our sample. While the average share of mining in GDP is 12.7 percent for the sample as a whole, it is 24.7 percent for the 19 Middle East countries alone, and only 8.2 percent for the non-Middle Eastern component. Thus, the possibility of structural differences between the two subsamples arises if equation (9.1) is used.

Chelliah included the mining share as an explanatory variable because of the high simple correlation between the tax ratio and the mining share. It is questionable, however, whether the mining share is the appropriate proxy measure. The share of mining in GDP does not explicitly represent the ability to tax foreign consumption of mineral production since a country could conceivably utilize a substantial portion of its mineral production for domestic purposes.

Chelliah maintained that the mining industry is relatively easy to tax owing to the presence of a few large firms and the necessity of expensive capital investment for mining operations. A similar argument could be advanced, however, regarding the ease of taxing large financial institutions or large land holdings such as those owned by United brands in Latin America. Yet another problem with the use of the mining share as the sole significant explanatory variable is that the resulting model does not provide policy information to a particular country as to how it could increase its tax ratio, since the country cannot readily change the share of mining in GDP.

Thus for several reasons, we constructed and tested another tax capacity model. It was our hope to improve the predictive value of the regression equation, to include a greater number of explanatory variables that would show statistical significance, and to test for structural differences that might set the Middle Eastern countries apart from other developing regions in this regard.

Following Chelliah, our model includes only those variables that indicate certain fundamental features of a developing economy that could possibly affect the ability of taxpayers to pay taxes or of the public authorities to collect taxes. On the basis of *a priori* reasoning, three broad tax capacity factors were hypothesized to affect the tax ratio:

(1) the general level of development;
(2) the 'openness' of the economy;
(3) the sectoral composition of national income.

The stage of economic development could, as discussed previously in reference to Chelliah's model, be measured by either per capita income (Y_p) or per capita nonexport income ($Y_p - X_p$). The difficulty of collecting taxes in kind may, however, effectively limit the amount of taxes that can be levied on the large subsistence sector found in most LDCs. The degree of monetization may, therefore, have some impact on the level of taxes that can be collected without encountering undue administrative difficulties. Such considerations are often of paramount interest in LDCs since the competence of tax assessors and collectors is often woefully inadequate. Thus, the degree of monetization, which is defined here as the ratio of the money supply (M_2) to the gross national product may be a reasonable measure of the general stage of development. Correlation analysis of the sample 67 countries indicates that there is no significant degree of collinearity between the monetization ratio and either of the income variables (Y_p or $Y_p - X_p$). Thus, if it seems desirable for *a priori* reasons to include both the monetization ratio and one of the income measures in the model, statistical difficulties should not ensue in the estimating procedure.

As indicated above, Chelliah considered three possible indicators for the degree of 'openness' of the economy: the export ratio, the export ratio excluding mineral exports, and the ratio of the sum of imports plus exports to GNP. Alternatively, the tax base of the foreign trade sector in a developing country may be largely determined by the level of imports, since the importation of consumer goods, particularly those of a luxury nature, is often subject to high rates of taxation. Consequently, it was decided to consider a variable indicating the size of this sector relative to GNP.

The foregoing measures of the foreign trade sector do not allow any differentiation for the type of commodity exported, the relative importance of the exporting country in world trade of that commodity, or the importance of the exported commodity in the economy of the exporting country. The ability to pass export taxes forward to the foreign consumer is largely dependent upon the price elasticity of demand for the commodity: an export tax on bananas, for instance, would be much less likely to be passed forward than an equivalent duty on a commodity such as petroleum or certain minerals essential for industrial processes.

Furthermore, a country may export a commodity for which demand is highly inelastic, such as industrial diamonds or tungsten ore, and still not be able to tax effectively the foreign consumer if that country does not supply a sizeable percentage of world trade in that particular commodity and if it is acting alone. Countries that each export a small amount of a good for which there is an inelastic demand may, of course, form a cartel for the purpose of controlling a significant portion of world trade – OPEC being the most obvious example of a successful cartel.

Even if a country enjoys a significant percentage of the world trade for a commodity with an inelastic demand, export taxes will yield little tax revenue unless the exported commodity constitutes a fairly large percentage of the country's GNP. If, for instance, the export of a commodity constitutes only one percent of the nation's GNP, then a 100 percent export duty would only increase the tax ratio by no more than one point.

Clearly, the construction of an index measuring the ability of a country to pass export taxes forward to foreigners must include all of these considerations. To this end, an 'index of the exportability of the tax burden' (EI) was constructed by combining these three factors into a multiplicative index and then summing the resultant index for all commodities exported by the particular country:

$$EI_j = \sum_{i=1}^{m} (E_i) \left(\frac{X_j}{X_t}\right)_i \left(\frac{X_j}{Y_j}\right)_i \tag{9.3}$$

where E_i = price elasticity of demand for commodity i; X_j = value of country j's exports of commodity i; X_t = value of world exports of commodity i; Y_j = GNP of country j; m = total number of commodities.

The sectoral composition of national income certainly could influence the tax ratio. It is often difficult to tax the agricultural sector due to such factors as the poor organization usually found in rural areas, the large subsistence sector and the geographical dispersion of the taxpayers. Therefore it is reasonable to expect that the existence of a large agricultural sector is associated with a low level of economic development; the data for the sample of 67 countries shows a negative correlation (-0.47) between the share of agriculture in GNP and the level of per capita income (Y_p). The share of mining in GDP, represented by the variable N_y, is another widely used indicator for the sectoral composition of the economy, but its exclusion in a tax capacity model is subject to the criticisms indicated above. It was decided, nevertheless to include the mining share in our model.

The level of development may be indicated by either per capita income (Y_p) or per capita nonexport income ($Y_p - X_p$), and by the degree of monetization. Alternative formulations using one or the other were used in this study. Similarly, the degree of openness may be measured by one or more (but not all) foreign trade variables (the export ratio, the export ratio excluding mineral exports, the sum of imports and exports to GNP, the import ratio, or the 'index of the exportability of the tax burden' (EI)). Various multiple regression models were constructed using different income variables and different combinations of the foreign trade variables, but not in the same equation.

9.4   The regression results

The various equations were fitted to the data for the entire sample of 67 countries and also to subsamples of Middle East and non-Middle East countries. The version that performed best, in terms of explaining variation in the tax capacity ratio, expressed tax capacity as a function of per capita non-export income, the shares of mining and agriculture in the national economy, the ratio of all trade to the size of the economy, the export elasticity index, and the degree of monetization:

$$\frac{T}{Y} = a_0 + a_1(Y_p - X_p) + a_2 N_y + a_3 A_y + a_4 \frac{F}{Y} + a_5 EI + a_6 \frac{M_2}{Y} \quad (9.4)$$

where T = tax revenue; Y = GNP; Y_p = per capita GNP; X_p = per capita exports; N_y = share of mining sector in GNP; A_y = share of agricultural sector in GNP; F = sum of exports and imports; EI = export elasticity index; M_2 = money supply.

Table 9.3 shows in columns (A), (B), and (C) respectively the results of the regressions run for the sample as a whole and for the subsamples of 19 Middle East countries and 48 other countries. As can be seen, using $\bar{R}^2$ as a criterion, Equation (9.4) performs well in all three regressions. However, while only the coefficients of the shares of mining and agriculture show statistical significance when the entire sample is included, a different picture emerges when the geographically differentiated subsamples are considered. Statistical evidence indicating a role for the income and trade variables in affecting variance in tax capacity is not strong. However, some significance for the export elasticity and monetization variables, especially in the Middle East, is indicated. The signs of the estimated coefficients are different for the two subsamples, with the negative signs found with the Middle East subsample being contrary to *a priori* expectations.

Table 9.3 *Regression results: revised tax capacity model with mineral sector as independent variable*

Estimated coefficient	Formulation		
	(A)	(B)	(C)
$Y_p - X_p$	−0.002	−0.006	−0.0025
	(0.53)	(1.20)	(0.59)
N_y	+0.48	+0.36	+0.32
	(8.17)	(4.24)	(4.80)
A_y	−0.12	−0.52	−0.065
	(2.09)	(3.96)	(1.41)
F/Y	−0.005	+0.53	−0.008
	(0.22)	(1.52)	(0.32)
EI	−0.0001	−0.0047	+0.0019
	(0.08)	(2.46)	(1.76)
M_2/Y	+0.027	−0.38	+0.099
	(0.45)	(3.96)	(1.42)
Constant	16.75	46.92	12.62
$\bar{R}^2$	0.722	0.866	0.602
n	67	19	48

In order to test for possible structural differences that set the Middle Eastern countries apart from other LDCs, a Chow test[12] was used to test the null hypothesis that both the 19 Middle Eastern and 48 other LDCs belong in the group described by the results shown in column (A) of *Table 9.3*. The results indicated that the null hypothesis could be rejected at the 99 percent confidence level: thus the Middle East countries are somewhat different in this regard from other LDCs.

As we have seen, a model described by Equation (9.4) seems to perform better than the Chelliah model. However, we have already indicated above objections to a model which relies heavily on N_y, the share of mining in national economies, to explain variation in tax capacity. This objection is accentuated by the results of the Chow test, since it is certainly with regard to the share of mining that the Middle Eastern countries as a group differ from other LDCs.

Thus, we rejected the argument that the mineral sector *a priori* is easier to tax and recalled that Chelliah seemed to be using N_y as a proxy for the export portion of the mineral industry. Thus, we revised Equation (9.4) by replacing N_y with the ratio of mineral exports to GNP. Because of collinearity problems, this also requires changing the measure of trade, F/Y; in its stead we used the ratio of imports to GNP:

$$\frac{T}{Y} = a_0 + a_1(Y_p - X_p) + a_2 A_y + a_3 \frac{X_m}{Y} + a_4 \frac{M}{Y} + a_5 EI + a_6 \frac{M_2}{Y} \quad (9.5)$$

where X_m = value of mineral exports;
$\quad\quad\ M$ = value of imports;
$\quad\quad\quad$ all other variables are the same as in Equation (9.4).

The regression results using this variation are shown in *Table 9.4* columns (A), (B), and (C) for the group as a whole and the subsamples. Again the

Table 9.4 *Regression results: revised tax capacity model with mineral exports as independent variable*

Estimated coefficient	Formulation					
	(A)	(B)	(C)	(D)	(E)	(F)
$X_p - X_p$	−0.0012 (0.27)	−0.0036 (0.59)	−0.0007 (0.16)	–	–	–
A_y	−0.20 (3.08)	−0.65 (4.34)	−0.071 (1.51)	−0.19 (3.36)	−0.62 (4.57)	−0.67 (1.75)
X_m/Y	+0.33 (6.86)	+0.28 (3.77)	+0.25 (4.92)	+0.33 (6.94)	+0.28 (3.83)	+0.25 (5.00)
M/Y	−0.095 (2.04)	−0.070 (0.93)	+0.25 (4.92)	−0.093 (2.04)	−0.078 (1.07)	−0.011 (0.29)
EI	−0.0042 (0.28)	−0.0056 (2.18)	+0.0011 (0.95)	+0.0004 (0.25)	−0.0054 (2.19)	+0.011 (0.99)
M_2/Y	+0.0018 (0.03)	−0.40 (3.54)	+0.093 (1.33)	−0.0016 (0.02)	−0.38 (3.62)	+0.089 (1.39)
Constant	22.65	55.78	12.96	22.09	53.53	12.68
$\bar{R}^2$	0.646	0.803	0.588	0.651	0.812	0.598
n	67	19	48	67	19	48

income variable shows no statistical significance. Thus regressions were also carried out after eliminating the income measure; these results are shown in columns (D), (E), and (F). On an adjusted basis, this last variant of the tax capacity model seems best at explaining variation in the dependent variable, if we allow the arguments made above against using a measure of the mineral sector as a whole.

All our modified equations seem to perform better than Equation (9.1), Chelliah's basic model. However, as we have seen, that model's results vary quite a bit depending upon the sample used. Thus, a fair comparison of Equations (9.1) and (9.5) requires using the same sample in each case. *Table 9.5* shows the regression estimates when these equations are applied to both

Table 9.5 *Comparison of regression results: Chelliah and revised models*

	Formulation					
Estimated Coefficient	47 countries			67 countries		
	Chelliah	Revised		Chelliah	Revised	
$Y_p - X_p$	+0.001 (0.38)	−0.0048 (1.20)	−	+0.0025 (0.73)	−0.012 (0.27)	−
N_y	+0.44 (5.45)	−	−	+0.540 (11.30)	−	−
X_y'	+0.05 (1.17)	−	−	+0.052 (0.86)	−	−
A_y	−	−0.10 (2.18)	−0.07 (1.81)	−	−0.20 (3.08)	−0.19 (3.36)
X_m/Y	−	+0.25 (2.95)	+0.26 (3.03)	−	+0.33 (6.86)	+0.33 (6.94)
M/Y	−	−0.03 (0.78)	−0.01 (0.31)	−	−0.095 (2.04)	−0.093 (2.04)
EI	−	+0.0012 (0.84)	+0.0012 (0.79)	−	−0.0042 (0.28)	+0.0004 (0.25)
M_2/Y	−	+0.038 (0.73)	+0.029 (0.56)	−	+0.0018 (0.03)	−0.0016 (0.02)
Constant	11.47	16.79	14.54	11.32	25.65	22.09
$\bar{R}^2$	0.376	0.497	0.482	0.708	0.646	0.651

Chelliah's original sample and our expanded sample. We would argue that Equation (9.5) is to be preferred. First, from the viewpoint of explaining variation in the dependent variable, it performs comparably well or better than the Chelliah model. Secondly it is conceptually preferable to link ease of taxing to exported minerals, rather than to the overall size of the mineral industry. Thirdly our regressions on both the sample as a whole and the two subsamples indicate enough evidence of statistical significance for all the *a priori* factors included in the model (with the likely exception of income) to retain them in the final version of the model.

Again, we are concerned with differences in tax capacity for Middle Eastern countries. Thus the Chow test was also applied to the regressions resulting from Equation (9.5). As with the use of this test mentioned above in connection with Equation (9.4), the indications point to structural differences separating the Middle East from other developing regions[13].

If this is in fact the case, then it is of interest to pinpoint some of the economic factors which may contribute to this disparity[14]. Perhaps the most obvious characteristic that may influence tax ratio is the existence of a large petroleum sector in a majority of the Middle East countries (12 out of 19) included in the regressions of the present study. It seems reasonable to assume that such an industry would provide a relatively large tax base from which a substantial proportion of the nation's tax revenue could be obtained.

More generally, it may be hypothesized that any developing country enjoying a sizeable endowment of mineral resources could obtain a significant percentage of total government revenue from this base and thereby enjoy a higher tax ratio than those countries lacking such mineral resources. Consequently, resource rich LDCs as a group might be significantly different from less fortunate LDCs when a regression model predicting the tax ratio is applied to them. To test this hypothesis, 26 of the countries in our sample were classified as 'resource rich' – that is, more than 20 percent of the total tax revenue in these countries was obtained from taxes levied on the most important mineral sectors[15]. However, when a Chow test was conducted in this case, the null hypothesis that both subsamples belonged to the same population could not be rejected[16]. While this leaves us with little positive evidence relative to the effect of a wealthy base of taxable minerals on the tax ratio of a country, neither does it lead us to reject a possible relationship out of hand. The lack of statistical evidence may result from the arbitrary nature of the groupings used. For example, while all the 'resource-rich' countries obtained major shares of their tax receipts from exported minerals, they are otherwise a very diverse group. They range from the very rich to the very poor, and, while all export minerals for which demand is generally price-inelastic, some have histories of consideable volatility in export earnings (such as the copper and bauxite exporters) while others (such as the petroleum and diamond suppliers) rarely experience severe declines in export receipts.

Other factors besides the presence of a particular type of export might explain the differences between two groups of countries (that is, resource rich and resource poor exporters). A sort of 'demonstration effect' may be operative within a group if the tax policies of a country are influenced by its neighbor's policies[17]. This might well prevail if the countries share a common colonial or cultural heritage, or if their similar past histories led to a similar attitude in their societies toward the demand for, and consumption of, public goods. Ceilings on tax rate structures may be affected by the rates in neighboring countries; for example land borders in many LDCs are poorly policed and easily crossed by smugglers taking advantage of opportunities found when wide disparities exist across these borders in the taxes on consumption goods.

Obviously, other potentially significant factors are present in the Middle East. We have already discussed one at length above – the Islamic heritage of the region and the traditional teachings of Islam about the collection and spending of public revenues.

As regards the six variables included in our regressions, *Table 9.6* shows the mean values of each variable for the Middle Eastern and non-Middle Eastern groups of LDCs. While it is with regard to mineral exports (X_m) that the greatest disparity between the two groups (33.00 percent in the Middle East versus a mean of 9.51 percent elsewhere) exists[18], there are also notable differences in other factors. For example, on average, the 19 Middle Eastern countries derive only about half as much of GNP from agriculture as do the other LDCs, and the mean value of the monetization ratio is more than 75 percent higher for the former group.

Table 9.6 *Mean values of regression variables, country sub-groups*

Variable	19 Middle East countries	48 other countries
T/Y	30.21	15.44
$Y_p - X_p$	297.13	237.20
A_y	16.35	30.00
X_m/Y	33.00	9.51
M/Y	33.84	23.78
EI	666.57	405.51
M_2/Y	42.92	24.46

In concluding this chapter, we would recall that the modified tax ratio model discussed above seems to perform better than earlier models in explaining variance in the dependent variable, but that it is clear that all these models show instability in their regression results when the sample being tested is changed. In our case, these indications led to a suspicion, somewhat confirmed by our results, that the Middle Eastern countries differ in some structural fashion from other LDCs relative to the determination of the tax ratio. On the other hand, we found no clear statistical evidence that this difference is primarily based on what is superficially at least the most obvious distinguishing characteristic of the region – the abundant presence of a major mineral export. Our attempts to isolate a measure of how easily a country can pass on part of its tax burden to foreign consumers resulted in an index of the demand elasticities for major exports (*EI*). However, difficulties arose in constructing an index for such a large group of developing countries that not only faithfully represented the concept behind the *a priori* arguments for such a variable, but also was based on consistently accurate data for the entire group. Further attempts at refining this type of index might prove useful in explaining the sorts of inter-regional differences we seem to have found[19].

In Part V we will discuss some of the differences between Middle Eastern and other LDCs and within the region itself, with an eye to the effects these may have on tax policies.

Notes

1 An excellent resumé of the most important studies may be found in Raja J. Chelliah, Trends in Taxation in Developing Countries, *IMF Staff Papers*, **18**, 288–293, (July, 1971). Much of our discussion is drawn from this source.

2 Jeffrey G. Williamson, Public Expenditure and Revenue: An International Comparison, *The Manchester School of Economic and Social Studies*, **24**, 43–56, (1961).

3 Sylvain Plasschaert, *Taxable Capacity in Developing Countries*, International Bank for Reconstruction and Development, Report No. **EC–103** (unpublished, Washington, 1962).

4 Harley H. Hinrichs, *A General Theory of Tax Structure Change During Economic Development*, (Cambridge: Harvard Law School, 1966), pp. 12–19.

5 Richard S. Thorn, The Evolution of Public Finances During Economic Development, *The Manchester School of Economic and Social Studies*, **35**, 19–53, (1967).

6 Jorgen R. Lotz and Elliot R. Morss, Measuring 'Tax Effort' in Developing Countries, *International Monetary Fund Staff Papers*, **14**, 478–497, (November, 1967).

7 Jorgen R. Lotz and Elliot R. Morss, A Theory of Tax Level Determinants for Developing Countries, *Economic Development and Cultural Change*, **18**, 328–41, (April 1970).

8 Chelliah, op. cit. (note 1) pp. 293–98.

9 Zambia, Chile, Venezuela, Zaire, Guyana, and Iran.

10 Raja J. Chelliah, Hessel J. Bass, and Margaret R. Helly, Tax Ratios and Tax Effort in Developing Countries, 1969–71, *International Monetary Fund Staff Papers*, **22**, 190–191, 204–205, (March, 1975). For simplicity, both studies are referred to in the text under Chelliah's name alone.

11 Data for 1966–68 are found in Chelliah, Trends in Taxation in Developing Countries, while 1972–76 data are found in Alan A. Tait, Wilfrid L. M. Gratz. and Barry J. Eichengreen, International Comparisons of Taxation in Developing Countries, 1972–76, *International Monetary Fund Staff Papers*, **26**, 128 (March, 1979).

12 Gregory C. Chow, Tests of Equality Between Sets of Coefficients in Two Linear Regressons, *Econometrica*, **28**, 591–605, (July, 1960). Using Equation 9.4, the sum of squares was calculated for the group as a whole, as well as for each subsample of countries. These were used to calculate an *F*-ratio for (p,q) degrees of freedom where p is the number of parameters in the regression and $q = n + m - 2p$, where n and m are the number in each of the two subsamples. $F(7,53)$ then was equal to the ratio $[(A - B - C)/p] \div [(B + C)/q]$ where A, B, and C are the sums of squares for the whole sample and the 2 sub-samples, in this case 9.27, which exceeded the critical value 2.98.

13 The sums of squares were calculated for the regressions based on Equation (9.5), both with and without the income variable included in the model. In the first case,

$F(7,53)$ was equal to 10.33 which is greater than the operative critical value of 2.98; in the second case, $F(6,55)$ was 12.24 and exceeded the critical value of 3.15. Thus in both cases the null hypothesis of no difference was rejected at the 99 percent level.

14 Roy W. Bahl also found a regional effect on the tax ratio in A Regression Approach to Tax Effort and Tax Ratio Analysis, *International Monetary Fund Staff Papers*, **18**, 602, (November, 1971). Bahl inserted a regionally based dummy variable into an equation that related the tax ratio to the shares of agriculture and of mining in GNP after arbitrarily grouping his sample of 49 countries into five regional subsamples. One of these contained six of the Middle Eastern countries considered here, in addition to Turkey. He concluded that after allowing for the effects of the mining and agricultural shares, the expected tax ratios were higher in the Middle East than for any other region except Tropical Africa.

15 The oil producers: Algeria, Bahrain, Brunei, Gabon, Iran, Iraq, Kuwait, Libya, Nigeria, Oman, Qatar, Saudi Arabia, Trinidad and Tobago, United Arab Emirates, and Venezuela, plus Bolivia, Chile, Guyana, Jamaica, Malaysia, Mauritania, Peru, Sierra Leone, Surinam, Zaire and Zambia.

16 The sums of squares were caculated for regressions based on Equation (9.5), both with and without the income variable included in the model, and using the distinction defining 'resource-rich' to separate the LDCs into subgroups of 26 and 41. With income included, $F(7, 53)$ was equal to 1.76, less than the critical value of 2.78; with income excluded $F(6,55)$ was 1.72, less than the critical value of 1.73. In neither case can the null hypothesis (that the two subgroups belong together) be rejected.

17 Bahl, op. cit. (note 14) p. 660.

18 With regard to the share of mining in GNP (N_y), the variable used by Chelliah, the mean value for 19 Middle Eastern Countries is 24.73 and for all other countries is 8.17.

19 In calculating the export elasticity index, some procedures to simplify maters were employed. First, an ordinal ranking of commodities (1 = most elastic demand to 4 = most inelastic demand) was used rather than actual elasticity values. Secondly, only commodities (mineral and agricultural) which comprised more than one percent of a country's total exports were included in the index.

PART V

Assessment of tax performance in the Middle East

General considerations relative to tax policy performance

This section will evaluate the recent tax policies of the sixteen Middle Eastern countries in the light of the data surveyed in Chapters 7 and 8. We are not seeking to find, or impose, an 'ideal' tax system, for either oil or non-oil exporting countries, individually or as a group: limitations imposed by the original data and the comparative categorizations employed would not lend themselves to a significant application of such an 'ideal' – even supposing such a thing existed.

Instead we will examine the comparative use in these countries of taxes, both as economic, and social, policy instruments. If, as economic policy instruments, taxes have been used to guide financial resources in the direction of the common goal of economic transformation and modernization, then which type of tax and which sectors of the economy have been mobilized to this end? If taxes are used as social policy instruments the major questions raised are those concerning equity: does the reality of income distribution have a bearing on the fiscal policies as they are applied in practice?

We will also look at whether fiscal policies conform to the general principles of Islamic society: be they in the form of *zakat* or more modern income and property taxes. These more general ideas will be covered in Chapter 10 while Chapters 11 and 12 will consider the oil and non-oil exporting countries respectively.

10.1 Mobilizing the resources of society

The simplest and most straightforward measure of the role played by the fiscal authorities in mobilizing the financial resources of a society is the ratio of tax revenues to some measure of national income, such as the GNP. Of course, this tells us nothing about how much or how effectively the government utilizes these financial resources. However, this work has focused exclusively on the collection side of fiscal policy, so here we can only consider the *potential* role of government measurable by the resources over which it is able to exert direct control.

At this point it is necessary to interject a cautionary note concerning the method of using the ratio of taxes to GNP as an indicator of tax effort.

Because of the unusual supply situation prevailing in the world petroleum market, oil exporters have been successful in enlarging and capturing the economic rent accruing to this resource. In a few low population exporters, this boost in the rent has a major effect both on government revenues and on GNP, that is, on both the numerator and the denominator of the tax ratio, with the impact on revenues being relatively greater.

Looking at *Table 10.1* it is clear that over three decades the ratio of taxes to GNP has risen in every country, and in some cases dramatically. In fact, the weighted average tax ratio nearly tripled (*Table 10.2*) to more than 35 percent of the aggregate gross product. This relative gain for the tax collector

Table 10.1 *Ratios of tax revenue to GNP (1950–1978) (percentage)*

Country	1950	1962	1968	1973	1978
Bahrain	12.6	33.5	32.4	55.7	42.1
Egypt	20.0	28.2	25.0	24.6	27.0[g]
Iran	4.4	19.0	19.1	25.4	38.0[g]
Iraq	18.4	27.8	34.0	65.9	52.1[g]
Jordan	12.9[b]	15.9	13.3	16.1	23.0
Kuwait	3.8	39.8	33.3	27.6	78.3
Lebanon	4.1	11.7	12.8	13.0	12.5[g]
Libya	19.6[b]	13.6	40.5	42.6	59.9[g]
Oman	NA	4.7	44.7	45.7	61.0
Qatar	6.3	47.0[d]	37.7[f]	40.1	82.4
Saudi Arabia	15.4	32.3	41.9	75.8	79.0
Sudan	10.7[c]	17.9	18.4	16.0	20.2
Syria	9.9	22.0	29.6	20.8	21.6[g]
United Arab Emirates	NA	21.0[e]	48.5	38.7	46.5
Yemen Arab Rep.	NA	3.6	4.9	8.4	14.1[g]
Yemen People's Dem. Rep.	15.7[a]	20.8[d]	11.5	20.5	21.8

Notes: NA indicates data not available
[a] 1951   [e] 1964
[b] 1952   [f] 1967
[c] 1955   [g] 1977
[d] 1960

Table 10.2 *Weighted average[a] tax ratios (1950–1978) (percentage)*

	1950	1962	1968	1973	1978
16 countries	13.1[b]	22.3	23.6	29.7	34.6
Oil exporters	9.2	23.3	27.1	42.1	49.3
Non-oil exporters[c]	15.8	21.6	21.1	20.1	23.0

Notes: [a] Ratios in *Table 10.1* are weighted by population to obtain averages.
[b] 13 countries only.
[c] Non-oil exporters include Libya in 1950 and 1962 and Oman in 1962.

was much greater, though, for the oil-exporting countries; as would be expected, the 1970s have seen oil-generated revenues growing much faster than the non-oil sectors of these economies. This divergence shows clearly in *Figure 10.1*. In the early 1950s, the two groups were graphically indistinguishable as regards tax ratio, though the weighted average for the non-oil countries was nearly 75 percent higher than for the oil countries. But

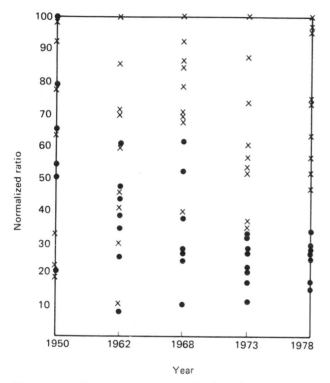

Figure 10.1   *Tax revenue to gross national product ratios 1950 –1978*

Notes: 100 = highest tax revenue ratio in a given year
      ×   Oil-exporting country
      ●   Non-oil exporting country

by the early 1960s, the latter countries had clearly moved to the forefront in this regard and by 1973, the oil exporter with the lowest tax effort ratio (Iran) had moved ahead of the non-oil exporter with the highest ratio (Egypt).

In the last chapter, we employed a broader sample of developing countries for the regressions testing our hypothesis in regard to the factors affecting the size of the tax ratio. The countries making up that sample for which recent tax revenue data are available are listed in *Table 10.3*. When their tax

Table 10.3 *Tax ratios: selected developing countries (1966–1968 and 1977)*

Country	GNP per capita (1977 dollars)	Tax ratio (%) 1966–68	1977
Algeria	1140	10.1	43.1[b]
Argentina	1950	13.4	12.2
Bolivia	650	8.2	9.4
Brazil	1400	22.9	19.9
Brunei	9190	34.1	58.0[a]
Burundi	130	11.5	13.9
Chile	1360	19.6	22.4
Colombia	760	12.5	10.8
Costa Rica	1450	13.1	16.9
Ecuador	830	13.4	9.9
Ethiopia	110	8.6	13.2
Gabon	1700	22.7	31.1
Ghana	380	15.8	29.6
Guatemala	830	7.9	10.2
Guyana	520	20.9	34.7
Honduras	420	11.3	13.6
India	160	13.4	10.1
Indonesia	320	10.1	18.5
Jamaica	1060	19.4	25.8
Kenya	290	14.4	15.0
Korea	980	15.4	15.6
Malaysia	970	19.3	22.6
Mali	110	13.2	17.2
Mauritania	270	13.7	23.0
Mexico	1160	7.1	13.2
Morocco	610	17.8	21.8
Nepal	110	4.5	6.4
Nigeria	510	16.2	39.2
Pakistan	200	8.8	10.7
Paraguay	750	10.9	10.8
Peru	720	14.2	14.2
Philippines	460	9.1	11.0
Rwanda	160	7.9	11.4
Senegal	380	18.1	17.1
Sierra Leone	200	16.0	16.2
Singapore	2820	13.2	17.4
Sri Lanka	160	17.7	17.8
Surinam	1500	25.7	26.2
Taiwan	1180	14.5	23.2
Tanzania	210	13.9	15.3
Thailand	430	12.4	12.0
Togo	300	11.3	25.0
Trinidad & Tobago	2620	15.2	21.1[b]
Tunisia	840	21.7	29.9
Turkey	1110	15.6	29.4
Uganda	220	12.8	13.2[b]
Upper Volta	110	10.2	14.2
Venezuela	2630	20.4	28.6
Zaire	210	29.4	17.0
Zambia	460	31.3	23.5

Notes: [a] 1975. [b] 1976.
Source: Government Finance Statistics Yearbook; Quarterly Economic Review, Economic Intelligence Unit, Ltd.

ratios are compared with those of Middle Eastern countries, it is clear that even the non-oil exporters among the latter rank highly in tax effort relative to other LDCs. For example, while only two Middle Eastern countries (Lebanon and the Yemen Arab Republic) had tax ratios below 20 percent in the late 1970s, 31 of the 50 LDCs listed in *Table 10.3* fell below this level. The other five non-oil exporters in the Middle East (Egypt, Jordan, Sudan,

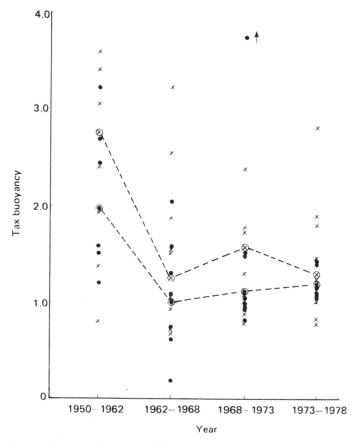

Figure 10.2   *Tax buoyancies 1950–1978*
× *Oil-exporting country*
● *Non-oil exporting country*
○ *Weighted average*

Syria and the Yemen People's Democratic Republic) had tax ratios between 20 and 29 percent, while the nine oil-exporters ranged from 38 percent (Iran) to 82.4 percent (Qatar). Elsewhere in the developing world, 14 countries were between 20 and 30 percent and only five had tax ratios in excess of 30 percent (three of these countries – Algeria, Gabon and Nigeria were OPEC members and a fourth, Brunei, was also a sizable oil exporter).

Very few LDCs in other parts of the world, therefore, matched or bettered the tax ratios of most of the Middle Eastern countries. Of those that did, the majority are heavily dependent on major mineral resources[1]. The regional predominance of high rax ratios in the Middle East shows up clearly in *Table 10.3*. Indeed it is only if we look at industrialized countries (*Table 10.4*) that we find many countries which match the tax effort ratios of the *non-oil* exporters of the Middle East.

Table 10.4 *Tax ratios: selected industrialized countries (1977)*

	GNP per capita (1977 dollars)	1977 tax ratio (%)
Australia	6775	28.2
Canada	8480	18.7
Denmark	9000	35.0
France	7210	35.1
Federal Republic of Germany	8375	28.2
Japan	6100	10.7
Netherlands	7700	47.0
Sweden	9425	41.4
United Kingdom	4420	31.5
United States	8760	18.2

Source: Government Financial Statistics Yearbook; International Financial Statistics Yearbook.

Referring back to our earlier note of caution, the fact that Oman has a tax ratio of about 60 percent while Syria's is about 20 percent does not imply that Oman tries three times as hard in this regard. The very high ratios of the Gulf area exporters have followed the oil prices rises of the early 1970s. Therefore, this ratio should be used only as an indicator if the relatively greater part of the country's national income falls under the direct control of the fiscal authorities.

A further limitation on the usefulness of the tax ratio is its essentially static nature. We are interested in how fiscal authorities adapt over time to changes throughout the national economy. Perhaps the best measure, therefore, would be an income elasticity of government revenue (G):

$$E = \frac{\Delta G/G}{\Delta Y/Y} \tag{10.1}$$

However, such a measure requires that the tax structure remain constant (and this would gauge the response of the structure to changes in the economy) or that all changes in the structure be separately accounted for (and this would gauge the response of the structure as a whole). Calculating the elasticity in this context is unfortunately not possible. The structures of

these countries have undergone major changes over time and the data
necessary to account for these changes are simply not available.

Therefore, we will define and use a less sophisticated measure of change,
tax buoyancy (B):

$$B = \frac{\text{percentage change in } G}{\text{percentage change in } Y} \qquad (10.2)$$

If the value of B is less than 1 during some time period, then government
revenues are growing more slowly than gross national product, and if B is
greater than 1, then revenues are growing faster (and consequently the tax
ratio will rise).

Buoyancies for the 16 Middle East countries are shown in *Table 10.5*.
These were calculated using average annual rates of growth in revenues and
in GNP for four time periods: 1950–62, 1962–68, 1968–73, and 1973–78.

These periods can be conveniently characterized as different, politically
and economically, one from another. The late 1950s were marked by
moderate economic growth worldwide and as the last decade of western

Table 10.5 *Tax buoyancies: Middle Eastern countries (1950–1978)*

Country	1950–1962	1962–1968	1968–1973	1973–1978
Bahrain	3.056	0.929	1.761	0.830
Egypt	1.592	0.709	0.957	1.153[j]
Iran	3.404	1.012	1.303	1.454[j]
Iraq	1.368	1.523	2.384	0.787[j]
Jordan	1.212[d]	0.642	1.533	1.450
Kuwait	3.582	0.662	0.796	2.824
Lebanon	3.223	1.262	1.031	0.472[j]
Libya	0.804[c]	1.866	1.068	1.804[j]
Oman	NA	3.229	1.026	1.206
Qatar	2.394[a]	0.680[f]	1.053[i]	1.903
Saudi Arabia	1.945	1.535	1.731	1.028
Sudan	2.691[e]	1.078	0.812	1.451
Syria	2.431	2.051	0.375	1.038[j]
United Arab Emirates	NA	2.551[b]	0.876	1.142
Yemen Arab Rep.	NA	1.559	1.548	1.117[j]
Yemen People's Dem. Rep.	1.508[b]	0.390[g]	7.313	1.069
Weighted average				
All countries	2.298	1.145	1.288	1.234
Oil exporters	2.751	1.253	1.551	1.293
Non-oil exporters	1.970	1.002	1.086	1.185

Notes: [a] 1950–1960   [f] 1960–1967
         [b] 1951–1960   [g] 1960–1968
         [c] 1951–1962   [h] 1964–1968
         [d] 1952–1962   [i] 1967–1973
         [e] 1955–1962   [j] 1973–1977
         1950–1962 includes only thirteen countries and Libya is considered to be a non-oil
         exporter.

political colonialism. The so-called Third World was still fairly quiet and most Middle East countries were just emerging from some form of colonial status (six were in fact still under direct British tutelage – Bahrain, Kuwait, Oman, Qatar, the UAE and South Yemen – and a seventh, the Sudan, became independent only halfway through this period). The 1960s saw rapid growth, fairly stable prices, and much more political activism among the developing countries. After 1968, the world economy was increasingly burdened with inflation. Then, of course, in 1973/74, oil prices quadrupled and the Middle East was the region most affected by the changes in the world oil market. Thus our divisions represent convenient, if somewhat arbitrary, political and economic benchmarks.

Table 10.6 *Oil and non-oil tax buoyancies (1950–1978)*

Country	Tax category	1950–62	1962–68	1968–73	1973–78
Bahrain	Oil	3.736	0.797	1.656	0.960
	Non-oil	1.944	1.239	1.963	0.541
Iran	Oil	5.675	1.443	1.525	1.567
	Non-oil	2.737	0.663	0.894	1.195
Iraq	Oil	2.535	1.448	3.183	0.837
	Non-oil	0.754	1.630	0.728	0.551
Kuwait	Oil	3.759	0.617	0.802	2.821
	Non-oil	2.183	1.338	0.726	2.866
Libya	Oil	NA	4.352	1.008	1.970
	Non-oil	0.761	0.742	1.268	1.208
Oman	Oil	NA	NA	1.006	1.184
	Non-oil	NA	0.303	1.440	1.531
Qatar	Oil	2.507	0.629	1.209	1.886
	Non-oil	1.130	1.925	0.188	2.624
Saudi Arabia	Oil	2.155	1.543	1.834	1.003
	Non-oil	1.159	1.487	0.930	0.284
United Arab Emirates	Oil	NA	4.566	0.896	1.229
	Non-oil	NA	2.955	0.775	0.321

Notes: See notes in *Table 10.5*.
NA indicates data not available or zero revenue at start of period.

Generally the highest buoyancies were calculated for the 1950s, a period which began (see *Figure 10.1*) with very low tax-to-GNP ratios. For oil and non-oil countries alike, the weighted average buoyancies were much higher then than during any of the later periods. The oil exporters consistently have the higher average over the entire three decades, though the gap between the two sub-groups has narrowed decisively, particularly during the 1970s (see

Figure 10.2). The recent high rates of growth of GNP (in current terms) throughout the region have undoubtedly served to lessen this difference.

These buoyancies, calculated for aggregate fiscal receipts, illustrate that tax authorities throughout the region have increased their share of national income at a faster rate than that of economic growth in general, though their relative gains have not proceeded at the same pace. However, they mark some of the differences found from one country to another which will be discussed further in Chapters 11 and 12. Also, they do not show as important differences in the way particular categories of taxes have undergone change.

Perhaps the most notable categorical differentiation separates oil-related taxes, largely paid by customers in importing countries, from all other levies, mostly paid by the residents of the taxing countries. As *Table 10.6* indicates, oil taxes have generally higher buoyancies than non-oil taxes; in 22 of the 32 data cells in the table where comparisons are relevant, the former's buoyancy is the greater. Oil tax buoyancies were generally at their peak in the 1950s; when they also led non-oil tax buoyancies in all exporting countries. In the 1970s, oil tax buoyancies have been more modest. This is explained by the data shown in *Table 10.1* and elsewhere above: in 1973 oil tax revenues already were quite large relative to GNP, and the price rises

Table 10.7 *Ratios of oil revenue to total government receipts (1950–1978)*

Country	1950 (%)	1962 (%)	1968 (%)	1973 (%)	1978 (%)
Bahrain	52.9	72.0	67.5	62.8	77.9
Iran	11.7	40.0	51.5	66.9	73.6
Iraq	17.3	58.9	57.2	80.9	85.5
Kuwait	81.7	94.6	92.3	92.8	92.6
Libya	0	7.6	78.4	75.1	83.2
Oman	0	0	95.8	94.3	91.3
Qatar	84.1	97.4	94.1	98.0	96.7
Saudi Arabia	72.7	85.2	85.5	92.5	89.1
United Arab Emirates	0	71.6	82.5	85.6	95.6

Note: See Notes, *Table 10.1*.

pushed both numerator and denominator in the buoyancy expressions up rapidly. Overall, the impression is that of a group of countries in which oil revenues came to dominate fiscal receipts during the 1950s, and where nothing has changed much in this respect, either in the 1960s and early 1970s when oil prices barely changed (but output sharply accelerated), or since. As can be seen from *Table 10.7*, the percentage of total revenue derived from oil in several exporting countries reached near peak levels by 1968 or even earlier. Some, like Kuwait and Saudi Arabia, have even seen a slight tendency toward fiscal diversification since 1973.

The burden of non-oil taxes falls on the domestic economy, with the partial exception of scattered and generally minor export taxes. In this regard, we have to consider the equitability of the types of taxes that are employed and the changes in the relative burden of different taxes over time. We will now survey the available data on income distribution in the Middle East, as this is a major factor in any discussion of equity.

10.2   Income distribution in the Middle East

Unfortunately, very few even reasonably reliable studies of the distribution of income across population classes are available for our group of countries. Questions concerning equity in tax incidence, or of the degrees of need for

Table 10.8 *Income distribution statistics: selected Middle Eastern countries*

Percentage of population	Egypt 1964/65	Iran 1959	Iran 1968	Iraq 1956	Lebanon 1955/60	Libya 1962	Sudan 1963
0–10	1.5	0.9	1.2	0.9	2.4	4.6	1.9
10–20	3.1	2.6	2.8	1.2	2.7	5.5	3.1
20–30	4.2	3.7	3.8	1.8	3.2	6.4	3.9
30–40	5.3	4.6	4.9	2.6	4.0	7.1	5.0
40–50	6.5	5.7	5.9	3.7	4.8	8.0	6.2
50–60	8.1	6.8	7.2	5.1	6.0	9.1	7.7
60–70	10.1	8.3	8.8	7.2	7.6	10.4	9.6
70–80	12.8	10.3	11.0	10.6	9.9	12.0	12.5
80–90	17.3	13.6	14.7	17.1	14.3	14.7	17.1
90–100	31.1	43.5	39.7	49.8	45.3	22.2	33.0
Measures of income inequality							
Gini coefficient	0.4337	0.5379	0.5018	0.6288	0.5370	0.2674	0.4460
Kuznets index	0.3316	0.3958	0.3726	0.5021	0.417	0.2032	0.3442
Standardized E index	0.2816	0.4540	0.3956	0.5483	0.4571	0.1162	0.2993

Source: Shail Jain, *Size Distribution of Income*, (Washington: International Bank for Reconstruction and Development, 1975).

the redistribution of income by the use of fiscal tools, are particularly hampered by the lack of such data. The available data were summarized by Jain in a recent World Bank publication[2], and *Table 10.8* shows the income distributions that he included for the Middle East. Though none of these figures are from recent studies, they do all refer roughly to the middle of the period covered in Chapters 7 and 8.

Gini coefficient		Kuznets index		Standardized E index		Percentage of income to highest quintile	
Ecuador	0.6826	Ecuador	0.5484	Ecuador	0.6328	Ecuador	72.0
Gabon	0.6439	Honduras	0.5084	Gabon	0.6032	Honduras	67.7
Iraq	0.6288	Iraq	0.5021	Honduras	0.5524	Gabon	67.5
Honduras	0.6252	Gabon	0.5000	Iraq	0.5483	Iraq	66.9
Brazil	0.6093	Brazil	0.4758	Brazil	0.5292	Brazil	64.5
S. Africa	0.5813	S. Africa	0.4695	Turkey	0.4734	S. Africa	62.0
Turkey	0.5679	Turkey	0.4368	S. Africa	0.4630	Turkey	60.6
Venezuela	0.5445	Venezuela	0.4295	Lebanon	0.4571	Lebanon	59.4
Iran (a)	0.5379	Lebanon	0.4179	Iran (a)	0.4540	Venezuela	59.0
Lebanon	0.5370	Costa Rica	0.4116	Costa Rica	0.4336	Costa Rica	58.6
Mexico	0.5248	Mexico	0.4021	Venezuela	0.4270	Iran (a)	57.1
Costa Rica	0.5207	Iran (a)	0.3958	Mexico	0.4137	Mexico	56.9
Philippines	0.5099	Philippines	0.3884	Iran (b)	0.3956	Philippines	55.4
Iran (b)	0.5018	Iran (b)	0.3726	Philippines	0.3925	Iran (b)	54.4
Indonesia	0.4625	Sudan	0.3442	Indonesia	0.3909	Indonesia	52.0
Sudan	0.4460	Indonesia	0.3368	India	0.3050	Sudan	50.1
Egypt	0.4337	Egypt	0.3316	Sudan	0.2993	India	48.9
India	0.4209	India	0.3116	Egypt	0.2816	Egypt	48.4
USA	0.4018	USA	0.2968	USA	0.2509	USA	44.7
Pakistan	0.3551	Pakistan	0.2674	Pakistan	0.2056	Pakistan	43.4
Yugoslavia	0.3474	Yugoslavia	0.2621	Yugoslavia	0.1872	Yugoslavia	41.4
Taiwan	0.3290	Taiwan	0.2432	Taiwan	0.1768	Taiwan	40.8
Korea	0.3045	S. Korea	0.2295	S. Korea	0.1492	S. Korea	39.2
Libya	0.2674	Libya	0.2032	Libya	0.1162	Libya	36.9
Poland	0.2635	Poland	0.2011	Poland	0.1099	Poland	36.1
Czechoslovakia	0.1938	Czechoslovakia	0.1463	Czechoslovakia	0.0598	Czechoslovakia	31.1

Notes: Iran (a) refers to 1959; Iran (b) to 1968.
All non-Middle East studies are national household surveys except: Gabon and Indonesia (income recipients); Ecuador (economically active population); S. Africa (population); Czechoslovakia and Poland (workers).
Survey periods were: Brazil (1970); Costa Rica (1961); Czechoslovakia (1964); Ecuador (1970); Gabon (1968); Honduras (1965); Indonesia (1971); Korea (1968); Mexico (1968); Pakistan (1967); Philippines (1965); Poland (1964); S. Africa (1965); Taiwan (1964); Turkey (1968); USA (1966); Venezuela (1962); Yugoslavia (1968).

Source: See Table 10.8.

Comparisons across the six countries covered by these studies should be made with some caution, not only because the survey years are different, but also because the sample bases are not the same. The Iraqi data relates to the population in general, while those for the other countries are for households. The Egyptian, Iraqi and Lebanese surveys purport to be national in scope, while those for Iran refer only to urban areas. The Libyan and Sudanese surveys were even more limited – their data were gathered only in the major city of each country (Tripoli and Omdurman).

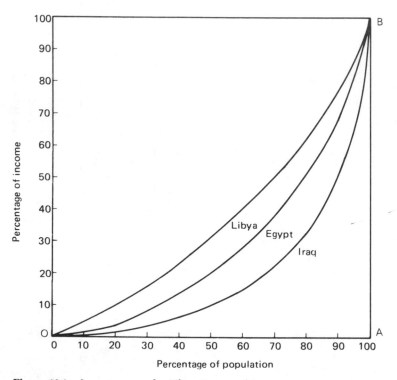

Figure 10.3 *Lorentz curves for Libya, Egypt and Iraq*

Table 10.9 compares these six countries with a select group of other countries at various stages of economic development, using four common measures of relative income equality. These measures were calculated in this manner: the first three indices shown are estimated after a Lorentz curve is fitted to the obse ed data (that is, the aggregate shares of income accruing to successive population deciles) using ordinary least squares regression techniques. As *Figure 10.3* illustrates, a Lorentz curve shows the relationship between cumulative population percentage shares (horizontal axis) and cumulative income percentage shares (vertical axis). If all members of the population received equal income shares, then the Lorentz curve would be the straight line OB (the line of perfect equality, while if all income went to one individual, the Lorentz curve would follow the path OAB (the line of absolute inequality).

The *Gini Coefficient* is the percentage of the area of the triangle OAB that lies between a country's Lorentz curve and the line of perfect equality. Its value can range from 0 to 1; the larger it is, the more the inequality in income distribution.

The *Kuznets Index* is computed by first dividing the population into 20 successive intervals of five percent each and then by determining how much each of these intervals deviate from perfect income equality. The absolute magnitudes of these deviations are then averaged and standardized; the resulting index lies between 0 and 1, with higher values indicating greater income inequality.

The *Standardized E Index* comes from a measure of entropy and has been adapted to developing inequality indices. The measure of entropy is the difference between the sum, over all the population, of the share of income going to each individual times the logarithm of the reciprocal of that share, and the sum, again over the entire population, of each individual's income share times the logarithm of that share. The resulting index is, as indicated by its name, standardized to range from 0 to 1, with higher values again showing greater inequality.

Whichever of these indices we examine in *Table 10.9*, which also includes the share of income going to the richest 20 percent of the population in each country, patterns that emerge are very similar. Of the six Middle Eastern countries for which Jain presented data, Iraq showed the greatest degree of income inequality, followed by Lebanon, Iran, Sudan and Egypt, with Libya having the least inequality according to this data. All countries but Libya fell within the range of values generally occupied by developing countries[3] – for example, Gini coefficients well above 0.4, or with 50 percent or more of national income going to the richest quintile in the population.

Though these studies do not allow any comparisons for determining changes over time (except for Iran), they do tend to confirm what the observer would expect to find[4]; that prerevolutionary Iraq (1956) should show the most inequality is hardly surprising, neither is the indication that Egypt, more than a decade into the presidency of Gamal Abd al-Nasr, shows more income equitability than does *laissez-faire* Lebanon. Some improvement might have been expected in Iran between 1959 and 1968, after the onset of land reform, but the two quoted studies refer to urban areas only. The modest Iranian gains (shown in *Table 10.8*) over the decade may not be conclusive evidence of change; for example, according to the data, the lowest three quintiles of the population moves up only slightly, from about 24.3 percent of national income to about 25.8 percent[5].

The modification of the distribution of income by fiscal policies in western capitalist states has been accomplished, on the one hand, through progressive income taxation and, on the other, by spending policies strongly oriented toward social welfare coupled usually with extensive transfer payments. The studies reported by Jain are of course of pretax income distributions. They can be of some help, at least for these six countries, in evaluating the possible effects of the tax structures on income equality. However, we will not be able to evaluate here the other side of the equation – the redistributive effects of government spending.

In summary, the relatively meager and somewhat outdated evidence indicates that the Middle Eastern pattern of income distribution is quite similar to that of the developing world in general. We might surmise that the differences which appear in the sub-sample of six countries might be found elsewhere in the region. For instance, if somewhat more equitability was present in the Egypt of Gamal Abd al-Nasr which had been following mildly socialist policy guidelines in the 1950s, then perhaps Syria and South Yemen might have similar patterns, while Jordan and North Yemen might look more like Lebanon. It is unfortunate that no data are available for any sparsely-populated oil exporter[6], since it is particularly difficult to place these countries in the spectrum of income distribution patterns.

10.3   Progressive and regressive aspects of the tax burden

If we return now to more strictly fiscal considerations, there are several broad categories of non-oil taxes that were used to make comparisons across our group of 16 countries in Chapters 7 and 8. These included personal income and profits taxes, inheritance and property taxes, customs duties and excise, sales and production taxes (see Appendix B for a definition of each category). Allowing for the imprecision necessarily present when trying to make comparisons based on data taken from widely divergent sources, we will try to draw some conclusions about how these taxes tend to affect the region's population.

As the last section indicates, it would seem fair to assume that during the period under consideration most Middle East countries had income distribution patterns that were similar to those prevailing throughout the developing world. Despite the paucity of hard data and the likely marginal improvements in income distribution during the 1970s (at least in many of the oil exporting countries), it is also reasonable to assume that distribution continues to be much more skewed than it is, say, in the industrialized countries of Europe and North America.

In these latter countries, the fiscal tool that has been most widely used to effect greater equity in income distribution is the graduated tax assessed on various forms of personal and corporate income. Such graduated taxes are on the law books of many Middle Eastern countries, in fact, only two countries by the late 1970s had no such tax – Bahrain and the UAE. All the rest had levies on profits and similar business income, and all but Kuwait, Oman, Qatar, and Saudi Arabia had in effect some form of personal income tax.

However, although theoretically both oil and non-oil exporting countries had similar tax rate structures, the relative impact of these taxes varied widely. For instance, in the late 1970s, Iran had a 20 percent maximum rate

Table 10.10 *Ratio of income taxes[a] to total government revenues: Middle Eastern countries compared to selected developing and industrialized countries (all figures percentages)*

Middle East – Average[b]: 6.3

Bahrain	0.0	Lebanon	6.2	Syria	9.9
Egypt	16.8	Libya	2.9	United Arab Emirates	0.0
Iran	10.4	Oman	1.5	Yemen Arab Rep.	5.1
Iraq	1.8	Qatar	0.3	Yemen People's Dem. Rep.	22.4
Jordan	12.0	Saudi Arabia	0.4		
Kuwait	0.02	Sudan	10.7		

Developing countries – Average[b]: 20.5

Argentina	6.1	Jamaica	29.7	Senegal	22.0
Bolivia	14.2	Kenya	35.0	Singapore	34.3
Brazil	16.3	Korea	28.2	Somalia	7.1
Burundi	15.9	Malaysia	35.9	Sri Lanka	15.1
Chad	18.5	Mali	20.8	Taiwan	16.9
Chile	16.9	Morocco	20.7	Tanzania	27.3
Costa Rica	16.1	Nepal	10.2	Thailand	17.3
Ethiopia	20.7	Pakistan	13.0	Togo	33.0
Ghana	19.7	Paraguay	11.0	Tunisia	15.9
Guatemala	12.4	Peru	13.4	Turkey	44.3
Honduras	18.9	Philippines	22.8	Upper Volta	16.8
India	21.7	Rwanda	14.3	Zambia	37.1

Industrialized countries – Average[b]: 34.8

Australia	63.7	Federal Republic		Sweden	18.1
Austria	19.7	of Germany	21.1	Switzerland	15.2
Belgium	38.8	Italy	18.3	United Kingdom	40.2
Canada	52.0	Japan	58.7	United States	57.0
France	18.7	Netherlands	31.1		

Notes: [a] Excluding oil royalties and oil company profits taxes.
   [b] Averages are numerical means.

Source: Government Finance Statistics Yearbook.

on personal and business income, while in Iraq, the maximum on both types was 75 percent. Despite this disparity Iran was realizing close to 10 percent of its revenues in this way, while Iraq's non-oil income taxes yielded less than 2 percent of total revenues. The corporate tax schedule was graduated as high as 55 percent in Kuwait and 50 percent in Qatar; in the latter, however, this tax is 12 times relatively more important than in the former.

If we compare the Middle East countries with the developing countries (listed above in Chapter 2) for which such income tax data are available for the late 1970s, then we find that all the oil exporters and most of the non-oil exporters rank rather low relative to LDCs in other parts of the world (*Table 10.10*). Only one of the countries covered in this study, the Yemen People's Democratic Republic, collects a share of its revenue from income taxes that is higher than the *average* share found among the comparison group of 36 LDCs. The industrialized countries rely on income taxes to an even higher degree, though in recent years many European countries have substituted value added taxes (theoretically levied on consumption, and therefore an indirect tax) for all or part of corporate profits taxes (which are classified in the direct tax category).

In several of the oil exporting countries, per capita incomes have begun to resemble or even surpass those prevailing in the industrialized countries. Nevertheless, in respect of the levies directly aimed at incomes (*Table 10.11*), there is, as yet, no real comparison between these two groups. As we

Table 10.11 *Income taxes as a percentage of national income: Middle East oil-exporting and selected industrialized countries*

Oil-exporters[a] – Average: 1.1			
Bahrain	0.0	Oman	0.9
Iran	6.0	Qatar	0.3
Iraq	0.1	Saudi Arabia	0.5
Kuwait	0.02	United Arab Emirates	0.0
Libya	1.8		

Industrialized countries – Average: 11.3			
Australia	24.0	Japan	7.5
Austria	7.3	Netherlands	17.5
Belgium	17.0	Sweden	8.3
Canada	10.8	Switzerland	3.2
France	7.7	United Kingdom	17.8
Federal Republic of Germany	6.5	United States	12.4
Italy	7.4		

Note: [a] Excluding oil royalties and oil company profits taxes.
Source: See *Table 10.10.*

indicated in Chapter 2, direct taxes in general, and income taxes in particular, tend to be underutilized in developing economies because of the difficulty of administration.

Several factors contributing to this problem were mentioned: the need for competent bureaucrats to oversee the fiscal program, the difficulty of assessing incomes in economies still operating, in the main, outside the cash sector, the need for considerable voluntary compliance (which depends to a considerable extent on how equitable the tax structure seems to those who are affected by it). There is no doubt that most of the Middle East countries have problems in the first regard. Countries with large numbers of skilled people, like Lebanon or Jordan, often cannot (or will not) pay salaries high enough to keep capable workers in civil service. Many of the richer countries, like the Gulf states, are still woefully short of skilled indigenous labor and the high salaries that attract expatriates to these countries are mostly to be found in the private sector.

As regards the second problem, there is still a fairly large traditional subsistence non-cash sector in nearly all Middle Eastern countries, at least in terms of the number of people involved. But this is a situation of rapid

Table 10.12 *Percentage of population in urban areas: Middle Eastern and selected developing countries (1960 and 1980)*

	1960	1980		1960	1980
Middle East					
Egypt	38	45	Libya	23	52
Iran	34	50	Saudi Arabia	30	67
Iraq	43	72	Sudan	10	25
Jordan	43	56	Syria	37	50
Kuwait	72	88	Yemen Arab Rep.	3	10
Lebanon	44	76	Yemen People's Dem. Rep.	28	37
Developing countries					
Bolivia	24	33	Mali	11	20
Brazil	46	65	Pakistan	22	28
Burundi	2	2	Philippines	30	36
Chad	7	18	Senegal	23	25
Ethiopia	6	15	Tanzania	5	12
Ghana	28	36	Thailand	13	14
India	18	22	Togo	10	17
Kenya	7	14	Upper Volta	5	9
Malaysia	25	29	Zambia	23	38

Source: World Development Report, 1980, (The World Bank).

change, especially in countries where the agricultural resources are sparse, which tend to be the oil exporting countries. The sharp absolute rise in income and profits taxes for nearly every country during the 1970s is evidence of the spread of the cash economy throughout the region. In fact, the relative size of the cash sector of most Middle Eastern countries is probably quite a bit larger than that in many of the African and Asian countries listed in *Table 10.10* as having a greater dependence on income and profits taxes than the Middle East. Within the region there are several anomalies in this respect. For example, Lebanon, the most urbanized non-oil exporter (see *Table 10.12*) also makes less use of income taxes than any other non-oil exporter except north Yemen. Iran, the least urbanized oil exporter, collects, relatively, the most from this fiscal source among the group of oil exporters. So we cannot explain the divergences among Middle Eastern countries in their ability (and willingness) to use income and profits taxes only on the basis of relative preponderance of the urban cash dominated sector of the economy.

The third problem – the need for voluntary compliance and its link with perceived equity – can perhaps be of help in explaining some of the regional differences. Some categories of taxpayers may have little choice but to pay the levies that are due – either because their incomes are easily subjected to scrutiny by the fiscal authorities, or because a type of automatic tax withholding system is in effect. Thus tax collections could be higher in a

Table 10.13 *Percentage of income tax receipts arising from business profits*

Country	Year	Percentage
Egypt	1977	75.1
Iran	1977/78	92.7
Iraq	–	NA
Jordan	1976	85.0
Kuwait	1978/79	100.0
Lebanon	–	NA
Libya	–	NA
Oman	1978	100.0
Qatar	1978	100.0
Saudi Arabia	1977/78	100.0
Sudan	1977/78	74.7
Syria	1976	84.7
Yemen Arab. Rep.	1977/78	58.9
Yemen People's Dem. Rep.	1978	73.9

country with comparatively few large and easily identified corporations than in one with a myriad of small enterprises of indefinite legal status, although both countries might be similar in the extent of industrial activity. Not only are profits taxes easier to collect in the former case; the salaries of employees of such large operations are more vulnerable to tax withholding at source. However, if it is clear that the fiscal authorities either cannot enforce (or choose not to do so) their collections outside certain parts of the economy, then certainly there are no incentives to pay unless one is caught. As we have indicated in Chapters 7 and 8, the entire category of income taxation in the Middle East is heavily tilted toward profits tax receipts (see *Table 10.13*).

Another way to approach the equity question is through the traditions and moral standards of the society in question. As we have seen in Chapter 5, Islam near its core has the roots of a system of taxation, and over a period of 1400 years an extensive body of legal literature has been built on questions relating to fiscal aspects of the state. Despite all the scholarly elaboration, a central theme is clear: every Muslim has obligations to the community at large and particularly to those less fortunate or weaker than himself, and avoidance is a sin. One way to meet these obligations has been *zakat*, one of the five pillars of Islam. In addition, the community or state has the right to enforce *zakat* at least in part, or, if necessary, to impose other fiscal levies on the faithful to meet its legitimate needs. These levies are morally binding on Muslims.

As *Table 10.14* shows, the vast majority of the population in the region we are considering adheres to Islam: probably 90 percent of the 150 million residents of these 16 countries. However, the data presented in Chapters 7 and 8 offer little evidence that traditional Islamic modes of taxation play a significant role at the present time. Only in three countries – Saudi Arabia, Sudan, and the Yemen Arab Republic – do the official sources of fiscal

Table 10.14 *Estimated Muslim percentage of total population: Middle Eastern countries*

Bahrain	75	Oman	85
Egypt	90	Qatar	75
Iraq	93	Saudi Arabia	88
Iran	98	Sudan	65
Jordan	85	Syria	85
Kuwait	75	United Arab Emirates	70
Lebanon	55	Yemen Arab Rep.	97
Libya	75	Yemen People's Dem. Rep.	95

Note: Total population includes expatriates, officially recorded and otherwise (authors' estimates). Period indicated is late 1970s.

statistics report *zakat* receipts, and even in these cases, the amounts are only a small part of government revenues. In the latter two countries, non-oil exporters, *zakat* and other traditional taxes have lately been accounting for about 2 percent of total receipts, while in Saudi Arabia, only a miniscule 0.1 percent is derived in this way.

But there are at least two reasons why these official statistics may understate the role that traditional Islamic teaching plays in determining current fiscal profiles. First, (as was discussed in Chapter 5) *zakat* obligations can be satisfied through voluntary almsgiving and although the community, acting through the official agencies of the state, may take steps to enforce the provisions of religious law, it should not eliminate the voluntary aspects of compliance. Therefore limitations have usually been placed on the state role, restricting it, for example, to half of the total obligation. Furthermore, there is no requirement that the state be involved specifically with the collection of *zakat*, although it should ensure that the faithful comply with the provisions of *zakat* and other religiously based taxes. In addition, *zakat* and *'ushr* have in the past been paid in kind rather than in cash, as was indicated in the examples cited above in Chapter 5. Thus, even if the religious obligations were being adhered to in a given country, the official tax records might record only a fraction of these payments.

Secondly, the traditional taxes, when being described in contemporary fiscal terms, are either wealth taxes (*zakat*), production taxes (*'ushr*), or poll taxes (*jizyah*). The argument could be made that other tax devices might well be in line with the spirit, if not with historical practice, of Islamic taxation. For example, the wealth of a merchant or landowner is fairly tangible, but that of a professional person is embodied in his or her training or skills. This 'wealth' cannot easily be taxed, but the income it generates can be identified.

Table 10.15 *'Religiously-appropriate' taxes as a percentage of total tax receipts and of national income*

Country	Total taxes (%)	National income (%)	Country	Total taxes (%)	National income (%)
Bahrain	0.0	0.0	Saudi Arabia	0.5	0.4
Egypt	21.3	6.1	Sudan	11.1	2.5
Iran	11.3	6.5	Syria	15.1	4.2
Iraq	2.2	0.2	United Arab Emirates	0.0	0.0
Jordan	13.5	3.1	Yemen Arab Rep.	7.0	1.0
Kuwait	0.1	0.1	Yemen People's Dem. Rep.	22.4	4.1
Lebanon	18.7	2.6			
Libya	2.9	1.8	*Average*: 16 countries	6.5	2.8
Oman	1.5	0.9	*Average*: Oil exporters	4.8	2.6
Qatar	0.3	0.3	*Average*: Non-oil exporters	16.5	4.1

Note: Averages weighted by GNP (1977).

Therefore judgment of the overall conformance of the fiscal system to Islamic ideals would seem to require some flexibility in defining what types of taxes should be considered. We would suggest that in addition to *zakat*, *'ushr*, and *jizyah*, as specifically defined, the following also would, arguably, be consistent with Islamic religious principles: non-regressive income and profits taxes, capital gains and inheritance taxes (wealth levies conveniently assessed on a one-time basis rather than on the annual basis of *zakat*), and various property related tax devices borrowed from non-Islamic sources (such as transfer and registration fees), taxes on the rental value of buildings and levies on major consumer durables, like automobiles[7]. These 'religiously-appropriate' taxes are shown as a percentage of total tax receipts and national income in *Table 10.15*. In only Egypt and the Yemen People's Democratic Republic do these taxes account for as much as a fifth of all government revenues. While the non-oil exporters use them more than do the oil exporters, only about 16.5 percent, by weighted average, of the former group's tax receipts originated in categories bearing some similarity to traditional Islamic levies.

On the other hand, if we look at buoyancies as a measure of change (*Table 10.16*), we find separate patterns for oil and non-oil exporters. Among the latter all but two countries (the two Yemens), the buoyancies for 'religiously appropriate' taxes were higher than for all tax revenues. In these cases, the various income- and wealth-related levies have become more prominent in

Table 10.16 *Buoyancies of all taxes and 'religiously appropriate' taxes (1950–1978)*

	All taxes	Religiously appropriate taxes
Bahrain	1.350	0
Egypt	1.155	1.251
Iran	1.695	1.535
Iraq	1.334	0.823
Jordan	1.219	1.299
Kuwait[a]	1.335	1.451
Lebanon	1.806	2.081
Libya	1.238	0.876
Oman[a]	1.795	NA
Qatar	1.623	NA
Saudi Arabia	1.463	0.993
Sudan	1.340	1.365
Syria	1.327	1.432
United Arab Emirates	1.199	0
Yemen Arab Rep.	1.501	1.367
Yemen People's Dem. Rep.	1.129	1.001

Notes: NA indicates data not available for at least one end-year or zero taxes in the initial year. Zero indicates no such taxes in either end-years
[a] 1962–1978.
[b] 1964–1978.

the fiscal profile during the last three decades. For the oil exporters' the prevailing picture is of lower buoyancies and slower growth rates for these taxes. The small part these taxes play (*Table 10.10*) in oil exporters receipts has been shrinking, rather than growing, in importance[8].

One major tax category remains for consideration – the levies that we might lump together as consumption taxes, principally customs duties and excise and sales taxes. For *a priori* reasons, these are usually considered as regressive taxes, hitting hardest at the poorest elements of society whose meager incomes are totally spent within the domestic economy where these levies apply. They are less onerous for the richer classes who may avoid some of their relative burden by saving part of their incomes, or by spending on such luxuries as foreign travel. In practice, however, the fiscal authorities have considerable leeway in designing the impact of these taxes. Basic consumer goods, such as food, for which the average and marginal propensities to spend by the poor are quite high, can be exempted, while luxury goods, often imported from abroad, can be taxed heavily. Because of this flexibility, making comparisons across a diverse group of countries is quite difficult. Not only must the specific tax structure of each country be considered but so must changes in a particular country over time. In our group we have such differing examples as Egypt, which not only exempts basic foodstuffs from import duties but further subsidizes the eventual market price for these goods, and the Sudan, which has been earning about 6 percent of all its fiscal revenues from the profits of the state-owned importing and marketing monopoly for sugar. The smaller Gulf states have had generally uniformly low flat rate tariff schedules which have remained the same for as many as 20 or more years, while countries like Iran, Iraq, and Syria have seen several major revisions in their tariff schedules during the same period.

Table 10.17 compares the relative importance of these easily administered and collected indirect taxes in the Middle Eastern countries and in selected LDCs in other parts of the world. The essential dichotomy present in the fiscal profiles of Middle Eastern countries is clear when we examine the data. Because oil exporters realized so much of their revenues from their principal natural resource, they used domestic consumption taxes much less than both their non-oil exporting neighbors and LDCs in general. The non-oil countries of the area (*Table 10.10*) do not use direct taxes to the extent that most other LDCs do and their reliance on indirect levies is generally greater. The average ratio of these consumer tax receipts to total receipts was only 4.7 percent for the nine oil exporting countries, but 51 percent for the other seven Middle Eastern countries.

Changes in the relative importance of customs duties and excise taxes can be seen in the buoyancy figures shown in *Table 10.18*. For only three countries, Jordan, Lebanon, and South Yemen (all non-oil exporters), were the buoyancies for this category higher than for all fiscal receipts. Thus, generally across the region these taxes have been becoming a relatively less important source of government revenues. However, the rate at which this change is taking place seems to be related to the major fiscal dichotomy – oil export earnings – among the countries.

Although these consumption oriented taxes are usually thought of as being somewhat regressive, a particular levy may be specifically designed to be progressive, and may be so in practice. Without a more detailed analysis than is possible here, we cannot generalize about such a diverse group as these 16 Middle East countries, or even about one country over time. However, it is interesting to note that in this region of the developing world at least, this administratively popular form of indirect taxation seems to be becoming less important in relation to other categories of taxation, even among those countries without an easily taxed resource such as oil. The data shown in *Tables 10.16* and *10.18* are consistent with a gradual shift towards direct taxes on income and wealth in the non-oil exporting countries.

Table 10.17 *Ratio of consumer taxes[a] to total government revenues: Middle Eastern countries compared to selected developing and industrialized countries (all figures percentages)*

Middle East – Average: 24.9

Bahrain	10.8	Lebanon	64.2	Syria	29.7
Egypt	36.7	Libya	6.5	United Arab Emirates	1.0
Iran	10.4	Oman	1.0	Yemen Arab Rep.	72.0
Iraq	8.4	Qatar	1.4	Yemen People's Dem. Rep.	48.9
Jordan	47.9	Saudi Arabia	0.7		
Kuwait	1.8	Sudan	57.7		

Developing countries – Average: 47.6

Argentina	37.7	Jamaica	52.5	Singapore	24.2
Bolivia	50.8	Kenya	53.2	Somalia	61.5
Brazil	34.3	Korea	60.8	Sri Lanka	41.2
Burundi	43.0	Malaysia	35.9	Taiwan	57.1
Chad	57.1	Mali	38.4	Tanzania	54.5
Chile	43.9	Mexico	32.3	Thailand	64.9
Colombia	35.6	Morocco	52.9	Togo	26.1
Congo	47.6	Nepal	59.0	Tunisia	48.9
Costa Rica	42.6	Pakistan	66.7	Turkey	36.4
Ethiopia	42.3	Paraguay	35.1	Upper Volta	62.9
Ghana	46.7	Peru	73.1	Venezuela	12.0
Guatemala	45.1	Philippines	54.7	Zambia	48.9
Honduras	47.2	Rwanda	48.5		
India	59.0	Senegal	68.7		

Industrialized countries – Average: 24.7

Australia	27.5	Federal Republic		Sweden	30.3
Austria	27.2	of Germany	23.8	Switzerland	28.9
Belgium	23.5	Italy	28.5	United Kingdom	25.0
Canada	22.9	Japan	24.7	United States	6.0
France	31.8	Netherlands	21.5		

Note: [a] Includes import duties and excise taxes on goods and services.

Source: See *Table 10.10.*

For the oil exporters, the buoyancies of what we have defined as 'religiously appropriate' taxes were higher than those of the consumer taxes in five countries over the same time periods – Iran, Iraq, Kuwait, Libya, and Saudi Arabia. In two more, Oman and Qatar, income and wealth taxes have been introduced so recently that we did not bother to present buoyancy figures in *Table 10.16*. Omani income tax revenues had replaced customs receipts by the late 1970s as the second largest revenue source (though a decidedly distant second – see *Table 7.18*). In Qatar, income tax receipts grew rapidly in the 1970s, though they are still only a tiny fraction of oil revenues. Neither Bahrain nor the United Arab Emirates have any form of

Table 10.18 *Buoyancies of consumer taxes (1950–1978)*

Bahrain	1.006	Oman[a]	0.444
Egypt	0.968	Qatar	1.032
Iran	1.355	Saudi Arabia	0.681
Iraq	0.755	Sudan[b]	1.452
Jordan	1.288	Syria	1.003
Kuwait	1.344	United Arab Emirates[c]	0.615
Lebanon	1.953	Yemen Arab Rep.	1.473
Libya	0.799	Yemen People's Dem. Rep.	1.651

Notes: [a]. 1962–1978
   [b] 1955–1978.
   [c] 1964–1978.

income or wealth taxation. On the whole then, for the oil exporting countries, direct taxes also seem to be gaining at the expense of indirect consumption-related taxes. However, none of these nine countries collects much less than three-quarters of its revenue from oil (see *Table 6.5*), making the shifts that take place among non-oil taxes rather unimportant by comparison.

Notes

1 This group includes eight oil exporters – Algeria, Brunei, Gabon, Malaysia, Nigeria, Trinidad & Tobago, Tunisia, and Venezuela; and eight exporters of four major minerals – Ghana, Guyana, Jamaica and Surinam (bauxite); Chile and Zambia (copper); Morocco (phosphates); Mauritania (iron).

2 Shail Jain, *Size Distribution of Income: A Compilation of Data*, (Washington D.C.: The World Bank, 1975).

3 For developed capitalist countries (that is, members of OECD), the Gini coefficients indicated by Jain range from about 0.44 in the Netherlands to about 0.32 for Australia.

4 Some fragmentary data are included in the World Bank publication *World Tables 1980*. The latest estimates for the percentage of income going to the poorest 20 percent in Egypt was 5.1 percent (mid 1970s), for Iran four percent (1970), for Lebanon four percent (mid 1970s) and for Sudan 5.1 percent (1968). This source also presents estimates for the percentage going to the richest five percent: Egypt – 22.0 percent, Iran – 29.7 percent, and Lebanon – 26.0 percent. In addition it has some indicators for Jordan: 6.3 percent of income going to the poorest quintile and 24.6 percent to the richest five percent in 1973. As can be seen these figures represent

no real advancement over those shown in *Table 10.8*.

5 The Libyan results reported by Jain are notable for the strange degree of equality they indicate – coefficients far below those for nearly every other *non-socialist* country (which Libya certainly was in 1962) for which Jain includes data. This egalitarianism is one of shared urban poverty, since 1962 was only Libya's second year as an oil exporter and long before oil revenues had any real impact on the vast majority of Libyans.

6 As indicated, the Libyan study does not shed much light on this question since it was carried out before oil was a major factor and since the quality of this study is even more questionable than that of the others.

7 State enterprise revenues, which equal or exceed in amount what is raised in many Middle Eastern countries by these taxes, cause us some difficulty. Much of such revenue is analogous to the profits tax levied on private business, but it also includes some oil-derived income and the revenue from the sales of state assets such as land. Because of difficulty in making comparisons across the group, it seemed best to leave these receipts out of the 'religiously appropriate' category. However, had they been included, they would have made a considerable difference for some countries. For example, in Syria, this category, without state enterprise revenues, accounted for 15.1 percent of total receipts in 1977. With them included, the share would jump to 60.2 percent but would include a sizeable amount of oil revenues.

8 It must be kept in mind that for the oil exporters, these income and wealth taxes not only are limited in scope but were often only recently imposed. Thus for Oman and Qatar, the years during which modest profits taxes have been in effect, did not seem a long enough period over which to present buoyancy comparisons in *Table 10.16*.

CHAPTER 11

Oil exporting countries

11.1 Bahrain

Bahrain is a decidedly minor oil exporter compared to the other eight countries discussed in this chapter. In fact, it produces much less than Egypt and Syria, which are classified as non oil-exporters in this work (cf. *Table 6.1*). However, our division of the Middle East into two groups was based on the relative importance of oil exports to a particular economy (not the absolute level of production) over the entire period of approximately three decades. For more than 20 years, Bahrain has exported about as much oil as it does today; these oil exports are nearly all the oil it produces, and clearly dominate other exports. In both Egypt and Syria, on the other hand, oil production, until quite recently, was not enough to cover domestic demand.

If then Bahrain technically belongs in the oil exporter group, its prosperity has always been more modest than that of its neighbors. Perhaps because of this, it has developed a more diversified economy, especially in comparison to the other smaller states along the Gulf. By the early 1970s Bahrain had clearly established itself as a regional service center and during the boom following 1973 such industries as banking, insurance and transportation have found the small island state an ideal location from which to do business throughout the oil producing region.

But, as *Tables 7.1, 7.2* and *11.1* show, the gradual diversification of Bahrain's economic base has not been matched by a broadening of its fiscal base. It is still without any type of tax on income or profits, despite the presence of burgeoning Arab and international business communities. The UAE is the only other state without these particular taxes. Long a major *entrepôt* for the Gulf, Bahrain historically has had low tariffs to encourage this transfer trade. However, the duties have remained minimal in the face of rapid growth in domestic imports and a sharp relative decline in reexports. The principal beneficiary of this policy now, is the Bahraini consumer.

Of course it has been higher oil prices that have allowed a minor producer like Bahrain to reduce its relative reliance on non-oil taxes, and because of this, it passes more of its fiscal burden to foreign consumers to the benefit of its own citizens. *Table 11.1* indicates that this has been done in the face of production cutbacks, which will stretch out the island state's modest reserves, while total receipts were up nearly 400 percent in the five years following 1973. This is also helped by the fact that, despite its oil exporter status, Bahrain has been able to exploit its strategic location in order to secure substantial economic assistance from its wealthier neighbors. Saudi Arabia has been particularly generous, and its recent agreement (1980) to fund the multibillion dollar construction costs of a long discussed causeway connecting the island to the mainland is only the largest of many Bahraini projects in which it is participating.

Table 11.1 *Bahrain: selected economic and fiscal statistics (1950–1978)*

	1950	1962	1968	1973	1978	
Population (thousands)	110	163	204	237	283	
GNP (millions of *dinars*)	13.5[a]	22.4[a]	37.1	84.0	585	
Annual oil production (millions of barrels)	11.0	16.4	27.5	24.8	20.0	
Total government revenues (millions of *dinars*)	1.7	7.5	32.8	46.8	246.3	
Percentage from:						
Oil taxes and royalties (%)	55.2	72.0	67.5	62.8	77.9	
'Religiously appropriate' taxes	0	0	0	0	0	
Consumer related taxes (%)	35.3	24.0	21.7	11.8	10.8	
Tax revenue/GNP ratio (%)	12.6	33.5	32.4	55.7	42.1	
Per capita						
GNP (*dinars*)	123	137	182	351	2067	
Oil receipts (*dinars*)	8.2	33	40	123	678	
Domestic taxes (*dinars*)	7.3	13	19	73	192	
Tax buoyancies						1950–78
All taxes		3.056	0.929	1.761	0.830	1.350
Oil taxes and royalties		3.736	0.797	1.656	0.960	1.465
'Religiously appropriate' taxes		0	0	0	0	0
Consumer related taxes		2.225	0.721	0.910	0.788	1.006

Note: [a] Estimated.

Source: See *Table 7.1.*

Booming oil revenues and foreign assistance have provided little incentive for the Bahraini government to look for new domestic sources of revenue. At least until now, the government has not needed more than it could obtain from foreigners (oil importers or aid donors). It has also followed what seems, on the surface, to be a successful policy of encouraging foreign corporations, especially in the service sector, to establish themselves in Bahrain by presenting the island state as some sort of nearly taxfree haven operating under *laissez-faire* principles. But it could certainly be argued that many of the institutions that have been attracted to Bahrain have been drawn more by its location, its access to communications and transportation and by its relative abundance (compared to its neighbors) of skilled labor, than by non-existent taxes on income, profits and property. Thus it would seem that modest levies in these regards would not detract from the appeal of Bahrain as a banking and commercial center.

But while the Bahraini government may not have lost vital revenues by avoiding any diversification of its fiscal structure, it has deprived itself of many of the policy tools that a broader tax base would provide. For example, an untaxed business sector means an implicit subsidy (relative to average world standards) to any nascent Bahraini industry, some of which, it would seem safe to assume, cannot survive without the continuance of that subsidy. It also means that, as far as tax authorities are concerned, all investments are treated the same, whether they be in the form of real estate speculation, or of industrial development which, in the long term, provides employment.

We have pointed out that traditional Islamic teachings require that the rich contribute out of their wealth to the community's needs, and have argued that by analogy at least the case can be made that a reasonable level of property and income taxation is consistent with these teachings[1]. Bahrain in recent times has used no such taxes; of the other states in the region only the much more oil-rich UAE do not utilize this form of taxation. Thus, its fiscal structure can be faulted on two grounds – both by the standards of modern economic policy and by Islamic tradition.

One last point ought to be made relative to the Bahraini statistics shown in *Table 11.1* – for nearly three decades the buoyancy of domestic taxation was greater than unity, indicating that tax receipts grew faster than GNP. However, since buoyancy from 1950 to 1978 was only 1.006, the lead of the former over the latter was not much.

It would seem appropriate at this point to indicate statistical anomalies that affect all nine countries in this chapter, especially as Bahrain is itself such an obvious anomaly. In using standards based both on western economics and on Islamic principles, problems arise from the inclusion of oil revenues.

First, and most obviously, these earnings greatly boost both GNP and total tax revenues; recently, they have raised the latter proportionately more than the former, but in the 1950s, and to a lesser extent in the 1960s, the situation was reversed. Thus, any ratios which involve one or other, or both, of these two measures (GNP and tax revenues) are subject to some distortion if compared to similar ratios for countries where the oil industry is a much smaller part of the economy (such as the seven countries discussed in the next chapter).

Secondly, oil is a natural and finite resource, the sale of which produces income in the current time period. That income can be used for whatever purpose its recipient determines, but at least theoretically the spending of such income is governed by economic principles relating to the use of capital gains income (especially when a windfall is involved – which is the way in which many western economists view the post 1973 Middle East situation). The prudent recipient of such income devotes as much as possible to the purchase of productive capital assets that will reproduce current income in the long run. In this way an exhaustible natural resource is transformed into a renewable resource, either natural, industrial, human or financial. Yet taxes on oil sales are represented in fiscal accounts exactly the same as taxes derived from any other industry or from any other sort of wealth. These oil revenues boost overall tax receipts, enormously in the cases of most of the Middle Eastern oil exporters, and tend to make other actual and potential tax sources seem less important both to those who set tax policy and to those who evaluate its performance *ex post facto*.

Thirdly, if we take the viewpoint of traditional Islamic teaching on taxation, *zakat* and *'ushr* were levied on what was essentially *reproducible* wealth (in other words, income). The revenues derived in this way were to be devoted to *current* needs – the defense of the state, the support of the poor and the maintenance of the community's necessary social appurtances. When we judge the fiscal performance of a portion of the Islamic community in this regard, we must be able to distinguish between taxes that relate to income derived from finite resources and those that relate to renewable resources.

In fact, we often cannot do so easily, despite the carefully reported statistics on oil-derived revenues for most of the Middle Eastern exporters. In some cases, oil taxes include revenues that should be charged against the renewable as opposed to the exhaustible side of the ledger; in other cases (much more frequent in occurrence), current and capital budgets are inseparable on the spending side and it cannot be estimated with any degree of accuracy where oil revenues are going.

As a result of this statistical difficulty there are a number of problems. From the viewpoint of the outside observer, there is first a dichotomy between the non-oil exporters (for which this problem does not exist) and those discussed in this chapter. Secondly, there is the broad spectrum that is found among oil exporters – on one extreme we have Qatar, with large oil fields and a tiny population (even including expatriates), and on the other, Iran and Iraq, diversified oil-producing economies whose combined populations are over 50 million. Thirdly, there is a tendency when interpreting the data shown in the tables of Chapter 7 to downplay the role of non-oil sources of fiscal revenues in the oil exporting countries. This is caused by the absence of complementary data relative to the uses of different types of tax revenue. In many cases capital spending is of course made possible by oil, while other taxes largely support the current budget. Fourthly, there is a further tendency to denigrate the role that traditional Islamic thinking on taxation may play in oil exporter fiscal policy decisions.

Table 11.2 Gross domestic product by industrial origin: oil exporting countries in the Middle East (1962–1978)

Country	Year	GDP	Mining	Other manufacturing	Agriculture	Construction	Services
					Percentage distribution		
Iran (billions of rials)	1962	351.2	14	12	28	4	38
	1968	658.8	17	13	21	5	37
	1973	1 860.9	32	14	13	4	33
	1977	5 365.7	37	11	9	9	31
Iraq (millions of dinars)	1962	695.9	31	10	20	3	32
	1968	1 100.7	31	10	15	3	35
	1973	1 626.4	35	11	12	4	34
	1976	4 856.8	51	7	7	7	22
Kuwait (millions of dinars)	1965	749.0	63	5	0.4	4	27
	1968	951.0	56	7	0.5	4	31
	1973	2 111.0	68	6	0.2	1	24
	1976	3 818.0	67	8	0.3	1	22
Libya (millions of dinars)	1962	172.4	23	5	9	6	47
	1968	1 110.7	58	3	3	8	25
	1973	2 246.2	50	3	3	12	30
	1978	5 911.5	55	3	2	11	26
Oman (millions of rials)	1970	106.8	67	0	16	10	7
	1973	169.4	56	1	10	14	20
	1978	892.8	57	1	3	10	30
Saudi Arabia (millions of riyals)	1962	8 673.0	46	9	10	2	31
	1968	15 975.0	46	10	6	6	30
	1973	99 314.9	78	6	1	3	20
	1977	223 746.8	57	4	1	14	22
UAE (millions of dirhams)	1973	11 392.1	70	2	1	.5	21
	1978	53 338.1	58	5	1	10	27

Note: Other manufacturing includes electricity, gas, and water.

From the viewpoint of those who make these decisions there are two very practical problems. First, there is the difficulty mentioned above that arises as a result of underestimating the usefulness of taxes as policy tools. Secondly, and following from the first, is the strong temptation for governments to avoid potentially troublesome domestic questions by adopting tax policies that are designed to promote short run internal tranquillity.

The magnitude of this statistical distortion in national income accounts can be seen from *Table 11.2*. For the seven countries for which more detailed national accounts figures are available, the share of the oil sector has ranged as high as 78 percent of GDP[2]. Only in Iran did it remain below half of GDP after the 1973/74 price increases, and despite rapid growth throughout the region in such sectors as construction and services, the oil industry is far more dominant in 1980 than it was in the 1960s when the region was much less diversified in terms of numbers of different types of economic activity taking place. The effects of increased oil prices (and in some countries, higher production levels) have been even greater on tax revenues than on GDP because the 1970s have also seen a radical realignment of the division of the price received for oil in world markets between governments and the oil companies.

11.2   Iran

Iran was, until its Islamic Revolution, by far the largest of the oil exporting economies in the Middle East; in the late 1970s it accounted for about 60 percent of the total population of these nine countries and its GNP was about 40 percent of the group's aggregate. It was also the most diversified economy, with the largest manufacturing, agricultural and service sectors (*Table 11.2*).

To some extent, this diversification is also reflected in Iran's fiscal profile. Although the share of oil taxes and royalties in total tax receipts climbed steadily through the 1960s and 1970s and from about 40 percent to nearly 75 percent just before the overthrow of the monarchy, the latter percentage was still lower than that found in any other major oil exporter (cf. *Table 6.5*).

Table 11.3 shows that as recently as 1968 Iran's revenues were derived equally from oil and from domestic taxpayers. During the following decade, oil receipts per capita grew at an average annual rate of about 38.8 percent, while domestic taxes per capita were growing at about 24.6 percent a year, only slightly faster than the 23.6 annual growth rate seen for GNP per capita. The taxes categorized as 'religiously appropriate' (income, profits and property taxes) maintained their relative importance in the government's revenue during this period. The domestic taxpayer 'gain' was mostly found in the consumer related taxes (customs duties and excises) which had dropped from about a fourth (1968) to barely a tenth (1977) of total revenues.

In trying to estimate the distribution of this gain within the Iranian economy, we cannot simply follow the conventional wisdom and say that the generally more progressive income and wealth taxes grew in importance relative to the generally more regressive taxes on consumption, and that, therefore, the 1968 to 1977 period saw the burden of the domestic tax structure tending to fall more heavily on those Iranians of greater economic means. Rather we must consider the major components of these categories of taxation individually.

Table 11.3 *Iran: selected economic and fiscal statistics (1950–1978)*

	1950	1963	1968	1973	1977
Population (millions)	16.28	22.77	27.08	31.30	34.27
GNP (billions of *rials*)	174.0	337.3	629.4	1832.7	5347.6
Annual oil production (millions of barrels)	242.5	487.0	1042.2	2152.2	2080.0
Total government revenues (billions of *rials*)	7.7	64.0	120.3	464.8	2034.3
Percentage from:					
Oil taxes and royalties (%)	11.7	40.0	51.4	67.0	73.6
'Religiously appropriate' taxes (%)	18.2	7.3	12.3	11.4	11.3
Consumer related taxes (%)	28.6	18.4	24.7	16.8	10.4
Tax revenue/GNP ratio (%)	4.4	19.0	19.1	25.4	38.0
Per capita					
GNP (thousands of *rials*)	10.7	14.8	23.2	58.6	156.0
Oil receipts (thousands of *rials*)	0.05	1.1	2.3	9.9	43.7
Domestic taxes (thousands of *rials*)	0.4	1.7	2.2	4.9	15.7
Tax buoyancies					1950–78
All taxes	3.404	1.012	1.303	1.454	1.695
Oil taxes and royalties	5.675	1.443	1.525	1.567	2.336
'Religiously appropriate' taxes	1.866	1.921	1.215	1.447	1.535
Consumer related taxes	2.628	1.502	0.898	0.919	1.355

Source: See *Table 7.3.*

As was indicated in Chapter 5, both the personal income and corporate profits tax schedules were sharply progressive in theory. However, most observers of the Iranian economy affirm that the burden of personal income taxes was easily avoided, in whole or in part, by many of those who, on paper, were most subject to these provisions. Aside from middle class employees of the governments and a few large private corporations, that is, of institutions withholding taxes from salaries, few Iranians paid anything like what they theoretically owed. In other words, the income tax legally exempted the poor, and in practice exempted the rich; leaving the middle class to shoulder the majority of the burden.

More important than personal income taxes have been those on corporate profits, which raised more than 160 billion *rials* in 1977/78. They increased about 20 fold since 1968, while personal income tax receipts, at about 50 billion *rials* in 1977/78, increased about ten fold during the same period. Whether these taxes were borne primarily by the owners of the corporations and other businesses, as would be the case if they are in reality direct taxes, or by consumers of these firms' goods and services in the form of higher prices, depends upon the demand elasticities.

Although it is not possible here to consider on a case by case basis the products of Iranian industry, there are at least two reasons to suspect that much of the profits tax ended up being paid by Iranian consumers. First of all, many of the country's industries saw little competition, either from abroad, because of protective tariffs and other import barriers, or at home where only a few firms made most items. Thus, the consumer found few substitutes for many of the products made domestically. Secondly, although the 1970s saw an increasingly wide variety of Iranian manufactures, most local firm activity was concentrated on products with tried and true markets – that is, import substitutes. For the most part, such goods are ordinary consumer goods in daily use, demand for which is generally inelastic. Therefore we would argue that the burden of this tax was probably falling more on the poorer and middle classes.

The taxes most obviously affecting consumers have been termed consumer-related – customs duties on imports and excise taxes. While these grew about seven fold, from less than 30 million *rials* to more than 210 million *rials*, between 1968 and 1977, this was considerably less than the 17 fold increase in total government revenues. As we can see from *Table 11.3*, these consumer related taxes slipped from being 24.7 percent of total revenues in 1968 to being only 10.4 percent by 1977; the buoyancy of this tax category over these nine years was only 0.908, indicating that they grew slower than did GNP.

Obviously, consumers gain when consumer taxes lose importance, but then the question is: which consumers? Again as with the income and profits taxes, an exact answer would require more detailed analysis than is possible here, but nevertheless we can surmise. As we discussed in Chapter 5, despite the apparently large gain in customs receipts during recent years, nonetheless, their growth was slower not only than overall tax revenues, but also than import values. For example, in the wake of the 1973/74 oil price rise, imports climbed from 233 billion *rials* in 1973 to 971 billion *rials* in 1977, or at a rate averaging about 43 percent a year; import duties during the same period grew by about 29 percent a year.

During the same time, the tariff structure underwent only marginal changes, so the explanation lies in the differentiated growth rates for different imports. Historically, Iranian tariffs have been directed at two types of commodities: those which are also produced domestically and are thus protected from competition under the so called infant industry argument; and those which are deemed to be luxuries, the consumption of which is to be discouraged by the tariffs. In this way scarce foreign exchange is diverted to more essential imports. Capital goods imported for the purpose of promoting industrial development have been spared from heavy tariffs. Purchases of goods led to Iran's import boom in the post 1973 period; but at the same time, such increases in this latter category did not add much to customs duty receipts. It would appear that individual consumers did not gain, at least in the short run, from this bias in the tariff schedule. Over the long term, if this policy of encouraging domestic industrialization was successful, individuals would benefit, in theory, from both the employment effect and from increasing efficiency in the domestic industries offered temporary protection from foreign competitors. But more immediately, those that benefit are the industrialists who can make their investments at cheaper costs (without tariffs) and realize their gains at higher prices (world prices plus tariffs).

The increased receipts from tariffs were obtained almost entirely from consumer goods, which with the exception of such absolute necessities as foodstuffs were often hit with levies of 100 percent *ad valorem* or more. Probably as with income taxes, those most directly affected by these charges were the middle income groups, and they would seem to have realized some gain, if in fact the relative burden of tariffs dropped during this decade[3].

Other sales related taxes have historically been limited to a few major excise levies. These have been on gasoline and other petroleum products, alcoholic beverages and automobiles. Generally hard to avoid, these taxes mostly hit the middle and upper income groups, though even poorer Iranians have been sharply increasing their consumption of petroleum products in recent years. Again however, we have the picture of a tax which affected the more prosperous elements of society becoming relatively less burdensome. Excises grew only a little more than five fold between 1968 and 1977, much less than any other major category of taxation.

In evaluating the fiscal policies followed in Iran we are faced with an apparent dichotomy: on the one hand, a violent revolution brought about by, amongst other things, economic dissatisfaction, which succeeded in overthrowing a long standing régime which had achieved a reasonable amount of economic modernization, and on the other hand fiscal policies which seem to have emphasized domestic diversification of tax revenue source in the face of greatly increased oil revenues from foreign consumers. During the mid 1970s, the one country among the oil exporters that managed to keep some tax pressures on the domestic economy, and in so doing tried to use fiscal policy tools, nevertheless failed, dramatically, to avoid revolution. One easily made if superficial reading of the lesson to be gained from this by other oil exporting states would be to avoid at all costs any serious increases in the domestic tax burden – to follow a policy of letting foreign oil consumers pay for all budgetary needs and therefore abandon fiscal policy as a means of affecting internal development. If the mightly Pahlavi empire, backed up by a very expensive military machine, fell before street rioters led by mullahs armed only with the Quran, how can weaker regimes in the Gulf states risk antagonizing their populations with higher domestic taxes?

We do not have any data which affirm either side of this question, but we would argue that the failure of Muhammed Reza Shah in fiscal policy was not in trying to use internal fiscal tools, but in ignoring certain economic 'facts of life' when designing and applying these tools. We have seen in Chapter 10 evidence of the heavily slanted pattern of income distribution that prevailed in Iran; we have argued in Chapter 7, and in this section, that recent taxes, both implicit (inflation) and explicit, have tended to exacerbate the problems that such an income distribution indicates.

In post 1973 Iran, the existing structure of the economy made the rich far richer, in real terms as well as apparently; the tax schedules did little to redress the imbalances. On paper, the poor seemed better off, but inflation eradicated most of their gains, especially in the urban areas. The domestic tax structure perhaps did them no real harm, but neither did they gain from it. The middle class, or many parts of it at least, were squeezed from both sides – they were obviously affected by inflation and often heavily hit by higher taxes. In the winter of 1978/79, it was the combined strength of the urban poor and of the middle classes that sent the Shah into exile.

Though on paper (cf *Table 11.3*) a superficial case could be made that Pahlavi had maintained the relative importance of the taxes we have grouped together as 'religiously appropriate' (income, profits and property taxes), religious Iranians were apparently not impressed. In fact, the monarchical régime did not argue that it was following Islamic taxation principles, and if it had, the claim probably would not have found many receptive listeners. So while undoubtedly the Pahlavi government did maintain a larger role for internal tax revenues than did other Middle Eastern countries during the 1970s, the policies that it followed showed little awareness of the preexisting imbalances within the Iranian economy or of the potential usefulness of domestic fiscal policy to correct or control these imbalances.

What then of Iran in revolution? We have discussed earlier in detail the traditional Islamic teachings on taxation, and the clerical government of the Ayatollahs certainly preaches the need to move towards the goal of an economy fully in accord with Islamic principles. In Chapter 7 we outlined some of the changes that were decreed in the immediate post revolution period regarding income taxes. These were designed to offer some relief to the poorest economic classes, and undoubtedly they did, but they were not true structural changes; rather, they belatedly, and partially, recognized the effects of inflation on tax brackets during the last two or three years of the imperial era.

Tax receipts have been affected by these adjustments in rates, but the major disruptions in many sectors of the Iranian economy since late 1978 have had a much greater impact. No data concerning either are yet available.

But dwarfing all domestic tax changes under the Islamic republic is what has happened in the oil sector. In the last complete fiscal year of the Pahlavi régime, 1977/78 (cf. *Table 11.3*), fully 73.6 percent of government revenues or some 1497 billion *rials* came from sales of oil on the world market. Though per barrel revenues accruing to the government during that year were only about a third of what they were by late 1980, two years of increasingly chaotic conditions had almost eliminated oil revenues as a major factor in the Iranian budget. Average daily output from Iranian oil fields is shown in *Table 11.4* over the post World War II period. Production reached its peak in the euphoria of higher 1974 prices, but good technological sense then dictated cutbacks to preserve the lifetimes of mature oil fields. These conservative estimates of the petroleum engineers prevailed through mid 1978; after that, the economic disruptions culminating in the successful revolution of early 1979 increasingly affected the oil fields[4].

Table 11.4 *Average daily output: Iranian oil fields (1945–1980) (thousands of barrels)*

1945	375.5	1976	5919.1
1950	664.4	1977	5234.0
1952	27.7	1978: I	5501.5
1956	541.8	II	5712.5
1960	1067.8	III	5927.5
1964	1710.7	IV	3804.5
1968	2847.5	1979: I	1180.6
1970	3845.5	II	3868.1
1972	5066.6	III	3766.3
1973	5896.4	IV	3380.4
1974	6056.4	1980: I	2631.9
1975	5384.6	II	1564.8

Source: Petroleum Economist.

The loss of Iran as a major supplier to the world oil market[5] caused panic, and prices in the spot market shot up. Eventually, stable prices in the neighborhood of $30, some 150 percent above 1977 prices, were established by early 1979. When some degree of normal operation was regained in Iranian oil fields in the spring of 1979, oil revenues were even greater than they had been before the revolution when production levels had been much higher. Since the Khomeini government had announced goals of both reducing oil output (and thus prolonging reserve lifetime) and of cutting back on government spending, the achieving of oil cutbacks, together with actual gains in revenue, represented major economic gains.

But this euphoria was short lived. In the majority Arab populated Khuzestan province, where most oil fields are located, labor unrest rather than government decreed conservation policies kept oil output levels to two thirds of what they were under the Pahlavi regime. During 1980, internal problems multiplied, and output plummeted, this time without any offsetting increase in oil prices. By late summer 1980, oil exports hit the zero level as output was only enough to meet domestic needs, and this was before the outbreak of fighting between Iran and Iraq which destroyed much of Iran's petroleum infrastructure. Iranian earnings from oil during 1979 fell 1 or 2 percent from the levels of the year before, but were still above $20 billion. However, government sources indicated by mid summer 1980 that the expected shortfall during the 1980/81 fiscal year would be much greater than had been expected and that revenues would be about half the anticipated level, possibly no more than $10 billion. These admissions, apparently meant to prod ministers into serious budget cuts, were, in fact, much too optimistic.

As far as oil revenues were concerned, in 1980 Iran was in a position that was similar in many ways to the one it occupied in 1950; that is, a leading exporting country, for which oil is the major element in its fiscal profile, that was on the brink of a long decline in its principal industry. It took 7 years in the 1950s for Iranian oil production to recover its pre-crisis levels, and Iran never again dominated regional exports because countries like Kuwait and Saudi Arabia secured the markets that Iran lost. Beginning in early 1979, Saudi Arabia filled much of the gap caused by the decline in Iranian production, but over the longer term, it may be other countries which supplant Iran. For instance, in Iraq production was up over 30 percent in 1979, a year in which it also replaced Iran as the world's second largest oil exporter; but much depends on Iraq's recovery from the 1980–82 war with Iran. Mexico, on the other hand, has no such problems in securing new long-term markets.

A prolonged internal crisis may have very long term fiscal repercussions for Iran. The leaders of the Islamic Republic may be forced toward rapid changes in the country's tax structure simply to make up for losses in oil revenues[6]. Although, as we have seen, Iran has historically made more use of non-oil tax sources than most of the other exporting countries, it still has not made nearly as much use of them as have most LDCs. Even after taking steps to curtail spending drastically, Iran in the early 1980s still seems likely to face serious internal tax problems.

11.3   Iraq

Iraq is the second largest economy among the region's oil exporters in terms of population and oil exports, and third largest in terms of GNP. Though its economy is not as diversified as Iran's (see *Table 11.2*), it is more varied than those of its southern neighbors in the Arabian peninsula. Because, in the Middle East, its available agricultural resources are second only to Egypt's[7] and its already fairly well-educated population is larger than that of the entire peninsula, it is generally conceded to have the brightest potential for economic development, given prudent use of oil revenues[8].

But this potential is not obvious in Iraq's fiscal profile. For more than 25 years, Iraq has collected close to 2 out of 3 *dinars*, or even more, of its tax revenues from oil; since the oil price rises of 1973/74, the proportion has

Table 11.5 *Iraq: selected economic and fiscal statistics (1950–1977)*

	1950	1962	1968	1973	1977
Population (millions)	5.12	7.32	8.86	10.41	11.91
GNP (millions of *dinars*)	182.0	604.1	899.3	1554.4	5392.5
Annual oil production (millions of barrels)	51.0	459.4	551.2	717.7	909.9
Total government revenues (millions of *dinars*)	33.5	168.2	305.4	1018.0	2810.2
Percentage from:					
Oil taxes and royalties (%)	17.3	58.9	57.2	80.9	85.5
'Religiously appropriate' taxes (%)	10.8	6.8	6.6	3.6	2.1
Consumer related taxes (%)	52.8	19.8	15.7	7.2	11.7
Tax revenue/GNP ratio (%)	18.4	27.8	34.0	65.9	52.1
Per capita					
GNP (*dinars*)	35.5	82.5	101.5	148.4	452.8
Oil receipts (*dinars*)	1.1	13.5	19.7	79.1	201.8
Domestic taxes (*dinars*)	5.4	9.5	14.8	18.7	34.1
Tax buoyancies					1950–78
All taxes		1.368	1.523	2.384	0.787	1.334
Oil taxes and royalties		2.535	1.448	3.183	0.837	1.871
'Religiously appropriate' taxes		0.958	1.458	1.095	0.366	0.823
Consumer related taxes		0.514	0.905	0.792	0.926	0.755

Source: See *Table 7.6.*

climbed to 5 out of 6 (see *Tables 7.6* and *11.5*). Since 1958 Iraq's various republican regimes have professed socialist ideals, but they have relied much less on internal taxation to achieve their ideals than did Iran's capitalist regime.

Unlike the situation in most other oil exporters, Iraq has generally been clearer in enunciating its intentions of keeping capital and current expenditures distinct, although these intentions have often only been honored in the breach. As indicated in Chapter 7, Iraq has published separate current and development budgets since 1950 (cf. *Table 7.7*). Initially, by law, 70 percent of oil revenues were to be spent on development and 30 percent on current expenses. After the revolution of 1958, the Qasim regime began 'borrowing' oil receipts for non-capital expenditures, allegedly to redress some of the immediate needs of the populace which had been ignored under the monarchy. By the mid 1960s, a *de facto* policy of splitting oil revenues equally between the two budgets had become official. Even this division was often violated in favor of current expenditures, most drastically during the 1974/75 fiscal year in the wake of the oil price rise and the reopening of military conflict between Arabs and Israelis in late 1973[9]. Since 1975,

Table 11.6 *Annual changes in official consumer price indices: Middle East countries (1973–1978) (%)*

	1973	1974	1975	1976	1977	1978
Oil exporters						
Bahrain	14.4	24.4	16.1	14.9	12.0	11.3
Iran	9.8	14.3	12.7	11.3	27.3	11.6
Iraq	4.9	8.3	9.5	10.3	7.7	4.5
Kuwait	8.4	13.2	8.9	5.5	8.2	9.0
Libya	8.0	7.4	9.2	5.4	6.4	29.4
Saudi Arabia	16.6	21.4	34.6	31.6	11.3	−1.6
Non-oil exporters						
Egypt	4.3	10.8	9.8	10.3	12.7	11.1
Jordan	11.1	19.4	12.0	15.3	10.8	6.9
Sudan	15.3	26.1	23.9	1.7	16.7	19.9
Syria	21.0	14.7	16.3	11.0	12.6	4.8
Yemen Arab Rep.	42.2	26.6	23.5	17.0	24.8	NA
Yemen People's Dem. Rep.	19.8	20.4	11.5	3.7	5.2	5.9

Note: Changes are those indicated during the year in question.

Source: International Financial Statistics, December 1980.

however, the development budget has clearly benefited from higher oil receipts. By 1977 for example, it had risen almost 250 percent over 1973 levels, almost entirely because of additions from the oil account, while the current budget was up to about 120 percent, as a result of slightly more growth in non-oil taxes (which have always gone to this budget) than in the oil revenue share.

Somewhat surprisingly, markedly similar buoyancies for both taxes in general and oil receipts in particular were found for the post 1973 interval than for any other part of the period under examination. In fact, Iraq was the only major oil exporter[10] (see *Table 11.5*) for which the post 1973 buoyancies were less than unity, indicating that GNP grew faster than did either total tax revenues or oil receipts. Though we pointed out earlier that the overwhelming role of oil in the economies of these nine exporting countries can frequently generate statistical anomalies that are difficult to explain correctly, these low buoyancies in Iraq after 1973 in the face of very sharp increases in oil revenues (averaging almost 131 percent a year over the four year period) are consistent with indications that the non-oil sectors of the economy were growing even faster[11] (*Table 11.6*). If this is in fact true, then the Iraqi economy may have attained the major gains, among the Middle East's oil exporters, from the first part of the 'OPEC revolution'.

Tables 7.6 and *11.5* tell the story of those revenues derived from domestic sources. Between 1950 and 1970, while GNP per capita grew by about 9.9 percent a year, the per capita receipts from all sources of domestic taxation grew by an average of about 7.1 percent a year, only a third of the annual gain in per capita oil receipts – 21.3 percent. The former sources brought in 5 of every 6 *dinars* in fiscal receipts in 1950; in 1977, this proportion had almost equally reversed in favor of oil revenues.

Both of the other major categories of taxation we have been using for comparative purposes fell sharply in relative terms. The 'religiously appropriate' taxes on income, profits and property that raised nearly 11 percent of Iraq's revenues in 1950 brought in barely 2 percent by 1977. The consumer related levies on imports and excises on selected products, which generated more than half the government receipts of 1950, brought in less than 12 percent in 1977.

The approximate five to one ratio of the latter to the former that prevailed throughout the period in question indicates maintenance of the initial preference of a generally regressive type of tax over a generally progressive type. This situation would be regrettable enough in the light of the income distribution data shown above in *Tables 10.8* and *10.9*. But there is also reason to believe that the static relationship between the two tax categories may actually have been more antagonistic toward any goal of more equality of distribution than may be apparent on the surface.

Iraq's income tax structure, like that found in many other LDCs, tends to be a burden primarily on a small part of the population – the generally lower portion of the middle income group that works for such institutions as the government which enforce income tax withholding regulations. Thus, on the one hand, this tax proves in practice not to be progressive, and on the other, not to be very helpful when vital agencies try to recruit and hold on to good employees.

The tariff schedule has held fairly constant in favoring absolute necessities and capital goods, concentrating on so-called luxury goods. The problem here is that the 'typical' Iraqi consumer is spending more and more of his or her income on these 'luxuries', while the richer elements continue to consume a sizable portion of their incomes outside the reaches of the tax collectors.

Thus, while we see on the face of the data an ostensibly static internal tax situation, in reality the 'progressive' portion hits more at the broadening lower middle income group. The consumption taxes, designed to tax supposed luxuries, have been affecting a larger proportion of the spending of a larger proportion of the lower income elements of the population. If this assessment is reasonably accurate, Iraq's 'static' domestic taxation has in fact become increasingly regressive over the last three decades.

What Iraq's fiscal direction was in the short-term past, given the latest data shown in *Tables 7.6* and *11.5*, is a relatively easy question to answer, at least through 1980. The post 1973 gains in oil revenues escalated sharply in the late 1970s, and not simply because of increased oil prices. As *Table 11.7* shows, production increased notably during this period, despite a general levelling out in what was previously a voraciously increasing demand of world markets. On the one hand, this was due to a very discreet policy of

Table 11.7 *Average daily output: Iraqi oil fields (1945–1980) (thousands of barrels)*

1945	100	1975	2248
1950	140	1976	2389
1955	688	1977	2493
1960	972	1978	2629
1964	1255	1979: I	3231
1968	1506	II	3371
1970	1566	III	3500
1972	1466	IV	3622
1973	1966	1980: I	3500
1974	1866	II	3533

Source: Petroleum Economist.

offering price cutting discounts, just marginal enough to win the increasingly important non-contract oil sales. On the other there was a program of production increases, especially after Iranian output levels faltered (cf. *Table 11.4*) at the onset of the anti Pahlavi revolution. During this period, Iraq replaced Iran as the world's second largest oil exporter. With the higher prices of 1979, Iraqi revenues soared, at least until September 1980, when its border war with Iran damaged the delivery infrastructures of both countries.

Although oil revenues might temporarily reverse their climbing trend[12], it does not seem likely that the 1980s will see any major change in their relative importance in Iraq's fiscal profile. Since the Iraqi government leaves less leeway for the private sector than do any of the neighboring oil exporters, a continued minimal use of fiscal policy tools may be of little significance concerning the direction the economy may take in the coming decade. However, if the role of the private sector is to be stressed more, the historic weakness of fiscal policy would assume a greater importance.

11.4   Kuwait

Kuwait's combination of a small population and a lengthy history of high oil production levels, and, therefore, of a high level of per capita income attained long before the oil price increases of 1973/74, put it into a special category among developing nations. The fiscal consequences of this were to preclude any perception, on the part of the government, of the need to develop non-oil sources of revenues. As *Tables 7.10* and *11.8* indicate, from the onset of the 50/50 profit sharing formula adopted by the oil companies in the early 1950s, Kuwait's oil receipts accounted for 95 percent of the total revenue of the state, a level which has been maintained now for nearly 30 years. During this time, only one other source of income has come to assume any importance relative to oil receipts, and this is the income derived from Kuwait's investments of its past surpluses (*Table 7.11*). This income will be discussed in Chapter 13.

Kuwait has on its tax law books a levy on business profits which, (as was indicated in Chapter 7), seems to be quite progressive, rising in 5 percent

Table 11.8 *Kuwait: selected economic and fiscal statistics (1950–1978)*

	1950	*1962*	*1968*	*1973*	*1978*
Population (thousands)	100	350	630	890	1200
GNP (millions of *dinars*)	160.0	460.0	793.0	2123.4	4188.0
Annual oil production (millions of barrels)	125.7	714.6	956.6	1103.2	765.5
Total government revenues (millions of *dinars*)	6.0	182.9	263.7	586.2	3277.8
Percentage from:					
Oil taxes and royalties (%)	81.7	94.6	92.3	92.8	92.6
'Religiously appropriate' taxes (%)	0	0.1	0.1	0.2	0.1
Consumer related taxes (%)	13.3	2.7	2.7	2.0	1.4
Tax revenue/GNP ratio (%)	3.8	39.8	33.2	27.6	78.3
Per capita					
GNP (*dinars*)	1600	1314	1258	2385	3490
Oil receipts (*dinars*)	49.0	494.3	386.3	611.1	2530
Domestic taxes (*dinars*)	11.0	28.3	32.2	47.5	201

Tax buoyancies					*1950–78*
All taxes		3.582	0.662	0.796	2.824	2.041
Oil taxes and royalties		3.759	0.617	0.802	2.821	2.087
'Religiously appropriate' taxes		[a]	0	1.612	2.610	1.451[b]
Consumer related taxes		1.793	0.607	0.462	1.032	1.264

Notes: [a] Zero base year; no calculation possible.
          [b] 1962–1978.
Source: See *Table 7.10*.

incremental steps to 55 percent of all net profits above KD375 000 (about $1.4 million), which would indicate fairly hefty tax levels even for medium size firms. In practice, however, this tax has so many loopholes in its provisions that most firms pay no tax at all. As we can see in *Table 7.12*, profits tax receipts in fiscal year 1978/79, (the most recent period for which data were available), came to the paltry sum of about 700 000 *dinars* (about $2.5 million – or about $2 per Kuwaiti resident). Property taxes, actually levied against estimated rental value, brought in five times as much as the profits tax. But even using our broad categorical definition of 'religiously appropriate' taxes, the aggregate of income and property taxes was responsible for only 1 *dinar* in 750 of the Kuwaiti government's receipts in 1978/79. The high buoyancies for these taxes indicated in *Table 11.8* relate to numerical changes in an essentially insignificant category which are high only in isolation from oil revenues.

Consumer-related taxes derived from import duties weigh more heavily on Kuwaitis. These raised ten times the combined receipts of profits and property taxes in 1978/79 – nearly 47 million *dinars* or about 40 *dinars* per resident. This came from a flat rate *ad valorem* duty of 4 percent on nearly all imports. Since Kuwait produces few consumer or capital goods, this is essentially a fairly general sales tax, affecting most necessities in the same manner as obvious luxuries. As such, it is regressive, burdening the poor more than the rich. Both economic theory and evidence from other countries indicate that the poor are only consumers and pay general sales taxes on nearly all their income, while the rich either save or else spend outside the local tax collector's purview.

In Kuwait, the situation may well be slightly different, since more than half the population consists of non-citizens who have come to Kuwait to work for short periods. Many of these people, perhaps 25–30 percent, hold basically middle class jobs, and probably save more than they would at home. The others do Kuwait's menial jobs, and, despite their low pay status relative to other residents of the state, save half or more of what they earn to send to dependents in neighboring countries. Thus in Kuwait it may well be that a general sales tax[13] is not in effect a heavy burden on the poorest portion of the population. However, it is probably still regressive, to the extent that the richest portion is least affected.

There are no real indications that Kuwait uses import duties as a serious revenue-raising device. Rather, it seems to be more in the category of fees for services rendered[14] – paying for the state's trade organizing and regulating apparatuses. *Table 11.9* shows that Kuwait and other sparsely populated oil exporters are much more like the industrialized countries or LDCs in general.

Kuwait has obviously shown no interest in using the conventional internal tax policy tools to any extent. Its tax structure not only has little effect on spending or investment[15] decisions at the present time, but the stability of its

Table 11.9 *Import duties as percentage of total taxes: Middle Eastern countries compared to selected developing and industrialized countries*

Middle East – Average: 19.3

Bahrain	10.6	Lebanon	41.3	Syria	18.1
Egypt	36.9	Libya	5.6	United Arab Emirates	1.0
Iran	8.2	Oman	1.0	Yemen Arab Rep.	68.5
Iraq	6.4	Qatar	1.4	Yemen People's Dem. Rep.	30.8
Jordan	41.6	Saudi Arabia	0.7		
Kuwait	1.3	Sudan	33.3		

Developing countries – Average: 19.5

Argentina	5.7	India	15.9	Rwanda	31.2
Bolivia	23.0	Indonesia	6.7	Senegal	41.4
Brazil	3.3	Jamaica	41.3	Singapore	8.2
Brunei	1.1	Kenya	22.7	Somalia	39.8
Burundi	20.5	Korea	17.0	Sri Lanka	13.1
Chad	44.0	Malaysia	15.1	Taiwan	28.7
Chile	6.3	Mali	18.8	Tanzania	13.9
Colombia	12.8	Mexico	4.9	Thailand	20.9
Congo	30.1	Morocco	18.6	Togo	15.7
Costa Rica	11.9	Nigeria	15.9	Tunisia	23.3
Ethiopia	24.4	Nepal	26.9	Turkey	16.3
Gabon	20.0	Pakistan	32.0	Upper Volta	44.3
Ghana	17.3	Paraguay	18.7	Venezuela	8.6
Guatemala	16.5	Peru	12.6	Zambia	5.0
Honduras	20.7	Philippines	21.6		

Industrialized countries – Average: 2.8

Australia	5.2	Federal Republic		Sweden	1.0
Austria	1.6	of Germany	0.03	Switzerland	5.9
Belgium	0.01	Italy	1.0	United Kingdom	9.3
Canada	6.6	Japan	2.3	United States	1.6
France	0.03	Netherlands	2.3		

Source: Government Financial Statistics Yearbook.

relative tax burden over the nearly 30 years covered in this study indicates that this situation is one of long standing.

The reason for this lack of interest is not hard to discern, either in Kuwait or in several other oil producers in the Middle East or elsewhere. It is not only that oil revenues have provided so much of the state's income up until now, but also that there are reasonable expectations that this situation will continue for many years to come. *Table 11.10* indicates how today's technology predicts the length of time over which present production levels can be maintained[16]. In few, if any, of the economically and politically more sophisticated countries of Europe, North America or the Pacific region, do many leaders consider seriously a time horizon extending as long as even ten years when fiscal policy decisions are being made. For Kuwait and several other oil exporting countries, oil receipts are not likely to diminish over the next 20 years. Therefore political leaders that look to diversification of the tax base now might well risk more unpopularity that would be more damaging to their regimes than delaying the inevitable move away from the almost absolute fiscal dependence on the oil sector for a few more years.

Unfortunately, this sort of attitude ignores a fact mentioned several times above: that taxes are not only a revenue raising device, but also serve as a multi purpose economic policy tool. To the extent that Kuwait eschews almost all direct taxation on personal and business incomes as well as consumption taxes which discriminate in their effect among various goods, its government forfeits a large part of its potential ability to affect the economic decisions of the private sector. Though this is a problem of long

Table 11.10 *Oil reserve lifetimes (reserves to output ratios): selected oil-producing developing countries*

Bahrain	13.2	Algeria	18.6
Egypt	17.0	Angola	23.2
Iran	54.8	Brunei	19.3
Iraq	35.2	Ecuador	13.7
Kuwait	75.4	Gabon	7.1
Libya	31.4	Indonesia	16.4
Oman	22.7	Mexico	57.5
Qatar	21.5	Nigeria	20.1
Saudi Arabia	47.9	Trinidad & Tobago	8.9
Syria	33.2	Tunisia	58.7
United Arab Emirates	43.9	Venezuela	21.0

Note: Ratios are calculated using 1979 production levels and estimated proven reserves as of 1 January 1980.

Source: International Petroleum Encyclopaedia 1980.

standing in Kuwait, given its maturity as a major oil based economy, there are reasons to believe that the abdication of the use of fiscal policy tools has had more serious implications since 1973. After the increase in oil prices which sharply boosted the already high Kuwaiti per capita receipts from this source, the government began in earnest a program of economic diversification which, while it was more modest than those being pursued in neighboring Iran, Iraq and Saudi Arabia, nonetheless involved billions of *dinars* and dozens of industrial projects. Implicitly, all new projects have been granted a major subsidy, relative to similar plants elsewhere in the world market, by being granted, in effect, an indefinite suspension from tax obligations; thus the likelihood (which is already strong in most LDC industrialization programs) is increased of long term subsidies to industries with doubtful credentials.

Secondly, also in the early 1970s, the Kuwait government realized that the large budget surpluses which it was already amassing (when oil prices were much lower), seemed to suggest conservation of its non-renewable natural resources – at least to the extent of keeping revenues in line with actually planned expenditures. The effects of this policy can be seen from the oil production figures of *Table 11.11*: output peaked in 1972 and had retreated almost 25 percent by 1974, the first year of the higher price regime. Though the government has not consistently followed these conservation policies[17],

Table 11.11 *Average daily output: Kuwaiti oil fields (1947–1980) (thousands of barrels)*

1947	44	1975	2085
1950	344	1976	2150
1955	1104	1977	1973
1960	1692	1978	2097
1964	2307	1979: I	2601
1968	2614	II	2571
1970	2988	III	2462
1972	3283	IV	2417
1973	3022	1980: I	2174
1974	2474	II	1553

Source: Petroleum Economist.

it has generally kept anticipated expenditures (for projects which were at least on paper) as a major criterion in the determination of production policy. Thus the government seems aware of the important links between tax revenue decisions and its development program, even if this awareness has not been translated into any broad application of fiscal policy tools.

11.5   Libya

Unlike the first four countries discussed in this chapter, Libya only became an oil producer during the period covered by this study. The data shown in *Tables 7.13* and *11.2* show the country's fiscal profile both before and after oil exports transformed its tax situation. An appreciation of how rapid this transformation was can be gained from an examination of the oil output figures: production began in 1961, and in that year Libya pumped an average of 19.2 thousand barrels a day, for which the government received 1.1 million *dinars*. Within 5 years, production reached 1.5 million barrels a day, putting Libya ahead of veteran exporter Iraq, and in 1970, average outflow was 3.3 million barrels a day which made Libya OPEC's third largest oil producer, behind only Iran and Saudi Arabia. During this decade, oil receipts paced government revenues, which from all sources amounted to only 11.5 *dinars* per capita in 1960, growing to 274 *dinars* per capita in 1970.

Indirect taxes, principally the consumer directed levies (import duties and excises), had predominated in the pre-oil era, and were responsible for four-fifths of total revenues as late as 1962/63, but by the end of the 1960s, their relative position had shrunk drastically, to only about one tenth of government receipts. During the 1970s, these taxes tended to maintain their position.

The only other tax of any note is that on income, both personal and corporate. As we have seen in Chapter 7, both types are subject to a progressive schedule, with the maximum rates being 35 percent on the

Table 11.12 *Libya: selected economic and fiscal statistics (1952–1977)*

	1952	1962	1968	1973	1977
Population (millions)	1.04	1.45	1.84	2.25	2.63
GNP (millions of *dinars*)	25	184	881	1928	5182
Annual oil production (millions of barrels)	0	66.5	951.5	796.4	758.0
Total government revenues (millions of *dinars*)	4.9	25.1	357	821	3105
Percentage from:					
Oil taxes and royalties (%)	0	7.6	78.4	75.1	83.2
'Religiously appropriate' taxes (%)	16.3	13.1	4.9	5.0	2.9
Consumer related taxes (%)	53.1	56.2	11.1	10.2	6.5
Tax revenue/GNP ratio (%)	19.6	13.6	40.5	42.6	59.9
Per capita					
GNP (*dinars*)	24.0	127	479	857	1970
Oil receipts (*dinars*)	0	1.3	152	274	982
Domestic taxes (*dinars*)	4.7	16.0	42	91	198
Tax buoyancies					1952–77
All taxes		0.804	1.866	1.068	1.804	1.238
Oil taxes and royalties		[a]	4.352	1.008	1.970	2.479[b]
'Religiously appropriate' taxes		0.689	1.074	1.098	0.996	0.876
Consumer related taxes		0.834	0.633	0.938	1.127	0.799

Notes: [a] Zero base year; no calculation possible.
[b] 1962–1977.

Source: See *Table 7.13.*

former and 60 percent on the latter. In addition, there is a very steep surtax, on all sorts of income, that theoretically rises to a maximum of 90 percent.

Though income tax receipts more than doubled between 1973 and 1977, their growth was slower than that of total tax receipts, GNP and national income. Despite the distortions discussed above that are introduced into comparisons between tax revenues from oil and non-oil sources and measures of national product and income, it seems likely to conclude on two grounds that the Libyan income tax is not nearly as effective a progressive tax as it would seem at first glance. In the first place, since it brings in only small returns (2.9 percent of total tax revenues in 1977, amounting to about 1.8 percent of national income), despite the high rates, few taxpayers pay anything near the full assessment that is theoretically due. This is clear even when we make generous allowances for the fact that it is not levied against the oil sector. Secondly, during the 1970s, when all portions of the Libyan eonomy were growing rapidly, income tax receipts, despite the progressive rate schedule, were lagging behind. As *Table 11.12* shows, this tax buoyancy during the 1973–77 period was less than unity.

Along with income and profits taxes, we have categorized property taxes as 'religiously appropriate'. Libya has been steadfast in its government's profession of the importance of applying Islamic principles throughout Libyan society, and in particular to the economy. However, as far as taxation is concerned, there are yet to be any discernible signs of movement towards Islamicizing the fiscal structure. The fraction of one percent realized from property taxes comes, not from an institutionalized form of *zakat*, but mostly from a levy on rental property. All together, the 'religiously appropriate' taxes which accounted for as much as a sixth of state revenues in the pre-oil era have steadily withered in relative importance as Libya's ability to tap foreign sources of fiscal income has grown.

Consumption-related taxes are still almost entirely import duties, reflecting Libya's overwhelming dependence on world markets for nearly all non-oil products. Though duties are generally at moderately high levels, there are a number of exceptions favoring such necessities as food. Also, under prescribed conditions, capital goods imports may qualify for exemptions. The larger part of these levies is paid on consumer goods therefore, especially durables and semi-durables, indicating that the brunt of their burden tends to fall on the middle class. Unlike income and property taxes, the consumer levies have had a buoyancy greater than one during the mid 1970s (see *Table 11.12*), indicating they have grown at a faster rate than GNP, though more slowly than oil revenues. Total imports increased more than tariff receipts during this period, but duties are concentrated on certain categories of commodities. From 1970 to 1977, capital goods imports grew fastest, followed by consumer goods and raw materials. For example, total imports by Libya from the industrialized OECD countries climbed at about 37 percent annually during this period, while consumer goods, the main source of tariff revenues, were up by about 34 percent a year.

Again, with Libya, we have a situation of the government mostly abdicating the possibility of using fiscal policy as an effective instrument of economic policy. It has not been total abdication as in Kuwait: even in the wake of the oil price increase of the 1970s, taxes on Libyan residents continued to supply more than 10 percent of state revenue. Pahlavi Iran actually used internal taxation to a greater extent, but not necessarily more effectively or equitably. In the light of its leader's strong devotion to the cause of devising some sort of 'third way' to economic development based on Quranic principles, it is surprising that, after a decade of revolutionary practice, Libya's fiscal profile should show so little evidence of Islamic influence. Steps in this direction could consist of prominent emphasis on income, profits, and property taxes and a tariff schedule that broadened the base of untaxed or lightly taxed commodities among the most widely consumed items.

Aside from strong Islamic motivations to make the internal tax structure more equitable, there are good reasons based on more secular considerations for the Libyan government to reexamine its fiscal arrangements. Although state enterprises, rather than private ones, dominate Libya's growing industrial efforts, publicly owned corporations (in the absence of central planning) take their cue from the climate prevailing in the market place in the same way as privately owned enterprises do. If these signals indicate a policy of little or no corporate taxation, they imply an unspoken subsidy, possibly indefinitely (for example, the lifetime of the oil exporting industry). The infant industry and comparative advantage arguments urge that even capital surplus countries like Libya should invest carefully, and in industries with strong promise of being able, eventually, to compete in world markets *without* subsidies.

11.6   Oman

Even in the company of its neighbors along the southern littoral of the Gulf – all desperately poor in any human or natural resources, aside from hydrocarbons – Oman stands out as an anomaly. Though it is only modestly endowed by Gulf standards (about $1500 in per capita oil receipts in 1978 versus $9200 in Kuwait and $11 300 in Qatar), it is certainly more fortunate than the vast majority of LDCs. The rather recent nature of Omani oil production (beginning in 1967) and the even more recent emergence of the country from an extreme xenophobia that blocked spending for economic and human development, despite the abdundance of revenues that followed increased production, mean that it has only a short history of pursuing the goals of social change.

In Oman, domestic fiscal policy has clearly not had a notable role in achieving these goals. Before oil production began, import duties supplied nearly all of the sparse revenues of the sultanate; these duties grew by about 8.7 percent a year over the period shown in *Table 11.13*. But at the same time, imports and gross national product climbed by averages of about 36.5 and 23.9 percent a year per capita – giving us the buoyancies of far less than unity for these consumer taxes shown in *Table 11.13*. Omani tariffs consisted in recent years of a flat rate of 2 percent on most goods with exemptions generally favoring capital goods which have increasingly dominated the trade sector in the 1970s. Thus, the brunt of this minor tax is borne by the nation's consumers.

Barely more important than import levies in the late 1970s were what we have been calling 'religiously appropriate' taxes; in Oman, this comprises a single tax, on the profits of non-oil companies. Though the revenues realized from this levy increased about ten fold in the five years following

Table 11.13 *Oman: selected economic and fiscal statistics (1962–1978)*

	1962	1968	1973	1978	
Population (thousands)	490	550	720	840	
GNP (millions of *rials*)	15.0	59.6	142.4	790.0	
Annual oil production					
(millions of *rials*)	0	87.9	106.9	114.7	
Total government revenues					
(millions of *rials*)	0.7	26.6	65.0	482.2	
Percentage from:					
Oil taxes and royalties (%)	0	95.9	94.3	91.3	
'Religiously appropriate' taxes (%)	0	0	1.1	1.5	
Consumer related taxes (%)	100.0	4.1	2.6	1.0	
Tax revenue/GNP ratio (%)	4.7	44.7	45.6	61.0	
Per capita					
GNP (*rials*)	30.6	108	198	940	
Oil receipts (*rials*)	0	46	92	524	
Domestic taxes (*rials*)	1.4	2.0	5.1	50	
Tax buoyancies					1962–78
All taxes		3.229	1.026	1.206	1.795
Oil taxes and royalties		[a]	1.006	1.184	1.117[b]
'Religiously appropriate' taxes		0	[a]	1.431	1.431[c]
Consumer related taxes		0.303	0.477	0.519	0.444

Notes: [a] Zero base year; calculation not possible.
      [b] 1968–1978.
      [c] 1973–1978.

Source: See *Table 7.18.*

the oil price rise of 1973 (see *Table 7.18*), and thus yielded a higher buoyancy for this category than for oil revenues, it still brought in only about 1 *rial* in every 60 accruing to government accounts in 1978.

Again we see the picture of a lightly populated country that has become almost totally dependent upon oil to generate official income. Oman's much shorter history of economic development and diversification, it seems safe to say, indicates fewer taxing opportunities, especially in the business sector. Like Bahrain, Oman has also been able to tap its richer neighbors, especially Saudi Arabia, for a sizable amount of concessional economic assistance.

Perhaps Oman should not be blamed too much for past failures to use fiscal policy but it should be careful not to follow the patterns set by richer (and earlier to export oil) neighboring Gulf states. In fact, in the late 1970s only Qatar was realizing more per capita ($32) than Oman ($24) from income taxes; the others, despite their higher levels of economic activity and generally greater economic sophistication, were far behind, for example Kuwait ($2.), and Bahrain and the UAE, neither of which had any such revenues.

11.7   Qatar

This least-populated of the oil exporting Gulf states stands with the richest countries in the world in terms of GNP per capita. The reason for this sets the tone for Qatar's fiscal situation. Very high oil revenues, and very few people, have resulted in this emirate's government accruing an annual income well in excess of its immediate needs. As a result, non-oil taxes have been superfluous and, aside from a few minor exceptions, Qatar has dispensed with them.

The data shown in *Table 11.14* actually somewhat understate the dominant role of the oil sector in generating Qatar's official revenues. Another consequence of the country's long history of budget surpluses has been the accumulation of a considerable amount of capital invested in foreign markets, especially since 1973. In the last section of this chapter we will discuss the fiscal implications of this situation, which exists in several other oil exporting countries. At this point it is enough to point out that the largest part of Qatar's current non-oil tax revenues are the fruits of past oil production. *Table 11.14* indicates that in 1978, for example, about 90 percent of state receipts come from oil and 10 percent from other sources, but from *Table 7.21*, we see that the income realized from Qatar's investments that year came to 618 million *riyals* (about $160 million) or about 7 percent of total revenues.

Most prominent in the miniscule 3 percent or so of Qatari revenues with no direct connection to present or past oil production, are the returns from the broad based *ad valorem* tariff of 2.5 percent. Since such things as foodstuffs and some capital goods are exempted from even this modest levy, the burden falls most heavily upon middle class consumers – that is, on the vast majority of Qatari citizens and on the minority of the expatriates who hold the better-paying jobs in the emirate. Less affected are the poor, mostly expatriates carrying out Qatar's menial and manual labor. As was indicated above in our discussion of Kuwait, these latter workers from the Middle East, east Africa, and south Asia have been attracted to the Gulf emirates by the prospect of being able to save much of what they earn. Thus, consumption taxes, which exempt the bare necessities, do not much concern them.

The only Qatari tax which falls into our 'religiously appropriate' category is a levy on business profits which had grown by 1978 to the modest amount of 25 million *riyals* (about $6.4 million) since its introduction in the early 1970s. Though the tax theoretically is graduated rather steeply to a maximum of 50 percent, the exemptions granted to several of the larger firms operating in Qatar, plus the modest size of most of the country's other enterprises, keep the returns from this tax small even if collections are scrupulously made from all potential taxpayers, which is hardly the case in reality.

Table 11.14 *Qatar: selected economic and fiscal statistics (1950–1978)*

	1950	*1960*	*1967*	*1973*	*1978*
Population (thousands)[a]	13	46	78	150	200
GNP (millions of *riyals*)	100	570	1162	4290	11 000.6
Annual oil production					
(millions of barrels)	12.3	63.9	118.2	207.9	175.9
Total government revenues					
(millions of *riyals*)	6.3	268	438	1720	9 059
Percentage from:					
Oil taxes and royalties (%)	84.1	97.0	91.8	93.2	89.9
'Religiously appropriate'					
taxes (%)	0	0	0	0.1	0.3
Consumer related taxes (%)	15.9	0.9	1.5[a]	0.8	1.4
Tax revenue/GNP ratio (%)	6.3	47.0	37.7	40.1	82.4
Per capita					
GNP (thousands of *riyals*)	7.7	12.4	14.9	28.6	55.0
Oil receipts					
(thousands of *riyals*)	0.4	5.7	5.3	11.2	43.8
Domestic taxes					
(thousands of *riyals*)	0.1	0.2	0.5	0.7	4.6
Tax buoyancies					*1950–78*
All taxes		2.394	0.680	1.053	1.903	1.623
Oil taxes and royalties		2.507	0.629	1.209	1.886	1.657
'Religiously appropriate' taxes		0	0	[a]	3.094	3.094
Consumer related taxes		0.481	1.452	0.538	2.646	1.032

Notes: NA indicates data not available.
　　　[a] Estimated.
Source: See *Table 7.20.*

Qatar, then, is quite similar in fiscal profile to several of its neighbors. Abundant oil receipts, especially in the 1970s have rendered potentially unpopular domestic taxes unnecessary, at least from the short run revenue raising viewpoint. However, a price is being paid for this abstention, though it is very difficult to assess how high that price will be in the long run. But

Qatar, like its neighbors, pursues an industrialization program, and its very avoidance of fiscal policy tools is an unintended fiscal policy, in that it subsidizes and shelters industrial projects which pay little or no taxes.

11.8 Saudi Arabia

By far the largest oil producer in the Middle East, Saudi Arabia, like other countries discussed in this chapter, has a fiscal profile which is overwhelmingly dominated by oil revenues, (*Tables 7.23* and *11.15*). Even in the late 1940s, before the changes in the relationship between the major international oil companies and their host countries brought on the so called 50/50 profit sharing arrangement that prevailed through the 1950s and 1960s, Saudi Arabia received more than two-thirds of its taxes from the oil industry. Between 1948 and 1978, oil production in the kingdom increased more than

Table 11.15 *Saudi Arabia: selected economic and fiscal statistics (1950–1977)*

	1950	*1960*	*1967*	*1973*	*1977*
Population (millions)	3.99	5.02	5.86	6.76	7.87
GNP (millions of *riyals*)	3000	6984	11 696	30 094	185 384
Annual oil production (millions of barrels)	278.0	599.7	1 113.7	2 773.6	3 023.3
Total government revenues (millions of *riyals*)	461	2257	4 895	22 800	146 471
Percentage from:					
Oil taxes and royalties (%)	72.7	85.2	85.5	92.5	89.1
'Religiously appropriate' taxes (%)	2.9	1.4	1.1	0.7	0.5
Consumer related taxes (%)	13.0	5.9	5.5	1.8	0.7
Tax revenue/GNP ratio (%)	15.4	32.3	41.9	75.8	79.0
Per capita					
GNP (thousands of *riyals*)	0.75	1.35	2.00	4.45	23.6
Oil receipts (thousands of *riyals*)	0.08	0.38	0.71	3.12	16.6
Domestic taxes (thousands of *riyals*)	0.03	0.07	0.12	0.25	2.0
Tax buoyancies					*1951–78*
All taxes	1.945	1.535	1.731	1.028	1.463
Oil taxes and royalties	2.155	1.543	1.834	1.003	1.520
'Religiously appropriate' taxes	1.040	0.973	1.237	0.808	0.993
Consumer related taxes	0.932	1.417	0.410	0.976	0.681

Source: See *Table 7.23.*

25 fold, while wide ranging changes in world markets induced revenue gains of more than 900 fold, as per barrel export returns went from about 1.4 *riyals* to about 45 *riyals* (and then on to about 100 *riyals* a barrel after the price escalations induced by the Iranian revolution in 1979).

The major oil discoveries occurred nearly 50 years ago, when Saudi Arabia had no other fiscal source more promising than the small tax imposed on every faithful (and usually poor) Muslim who made the arduous journey to Saudi Arabia in fulfilment of the Quranic obligation of *Hajj* – the pilgrimage to the Holy Cities of Mecca and Medina. Since then two generations of Saudi Arabian budgets have not found a serious substitute for, or supplement to, oil revenues.

For most of that time, Saudi Arabia was, like most LDCs, quite poor and with little in its economy worth much attention from tax collectors. During the 1950s and 1960s, oil production increased quite steadily, at an average rate of a little over 10 percent a year, while per barrel returns from oil were fairly steady. As *Table 11.15* shows, the buoyancies during this period for all taxes and for oil taxes alone were very similar, at a value close to 1.85, indicating that oil taxes pushed total revenues up almost twice as fast as GNP.

More recently, of course, Saudi Arabia has embarked on a massive wide based program of economic development and diversification, with considerable attention to the non-oil industrial sectors and to agriculture. The result of this has been a spurt in economic growth that shows up in changes in such standard economic measures as GNP, changes that are historically unprecedented outside a few other oil exporting countries. Though the kingdom's oil revenues have grown in a spectacular fashion, about 44 percent a year during the mid 1970s, GNP kept pace – paradoxically resulting in the lowest values of the modern period for tax buoyancy occurring during the mid 1970s, just about equal to unity. However, despite this diversification, by the late 1970s, there was no sign that it had been accompanied by a broadened tax base. As can be seen from *Table 11.15*, oil revenues were a slightly smaller part of the government's receipts in 1977 than they had been in 1973, though in 1978 they were slightly ahead of where they had been, in relative terms, in 1968[18].

As far as 'religiously appropriate' taxes are concerned, Saudi Arabia probably has been more persistent than any other Middle Eastern country in trying to use Islamic guidelines to determine both its economic direction and the economic policies which it will employ. This has followed from the kingdom's maintenance of *shari'a*, Islamic law, as the sole guideline for the judicial system.

In fiscal matters this would indicate a prominent role for traditional Islamic taxes, or at least for taxes which are reasonably closely analogous. Thus, our 'religiously appropriate' category should be a useful tool for the purpose of making comparisons. The official religion of Saudi Arabia is

Wahhabi Islam, a most orthodox *Sunni* sect, and *Sunni* teaching has rather consistently indicated a prominent role for the community and its institutions in overseeing, and enforcing, if necessary, the religious obligations of individual Muslims.

In fact, during the lifetime of the Saudi kingdom, *zakat* has been enforced and its returns have been officially reported (see *Tables 7.23* and *7.24*). These returns, together with analogous taxes (which include non-oil income and profits taxes), have been lumped together already in the 'religiously appropriate' category (cf. *Table 10.15*).

We have shown in this table what Middle East countries are collecting under this guise in tax revenues, and we repeat the figures for convenience in *Table 11.16* so that we can make comparisons between Saudi Arabia and other Middle East countries, and Islamic countries in other parts of the world.

Table 11.16 *'Religiously appropriate' taxes as percentage of total tax receipts: selected Islamic countries*

Middle East			
Bahrain	0.0	Oman	1.5
Egypt	21.3	Qatar	0.3
Iran	11.3	Saudi Arabia	0.5
Iraq	2.2	Sudan	11.1
Jordan	13.5	Syria	15.1
Kuwait	0.1	United Arab Emirates	0.0
Lebanon	18.7	Yemen Arab Rep.	7.0
Libya	2.9	Yemen People's Dem. Rep.	22.4
Elsewhere			
Afghanistan	27.0	Mauritania	20.0
Algeria	24.1	Morocco	24.8
Bangladesh	5.5	Niger	28.7
Brunei	0.5	Pakistan	11.5
Chad	20.0	Senegal	22.9
Gambia	13.0	Somalia	9.2
Indonesia	13.0	Tunisia	20.6
Malaysia	16.0	Turkey	50.8
Mali	25.5	Upper Volta	14.6

During the 30 or so years with which we are concerned, Saudi Arabia has never used these religiously based taxes to collect more than about 1 *riyal* in 35 of the kingdom's total revenues. Despite the clear and obvious surge in domestic personal and corporate wealth and income during the 1970s, the relative importance of these tax sources has actually sharply declined, from about 1.1 percent in 1968/69 to only about 0.5 percent in 1977/78. Under *Sunni* teaching the state may collect about the same amount as the voluntary quota (1.25 percent of wealth). If we take this as a guideline we could only assume that voluntary contributions approximately match official *zakat* collections, that is another 75–200 million *riyals* in 1977/78, or about 0.05 to about 0.15 percent of the total receipts. When we use national income statistics, no matter how much allowance we make for the distortions introduced into them by a relatively short-term phenomenon (a highly-priced exhaustible resource being intensively exploited), it is obvious that Saudi Arabia's receipts under our broadly defined 'religiously appropriate' category are not in line with what might be expected.

Among Islamic countries (see *Table 11.16*) Saudi Arabia can only be compared with the other major oil exporters; the average percentage in the late 1970s for these nine countries was about 2.1 percent, more than four times the relative share that these taxes had in Saudi Arabia – 0.5 percent. The seven non-oil exporting countries in the Middle East averaged about 13.5 percent for the 'religiously appropriate' taxes. Outside the region comparable data is available for 18 countries with Muslim majorities ranging from the Atlantic (Gambia) to the Pacific (Malaysia), and including some oil exporters (Algeria, Brunei, Indonesia, Malaysia, and Tunisia). From the viewpoint of religious taxes, this group is quite diverse; on the whole, it is obvious that these taxes are relatively much more important outside the region of the Islamic heartland[19] than they are anywhere in the Middle East. The average for the group is 19.3 percent of government income originating in the 'religiously appropriate' categories; with the exception of Brunei, the oil exporters are grouped around this mean, from a low of 13.0 percent in Indonesia to a high of 24.1 percent in Algeria.

Saudi Arabian finances in the early 1980s are characterized by: no income tax on citizen or expatriate, Muslim or non-Muslim; a business profits tax which is superficially highly progressive, but which in practice during the late 1970s was responsible for less than 0.5 percent of fiscal collections, and this in a country whose booming business sector was probably second to few in the world in growth and profit margins; and official *zakat* collections which have shown only modest growth, and which still only amounted to about 12 *riyals* (about $3.75) per capita in 1977/78. However lenient the standards that are used, Saudi Arabia, like the other oil exporters, has not seriously begun a program of using Islamic guidelines to structure fiscal policy.

For the other major category of domestic taxation, the so-called consumer related taxes, a picture of steadily eroding relative importance also emerges. The decline has been even more dramatic than for the income, profits and property taxes. As *Table 11.15* shows, customs duties and excises amounted to about 5.5 percent in 1968, less than two percent in 1973, and only 0.7 percent in 1977. As we have indicated in Chapter 7, during the tremendous export boom of the mid 1970s, customs levies were up by only about three fold while imports were climbing some twelve fold. Excises have continued to be minor, even when compared to the low rate customs duties, which exempt most necessities and capital goods.

What has been stated above can only be repeated here: conscious fiscal policy which would affect the domestic sectors of the Saudi Arabian economy has received so little attention, before and after the 1973/74 oil price increase, that observers can fairly decry its absence in the Saudi Arabian fiscal profile. It is obvious that Saudi Arabia will continue to generate budget surpluses as long as its strategic oil export policy remains the same as in the 1970s, to pump enough oil to stay, as far as is possible, the dominant price setting power in OPEC councils[20]. But this is still not sufficient reason to ignore the potential uses of domestic fiscal policies in guiding economic development.

Economic reality must be stated clearly. Saudi Arabia is not still another small oil producing entity whose small population and relatively large output makes it into a statistical freak as regards per capita national income, like those along the Gulf (such as Kuwait, Qatar, or the UAE) or elsewhere (such as Brunei or Trinidad and Tobago). Though its population is not large, Saudi Arabia is a major world economic power. Unlike other such powers it does not face the immediate need to raise sizeable portions of its operating revenue from its own residents. However, if short run domestic interest does not require careful consideration of (non-oil) fiscal policy, long run domestic (and international) interests do have such a requirement. We need not repeat again what has been said already concerning the ways in which the lack of fiscal policy relative to internal development becomes in effect an unintended fiscal policy.

Internationally, Saudi Arabia with no real rivals has moved into the major price setting role in OPEC. This has meant in effect that, at a given point in time, it has adjusted its output in order to balance the market, and/or in order to maintain the price it considers appropriate in the late 1970s, Saudi Arabia has produced far more oil than it needed to meet its revenue needs,

Table 11.17 *Average daily output: Saudi Arabian oil fields (1946–1980) (thousands of barrels)*

1946	164	1976	8577
1950	547	1977	9203
1955	977	1978	8283
1960	1314	1979: I	9780
1964	1897	II	8784
1968	3043	III	9773
1970	3799	IV	9766
1972	6016	1980: I	9785
1973	7596	II	9770
1974	8480		
1975	7075		

Source: Petroleum Economist.

and in so doing has added considerably to its accumulated foreign investments (compare *Tables 7.25* and *11.17*). We will discuss in Chapter 13 some
of the interlocking relationships between world markets (oil and financial)
and the domestic revenue needs of Saudi Arabia and other capital surplus
oil-exporters.

11.9   United Arab Emirates

Primarily a marriage of convenience, the federation of the seven sheikhdoms
of the lower Gulf – Abu Dhabi, Ajman, Dubai, Fujairah, Ras al-Khaimah,
Sharjah and Umm al-Quwain – was formed by the erstwhile protecting
power, Britain, prior to achieving full independence. The marriage has
survived its first decade to the surprise of many observers, and in many ways
the union has even thrived, and the highly visible trappings of the federal
government are both international and domestic.

However, as regards the major governmental function with which we are
concerned here, taxation, the union is no stronger in the early 1980s than it

Table 11.18 *United Arab Emirates: selected economic and fiscal statistics
(1964–1978)*

	1964	*1968*	*1973*	*1978*
Population (thousands)	151	178	320	710
GNP (millions of *dirhams*)	400	1250	11 400	53 400
Annual oil production (millions of barrels	67.5	182.6	552.2	660.5
Total government revenues (millions of *dirhams*)	84	606	4 408	24 833
Percentage from:				
Oil taxes and royalties (%)	71.6	82.5	85.6	95.6
'Religiously appropriate' taxes	0	0	0	0
Consumer related taxes (%)	15.0	6.61	1.36	0.98
Tax revenue/GNP ratio (%)	21.0	48.5	38.8	46.5
Per capita				
GNP (thousands of *dirhams*)	2.6	7.0	35.6	75.2
Oil receipts (thousands of *dirhams*)	0.4	2.8	11.8	33.4
Domestic taxes (thousands of *dirhams*)	0.16	0.6	2.0	1.5
Tax buoyancies				*1964–78*
All taxes	4.178	0.876	1.142	1.198
Oil taxes and royalties	4.566	0.896	1.229	1.273
'Religiously appropriate' taxes	0	0	0	0
Consumer related taxes	1.938	0.192	0.898	0.615

Source: See *Tables 7.26, 7.28* and *7.29.*

was at its foundation. With the exception of the postal service and a few new or integrated agencies charging fees for services rendered, the federal government was given no revenue raising capability of its own under the constitution worked out in the early 1970s. At that time, only two emirates, Abu Dhabi and Dubai, were producing oil, but the other five had hopes of discoveries; thus, oil revenues were left to the individual emirates. So too were the receipts from the seven dissimilar tariff schedules that were in effect at the onset of union.

During the 1970s, there was no change in this basic situation; thus the data shown in *Tables 7.26* and *11.18* reflect the receipts of the separate emirates, and not the revenues available to the federal government. The latter come mostly as freely offered contributions from the emirates, which in practice has meant contributions from Abu Dhabi, since Dubai, the only other oil exporter of any other size, has generally held itself aloof from most federal activities.

Table 11.19 *United Arab Emirates: federal government revenues (1973–1979) (millions of dirhams)*

	Total	Federal sources	Emirate contributions
1973	419.8	17.1	402.7
1974	800.5	21.0	779.5
1975	1700	54.6	1722.4
1976	3108.6	102.7	3005.9
1977	6015.1	220.8	5794.3
1978	6973.9	160.5	6813.4
1979	8416.1	216.1	8200.0

Source: Government Finance Statistics Yearbook, 1980.

Table 11.18 indicates the revenues that were actually received by the federal government during the mid 1970s. During this period the government's own sources did not raise more than 5 percent of the total receipts. Abu Dhabi, which dominates the union politically, has shown increasing willingness to fund federal activities; if we compare *Tables 7.26* and *11.19*, we can see that this emirate used about 5 percent of its own estimated revenues for federal budget contributions in 1974, but this proportion rose to about 15 percent in 1976 and probably to about 30 percent in 1978. The biggest factor in motivating Abu Dhabi's increased contributions has obviously been the military defense of the federation; this portion of the budget climbed from about 13 percent in 1973 to more than 49 percent by 1979 (see *Table 11.20*)[21].

Although the problem of lack of data has eased considerably in this region throughout the 1970s, even in relative statistical wastelands such as Oman, Qatar and the Yemens, the UAE has resisted any such change. Despite the wealth of the country, and its subsequent ability to improve greatly the working data needed for policy action by its own officials, the individual emirates, especially the more wealthy ones, are wary about sharing improved fiscal data with outsiders. The problem is of course compounded by the fact that there is not one fiscal policy for the UAE but eight: one followed by the federal budget authorities and seven determined by each of the separate emirates.

Table 11.20 *Federal budget allocations to major functions (1973–1979) (millions of dirhams)*

	1973	1976	1979
Defense	57.6	312.0	4000.0
Education	73.4	354.9	924.7
Health	26.1	150.1	687.5
Welfare	20.5	136.2	254.1
Economic services	49.1	576.7	432.1
General public services	131.1	840.0	1469.5
Other	–	26.0	223.4
Total	400.9	2513.9	8091.6

Source: See *Table 11.19.*

Though we must make these objections as to the available data for the UAE, these major limitations do not seriously limit the analysis we will present. Though precision may not be possible when we break down UAE revenue sources by category, it is obvious that nearly all funds originate in the oil sector, and that the UAE fiscal profile is very similar in this regard to its immediate neighbors, Kuwait, Qatar, and Saudi Arabia, which we have already discussed. During the period for which we have sufficient data, oil revenues have accounted for 75 percent or more of total revenues (that is, emirates and federal sources together).

The only other major levy during this period has been on imports. As we have indicated above, tariffs have not been, and still are not in the early 1980s, within federal jurisdiction; thus, there is not a unified federal tariff schedule. In fact, the determining factor in the UAE as regards tariffs has always been the charges made at its best natural port, Dubai, where the major consideration continues to be the effect of tariffs on goods which are to be reexported, either in bulk or by individual visitors or, in some cases, by smugglers. In other words, whatever method we might use to determine the average effective tariff for the UAE, it would prove on an *ad valorem* basis to be quite similar to the Dubai tariff schedule.

While it might seem unfair to dismiss past UAE fiscal policy too quickly without citing much statistical evidence, the fact is that precision in this regard is not possible. We must draw general impressions from the data that are available. The UAE, on either the federal or emirate level, has yet to make any attempt to tax personal or business incomes and in this regard it is similar only to Bahrain. As we have seen above, the other sparsely populated oil exporters have at least a profits tax on the books. The UAE is the world's richest Islamic state in terms of per capita national income, and yet it levies on its residents no tax that would fall within the group of property and income taxes that we have categorized as 'religiously appropriate'.

The broad-based import duties acted pretty much like general sales taxes in the 1960s before the UAE's independence; as such, they were probably rather regressive in effect. Several factors have tended to mitigate this circumstance during the 1970s. First, many goods have been exempted from tariffs since the oil boom began in earnest, especially necessities such as foodstuffs. Secondly, most other duties have been reduced. Thirdly, in the UAE, as in other small population Gulf states, the poorest classes are immigrant workers from elsewhere in the Middle East or from countries around the Indian Ocean. They come to the Gulf to do whatever menial work they can find, for which they are paid wages far higher than they would earn at home. In return they live for relatively short periods in extreme privation while they save most of their earnings and send them home. They buy very little and pay nearly nothing in consumption taxes as a result. Thus the burden of this tax in the UAE as in other Gulf countries tends to fall mostly on the middle class. This would include most of the perhaps 200 000 citizens of the various emirates and some 25 to 30 percent of the 600 000 or so foreigners who live and work in the UAE.

As we have seen above, nearly all official revenues, aside from these customs receipts and from fees for services rendered by various agencies of the federal emirate governments, are oil-generated. Oil output has been fairly steady in the UAE as a whole during the mid and late 1970s (see *Table 11.21*). The hopes of the so called northern emirates (that is, north of Abu Dhabi), which were so bright in the early 1970s, have so far proved fruitless apart from Dubai's success. Thus, Abu Dhabi has continued to dominate the federal structure, with Dubai using its comfortable revenues to go its own way. Neither major oil producing emirate has shown any willingness to assign its revenues to the federal authorities in whole or in part, with Abu Dhabi preferring continuation of the initial mechanism of annually determined contributions whilst Dubai ignores the federal structure as much as possible. All other revenues of the individual emirates could be transferred to the federal government without any improvement in the latter's fiscal independence to any notable extent. It would seem unlikely that the central government will ever gain the dominant role needed to bring about a unified fiscal policy without achieving control of the principal source of revenues; why then bother with minor existing and potential taxes[22]?

The continued lack of a domestic tax policy in the UAE carries with it the strong likelihood of the same sorts of problems that we have discussed already in relation to other oil exporters with small populations. Abandonment of non-oil taxes as tools of economic policy sharply constricts any contemporary government's options for influencing the course of development. In the UAE, the problem we have discussed above in relation to the

Table 11.21 *Average daily output: United Arab Emirates oil fields (1962–1980) (thousands of barrels)*

Year	Total Emirates	Abu Dhabi	Dubai	Sharjah
1962	14	14	–	–
1964	187	187	–	–
1968	497	497	–	–
1970	779	693	86	–
1972	1202	1051	151	–
1973	1525	1305	220	–
1974	1678	1414	241	23
1975	1694	1402	254	38
1976	1932	1592	313	37
1977	2014	1667	319	28
1978	1831	1447	362	22
1979: I	1826	1455	358	13
II	1824	1445	367	12
III	1834	1459	361	14
IV	1839	1494	330	15
1980: I	1723	1365	346	12
II	1719	1365	344	10

Source: Petroleum Economist.

absence of taxes on corporations being possibly an unintended fiscal policy is multiplied seven-fold, since each emirate has been, to no small extent, following an indepenent program of encouraging industrial development. Although the poorer emirates are generally dependent on Abu Dhabi for financial assistance and subject to its veto on projects needing aid, it is possible nevertheless that the same industry can be developed simultaneously in all emirates: seven factories existing for some time by dint of various subsidies, including the implicit one due to the absence of taxation. If the UAE had a well structured federal fiscal policy this development duplication could have been avoided.

Other governments have used tax policies with some success to encourage foreign investment in the poorer regions most in need of broadening their economic bases. The UAE, with no corporate taxes, has no fiscal incentives to encourage investment location in Fujairah, for example, instead of Abu Dhabi[23]. With no taxes on income or property, it loses its options in this regard to encourage investment in the country's promising agricultural region, rather than in the speculative real estate markets of the principal urban areas. With uniformly low taxes on consumption (through import duties), luxury goods for Abu Dhabi are treated the same as capital goods intended for Ajman. With its reliance on foreign oil consumers, the United Arab Emirates, like several of its neighbors, does little to further the long-established Islamic tradition of state reinforcement of the Quranic ideal of the community bearing major responsibility for its own less economically fortunate citizens.

The overall picture of the nine oil exporting countries is one of little concentrated interest in non-oil fiscal sources. This was true in the pre 1973 period when Saudi Arabia and Iran, both of whom have medium sized populations[24], were ranked alongside the world's poorer nations, and it remains true for the period following 1973 when they were all received into the councils of the rich, where Kuwait and Qatar were already established. In the next chapter we will continue this discussion for the seven non-oil exporters. Then we will consider in Chapter 13 two questions that particularly impinge on oil export and oil revenue considerations in the 1980s. The first is the increasing revenue that oil exporters are realizing from the investment of surplus funds earned from previous oil exports. The second is the rising domestic demand for petroleum products. These two questions have opposite effects on oil production and oil revenue decisions; and, of course, each also has an impact on world oil supply.

Notes

1 As was indicated above in Chapter 5, there is considerable variation even within 'orthodox' or *Sunni* Islam, with its four widely accepted schools of law, as to the practical interpretation of the injunctions related to *zakat*. Thus, there is no universally recognized standard for the role of the state. When the horizons are expanded to the *Shi'i* minority (ten to 15 percent of the Muslim community), and especially to some of this group's more heterodox sects, this variation becomes even greater. Many of the *Shi'i* demand that the state leave *zakat* alone, claiming that its payment must be voluntary if it is to fulfil the religious obligation. For example, the Zia regime in Pakistan was frustrated during the summer of 1980 in its attempts to Islamicize the fiscal structure. *Shi'i* rioters protested against compulsory annual levies on savings accounts.

Bahrain finds itself in a somewhat awkward situation as regards religious levies since the regime is *Sunni* Arab and a large portion (perhaps even a majority) of the citizenry is *Shi'i* (Iranian and Arab). Thus any attempt to incorporate *zakat* and other traditional Islamic levies into the official tax structure could provoke inter-communal difficulties. However, this hardly precludes the use of officially religiously neutral income or profits taxes, nor for that matter even the *zakat* concept. After the Pakistani rioting, it was reported that President Zia agreed to allow those who objected to the law file for exemptions on the grounds of religious conscience.

2 Of the other three oil producing economies, only in Bahrain would the oil sector be smaller than the rest of the economy. The authors' estimates for the share of GDP accounted for by oil in these countries during the late 1970s are as follows: Bahrain, 25–30 percent; Qatar, 70–80 percent; UAE, 65–75 percent.

3 As was noted above in Chapter 5, preliminary data released in the last months of the defunct monarchical regime indicated that consumer goods imports actually grew faster than those of capital goods during the mid 1970s oil boom. Still the near tax exempt status of the latter means that consumer goods were responsible for the additional customs receipts.

4 For Iran, and for the countries that follow in our discussions in this chapter, we halt our considerations before the outbreak of the Iran–Iraq war in the third quarter of 1980. For the non-participants, this has the effect of closing discussion at the beginning of the latest world-wide cycle in the petroleum market, which is largely exogenous in generation and effect to the analyses of domestic calculators of fiscal policy. But for Iran, post-September 1980 oil production and revenue receipts are only further disruptions in a chaotic pattern beginning with the birth pangs of the Islamic Republic. That is, re-establishment of peace is certainly no reassurance of normalcy in Iran's oil industry in the short run.

5. For several weeks in late 1978 and early 1979, Iran had no oil to export; its domestic needs were between 500 000 and 700 000 barrels a day. This situation was repeated again after the onset of war with Iraq.

6 Such problems seem inevitable even without more drastic happenings such as the loss of the largely Arab-populated Khuzestan region, which contains most of Iran's oil fields, to a secessionist movement.

7 And possibly also to those of the Sudan.

8 Especially after the onset of economic chaos in Iran at the close of the 1970s.

9 At that time, as had often happened earlier, the urgencies in the current budget were military in nature.

10 This was also true for Bahrain; see *Tables 11.1* and *11.5*.

11 This would also be consistent with inflation, but there is no particular evidence that inflation has been a worse problem in Iraq during the post 1973 period than it has been elsewhere in the region (see *Table 11.6*).

12 As indicated above, the effects of the Iran–Iraq war are not being considered here; this arbitrary decision on the part of the authors puts an end to the data period being included herein. While Iraqi production plummeted during the war as a direct result of the military situation, it is not clear that peace might not quickly restore 'normalcy'. This is unlike the situation in Iran, where pre-war confusion had already badly disrupted the oil industry.

13 Which does exempt several absolutely basic necessities.

14 Fees for services rendered are mostly treated in Chapters 7 and 8 as 'other indirect taxes', though in no case does the latter category include import duties. However, our argument is that for states like Kuwait, Qatar and the UAE, the low duties represent *only* such fees and neither revenue raising nor consumption regulating devices.

15 Outside the oil industry.

16 That is, any improvements in either technology or discovery would add to reserve lifetimes at existing output levels.

17 A further point of argument has to do with whether 'actually planned expenditures' considerably exceeded what would be prudent development spending levels. Aside from pointing out the importance of such considerations in all the countries (except probably Bahrain) discussed in this chapter, we will not enter into discussions of this question.

18 In fact, the statistics may be somewhat deceiving when comparisons between 1972/73 and 1977/78 are being made. As can be seen from *Table 7.23*, the biggest non-oil tax increase during the mid 1970s was in the 'catch-all' category, other indirect taxes, used generally in this work for such things as stamp duties and receipts from fee-charging government agencies (other than state enterprises). However, the almost 15 fold increase in Saudi Arabian receipts in this category

over a 4 year period seems to result, at least in part, from growth in the kingdom's overseas investment portfolio and its returns (see *Table 7.25*). For other oil surplus countries we have tried either to isolate such income from tax receipts entirely or at least to consign it to state enterprise returns. The nature of officially reported Saudi Arabian statistics made it impossible both to make this distinction and to know exactly how much of a statistical problem was involved. If we were able to exclude such receipts (or alternatively, to consider them as oil generated), then the percentage of oil revenues in total revenues in 1977/78 would be several percentage points higher.

19 The one exception is Brunei, which, like many of the Gulf emirates, has a small population (200 000) and large oil production (about 210 000 barrels a day). The exact origin of Brunei's fiscal revenue is not easy to identify, but nearly all the returns from its only income tax, one on business profits, comes from the oil sector. Thus, what we have called 'religiously appropriate' taxes probably raise well less than 1 percent of Brunei's revenues.

20 Which is not to say that Saudi Arabia has always achieved tactical sucess.

21 In addition to the figures shown here for the federal budget, members of the union (such as Ajman, Fujairah, and Umm al-Quwain) have been successful during the 1970s in attracting grants for local current needs and especially for development projects. Some donors have been without the federation, but Abu Dhabi and Dubai have also been sources of funding and this has by no means always been through the mechanism of the federal budget.

22 Some observers of the UAE have commented that as long as the current federal structure is in place, little change

can be expected. But if the rivalry between Abu Dhabi and Dubai leads to the secession of one (most likely to the latter), then the remaining oil producer could force the 5 poor emirates into a much tighter federation or even eventually into total dissolution.

23 Which is not to say there are no alternative tools which allow the government the means to affect the location of investment. In the UAE as elsewhere in the Gulf states, most foreign investment involves joint ventures, with the government playing a role. However, the two rich emirates tend to keep these ventures for themselves; the federal authorities have had only limited autonomy in redressing regional imbalances.

24 Iran in the early 1980s is an anomaly in this regard. Obviously a resource-rich, if income-poor, country prior to 1973, it was despite its large population treated among the oil-determined *nouveau riche* between 1973 and the anti-imperial revolution. In 1979, both oil production and all sorts of other non-agricultural activity have fallen so much that the major sources of internationally comparative data regarding national income, the International Monetary Fund and the World Bank, have suspended their estimates of these statistics. With Muhammed Reza Pahlavi still firmly in control in 1977, GNP was estimated to be some $75.7 billion, or about $2210 per capita, which for example was 41 percent above the estimated level of $1570 per capita for Iraq. Three years later, at the outbreak of war between the Islamic republic and the secular Ba'thi republic of Iraq, Iranian oil production had fallen 70 percent from 1977 levels (see *Table 11.4*), Iraqi oil production had jumped 42 percent over the same base (see *Table 11.7*), and of course oil prices had more than doubled.

CHAPTER 12

Non-oil exporting countries

12.1   Egypt

By the late 1970s, Egyptian oil production had reached higher levels than those found in three of the countries discussed in the last chapter – Bahrain, Oman and Qatar. By 1980, it had also surpassed the faltering Iranian oil industry. However, by the criteria we have been using, Egypt is categorized as a non-oil exporter throughout the period under discussion; that is, oil revenues have not played a significant role in Egypt's fiscal accounts during most of this time.

From published statistics we cannot identify exactly how much the oil industry has paid to the Egyptian government. In *Tables 8.1* and *8.2* most of these payments are included under the category 'business profits taxes', however, using production figures we can make some rough estimates. From 1950 to 1973 oil revenues grew steadily and probably somewhat faster than overall tax receipts; they amounted to perhaps 2 percent of total receipts in 1950, with their share growing to perhaps as much as 4 percent before the 1973 oil price increases. Production has grown about twice as fast (15.5 percent) each year during the 1973–79 period as it had on average during the preceding 23 years (about 7.9 percent a year). This growth, coupled with the multifold increase in per barrel returns to the treasury, probably brought oil receipts above 10 percent of total taxes by 1976 or 1977 and above 20 percent by the end of the 1970s. Current projections indicate export levels close to one million barrels a day by the mid 1980s which would generate more than 7500 million pounds in revenue for the government. It would seem likely that Egypt will become much more dependent on oil taxes; but in this section we will focus on other taxes which have provided the vast majority of fiscal receipts through the 1970s.

As the statistics shown in *Table 12.1* indicate, in a period when Egypt was undergoing considerable economic and social change, several of the more general characteristics of the fiscal sector do not show any drastic transformations. For example, although there was an upward shift in the ratio of tax revenues to GNP in the early years of the regime of President Gamal Abd al-Nasr, the relative gain was notably smaller in Egypt than it was in any of the other countries discussed in this chapter. The government's share only moved from about 20 to 25 percent of GNP despite a pronounced tilt during the 1950s and 1960s toward boosting the public sectors of the economy in pursuit of the goal of Arab Socialism. In decidedly non-socialist Jordan for example, the relative tax share about doubled, from 13 percent to almost 25 percent. Middle Eastern countries (both oil and non-oil exporters) tend to do better than other LDCs as regards tax effort, that is, the share of taxes in GNP: Egypt compares well with other non-oil countries (cf. *Table 10.1*) but not so well with oil exporters.

Table 12.1 *Egypt: selected economic and fiscal statistics (1950–1977)*

	1950	1962	1968	1973	1977
Population (millions)	20.46	27.26	31.69	35.62	38.74
GNP (millions of pounds)	918.0	1684.6	2584.8	3625.5	7139.0
Annual oil production (millions of barrels)	16.3	32.3	67.1	93.4	150.5
Total government revenues (millions of pounds	183.2	474.8	645.3	892.5	1930.0
Percentage from:					
'Religiously appropriate' taxes	17.7	16.0	20.5	22.1	21.3
Consumer related taxes	52.5	38.8	38.5	33.7	36.9
Tax revenue/GNP ratio	20.0	28.2	25.0	24.6	27.0
Per capita					
GNP (pounds)	44.9	61.8	81.6	101.8	184.3
Domestic taxes (pounds)	9.0	17.4	20.4	25.1	49.8
Tax buoyancies					1950–77
All taxes	1.592	0.709	0.957	1.153	1.155
'Religiously appropriate' taxes	1.414	1.316	1.183	1.095	1.251
Consumer related taxes	1.073	0.691	0.561	1.302	0.968

Source: See *Table 8.1.*

For Egypt and the other countries discussed in this chapter, our focus is of course on domestically generated tax revenues. As far as this is concerned the per capita burden on Egyptians is close to the non-oil group average (*Table 12.2*) in absolute terms, if somewhat more onerous, in relative terms, than in the other six countries.

It should be noted that while the oil exporters rely on domestic sources for as little as 5 percent of their tax revenues, the seven non-oil countries are totally dependent on domestic taxes. Despite these latter countries' much lower levels of national income, several of them impose tax burdens on their citizens that are comparable with the burdens borne by residents of their much richer neighbors. Egypt, for example, and more particularly Jordan and Syria, rank with Iraq, Oman and Iran in terms of the absolute size of per capita domestic taxes.

The two major categories of taxation shown in *Table 12.1* were fairly stable over the entire time period under consideration. Egypt makes no formal use of traditional Islamic levies such as *zakat* or *'ushr* in its fiscal structure, but the approximately one fifth of all revenues raised under the broader heading of 'religiously appropriate' taxes, places it very high among Middle Eastern states as far as this category is concerned (cf. *Table 11.16*). Throughout these three decades the largest part of this category has

Table 12.2 *Per capita domestically-generated tax revenues: Middle East countries (US dollars)*

	Per capita GNP ($)	Per capita tax revenues ($)
Oil exporters		
Bahrain	4 435	412
Iran	2 210	222
Iraq	1 533	116
Kuwait	12 690	731
Libya	6 655	669
Oman	2 721	145
Qatar	14 187	384
Saudi Arabia	6 695	567
United Arab Emirates	19 425	388
Average[a]	3 332	278
Non-oil exporters		
Egypt	470	127
Jordan	775	178
Lebanon	900	112
Sudan	377	76
Syria	907	196
Yemen Arab Rep.	536	76
Yemen People's Dem. Rep.	320	70
Average[a]	524	119

Notes: Time period is the late 1970s.
    [a] Averages are weighted by population.

consisted of business profits taxes, which accounted for about 75 percent of all such tax revenues in the late 1970s. In part, the relative stability of these taxes in the total fiscal profile is explained by similar stability among the major sectors of the economy. *Table 12.3* shows that while Egyptian industry underwent considerable growth in both extent and diversity during the 1960s and 1970s, it maintained approximately the same position *vis-à-vis* agriculture in the late 1970s as it did in the early 1960s.

Table 12.3 Gross domestic product by industrial origin: non-oil exporting countries in the Middle East (1962–1977) (percentages)

Country	Year	GDP at market prices	Mining	Other manufacturing	Agriculture	Construction	Services
Egypt (millions of pounds)	1962	1 684.4		22	25	5	41
	1968	2 696.4		20	26	4	37
	1973	3 663.0		19	29	3	37
	1977	7 341.7		23	24	4	38
Jordan (millions of dinars)	1962	118.9		11	18	5	62
	1968	156.1		16	10	6	62
	1973	218.3		16	8	7	62
	1977	477.6		16	9	6	53
Lebanon (millions of pounds)	1962	2 941.0		15	12	5	68
	1968	4 273.2		15	10	5	70
	1973	7 100.0		17	10	4	70
Sudan (millions of pounds)	1962	456.2	0	8	50	5	25
	1968	647.8	0	11	37	4	41
	1973	1 246.2	0	10	41	5	39
	1977	2 091.0	1	8	40	3	43
Syria (millions of pounds)	1963	3 980.0	0	16	30	3	51
	1968	5 514.0	1	16	23	3	56
	1973	9 413.0	3	18	18	4	57
	1977	26 132.0	3	16	20	7	54
Yemen Arab Rep. (millions of rials)	1970	1 399.0		5	53	5	39
	1973	2 514.0		6	50	5	39
	1976	5 181.0		6	44	4	45

Sources: *Yearbook of National Account Statistics; World Tables.*

From *Table 12.1*, it would seem that consumer related taxes have dropped considerably in relative terms, by about a third since 1950, with most of the decrease coming in the 1950s. However, it was mentioned in Chapter 8 that Egypt has employed a complex structure of market control devices that have the effect of subsidizing the prices of some consumer goods out of the profits realized on the sales of other items by government monopolies. Some of these receipts are clearly excises, such as those obtained from sales of coffee and tea; others are more like production taxes, such as those gained from cottonseed. The net receipts have risen from a few million pounds in the early 1960s to almost £E200 million by the late 1970s, becoming one of the government's three most important revenue sources. These receipts are included in *Table 8.1* as other indirect taxes, but if we include them along with customs duties and excises as consumer related taxes, then the share of this category increases notably, to about 41 percent in 1962, 50 percent in 1968, 47 percent in 1973, and to about 46 percent in 1977. In other words, a pattern emerges showing a much smaller diminution of the share of this tax category than is indicated in *Table 12.1*, Correspondingly, the tax buoyancy for these taxes would be higher than the value of 0.968 indicated in the table for the 1950 to 1977 period, perhaps more closely equal to about 1.1 after making this adjustment.

Thus, sharply progressive income and profits taxes have become slightly more prominent in Egypt's fiscal profile during the 1960s and 1970s, while the consumption based taxes which can be regressive in effect have declined relatively by an approximately corresponding amount. We have seen that Egypt still relies less on income taxes and more on consumption taxes than most industrialized nations (cf. *Tables 10.10* and *10.17*). However, compared to other LDCs and especially to other Middle Eastern countries, it makes more use of income and wealth based levies. While our only income distribution data for Egypt is a little out of date (cf. *Tables 10.8* and *10.9*), these also indicated a situation more economically equitable than that prevailing in the 'typical' LDC. We might cautiously conclude from what we know about income distribution and income taxes that the situation is a little better in Egypt than elsewhere, in the developing world in general, and in the Middle East in particular. Taxes on personal incomes exempt the poor and, as elsewhere in the region, tend to hit hardest at the urban middle class, rather than at the rich, but more than three pounds in four arising from the 'religiously appropriate' category come from business rather than personal levies.

A few points also should be made about the much more fiscally important consumption based taxes – customs duties and excises, plus, in the expanded sense of the term used in this section, the returns from the government price differential system. As in other LDCs aspiring to a greater degree of industrialization, Egypt's tariffs favor capital goods with full or partial exemptions and are heaviest on luxuries and items which are also produced domestically. Excises follow the usual pattern of levies on fuel, beverages and tobacco products. Thus, in this regard, this category is a burden that tends to fall heaviest on the urban middle and working classes – that is, a generally regressive form of taxation. However, as we have seen above, under the republican regime, Egyptian governments have also intervened in a countervailing manner in the markets for many common consumer items. On the one hand, government monopolies control such items as sugar, coffee and tea, and from these sales considerable profit is realized. In turn, subsidies are granted from these funds to such staples as cereals and cooking fuel.

This system has been criticized by outside economic observers (in particular, the IMF) for being both very expensive and for introducing distortions in the market place that tend to exacerbate Egypt's chronic trade deficits. Whatever the merits of these criticisms, the purely fiscal effect seems to be considerable mitigation of a situation in which a regressive category of taxation was used to produce close to half the domestic revenues of the government.

An ideal solution to the critics' charges which would also maintain a progressive tilt to the tax structure, would be to increase further the role of income and property taxes relative to that of consumption taxes. But we have discussed the political and institutional problems that LDCs encounter with such broad based direct taxes. Furthermore, we have also seen that, compared to LDCs in general, (and especially compared to some of its oil-rich neighbors), Egypt already collects a high proportion of its revenues from income and property taxes[1], so to advise such a transformation would not at first glance seem very practical.

However, the Egyptian situation in the 1980s does allow for this possibility. As was indicated above, the long established Egyptian oil industry seems finally about to boost the country at least into the ranks of middle-level oil producers. In 1980, every 100 000 barrels in additional daily production would bring some £E850 million a year to government coffers, or about four times what was realized through the business profits tax in 1977. The annual increment in recent years has been almost 100 000 barrels a day: 1974 – 235 000; 1975 – 305 000; 1976 – 328 000; 1977 – 412 000; 1978 – 541 000; 1979 – 610 000; 1980 (January–June) – 705 000.

If Egypt continues to enjoy expansion in its oil production and export levels, then the fiscal consequences depend upon the extent to which the revenues generated are net additions to government receipts. If direct taxes are maintained at the levels prevailing in the late 1970s, oil revenues would tilt the fiscal profile away from its historical domination by consumption based and other indirect taxes. Part of the increased revenues could be used to support a gradual phaseout of current market distorting fiscal practices.

On the other hand, Egypt could fall prey, in a period of oil prosperity, to a temptation to restructure its fiscal system in the pattern of the nine countries discussed in the last chapter. Ample oil revenues could lead to a weakening of the effectiveness of fiscal policy tools – that is, a popular political policy would have negative economic implications.

Egypt in the early 1980s stands on a fiscal threshhold. A relative dearth of easily taxable resources in the past has led it to develop a fairly diversified range of taxes. Now the prospects of an expanded petroleum sector offer it the chance both to relieve past capital constraints and to adjust the tax structure in the interests of equitability and efficiency. To accomplish this, however, the government must view the oil windfall primarily in terms of a breathing space in which to reorganize the national economy so as to increase its capacity to be self-sustaining, and not largely as an opportunity to transfer to foreign consumers the burdens currently borne by domestic taxpayers.

12.2   Jordan

One of the poorest countries in the region (to say nothing of the world) at the start of the period we have been considering, Jordan is one of the most frequently cited 'success stories' among LDCs, though perhaps a more modest example than, for example, Taiwan or Singapore. It began the period in 1950 with a per capita GDP of perhaps $50, and was hopelessly saddled with as many refugees as permanent residents as a result of the dispossession of the Palestinians during the first Arab–Israeli war. Total domestic fiscal resources available annually to the Jordanian government ran to barely $10 per capita (see *Table 12.4*) during the early 1950s, an amount that was approximately matched by foreign economic assistance.

As a result more of its human resources than any other single factor, per capita GDP was close to $1200 by 1980 and had grown an average of nearly 11.2 percent a year over three decades. Real growth during the 1970s has been estimated to have been about 6.5 percent in per capita terms, which puts it just behind South Korea (7.6 percent) and Singapore (6.6 percent) and ahead of Hong Kong (5.8 percent) and Taiwan (5.5 percent).

Tax revenues have more than kept pace with the overall economy during this period. As can be seen from *Table 12.4*, the buoyancy recorded for all taxes between 1952 and 1978 was almost 1.22 and the ratio of tax revenue to GNP almost doubled, from 12.9 percent to 23.0 percent.

In examining resource poor Jordan's successes relative to other non-oil countries in the region, it is difficult to single out any fiscal policies that could be credited specifically with contributing to this picture of rapid growth. In fact, Jordan's fiscal history is not very different from that of its neighbors – a tax buoyancy greater than unity, a small but generally growing (in relative terms) role for direct taxes, duties and excises with both sumptuary and domestic industrial protection aims that continue to dominate the government's accounts. What does distinguish Jordan from most of its LDC neighbors over the past 30 years has been its persistent success in securing sizable amounts of foreign economic assistance. Throughout this period, this aid has matched or exceeded domestic revenues nearly every year. In effect, this has allowed the latter to be devoted to the current budget, mostly services such as human resource development and social welfare, while foreign sources have paid the bills for the capital (development) and military budgets. In recent years, this has allowed the government

Table 12.4 *Jordan: selected economic and fiscal statistics (1952–1978)*

	1952	1962	1968	1973	1978
Population (thousands)	1315	1770	2150	2540	2980
GNP (millions of *dinars*)	42.5	118.9	197.3	287.0	707.1
Total government revenues (millions of *dinars*)	5.5	18.9	26.3	46.2	162.8
Percentage from:					
'Religiously appropriate' taxes	10.9	16.4	7.2	8.7	13.5
Consumer related taxes	40.0	33.9	54.8	43.3	47.9
Tax revenue/GNP ratio	12.9	15.9	13.3	16.1	23.0
Per capita					
GNP (*dinars*)	32.3	67.2	91.8	113.0	237.3
Domestic taxes (*dinars*)	4.2	10.7	12.2	18.2	54.6
Tax buoyancies					*1952–78*
All taxes	1.212	0.642	1.533	1.450	1.219
'Religiously appropriate' taxes	1.645	−0.890	2.063	1.721	1.299
Consumer related taxes	1.039	1.642	0.873	1.583	1.288

Source: See *Table 8.5.*

expenditures to GNP ratio to be close to 50 percent, or twice the tax/GNP ratio – well above what it is in any of the non-oil exporters we are considering in this chapter. As *Table 12.5* shows, using three criteria (official development assistance (ODA) per capita, and the ratios of ODA to GNP and to government tax revenues), Jordan is consistently at the top of the rankings, not only of the Middle Eastern countries we have discussed, but also of LDCs in general.

At least through 1980, Jordan has continued to receive large amounts of aid, despite the fact its GNP per capita is now well up in the middle income range for LDCs. Other countries that have experienced similar economic growth in the past have found that economic assistance falls off sharply with new-found prosperity. For example, assistance to Korea peaked in 1972 and

Table 12.5 Selected measures of official development assistance: Middle Eastern and other selected developing countries

Country	GNP per capita 1977 ($)	Total ODA[a] 1971–1978 ($)	ODA per capita 1971–1978 ($)	Ratio of 1977 ODA to: GNP	Government revenues
Bahrain	4050	286	1157	2.6	6.3
Egypt	340	10923	297	20.1	31.6
Jordan	940	2354	885	23.3	103.9
Lebanon	900[b]	455	164	2.5	19.9
Oman	2510	480	636	2.9	4.2
Sudan	330	1408	91	3.9	22.1
Syria	860	3051	422	9.5	24.5
Yemen Arab Rep.	510	1070	205	9.8	87.6
Yemen People's Dem. Rep.	350	471	284	16.7	99.0
Bangladesh	80	4447	58	14.0	134.6
Bolivia	480	545	113	3.8	24.3
Chad	130	1937	485	11.1	98.4
Ghana	370	587	60	2.3	9.2
Honduras	420	320	105	4.0	29.4
India	160	9696	16	1.1	8.7
Jamaica	1060	289	143	1.5	4.1
Kenya	290	1051	80	3.8	22.2
Korea	980	2100	60	0.7	3.9
Pakistan	200	5076	73	3.6	26.5
Rwanda	160	530	127	13.3	101.1
Tunisia	840	1427	256	4.1	13.4
Turkey	1110	1058	27	0.2	0.9

Notes: [a] From OECD and OPEC donors, as well as multilateral agencies.
[b] Estimated.

Sources: *Geographic Distribution of Financial Flows to Developing Countries and Development Cooperation: 1979 Review* (OECD); *Government Finance Statistics Yearbook* (IMF); *World Bank Atlas 1979*.

by the late 1970s was perhaps only a fourth what it had been in real terms a decade earlier. For all practical purposes, Taiwan ceased receiving such aid in the early 1970s.

For political reasons Jordan is unlikely to face a rapid phaseout of ODA from either of its major sources; over the 1971/78 period, about 49 percent came from OPEC and 20 percent from the United States. However, if the country continues to enjoy as much real growth as it did during the 1970s, it would seem unlikely that in the future annual ODA will match tax revenues or be equal to about a quarter of GNP. It is important, therefore, that any relative drop in ODA be somewhat offset by increases in domestically originating tax revenues[2]. This need not involve drastic change in the overall thrust of the government's tax policies. For example, the buoyancy over the decade 1968 to 1978 was approximately 1.5, while GNP (in current terms) grew by about 13.6 a year; at the same time the tax revenue to GNP ratio almost doubled, from 13.3 percent to 23.0 percent. *Table 12.6* shows that with a much lower buoyancy (close to 1.25), the tax ratio would rise to close to one-third of GNP for the growth rates shown by the end of the 1980s.

Table 12.6 *Projected tax ratios: Jordan (1985 and 1990)*

Assumed rate of growth in GNP (current terms) (%)	Assumed tax buoyancy	Projected tax to GNP ratio (%)	
		1985	*1990*
13.6	1.5	34.6	46.2
	1.35	30.6	37.7
	1.2	27.1	30.6
11.5	1.5	32.7	42.1
	1.35	29.5	35.2
	1.2	26.6	29.4
9.5	1.5	31.0	38.3
	1.35	28.4	33.0
	1.2	26.0	28.3

However, if general fiscal policies continued to be used as they have been, this will allow a considerable relative increase in domestic revenues. Specific policies for the 1980s must be carefully tailored to promote economic growth and at least to avoid antagonizing a likely regressive tilt in Jordan's tax structure. For example, though Jordan saw some growth in the role of business profits taxation during the 1970s, it was also using partial exemptions from these taxes to encourage greater investment. Such incentives are worthwhile if they are used with care, for example, in the early less profitable years of an enterprise. But other countries have found that tax holiday policies may encourage ventures that are indefinitely dependent upon the implicit subsidy of foregone taxes or attract somewhat 'fly-by-night' investors – highly mobile industries that can easily move to a new location at the end of the tax holiday. In neither case is much business activity ever added to active tax rolls.

As mentioned earlier, personal income taxes in Jordan, as elsewhere in the Middle East, are progressive in theory, but in fact this is true only for middle income levels downward. The rich tend to be self employed and/or recipients of unearned income, and thus are able to avoid all but a fraction of the taxes that are due. With continued economic growth, more and more Jordanians join the middle (taxpaying) class, thus increasing collections from this source. However, unless the government also succeeds in raising its collections from those elements now avoiding this tax, it will surely find itself faced with considerable resentment on the part of those who have no choice but to pay. Such tax resentment was at least a minor factor in mobilizing the urban middle class to the anti-Pahlavi cause in Iran.

The role of consumption related taxes remains high in Jordan and changes in their relative importance have followed no particular trend in the last 30 years (*Table 12.4*). However, they are no more prominent in Jordan than in Egypt (when this category is adjusted to include price differential returns in the latter country), and they are relatively less important than they are in Lebanon, Sudan and the Yemens. One argument in favor of these taxes is that they are perhaps the most effective levy that can be made against a very important type of income received for many Jordanian families; remittances from the thousands of emigrants who work in the Arabian peninsula or the United States[3]. A tax levied directly against such remittances would lead either to less funds remitted or to extra legal methods of sending them. Consumption taxes tend to encourage spending this income on untaxed or lightly taxed items[4].

Perhaps a more reasonable goal for Jordanian fiscan authorities than merely reducing the relative role of these taxes would be to keep them under frequent review with the intention of striving to keep them as progressive in effect as possible. This can be done by lowering the rates levied on necessities and increasing those on luxuries. 'Necessities' and 'luxuries' are relative terms, and their composition can be changing rapidly in a society undergoing considerable economic growth. Efficient fine tuning of the effect of consumption taxes, of course, requires adequate and up to date information on patterns of consumption and on income distribution.

12.3   Lebanon

In discussing the fiscal structure in Lebanon, as with almost anything else of substance in that unfortunate country, it is not possible to do so in a vacuum and ignore the effects of the civil war that has been going on since 1975. That is why in Chapter 8 we have included some estimates for tax receipts after the outbreak of war. Though no official data are available later than 1975 and such estimates as are available are highly variable in quality, to look at Lebanon's fiscal profile only up until 1975 could easily result in distorted impressions.

For Lebanon, perhaps more than any other country in recent history, had been following a model of economic development that, with some justification, has been termed *laissez-faire* capitalism. And it had been following that model with more than a little success according to most observers. As *Table 12.7* shows, per capita GNP grew at an impressive annual average rate of 4 percent from 1950 to 1973; in the late 1960s and early 1970s, this growth had accelerated to nearly 8 percent a year. Particularly after the closing of the

Table 12.7 *Lebanon: selected economic and fiscal statistics (1950–1978)*

	1950	1962	1968	1973	1978
Population (thousands)	1650	2070	2340	2660	3010
GNP (millions of pounds)	1858	3083	4468	7405	8000
Total government revenues (millions of pounds)	75.6	360.1	573.1	963.9	1000
Percentage from:					
'Religiously appropriate' taxes	18.5	17.5	21.5	20.3	20.0
Consumer related taxes	52.2	49.6	48.5	48.8	56.5
Tax revenue/GNP ratio	4.1	11.7	12.8	13.0	12.5
Per capita					
GNP (pounds)	1126	1489	1909	2783	2658
Domestic taxes (pounds)	45.8	174.0	244.9	362.4	332.2
Tax buoyancies					1950–78
All taxes		3.223	1.262	1.031	0.472	1.806
'Religiously appropriate' taxes		3.095	1.858	0.917	0.251	1.791
Consumer related taxes		2.323	1.201	1.042	1.912	1.538

Source: See *Table 8.8.*

Suez Canal in the June 1967 War changed Middle East transport patterns, Lebanon showed clear signs of becoming a regional manufacturing center, in addition to continuing to play its well established commercial and financial roles. Lebanese exports, which had long lagged far behind its imports, began an impressive spurt and indicated bright promise of closing or even reversing the traditional trade deficit. Much of this additional trade came from sales of Lebanese manufactures[5] in the growing markets of the oil exporting countries of the Gulf region. The rapid growth of Lebanese exports over the 20 years up until 1973 (the last year for which any detailed data are available) was paced by manufactured goods, the sales of which went from $8.98 million in 1953 to $358.26 million by 1973 (*Table 12.8*). The almost three-quarters share of manufactures in Lebanese exports was unmatched anywhere else in the Middle East (*Table 12.9*).

All this economic change and growth came with the Lebanese government playing only a minor role. As *Table 12.7* shows, throughout the 1960s and early 1970s, the tax revenue to GNP ratio hovered around 12 percent, a

Table 12.8 *Lebanese exports (1953–1973) (percentages)*

Category	1953	1959	1965	1970	1973	Average annual rate of growth
Food, beverages and tobacco (%)	42.8	47.0	42.0	29.3	20.3	11.8
Manufactured goods (%)	35.0	40.8	45.6	63.4	71.3	20.2
Raw materials (%)	22.2	12.1	12.4	7.3	7.3	9.8
Total ($ millions)	25.66	39.96	85.38	197.83	502.47	16.0

Source: Askari and Cummings, *Middle East Economies in the 1970's: A Comparative Approach* (New York: Praeger, 1976), p.243.

Table 12.9 *Composition of exports: selected Middle East countries (1973) (%)*

	Food, beverages and tobacco (%)	Manufactured goods (%)	Raw materials (%)
Bahrain	4.2	22.6	73.2
Egypt	18.8	25.4	55.8
Iran	2.3	4.9	88.2
Iraq	6.1	2.9	91.0
Jordan	28.0	20.2	51.8
Kuwait	0.8	6.8	92.4
Lebanon	20.3	71.3	7.3
Sudan	13.5	0.3	86.0
Syria	16.9	16.1	66.9
Yemen Arab Rep.	26.3	1.0	71.0

Source: See *Table 12.8.*

value far below what we have seen for other countries in the region and elsewhere in the developing world[6]. If Lebanese fiscal policies had anything to do with encouraging growth, it would seem that the magnitude rather than the type of taxation would be the critical element. Lebanon has employed as full a range of different types of taxes as any of its neighbors, and it has actually raised a larger share of government revenues from progressive income and profits taxes than any other country that we are considering except Egypt and South Yemen. But these taxes took a notably smaller share of national income in Lebanon than they did in most of the other non-oil exporters (*Table 10.15*).

In the early 1970s, Lebanon adopted fiscal policies aimed at promoting exports. New enterprises engaged in the production and/or assembly of manufactured goods for export were granted tax holidays on profits, and foreign investors were offered exemptions from certain investment and labor regulations. However, most of these devices were put into operation well after the export boom was underway, and in many cases they had had little or no effect before civil war disrupted the national economy. Thus, it would be difficult to ascribe to them more than a peripheral role in the economic events of 1967 to 1975. Far more likely, the already existing low taxes and general lack of business regulation encouraged the boom more than any program of exemptions.

Though the religio-communal aspects of Lebanon's internal conflicts receive most of the attention of observers and commentators, most also admit the existence of an important economic dimension. Though this is not the place for a detailed analysis of this situation, we should at least present a brief summary.

Like its Middle East neighbors, Lebanon during the post World War II period has gone through a period of rapid economic and social change. Unlike most of its neighbors, it saw very little internal political change – no revolutionary or even moderately reformist regime came to power during the period. The country experienced considerable economic advancement, at least in terms indicated by aggregate and average measurements. But there have been ample indications that the country's prosperity was not widely shared. Unfortunately, data pertaining to this are sparse. We have referred above to one study of income distribution, but this covers a period more than 20 years ago. These figures (see *Tables 10.8* and *10.9*) show a Lebanon that was second only to pre-revolutionary Iraq, among the half dozen Middle Eastern countries for which there were data, in the degree of imbalance in income distribution. About 60 percent of national income went to the richest fifth of the population, while only about 12 percent went to the poorest two fifths. We have no comparable figures that are any more recent to indicate whether the prosperity of the 1960s and early 1970s did anything to redress this imbalance, but we can consider whether the tax structure might have played a role.

As indicated in Chapter 8, Lebanon has had progressive income and profits taxes. However, both the difficulties in collecting such taxes (a problem shared with its neighbors) and generally low tax rates (unlike those of most of its neighbors) have combined to make these levies of relatively little importance in Lebanon. All of the non-oil exporting countries use these taxes more intensively (cf. *Table 10.10*); while Lebanon in the 1970s was raising about 6 percent of its revenues from these sources, Egypt was raising about 17 percent, Jordan 12 percent and Sudan 11 percent. If we compare income tax receipts to national income, the relative lightness of the burden of these taxes on Lebanese taxpayers is shown in ever greater contrast – Lebanon's tax revenue to GNP ratio is only about half that of most of its neighbors.

Wealth taxes were also quite light throughout this period. There were no taxes on invested capital (or from the returns) and very low levies on capital gains (which were in any case hard to collect). Despite the long running real estate boom before the civil war, all taxes on real estate continued to bring in less than half as much revenue as those on automobiles.

Consumption taxes, hitting hardest at the urban working and middle classes, have dominated Lebanon's fiscal profile throughout the period in question. During the 1960s and 1970s, these taxes grew notably faster than both total receipts and the income and property levies lumped together in the 'religiously appropriate' category.

All in all, we see a picture of a country with rather severe imbalances in its income distribution in the 1950s, even by LDC standards, and a tax structure at that time, and since, that would do little to correct existing imbalances. Also modifications in taxes during the 1960s that mostly favored those who were already realizing the biggest gains from the economic boom, entrepreneurs and real estate owners[7]. Certainly, whatever else may have been going on in the Lebanon, it seems reasonable to assume that the country did not use fiscal policy to redress income imbalances to any notable extent. A prime problem facing any post civil war Lebanese regime will be how to alleviate this problem while reigniting an economic boom that clearly was sustained by a tax structure which put its burdens mostly on the urbanized working and middle class.

12.4   Sudan

Though the Sudan is still one of the poorest countries in the Middle East (see *Table 12.2*), its long term economic prospects are considered by most observers to be quite good. It is larger than any other country we are examining; with more than 2.5 million square kilometers, it covers more than the combined area of Saudi Arabia (the second largest country in the Middle East), Jordan, Kuwait, Bahrain, Qatar and the UAE. Although recent discoveries offer the prospect of the Sudan becoming a modest oil exporter by the late 1980s, it is another natural resource, cultivable land, that appears to hold the key to economic development.

In short, the Sudan has perhaps more potentially productive agricultural land, given currently available technology, that is not used (or severely underused) than any other country in the world. For a transformation into the 'breadbasket of the Middle East', a lot of reliance is to be placed on massive infusions of external economic assistance, especially from the neighboring capital-surplus oil exporters, as the Sudanese economy is hard pressed to generate domestically the investment funds needed to escalate agricultural production. Although the tax revenue to GNP ratio almost tripled between 1955 and 1977, with an overall buoyancy of about 1.37, the only Middle Eastern country with less in per capita tax receipts than the Sudan during the late 1970s was South Yemen (*Tables 12.2* and *12.10*).

Table 12.10 *Sudan: selected economic and fiscal statistics (1955–1977)*

	1955	1962	1968	1973	1977
Population (millions)	195.5	12.57	13.84	14.96	16.95
GNP (millions of pounds)	300.0	415.7	577.2	1246.0	2224.0
Total government revenues (millions of pounds)	32.0	74.4	105.9	199.6	451.0
Percentage from:					
'Religiously appropriate' taxes	10.6	6.5	8.7	11.8	11.1
Consumer related taxes	46.9	54.8	55.4	59.7	57.7
Tax revenue/GNP ratio	10.7	17.9	18.4	22.0	29.0
Per capita					
GNP (pounds)	29.4	33.1	41.7	83.3	131.2
Domestic taxes (pounds)	3.1	5.9	7.6	13.3	26.6
Tax buoyancies					*1955–77*
All taxes		2.691	1.078	0.812	1.126	1.340
'Religiously appropriate' taxes		1.061	2.037	1.246	1.209	1.365
Consumer related taxes		3.214	1.112	0.915	1.256	1.452

Source: See *Table 8.13.*

As was pointed out in Chapter 8, the Sudanese tax profile remains that of a typical subsistence level agricultural economy. The continued dominance of agriculture can be seen in *Table 12.3*; more than in any other country in the Middle East, except North Yemen (and probably also South Yemen, for which no official data are available), the share of agriculture in GNP still far outweighs all other private sectors (that is, excepting the inflated government services sector). By way of comparison, in both Egypt, which shares the rich Nile Valley with the Sudan, and Syria, another major agricultural economy, the industrial and agricultural sectors have approached each other in the relative importance of their contributions to GNP over the last generation. In the Sudan, on the other hand, we continue to find one of the only two Middle Eastern economies which have less than 10 percent of their GNP originating in the industrial sector[8].

The specifics of Sudan's fiscal profile are contained in *Tables 8.13, 8.14* and *12.10*. Indirect taxes have gradually *increased* in relative importance since the early 1950s; in most LDCs in the Middle East and elsewhere, the tendency has been for indirect taxes to have remained stable or to have experienced a modest decline in this regard. In part, this circumstance has arisen in the Sudan, not because of a relative lessening in the importance of direct taxes, but because of changes in state enterprise revenues. While these earnings rose about nine fold over the 1952–1977 period, their relative importance was off about 60 percent. Most of these enterprises are part of the large network of agricultural schemes, and the government has greatly preferred taxes on consumers to those on producers (taking a larger share of the profits of the schemes would act, in effect, as a tax on the incomes of the farmers who participate in these schemes). On the other hand, the buoyancy of nearly 1.5 indicated for consumer-related taxes, the largest grouping within the indirect category, indicates that the growing role of indirect taxes is not merely a question of policies favoring a relative decline in state enterprise revenues. The Sudanese consumer has been the easiest taxpayer to reach throughout this period, and the buoyancies of consumer related taxes have consistently led those for all taxes.

In our earlier discussion of the Sudan in Chapter 8, we indicated that it was one of the few countries for which there existed some officially reported data on specifically Islamic taxes. *Table 8.15* shows some figures for three such levies – *zakat*, *'ushr*, and the tribute or head tax – all of which have had limited use by local fiscal authorities. In comparing the Sudan to its neighbors, three points should be made. Although the Sudan, unlike most of its neighbors, had these traditional levies on its law books before the resurgence across the Middle East of interest in Islamic economic principles in the late 1970s, these specifically religious sources of revenue were decidedly minor in nature. In 1969/70, the last year for which separate data are available, only about £1.15 million were realized in this fashion – about 25 percent of total local government revenues and less than two percent of all government revenues. Secondly, these taxes were being used only by local authorities in a country where nearly all taxes were collected by national authorities. Thirdly, these taxes obviously declined in importance over the period in question; they accounted for more than 1.9 million pounds and 90 percent of local revenues in 1957/58.

Thus, the Sudan could hardly be singled out as a country where Islamic principles played a significant role in the formulation of its tax policies. If we broaden our considerations to include the category of 'religiously appropriate' taxes, then the amounts collected are considerably greater. Nevertheless, the percentage of all tax revenues raised through income and wealth taxes in the Sudan is the second lowest among the region's non-oil exporters (see *Table 10.15*), although the buoyancy of almost 1.4 for this category indicates that it grew somewhat faster than taxes in general.

Assessing the relative burden across the income profile of Sudan is of necessity a speculative venture in the absence of much reliable data on either income distribution or the impact of various taxes on Sudanese households. Not only is the information on income distribution in the country somewhat out of date (cf. *Tables 10.8* and *10.9*), but it is derived from a survey in only one city, Omdurman. This showed the Sudan to be marginally better off as regards distribution than other Middle East countries (except for Libya) for which data were available, but still within the range of such indicators as the Gini coefficient where most LDCs are found.

As mentioned above in Chapter 8, the Sudan has income and profits taxes that are steeply progressive in theory. However, large initial exemptions and difficulties in collecting more than a small portion of what is due from selfemployed individuals or from those whose incomes are derived from non-labor sources leads to the reasonable assumption that most of the burden of the income tax falls on the small middle class – which in the Sudan is mostly comprised of government employees. It has been pointed out that two sources of revenue not classified as direct taxes in *Table 8.13* – the levies on agricultural schemes – are in effect very much like income taxes on the agricultural sector. By the late 1970s, these levies probably were bringing in about half as much as were those on incomes and profits, but it is not clear how their burden is apportioned among the rural population – landlords, small freeholders and agricultural laborers.

Like many other LDCs, the Sudan has tended to construct its schedule of import duties (the largest single category of taxes) to favor capital goods over consumer goods. The burden of these taxes (plus that of the excises on domestically produced consumer goods) thus tends to fall heavily on those groups most affected by the income tax – the urban middle class. However, the consumption levies are almost certainly more widely felt than are income taxes since many Sudanese who escape the brunt of the latter, such as merchants and property owners, are among the most prominent consumers of heavily taxed items. Nor is the effect of onsumption taxation limited to the small proportion of the population found in urban areas (cf. *Table 10.12*). A large part of Sudanese agriculture is firmly entrenched in the cash sector, and many of the food and non-food items purchased by the farmers who grow cotton, gum arabic and groundnuts carry with them some kind of consumption tax.

12.5   Syria

At first glance, the Syrian fiscal profile shows a considerable degree of variability as far as the major categories are concerned (cf. *Table 8.17*). For example, direct taxes in 1950 accounted for less than 14 percent of government revenues; by 1958, their share had ballooned to nearly 39 percent, only to fall to less than 25 percent by 1970. Then a rapid increase took them to more than 36 percent only two years later before falling back to 15 percent by 1977. Both indirect taxes and state enterprise revenues showed similar relative volatility, making it difficult to identify overall trends during the three decades in question.

At least part of this problem can be traced to statistical sources. Syria is now a minor oil exporter, but until production began in the early 1960s, its oil related revenues consisted primarily of transit fees collected on the through-put of two major pipelines that cross Syria from oil fields in Iraq and Saudi Arabia. To a much lesser extent, there were also exploration fees paid by companies prospecting in Syria. All this revenue was reported in Syrian fiscal documents as royalty income, which in the categories employed in this work is included under direct taxes. When domestic production began, receipts were at first counted as royalties. However, an increasing proportion of Syrian oil earnings in the 1970s were channeled through the General Petroleum Authority, a state owned corporation. As *Table 8.17* shows, by 1977, no royalty earnings are indicated. All oil income in that year was classified as state enterprise receipts, which accounted for more than 45 percent of all government revenue.

Table 12.11 *Syria: oil production, exports, and export earning (1968–1979)*

	Oil production	Oil exports	Oil export earnings
	(thousands of barrels/day)		(millions of S£)
1968	27.2	15.8	29.8
1970	83.1	64.8	128.7
1972	117.2	77.1	200.2
1973	110.4	82.7	291.3
1974	130.7	117.3	1607.5
1975	192.7	189.4	2376.6
1976	195.2	183.3	2585.7
1977	174.0	150.6	2436.0
1978	171.0	154.2	2583.0
1979	165.0	147.0	4449.0

Sources: International Financial Statistics; Quarterly Economic Review of Syria and Jordan.

Since it is not possible to isolate oil income in a consistent fashion from published sources, the procedures we have followed in discussing the other countries in this and the previous chapter are less useful in the case of Syria. *Table 12.11* shows oil production and export earnings since 1968; while the latter series is useful in indicating the relative importance of oil to the economy as a whole and to government receipts, it must be kept in mind that the export value of oil and the tax revenue generated by its production are not identical. Nevertheless, it is reasonable to conclude that, since Syria renewed its exports of oil in 1974 after repairing the damage of the October 1973 war, the oil industry has generated between 35 and 40 percent of the nation's tax revenues. This is a considerably smaller relative share than that played by oil in any of the nine exporting countries treated in the previous chapter, but nearly twice as large as the role of oil in Egyptian budgets during the late 1970s (though Egyptian oil production at this time was about three times Syrian levels)[9].

Table 12.12 *Syria: selected economic and fiscal statistics (1950–1977)*

	1950	*1962*	*1968*	*1973*	*1977*
Population (millions)	3.21	4.84	5.87	6.69	7.84
GNP (millions of pounds)	2185	3950	5325	9446	28 084
Annual oil production (millions of barrels)	–	–	30.3	36.1	74.8
Total government revenues (millions of pounds)	216	867	1575	1969	6 067
Percentage from:					
'Religiously appropriate' taxes	11.7	17.7	11.1	13.5	15.1
Consumer related taxes	64.4	45.9	20.2	25.8	29.7
Tax revenue/GNP ratio	9.9	22.0	29.6	20.8	21.6
Per capita					
GNP (pounds)	680	816	907	1371	3582
Domestic taxes (pounds)	67.3	179	268	286	774
Tax buoyancies					*1950–77*
All taxes	2.431	2.051	0.375	1.038	1.327
'Religiously appropriate' taxes	3.206	0.449	0.716	1.150	1.432
Consumer related taxes	1.739	−0.765	0.849	1.292	1.028

Source: See *Table 8.17.*

If we adjust the figures of *Table 8.17* by moving oil receipts to the direct tax category (either as a profits tax on the state owned oil company or as royalties), then direct taxes would account for 50 to 55 percent of government revenues, while the state enterprise category would drop to 5–10 percent of the total. However, this move would not affect the tax groupings employed in *Table 12.12*. As was indicated earlier, the 'religiously appropriate' heading was used to bring together those taxes on individuals or businesses that were either specifically within the traditions of Islam or which might be seen as analogous to Islamic taxes. Thus we excluded oil taxes which are mostly paid by foreign consumers. As can be seen then, from *Table 12.12*, 'religiously appropriate' taxes climbed from about 11 percent of total receipts in 1968 to about 15 percent by 1977 – that is, during the period that Syria became an oil exporter. At late 1970s levels, Syrian fiscal reliance on these sources was considerably higher than we found in the major oil exporters (see *Table 10.15*), but still slightly below average among the seven non-oil countries. However, unlike any of the three countries with higher shares for these taxes (South Yemen, Egypt and Lebanon), Syria has seen them grow considerably faster than other revenues during the 1970s.

As regards the other category we have been using, consumer related taxes, Syria saw a very sharp drop in its relative reliance on such sources in the 1950s and 1960s and some upward adjustment during the 1970s. Still, at about the 25 percent level in the late 1970s, Syria was using them relatively less than both its non-oil neighbors in the Middle East and LDCs in general (cf. *Table 10.17*). Closest to Syria in this regard is Egypt; both countries have somewhat sophisticated economies for the region (that is, more opportunity to tax various kinds of economic activity) as well as oil revenues to help ease the common LDC dependence on consumption taxation.

In trying to evaluate the impact of taxation on Syria's population, there is a lack of even the rudimentary information on income distribution that was discussed in Chapter 10 for a few of its neighbors. Income taxes have been progressive in theory, but several factors have tended to nullify this effect in practice. First, in Syria as in many LDCs, much of what is due in income taxes is avoided, especially by the wealthy, who tend to be self-employed. Secondly, the tax structure employed by Syria has had one of the lowest maximum rates in the region – only 12 percent due on wages and salaries above £4000 a month[10]. Thirdly, government employees, by far the largest group of income tax payers, were (at least through the mid 1970s) being assessed a flat 4.44 percent, rather than subjected to the official sliding scale. Thus, in practice, few Syrians have paid income taxes at rates in excess of this flat rate for civil servants, and what has been in theory a mildly progressive tax on all wage earners but the very poorest[11] has been in fact a rather small flat rate tax on a small part of the population. The result is the minor role for income taxes in the overall fiscal profile; they amounted to only a bit more than 1 percent of total government revenues (cf. *Tables 8.17* and *8.18*) through the early and mid 1970s.

Business taxes (a wide range of different levies on various sorts of profits and returns on investments) have been much more significant, realizing about six times as much revenue as personal income levies in the 1970s. Rates have been much more steeply progressive (up to 46 percent) for both proprietorship and incorporated types of firms, though it seems unlikely that few if any businesses pay anything near what is theoretically due[12]. It must be recalled that, outside the oil sector, few sizable foreign owned enterprises (the most likely candidates in other LDCs to pay taxes in approximate line with what is theoretically due) operate in Syria, which has pursued both nationalizing and socializing economic goals more or less consistently for the last two decades. However, since the private domestically owned business sector has survived and even prospered within sharp limits, business related taxes (even if theoretically underpaid) probably introduce some degree of progressivity into the overall income tax category.

Consumption related taxes have been about equally divided between customs duties and domestic excises until the mid 1970s when the former became notably more important revenue earners. Since duties on imported necessities are generally low and the Syrian economy is largely self-sufficient in major consumption items (food, textiles, fuel) found in lower income family budgets, these taxes in effect probably are progressive, at least up through middle income levels.

One series of commodity taxes, on certain agricultural products, is not in its effect a consumption tax, since it is levied on exports. Given demand elasticities for these commodities in world markets, most of their burden is shifted backward onto the producers as an implicit income tax. Though they grew significantly more slowly over the period in question than did urban oriented income and profits taxes (at an average of about 9 percent a year versus some 15 percent a year for the latter, and thus fell in relative importance from about 12 percent of total receipts in 1950 to about 3 percent in 1977), inclusion of them with income, profits and property taxes in the 'religiously appropriate' classification does have a notable effect on the figures shown in *Table 12.12* for this category. For example, this enlargement would mean about 24 percent of all taxes coming from this source in 1950, with a slight rise to about 26 percent by 1962, then a drop before levelling off between 16 and 19 percent during the late 1960s and 1970s.

The buoyancy figures in *Table 12.12* show the uneven growth pattern in Syrian taxes relative to the economy as a whole – buoyancies well above 2 for roughly the first two-thirds of the period in question and well less than 1 from 1968 to 1977. Ironically, taxes have tended to grow faster relative to GNP during the country's capitalist oriented periods, especially the early and mid 1950s, as opposed to the more socialist periods. The buoyancies of 'religiously appropriate' and consumer related taxes differ sharply, with the former generally leading overall tax buoyancies, while the latter tend to lag behind. However, if producer taxes are treated as 'religiously appropriate'[13], the buoyancies of the two categories are closer, with the figure for the revised religious taxes dropping to about 1.2 for the period as a whole.

Commenting on Syrian tax policies at present and in the future encounters the same major non-political problem as Egypt – the future role of oil and oil generated tax revenue in an economy which, up until now, we have classified as non-oil in character. As indicated above, the recent performance of this sector has been unsatisfactory, except in two respects over which Syria has little or no control – world demand and market price. Only higher prices in the wake of the concerted OPEC (of which Syria is not a member) price action of 1973–74[14], the wild gyrations in the spot market for oil after the demise of the Pahlavi regime in early 1979, and the Iran-Iraq war of 1980–82, has allowed Syria to boost its oil revenues and to maintain them at high levels. Both production and exports declined in the last half of the reently ended decade (cf. *Table 12.11*). For several years, the official government position has been that major discoveries which will add considerably to the country's reserves, production and exports are 'only around the corner'. While the government's use of such propaganda is understandable, regardless of geological fact, many neutral observers of hydrocarbon potential tend to agree that Syria's future could indeed be very bright, though political barriers to exploration by major international oil companies are then cited as dampening factors to such optimism.

If either chance discovery, which has happened in a huge way elsewhere in the Middle East, or a change in political attitudes (as in Sadat's Egypt) results in a significant increase in known Syrian hydrocarbon deposits of commercially explorable quality, then the fiscal picture for the 1980s becomes very optimistic. In such circumstances, advice to Syria parallels what was said above in this chapter about Egypt, where petro-prospects are already bright. In short, try to keep such additional receipts as *net receipts* insofar as is possible, earmarking real gains for investment spending, and not substituting for domestic fiscal sources to support current needs.

Oil, natural gas and related products are non-renewable resources; thus the income they generate is a one time phenomenon unless this income is reinvested in projects that will perpetuate current income streams. Unlike Saudi Arabia and Kuwait in the 1950s, Libya and Abu Dhabi in the 1960s, Oman in the 1970s, Syria and Egypt in the 1980s and 1990s already enjoy a relatively advanced (as compared to LDCs in general) level of education, public health, housing, water distribution, and transportation.

Thus, financing major expansions in those items, typically found in LDC current budgets, entirely out of additional oil revenues (to the point of allowing existing domestic tax sources to wither away) must be seen as economically unwise, no matter what may be the short term political advantage. Syrian (and Egyptian) fiscal policy makers would more wisely treat major oil discoveries in the same fashion that their compatriots in such places as Japan, Taiwan, South Korea, Hong Kong and Singapore during the last 25 years have treated other (temporary) comparative advantages as brief opportunities to add significantly to the nation's otherwise meager base of renewable resources.

If, on the other hand, Syrian oil hopes evaporate, even in the face of a wide open exploration process, then the country must resolve itself to adjusting to a more conventional LDC fiscal situation. Unfortunately, Syria has already shown signs of ignoring that possibility. As indicated earlier, unofficial figures allow the estimate that by the late 1970s Syria's not very significant oil industry (in Middle East terms) had approached the 50 percent mark as a source of fiscal revenues. Yet projections of domestic demand for hydrocarbon products show that this alone will virtually eliminate exports as early as 1986 or 1987 (unless successful exploration allows an expansion in production)[15]. Any national projection of Syrian fiscal policy over the next decade must allow for the strong possibility that geological realities may well permanently eliminate oil export revenues in the relatively short term.

12.6   Yemen Arab Republic

This section brings us to the first of the two 'orphans' of the Middle East – the twin Yemeni states. Not only are these two countries the poorest in the region, but statistical information for them is also the sparsest among the states we are discussing. As can be seen from *Table 8.20*, the earliest detailed official fiscal data available is for 1966/67, though unofficial estimates allow us to go back a bit further in *Table 12.13*.

The major event in the north Yemeni economy during this period has been the remittance boom. Estimates are that as much as half the adult male labor force of the country has found more or less permanent employment in one of the neighboring oil exporting states, especially in Saudi Arabia where perhaps one million Yemenis were working in the late 1970s. Though it is difficult to estimate precisely how much these remittances come to, there are indications that they increased eight times in the first years of the oil price rise – from about 575 million *rials* in 1972/73 to about 4560 million *rials* in 1976/77[16], approximately one third of the GNP. Observers agree that while some of these remitted funds have been spent on capital improvements in what remains Yemen's only productive sector to speak of, agriculture, most are spent on imported consumer goods. Thus the net effect of emigration has been a decline in the volume of productive activity, even while GNP was climbing perhaps ten fold during the 1970s.

During the period, north Yemen's fiscal profile remained rather constant with indirect taxes (mostly import duties) accounting for the bulk of government revenue. The buoyancy figures indicate that taxes grew about 50 percent faster than the economy as a whole.

We have discussed the officially reported data for *zakat* in north Yemen in Chapter 8. Like the two other countries for which similar information is available (Saudi Arabia and the Sudan), the Yemen Arab Republic has seen a relative decline in the importance of this traditional Islamic levy during recent times. For example in the mid 1960s, *zakat* accounted for nearly one-eighth of the government's total receipts; by the late 1970s, this proportion had fallen to less than one-fiftieth. The buoyancy for *zakat* alone over the period shown in *Table 12.13* was only about 0.85, barely half the total value for taxes in general. However, because of the adoption of contemporary forms of direct taxation (on profits and personal incomes) which can be included in our broader 'religiously appropriate' category, the buoyancy for this grouping is much larger than that for *zakat* alone.

Since 1973, the already small share of direct taxes (identical with the 'religiously appropriate' category for north Yemen) has been squeezed even more as imports and import duties have grown tremendously – respectively by about 71 percent and 70 percent a year on average, between 1973 and 1977. During this period, as well as during the preceding five years, the consumer related taxes, among which import duties have been the most prominent, grew notably faster than taxes as a whole, as the buoyancy figures in *Table 12.13* show.

Table 12.13 *Yemen Arab Republic: selected economic and fiscal statistics (1962–1977)*

	1962	1968	1973	1977
Population (millions)	4.22	4.70	5.08	5.52
GNP (millions of *rials*)	560[a]	1050	3279	13 500
Total government revenues (millions of *rials*)	20[a]	52	275	1902
Percentage from:				
'Religiously appropriate' taxes	10.0[a]	11.7	12.0	7.0
Consumer related taxes	77.5[a]	59.2	70.1	72.0
Tax revenue/GNP ratio	3.6[a]	4.9	8.4	14.1
Per capita				
GNP (*rials*)	133	223	645	2445
Domestic taxes (*rials*)	4.7	11.1	54.1	345
Tax buoyancies				*1962–77*
All taxes		1.559	1.548	1.117	1.501
'Religiously appropriate' taxes		1.848	1.573	0.981	1.367
Consumer related taxes		1.098	1.732	1.491	1.473

Note: [a] Estimated.

Source: See *Table 8.20.*

Only the most general assessment can be made of the impact of the Yemen Arab Republic's tax policies on its population. With little information on the demography and even less on the income distribution pattern of the country, we can only examine the tax structure relative to certain assumptions about these factors. North Yemen is the least urbanized country of the region, with well over 80 percent of the population still on the land. Yet the dominant agricultural sector has been stripped of half or more of its adult male labor force. Rural income has become much more a question of remittances from emigrants than earnings from farm production.

Direct taxation (except for *zakat*) is primarily aimed at the small urban population. In north Yemen, as in many other LDCs, the personal income tax is paid by few non-government employees. As indicated in Chapter 8, a combination of deduction allowances and a low maximum rate keeps this tax from being onerous for the few who pay it; in 1977/78 it realized less than 40 million *rials*, about 2 percent of government revenue. Business profits taxes are mostly paid by the few modern type enterprises in the country and are difficult to collect in the large sector made up of traditional entrepreneurs such as the merchants.

Indirect taxes are mostly levied on goods of foreign origin in the form of import duties or excise taxes (e.g., on petroleum products and automobiles). Although we have no evidence in this regard, it is not unlikely that these taxes in present day north Yemen are less regressive in effect than they would be in most LDCs. They are a relatively easily administered levy on a type of consumption which is largely supported by emigrant remittances. Unlike taxes assessed directly against such transfers or against their recipients' incomes, they do not have a direct negative effect on remittances (which would also be easier to send into the country by extralegal means than are dutiable commodities). With lighter duties on necessities (many of which like cereal grains have to be imported as a result of migration of so many rural Yemeni workers) and heavier duties and excises on less essential items, these taxes do have a selective impact across the country's family income spectrum. Also benefitting to some extent from lower duties are capital goods including farm equipment, the importation of which has partially, if unevenly, compensated for rural depopulation[17].

One last remark relative to the Yemen Arab Republic's fiscal profile bears repeating. Though obviously the country is very poor, its tax effort must be rated as well below similar countries in the Middle East (though not so low as many LDCs elsewhere (cf. *Table 10.3*). Tax effort, as measured by the tax revenue to GNP ratio did rise sharply after 1973, from levels among the lowest in the world. Since north Yemen has been fairly successful in obtaining large scale economic assistance from its wealthy neighbors and elsewhere, it remains to be seen whether the government will continue this enhanced tax effort at current or higher levels or let the tax ratio drop back toward pre 1973 levels.

12.7 People's Democratic Republic of Yemen

Without its northern neighbor's rather extensive (in Arabian terms) endowment of arable land, south Yemen is now clearly the Arab state with the poorest prospects for economic development. In earlier years, this bleak prognosis was masked by the activity of Aden and its harbor. Long a major port of call between Europe and the Orient, Aden was the location of one of the Middle East's first oil refineries, built in 1954 by the British Petroleum Company, primarily as a source of bunkering fuel for the hundreds of ships calling on the port each year. As recently as 1967, the refinery accounted for more than 80 percent of all industrial activity in the collection of British territories and protectorates that became independent as south Yemen. Then came the June 1967 war, the closure of the Suez Canal and the era of the supertanker. Even after the reopening of the canal in 1975, Aden's recovery as a port was undistinguished. The refinery, finally nationalized in 1977 after several years as the biggest capitalist exception in an increasingly socialist

Table 12.14 *Yemen People's Democratic Republic: selected economic and fiscal statistics (1951–1978)*

	1951	1962	1968	1973	1978
Population (thousands)	820	1100	1360	1570	1810
GNP (millions of *dinars*)	14	25	68	75	200
Total government revenues (millions of *dinars*)	2.2[a]	5.4	7.8	15.3	43.5
Percentage from:					
'Religiously appropriate' taxes	30.9	29.0	25.6	20.7	22.4
Consumer related taxes	13.6	31.2	35.5	49.6	48.8
Tax revenue/GNP ratio	15.7	21.6	11.5	25.5	21.8
Per capita					
GNP (*dinars*)	17.1	22.7	50.0	47.7	110.5
Domestic taxes (*dinars*)	2.7	4.9	5.7	9.7	24.0
Tax buoyancies					1951–78
All taxes	1.508	0.390	7.313	1.069	1.219
'Religiously appropriate' taxes	1.393	0.269	4.873	1.162	1.001
Consumer related taxes	2.492	0.707	11.237	1.054	1.651

Note: [a] Includes estimates for Aden Protectorate revenues.

Source: See *Table 8.23.*

economy, continues to languish at a small fraction of capacity production, hardly the factor in south Yemen's fiscal accounts that it once was. For example, from 1973 (when the refinery was already underused) to 1977, the value of petroleum imports rose only from $28 million to $46 million; given price increases, this represents a drop in volume of 50 percent or more.

Yet despite these economic misfortunes, south Yemen saw per capita GNP more than double between 1973 and 1978, whereas it had actually fallen during the previous five years (cf. *Table 12.14*). This 'boom', however, is deceptive; its origins are totally external. As is the case with the

Yemen Arab Republic, the People's Democratic Republic of Yemen is an exporter of labor and has become heavily dependent on emigrant remittances. Even less is known about the extent of emigration in the latter than in the former, but if we compare what is known about net remittances to each country, we can estimate that there are between 200 000 and 300 000 adult male south Yemenis in Saudi Arabia, the Gulf states and elsewhere. According to the International Monetary Fund, by 1978, net private unrequited financial transfers came to more than 88 million *dinars*; nearly all the funds involved in this category were emigrant remittances. This figure amounts to about 45 percent of south Yemen's GNP.

As a result of the different social and economic systems in the two Yemens, there is a major distinction in the way the recipients in each country use them. As observers[18] have noted, at least a sizable portion of the remittances sent to north Yemen are spent on capital goods, especially for agriculture and small scale industrial enterprises, such as repair shops. In addition, the visitor to the Yemen Arab Republic is impressed by the number of farm vehicles (small pick-up trucks, four wheel drive jeeps, etc.) that have been brought back by returnees. Though even in north Yemen most transfers are spent on consumer goods, in south Yemen, socialism affects the rural areas where collectivism is the goal and private investment is not very attractive. Thus, not many of the funds remitted to south Yemen are devoted to capital investment by the recipients or by those returning.

Though we have longer fiscal data series for south Yemen (cf. *Table 8.23*) than for its northern neighbor, it should be recalled that in the preindependence period, only the rather tiny area of Aden Colony was under the watchful eye (and pen) of the British bureaucracy. For the hinterland we have compiled such estimates as are available and these do not fit precisely, for all years, into the categories used in *Tables 8.23* and *8.24*. Nonetheless, we can point out certain patterns in the country's fiscal structure – for example, the fairly consistent shares of direct and indirect taxes before and after independence, the tax revenue–GNP ratio that was about the same in 1978 as it had been in 1962. Beneath these more general statistics, there were significant changes beginning with independence.

During the British period, most tax receipts came from (and most government spending went back to) the immediate area of Aden, an important military outpost that merited fairly sizable subsidies from the colonial power. With the local spending requirements being quite low (the much larger protectorate area was fiscally autonomous), so were local taxes; no profits taxes on the refinery or the lucrative free port activities, most imports were duty free, excises were limited and modest. After independence, the new government had the task of unifying what had been a group of 24 autonomous shiekhdoms into one nation and, consequently, faced major infrastructural needs to serve a sparsely settled country stretched along a 1000 kilometer littoral. Given the meagerness of its own resources, the government imposed new taxes (such as that on profits) or increased existing ones (such as import duties). From 1968, the year after independence (when the tax revenue–GNP ratio fell to only half what it had been in the early 1960s), to 1973, tax revenues almost doubled while GNP increased only about 12 percent. The heavy drag of these new taxes in a deteriorating economy, along with other policies of south Yemen's socialist government, virtually eliminated a large part of the private sector of the economy.

With the nationalization of the refinery in 1977, all sizable industrial enterprises are now in the public sector, but they are still liable to profits taxes, as well as to paying a portion of their post tax profit to the state (shown in *Table 8.23* as returns from state enterprises). Thus in the late 1970s, these firms are the source of about 40 to 45 percent of the government's revenue.

Personal income taxes, in south Yemen as elsewhere in the region, are theoretically quite progressive but in practice are paid by only a small proportion of the work force, in this case employees of the government and of state corporations. One difference in south Yemen – there are few, if any, rich self-employed citizens to avoid the burdens of this levy.

Customs duties and excises on a few locally produced goods (most prominently petroleum products) generate about half of fiscal revenue and these are by far the broadest base tax. Since emigration has affected all parts of the country, so do emigrant remittances. In both Yemens, remittances increased similarly after 1973; by perhaps ten fold over 4 or 5 years. But in north Yemen, an import surge has seen customs receipts climb by roughly the same order of magnitude. In south Yemen both imports and the duties on them have grown more modestly, while imports were up 220 percent between 1973 and 1978, customs receipts were up 150 percent. This indicates that in south Yemen rather more of the remittances go for locally produced goods and/or imports which are less heavily taxed (in both cases, this would probably mean food and similar necessities). As indicated earlier, there are fewer opportunities and incentives in south Yemen to use remittances for capital goods, so only the government portion (that is, taxes on the spending of these funds) is likely to become available for any type of domestic investment. It would seem that the north Yemeni government manages to channel a larger proportion of its emigrants' remittances into the public coffers than does its counterpart in south Yemen.

Of all the countries discussed in this chapter, it is probable that in the People's Democratic Republic of Yemen tax policies are least likely to be predominant in the pursuance of any major economic goal. Progressive income taxes as a means of redistributing income are hardly effective in a society where no one can earn (legally) more than a few times the income of the poorest citizen; the remnants of Aden's always small 'wealthy' class – mostly merchants – have long since had their businesses nationalized and/or have departed the country. Profits taxes are almost exclusively levied on government corporations; in the decision processes of the managers of these enterprises, the influence of taxes must surely be much less than it would be in privately owned firms. Property and wealth taxes are minor items when such a large part of the productive assets of the country is socialized. Duties and excises can be used to influence spending decisions, but other government policies have been more important here; for example, it is not the level of duties on machinery that determines whether a rural south Yemeni family with remittance income from abroad uses it to mechanize some farm operation, but the degree of socialization in agriculture that the government is pursuing.

Notes

1 Ironically, Egypt has historically been one of the more 'secular' countries in the Islamic world. Yet its tax profile shows much more reliance on the 'religiously appropriate' taxes than many of its more formally orthodox neighbors.

2 Obviously, not all ODA losses have to be matched by tax increases. For example, non-concessional financial flows can also substitute, and *ceteris paribus* it would be expected that a rapidly growing economy such as Jordan's would be attractive to such flows. Undoubtedly, the key elements in this regard will be the internal stability of Jordan and changes in the level of external threats to its territorial integrity.

3 The importance of these remittances is obvious: in 1971, they amounted to 5.7 million *dinars*, but by 1978, this had grown to 163.5 million *dinars*, according to the official figures reported by the IMF in the *Balance of Payments Yearbook*.

4 Such as necessities (including education) for the poorest families receiving them, or small capital goods like agricultural machinery for others.

5 Two of the authors have discussed this period of recent Lebanese economic history in some detail in *The Middle East Economies in the 1970s: A Comparative Approach*, Chapters 7 and 11.

6 In fact this ratio may be far smaller. In a recent article in *The Arab Economist* (January 1981), Prof. André Chaib of the American University of Beirut argued that Lebanese GNP estimates before the civil war were too low, and that in the early 1970s it may have been twice as high as official estimates. If so, of course, then tax to GNP ratios are actually only half what is indicated in *Table 12.7*.

7 In addition, the Lebanese budget clearly favored certain parts of the country (especially the cities) over others (especially the south) as regards major projects. Though we have not discussed the spending side of fiscal policy in this work, we have examined this aspect of Lebanon elsewhere (cf. Askari and Cummings, op. cit. (note 5) Chapter 13).

8 The other being the Yemen Arab Republic; though no GNP data are available by sector for the Yemen People's Democratic Republic, the large oil refining industry in that country undoubtedly puts the industrial sector's share above ten percent.

9 Though generally reported prospects for the oil industries of the two countries indicate they may reverse this situation by the mid 1980s. Syria on the one hand faces stagnant production with rapid growth in domestic demand, while Egypt's exploration program has yielded very optimistic estimates of future production.

10 With an additional ten percent surtax imposed for defense purposes.

11 Exemptions varied with family size. No tax was due (1976) from an unmarried taxpayer with monthly wages less than £100, on up to less than about £450 a month for the married wage-earner with seven or more children.

12 That portion of the profits of state owned corporations paid to the government are recorded as receipts from state enterprises.

13 They can arguably be quite like *'ushr* (tithe) in intent and effect, at least for major cash crops.

14 Where Syria was at least arguably a
political participant as a result of its
participation in the partially successful
joint effort with Egypt to dislodge Israeli
military occupation forces during the
October 1973 Arab-Israeli war.
15 For example, the Syrian Deputy Prime
Minister for Economic Affairs was quoted
(*Middle East Economic Survey*, 15
September, 1980) as predicting
consumption of 9.1 million tonnes by
1985 and 14.5 million tonnes by 1990.
Current production (1980) is about nine
million tonnes.

16 See Jon C. Swanson, Some Consequences
of Emigration for Rural Economic
Development in the Yemen Arab
Republic, *Middle East Journal*, (Winter
1979). Remittance estimates given by
Swanson are consistent with balance of
payments figures for net private
unrequited transfers published in
International Financial Statistics and the
Balance of Payments Yearbook.
17 See Swanson, Ibid.
18 Including Swanson, Ibid.

Regional problems in fiscal policy

13.1   A future regional fiscal policy problem of international consequence

Governments have two principal objectives in designing their tax policies: first, and most obviously, there is the task of raising enough revenue to pay for those current and capital expenditures which, using various criteria, have been determined to be necessary and/or desirable; secondly, taxes can be very effective tools for steering the overall development of an economy in directions which have been assigned high priorities.

For political reasons at least, it seems likely that most governments, in both developing and already industrialized economies, will rate rather more highly the first of these objectives; especially if their major concerns are of a short run nature: for example, survival of the regime. In this regard, low taxes in broad based categories (such as those on consumption or personal income) improve any government's prospects for continuation, *ceteris paribus*. However a regime's chances of survival might also be questionable if there is sluggish economic development caused by low taxes and, therefore, little government spending.

It is not difficult to understand why a government would opt for raising its revenues (and therefore its spending power) by the least painful of the available options, as judged from a political viewpoint. As we have seen in Chapters 7 and 11, in the oil exporting countries of the Middle East, this has generally meant an increasing dependence on revenues directly arising from oil production – that is, taxes whose burden falls almost entirely on foreign consumers. No doubt there are limits as to how far these distant ratepayers can be pushed before questions are raised concerning the continuation of the *de facto* military alliances which have been needed to assure the survival of the regimes in the oil exporting countries. However, through the 1970s at least, it has probably seemed to the political leadership of the oil exporters that foreign taxpayers tend to be more patient, or at least are slower to react in potentially disastrous ways, than those closer to home.

As *Table 13.1* indicates, oil revenues have generally grown faster than those from other sources throughout the interval we have been discussing. This table not only shows the increases during the periods before and after the oil price rise of 1973/4, but also shows the relationship of these changes to those in non-oil taxes. With few exceptions over the time period shown, oil taxes grew much faster.

Another method of comparison can be based on the figures of *Table 6.5*[1]. Generally, these figures indicate increasing reliance on oil related taxes. Especially since the major changes during 1973/74, even countries like Iraq

Table 13.1 *Oil tax and non-oil tax average annual growth rates (1950–1977) (%)*

Country	1950–1962	1962–1973	1973–1977	1950–1977
Oil taxes				
Bahrain	16.1	16.7	57.5	21.7
Iran	29.4	25.5	48.1	33.0
Iraq	26.7	21.2	30.7	25.0
Kuwait	34.6	11.0	44.9	25.7
Libya	[a]	69.2	43.1	61.7[i]
Oman	[a]	78.4[f]	67.5	74.0
Qatar	47.6[c]	14.8[g]	47.8	30.8
Saudi Arabia	18.6[d]	20.2	81.3	26.4[k]
United Arab Emirates	[a]	62.9[b]	66.9	64.3[l]
Non-oil taxes				
Bahrain	7.9	20.6	31.3	16.2
Iran	17.0	14.8	35.6	20.2
Iraq	7.8	9.4	19.9	10.2
Kuwait	13.2	12.6	46.8	17.5
Libya	18.1[e]	18.4	24.9	20.2[i]
Oman	NA	20.4[f]	68.9	40.4[j]
Qatar	11.6[c]	20.6	65.0	22.8
Saudi Arabia	9.5[d]	14.5	45.9	15.7[k]
United Arab Emirates	NA	38.6[b]	45.3	40.9[l]
Ratio of oil tax to non-oil tax growth rates				
Bahrain	2.04	0.81	1.84	1.34
Iran	1.72	1.72	1.35	1.63
Iraq	3.42	2.26	1.54	2.45
Kuwait	2.62	0.87	0.96	1.47
Libya	[b]	3.76	1.73	3.05[i]
Oman	[b]	3.84[f]	0.98	1.83[j]
Qatar	4.10[c]	0.72[g]	0.74	1.35
Saudi Araba	1.96[d]	1.39	1.77	1.68[k]
United Arab Emirates	[b]	1.63[b]	1.48	1.57[l]

Notes: NA Data not available.
[a] Increase from base of zero
[b] Ratio not calculable
[c] 1950–1960
[d] 1947–1962
[e] 1952–1962
[f] 1967–1973
[g] 1960–1973
[h] 1964–1973
[i] 1962–1977
[j] 1967–1977
[k] 1947–1977
[l] 1964–1977

and Iran, which had been diversifying their tax bases, have again shifted toward more relative dependence on oil revenues. For example, Iraq was receiving almost half its taxes from non-oil sources as late as 1972/73, but after this the price rises quickly boosted oil receipts to a share of more than 80 percent. Non-oil taxes have not declined: Iraqi customs revenues, for example, in 1977 were almost 390 percent above 1972 levels, while excises were up about 120 percent and income taxes by 81 percent during the same period. But these levies have simply not grown as fast as have oil revenues.

Table 13.2 *Officially held overseas investments and returns (1960–1978)* *(millions of US dollars)*

	1960	1966	1970	1973	1978
Investments					
Iran	53	121	77	976	15 000
Iraq	259	326	462	1528	11 000
Kuwait	822	1479	1636	3700	35 000
Libya	82	339	1590	2109	5000
Qatar	25^a	80^a	150	287	3000
Saudi Arabia	184	813	893	4590	67 000
United Arab Emirates	0	25^a	100^a	500	10 000
Returns					
Iran	1.3	6.0	10.0	50.1	1300^a
Iraq	7.3	12.9	23.0	62.2	1000^a
Kuwait	26.6	50.4	89.0	301.7	2000^a
Libya	0.2^a	14.0	96.9	114.6	400^a
Qatar	1.1^a	2.7^a	6.3^a	17.4	260^a
Saudi Arabia	4.0	26.9	61.1	209.4	5310^a
United Arab Emirates	0	1.1^a	3.2^a	20.0	1000^a

Notes: Figures refer to 31 December of the year indicated.
^{a} Estimated.

Sources: Various, including International Monetary Fund and government publications, as well as authors' own estimates.

Some oil exporters have found themselves with sizable budget surpluses, even while lightening considerably the relative domestic tax burden. As a result, state owned foreign investments in several Middle Eastrn countries have accumulated very rapidly during the 1970s, as can be seen from *Table 13.2*. These investments of course are earning returns for their holders and in some cases, these returns have already become substantial. At least two oil exporting countries have already institutionalized their foreign investment programs – Kuwait's 'Fund for Tomorrow' and the Abu Dhabi Investment Authority – plowing back all the returns into new investments with the intention of providing livelihoods for their citizens after oil production ceases. Qatar appears to have similar intentions, while Saudi Arabia, which has much more ambitious hopes than its neighbors along the Gulf for domestic economic diversification extending into the post petroleum era, has also shown interest in building a sizable portfolio of foreign investments as part of this diversification strategy. Libya's small population gives it the option of pursuing a similar policy, though up to the end of the 1970s, this did not seem to be a major factor in Libyan government plans.

The overall size of these overseas investments has been a matter of considerable speculation and controversy in the financial circles of the industrial nations. By no means do we intend the most recent figures shown in *Table 13.2* to be taken as definitive estimates; rather they represent our own working estimates as derived from various sources[2].

Just how important these have already become can be seen from the figures shown in *Table 13.3*. These are presented on a *per citizen*, rather than *per inhabitant* basis on the grounds that only citizens have any reasonably enforceable claim over the long run on a country's resources. Of course for many of the smaller states that are oil exporters, if a distinction is made between residents and citizens, a considerable difference results when average returns are being calculated[3]. For example, in the late 1970s, we are using estimates that the citizen to total population ratio is only about 21 percent in the UAE, about 36 percent in Qatar and about 40 percent in Kuwait; even these estimates may be over generous for the first two countries, as may be our estimate of the citizen population of Saudi Arabia. *Table 13.3* also includes the estimates of the citizen populations that we used in making our calculations[4].

The overall impression that is gained from a perusal of *Table 13.3* is one of tremendous increase in this non-tax source of government revenues, that is, of major returns now being realized from the invested (oil-generated) budget surpluses of the past. This raises a question we must consider at this point. It is quite conceivable that as early as the mid 1980s, these investments alone could be generating the revenues needed to cover the current expenses of some of the smaller countries along the Gulf littoral.

Per citizen returns in Kuwait increased more than 5.5 fold from 1973 to 1978 – that is, at some 41 percent a year averaged over the period. By 1978, these investment returns alone were amounting to only about 10 percent *less* than the per capita GNP in Czechoslovakia, to about 12.5 percent and 25 percent *higher* than per capita GNP in the USSR and Ireland respectively (see figures shown in *Table 13.4* for ease of comparison).

For the UAE, the results were even more spectacular, with an almost 40 fold increase in five years, or an annual average growth rate of almost 110 percent. Per citizen returns in 1978 were about equal to per capita GNP in Finland and only 5 percent below Austrian levels; the UAE led the United Kingdom by 32 percent and Italy by 74 percent.

Table 13.3 *Per citizen returns from state-owned overseas investments[a] (1960–1978)*

		1960	1966	1970	1973	1978
Iran	Citizens (thousands)	21 434	25 789	29 146	32 136	35 510
	Per citizen returns (dollars)	0.06	0.23	0.34	1.58	36.6[b]
Iraq	Citizens (thousands)	6 870	8 310	9 440	10 410	12 770
	Per citizen returns (dollars)	1.06	1.55	2.34	5.97	78.3[b]
Kuwait	Citizens (thousands)	142	254	347	387	460
	Per citizen returns (dollars)	187	198	257	780	4 350[b]
Libya	Citizens (thousands)	1 349	1 643	1 843	2 037	2 400
	Per citizen returns (dollars)	1.50[a]	8.51	52.6	56.2	250[b]
Qatar	Citizens (thousands)	36	45	52	58	70
	Per citizen returns (dollars)	30.5[b]	60.0[b]	14[b]	300	3 715[b]
Saudi Arabia	Citizens (thousands)	3 100	3 660	4 085	4 530	5 200
	Per citizen returns (dollars)	1.29	7.35	15.0	46.2	1 020[b]
United Arab Emirates	Citizens (thousands)	80	93	107	120	150
	Per citizen returns (dollars)	0.00	11.1[b]	29.4[b]	167	6 667[b]

Notes: [a] The number of citizens and the reported or estimated total population are for our purposes assumed to be the same in Iran and Iraq for all years, as well as for Libya in 1960. For Kuwait (all years) and Libya after 1960, official census figures are used to estimate the proportion of citizens in the total population. Saudi Arabia and the United Arab emirates have conducted censuses, but observers have cast serious doubt on the officially reported results; our estimates are strictly non-official. Qatar has never had any sort of official census. On the whole, we have preferred to quote *higher* figures for estimated citizen populations when conflicts arose among various calculating methods.
 [b] Estimated.

Source: Returns are as quoted in *Table 13.2.*

Table 13.4 *Per citizen investment returns in major Middle Eastern oil exporters and per capita GNP in selected industrialized and developing countries (1978) (US dollars)*

Middle East

Iran	37	Libya	250	Saudi Arabia	1020
Iraq	78	Qatar	3715	United Arab Emirates	6667
Kuwait	4350				

Industrialized countries

Australia	7920	Federal Republic of Germany	9600	Spain	3520
Austria	7030	Greece	3270	USSR	3700
Canada	9170	Ireland	3470	UK	5030
Czechoslovakia	4720	Italy	3840	USA	9700
France	8270	Poland	3660	Yugoslavia	2390

Developing countries

Argentina	1910	India	180	Morocco	670
Brazil	1570	Kenya	320	Taiwan	1400
China	460	Malaysia	1090	Thailand	490
Egypt	400	Mexico	1290	Zaire	210

Source: See *Table 13.2* for Middle East; other countries – World Bank.

Per citizen earnings in Qatar were up by more than twelve fold between 1973 and 1978. On this basis, the investment returns to the average Qatari were slightly higher than Poland's per capita GNP and about 14 percent above Greek levels. Saudi Arabia, with a much larger citizen population than the Gulf states, saw its investment returns on a per citzen basis multiply well over 20 fold during the 1973 to 1978 period. In 1978, when Saudi Arabia's rapidly growing importance in the world economy had at last earned it a permanent place in the guiding councils of the IMF, its per citizen returns alone were equal to about two-thirds of Brazilian per capita GNP and more than 120 percent higher than that in the world's largest nation, China.

More significant than what has happened during the 1970s is what will be happening in the 1980s. It is reasonable to expect that, in light of disruptions in the oil markets by the Iranian revolution and the Iran–Iraq border war, the large financial surpluses of the Gulf states continued into 1981 and even later at possibly even higher levels than those projected in the First National Bank of Chicago study that was referred to above. We have made some projections of our own about the possible growth paths of these investment portfolios, and the results are shown in *Table 13.5*. Our assumptions about population growth and about the rates of return to be earned on the portfolios have been rather conservative: we have assumed that population growth will continue at very high levels, amplifying the denominators in per citizen ratios, and that this return from the portfolios will be rather low; in the range of historical rates actually earned during the 1970s which is well below the record high prevailing rates of 1980 and 1981.

The continued accumulation of capital assets is more of a problem, since the very high rates of growth that were recorded during the 1970s were in part due to the relatively low base from which these countries began the decade. Thus we have not used the very high recent (post 1974) growth rates in some countries, even for setting upper limits to the range of growth rates. The lower limit is in some cases (Iran, Iraq, Libya) only about the equivalent of current rates of return and thus represents further investment only of the earnings on current holdings. Since both Iraq and Libya ran strong balance of payments surpluses in the late 1970s, this is both reasonable and conservative. For the oil exporters in the Gulf region, our lower limit assumes reinvestment of earnings, roughly matched on average by an equivalent amount of 'new' investments. The upper limits in all cases are rather arbitrarily chosen, and represent our estimates of likely maxima that could be reached during the early and perhaps mid 1980s, though not very likely to be maintained over the entire decade and a half[5].

We could summarize the assumptions used to calculate the figures shown in *Table 13.5* as follows. The citizen population growth rate, applied to estimated future numbers of *citizens*, will probably drop from present historic highs during the next 15 years as the birth rate drops, but this could

Table 13.5 *Projected per citizen returns from state-owned overseas investments: 1985, 1990 and 1995*

Country	Assumed population rate of growth (%)	Assumed investment rate of return (%)	Range of rates of growth of invested assets (%)	Per citizen returns ($)		
				1985	*1990*	*1995*
Iran	3.0	7.75	7–12	42.7 to 58.0	51.7 to 89.5	62.2 to 136.0
Iraq	3.35	8.35	8–20	97.9 to 204.6	122.0 to 431.9	152.0 to 911.4
Kuwait	3.4	7.5	12–25	9988 to 21544	14886 to 55602	22196 to 143563
Libya	3.4	5.9	6–25	146.3 to 463.8	165.6 to 1197	187.5 to 3092
Qatar	3.5	5.85	12–25	4359 to 9402	6450 to 24093	9563 to 61855
Saudi Arabia	3.5	6.7	12–25	1500 to 3235	2225 to 8313	3303 to 21362
United Arab Emirates	3.6	7.5	12–25	8635 to 18627	12759 to 47659	18794 to 121557

be matched by any easing of naturalization regulations in the smaller countries. So the estimated citizen populations in 1985, 1990, and 1995 are probably fairly accurate, or a little on the high side. The rate of return used for each country is based on its recent history (cf. *Table 13.2*), and is thus very conservative by the standards of the late 1970s and early 1980s. Since inflation is likely to keep interest rates high at least through 1985, we can guess that our assumptions lead to projections that are likely to be low for investment earning in 1985. Beyond that date, it is hard to make any justifiable estimates one way or the other, and the historically derived (and relatively low) figures of *Table 13.5* seem to be the most reasonable projections that can be made.

The accuracy of the estimated rates of growth for accumulated assets vary from country to country, as well as over the period. For example, after its revolution in 1979, Iran spent some assets, and then as a result of the conflict with the United States, a large portion of overseas holdings were indefinitely tied up in litigation. The policies of the Libyan government towards surpluses have been erratic. At times, it seems a careful investor in European markets, while at others most extra funds are plowed into various political and military ventures to gain influence in the developing world. As an oil-exporter of considerable production potential (cf. *Table 6.1*) and low population, under a more conservative regime Libya could be banking hundreds of millions of dollars a year. Iraq, during the 1970s, has been relatively cautious in its domestic spending policies, while rather steadily increasing its oil production; the result, particularly in the months following the Iranian revolution, was rapid growth in Iraqi foreign investments. Then came the Iran–Iraq war of 1980–82 and a major indefinite interruption in Iraqi oil production. Thus, for at least these three countries, recent history makes it very risky to predict the path of overseas investment policy even over the very short term.

For the peninsular Arab monarchies, however, it is possible to hazard at least a few guesses[6]. To the extent that any of these countries have announced policies regarding their foreign portfolios, we have already discussed Kuwait and Abu Dhabi; both of these have well-defined goals of integrating these investments into overall programs of economic diversification. Each has made it clear that they have no intention to withdraw any of these investment earnings for some time to come. If Qatar and Saudi Arabia do not have such publicly discussed policy arrangements, nevertheless this also appears to be their intention. Therefore, our minimum estimates shown in *Table 13.5* of 12 percent annual additions to accumulated assets seem to be modest, especially since recent rates of return have been far above 10 percent a year. In addition, these peninsular countries have usually found themselves gaining from world supply interruptions, related first to the Iranian revolution, and secondly to the Iran–Iraq war. The gains in revenues have mostly boosted existing budget and international payments surpluses, not imports, and thus the growth in overseas portfolios. Thus, at least during the early 1980s, it would seem reasonable *ceteris paribus* to project annual increases in these portfolios that average several percentage points above the minima of *Table 13.5*. After 1985, prudence would dictate projections of growth rates closer to the 12 percent level.

All in all then, we could fairly use the high estimates through 1985 in *Table 13.5*, which would then signal mid range values for 1990 and 1995, even with a drop-off in the late 1980s toward the minimum indicated rates of growth for portfolios. Any diminution of the population explosion or continuation of current high interest rates would tend to increase per citizen returns in the late 1980s and early 1990s.

The projections shown in *Table 13.6* are very conservative, using the lower end of the growth scale for portfolios throughout the entire period. These figures focus our attention on the four oil exporters for which investment earnings are already sizable in relationship to their other official receipts.

Table 13.6 *Future investment returns and current budget expenditures (millions of dollars)*

Country	1978 Budget estimates			Projected investment returns[a]		
	Total revenues	Expenditures	Investment returns	1985	1990	1995
Kuwait	11 850	6 260	2000	5800	10 225	18 025
Qatar	2 340	1 815	260	390	685	1 200
Saudi Arabia	43 100	32 765	5310	9925	17 500	30 825
United Arab Emirates	6 460	6 250	1000	1660	2 925	5 150

Note: [a] Projections made at the lower ends of the growth scales shown in *Table 13.5* for accumulation of assets.

For Kuwait, we can see an almost immediately developing situation, in theory at least, of a rentier economy. By 1985 at the latest, Kuwait should be earning more from its investments than it was spending for all purposes during the late 1970s. It is very difficult to project spending needs into the mid 1980s, but it should be kept in mind that in the 1970s, Kuwait and other peninsular states were spending heavily on many non-recurring items, some of which are truly unique, and many others which, given normal depreciation situations, will not recur for some time[7]. So it is quite possible that sometime in the late 1980s, the Kuwaiti government could, if it wished, begin to draw on its investment earnings as a substitute for the bulk of the tax revenues which it currently receives from the oil sector.

None of the other peninsular countries will find themselves in the same situation of being able, nearly, to replace tax revenues with investment earnings quite so rapidly. But with a continuation of the surplus generating situations of the late 1970s into the 1980s, each of these countries is following the Kuwaiti lead. This situation will develop even more rapidly if any of these countries turns toward more conservative domestic spending policies, for example, by scaling down some of the more elaborate industrial development proposals now on planning ministry drawing boards. On the other hand its realization will be slowed by any prolonged world recession that reduces oil demand and revenues.

Our point, however, is not to speculate on how soon these countries could begin to live solely on their dividends. The answer to that is, of course, *now* – provided some of them were willing to cut back their living standards somewhat, and risk much lower military equipment outlays. Assuming that the following were to happen: the departure of non-citizens; a medium level of portfolio growth from 1978 to 1982; inflation of 10 percent a year; and a multiplier factor of only two; rough calculations would then indicate that the earnings of these portfolios would support the following levels of GNP per citizen in, say, 1982 (in *constant* 1978 dollars): Kuwait – $12 700; Qatar – $5575; Saudi Arabia – $1850; and UAE – $11 050. A further reduction in annual returns of 15 percent would allow for sufficient reinvestment to maintain indefinitely real per citizen GNP in real 1978 prices – by 1982 – which would peg Kuwait's real GNP to about where it was in 1975, Qatar and Saudi Arabia to their 1973 levels, and the UAE to where it was in 1974. In terms of what citizens have becomed accustomed to, this would only be an unacceptable alternative for Saudi Arabia.

We merely wish to stress that these massive amounts of overseas investments are generating earnings that loom ever larger in the total annual receipts of these governments, and that they raise four questions for tax policy makers that seriously impinge on the subjects we have been considering. First, if so much money is earned by overseas investment of past oil-generated fiscal surpluses, why look seriously for domestic alternatives to the existing oil taxes? Secondly, as time goes on and past surpluses, prudently invested, are producing (indefinitely) an income stream so large relative to earnings from current oil production, why sell so much of a finite resource? Thirdly, if overseas investments are so reliable a source of return why undertake many of the more doubtful domestic industrialization projects that have been proposed? Fourthly, if many of the latter are clearly somewhat imprudent in nature, why spend so much on them, why import so much, why buy so much from the industrialized returns, why try to generate so much revenue in the first place?

We have been arguing throughout this chapter that the major oil exporting countries have not generally paid much attention to non-oil tax sources, largely abdicating the role that domestic fiscal policy can play in guiding their economic development. The rapid growth in overseas investment earnings hardly augurs well for an improvement in this situation, at least in the four countries listed in *Table 13.6*. Already by the late 1970s, these portfolio returns had by far eclipsed non-oil domestic taxation (*Table 13.7*); even for Iraq investment earnings in the late 1970s were more than two-thirds the amount of all other non-oil revenues.

Since the four countries with the largest budget surpluses have shown no interest in using their portfolio earnings at this time to support current or capital budget spending, but have reinvested these earnings, the sheer size

Table 13.7 *Non-oil tax revenues and investment earnings (1973–1978)* *(millions of dollars)*

	Non-oil tax revenues[a]			Investment earnings		
	1973	*1976*	*1978*	*1973*	*1976*	*1978*
Kuwait	142	342	876	302	1125	1900
Qatar	12	31	77	18	110	160
Saudi Arabia	257	415	490	210	2890	5310
United Arab Emirates	150	228	310	20	177	1000

Note: [a] Excludes oil taxes and investment earnings.

and rapid growth of these earnings need not result in further diminution in the relative importance of non-oil taxes. On the other hand, neither continued oil production at late 1970s levels, nor maintenance in real terms of oil earnings during that time means that some of these governments could not, as policy, choose to increase the importance of domestic taxes.

However, the questions posed two paragraphs above concerning domestic policies would indicate that the 1980s are not likely to see any major shifts in the fiscal profiles of the major oil producing states. We cannot so easily dismiss the questions relating to net Middle Eastern oil inputs into world oil markets.

But oil revenues, in the sense of earnings from foreign 'taxpayers', cannot be discussed simply in an international context. The limiting factor, on a country by country basis, is, ultimately, *production*, which is primarily determined by available technology, then availability, in practice as opposed to theory has to be considered, and then *domestic* factors, in this context, domestic demand which until recently has been dismissed as only of peripheral concern.

13.2   Oil depletion and tax revenues

There remains one last point of regional significance to be made in this section. In discussing the major oil exporting countries in Chapter 11 and the two minor exporters, Egypt and Syria, in Chapter 12, it was mentioned several times that oil, in the final analysis, is a wasting resource. Furthermore, domestic demand for oil has been rising sharply and will probably continue to do so for at least several years. Those countries now depending upon it for major portions of their fiscal revenues must, therefore, eventually expect to see the diminution of these revenues and plan accordingly.

Among the countries we have been discussing, we can distinguish three groups where future oil production is concerned. The first, comprising Saudi Arabia, Kuwait, the United Arab Emirates and probably Oman, faces only distant prospects of decreased production and will undoubtedly even in the year 2000 still be experiencing relatively low domestic demand. For this group, the current situation of fiscal surplus may thus be extended indefinitely as the following factors interact:

(1) at least constant real prices, if not modestly increasing ones, are found in the world oil market;
(2) increasing revenues from investment of previous surpluses, as discussed in the previous section; and
(3) spending pressures ease for infrastructure investment.

In short, these countries have plenty of time to get their fiscal houses in order before oil revenues begin to shrink.

The second group comprises Iraq, Libya and posibly Qatar, where rising domestic consumption and/or falling production will start to impinge noticeably on oil revenues by the end of the century. Unless real oil prices rise a fair amount or current economic diversification programs broaden their tax bases, or both, these countries will at that time be faced with potentially serious budget problems.

The third group will find itself with these problems much sooner. Bahrain and Syria, and possibly Egypt and Iran, will soon have little oil for export – according to some projections, by the early 1990s. Considering these countries in turn, Bahrain has made no real attempt to broaden its tax base, despite a long-standing program of economic diversification, as we have seen above in Chapters 6 and 11. Iran, before the Islamic revolution of 1978/79, was collecting more taxes from non-oil sources than any other major oil producer; this still meant, however, that oil provided about five-sixths of government revenue. Both Egypt and Syria are relatively recent oil exporters, but Syria at least was rapidly becoming dependent on these revenues during recent years. In Chapter 12, a warning was expressed that these newer exporters should avoid in their future tax profiles the overwhelming dominance of oil revenues that has characterized the traditional exporters.

With regard to the overall question, it is illustrative briefly to consider the possible scenario of future oil production and consumption that is outlined in the data shown in *Tables 13.8* to *13.11*. *Table 13.8* indicates the discovered

Table 13.8 *Estimated petroleum and natural gas reserves and life of reserves: Middle East countries*

Country	Estimated reserves[a]		Life of reserves[b]	
	Petroleum (thousand barrels)	Natural gas (billion cubic feet)	Petroleum (years)	Natural gas (years)
Bahrain	225	9 900	12.5	102.1
Egypt	2 900	2 970	13.5	38.6
Iran	57 500	388 500	122.7	1330.5
Iraq	30 000	27 550	31.5	444.4
Kuwait[c]	67 930	33 125	110.8	283.1
Libya	23 000	23 800	35.3	203.4
Oman	2 340	5 015	22.8	238.8
Qatar	3 585	65 260	20.8	598.7
Saudi Arabia[c]	168 030	95 575	44.3	181.7
Syria	1 940	3 180	32.1	3180.0
United Arab Emirates	30 410	22 530	47.8	98.0
World	648 525	2 744 340	29.7	51.0

Notes: [a] Estimated proven reserves as of 1 January 1981.
       [b] Ratio of reserves to 1980 production.
       [c] Includes half share of partitioned Neutral Zone.

Sources: *Oil and Gas Journal*, (December 29, 1980); *Petroleum Economist*, (August 1981).

Table 13.9 *Estimates for petroleum production: 1978–2000[a] (thousand barrels/day)*

Country	1978	1980	1985	1990	1995	2000
Bahrain	56	49	40	35	32	28
Egypt	465	585	1 000	1 000	1 000	1 000
Iran	5242	1280	4 000	3 800	3 500	3 300
Iraq	2562	2600	4 000	4 000	4 000	4 000
Kuwait	2098	1675	3 000	3 000	3 000	3 000
Libya	1983	1780	2 000	2 000	2 000	1 800
Oman	320	280	300	280	270	270
Qatar	487	470	500	450	425	375
Saudi Arabia	8292	9895	12 000	12 000	12 000	12 000
Syria	170	165	250	250	225	225
United Arab Emirates	1834	1740	2 000	2 000	1 900	1 900

Notes: [a] 1978 and 1980 figures represent actual production figures. Other figures are projections of maximum, technically advisable output levels made by the authors on the basis of 1981 estimated reserves, production during the 1970s, and conservative allowances for further discoveries.

Sources: *Petroleum Economist*; *International Petroleum Annual*; Oil Consumption, Production and Trade in Developing Countries; *OPEC Review* (Autumn 1979).

proven reserves in these 11 countries of both oil and natural gas; that is, reserves that have been measured by various established techniques and which are economically recoverable using presently employed methods. It can be seen that the reserves to output ratios (the so-called reserve lifetime ratios) for oil run from as little as 12.5 years in Bahrain to more than 100 years for Kuwait and Iran[8]. Of course, these figures do not tell us how long oil will be produced. As an oilfield matures, production must be gradually reduced. In addition, proven reserves are by no means reduced each year by the amount of production that occurred, even in such long-time exporters as

Table 13.10 *Estimates for domestic petroleum consumption: 1980–2000[a]* *(thousand barrels/day)*

Country	1980	1985	1990	1995	2000
Bahrain[b]	10	14	17	21	25
Egypt	240	305	423	588	818
Iran	660	1045	1660	2637	4189
Iraq	220	340	531	827	1290
Kuwait	38	60	94	149	236
Libya	100	169	313	579	1071
Oman[b]	11	13	17	22	30
Qatar	10	14	22	36	58
Saudi Arabia	370	458	839	1535	2808
Syria	115	131	181	250	346
United Arab Emirates	45	67	108	178	285

Notes: [a] Estimates are made by the authors after assessment of the sources listed.
[b] Bunker sales excluded.

Sources: 'Domestic Energy Requirements in OPEC Member Countries', *OPEC Papers* No. 1 (August 1980); 'Energy Demand Forecasts for the Arab Countries in 1985, 1990 and 2000', by A. T. Sadik, H. Saleh, and M. Al-Badrawi, in *Energy in the Arab World* (Volume 2).

Bahrain. New fields are discovered and measured, old ones are re-evaluated, and new technology upgrades probable and possible reserves to the status of proven reserves. Furthermore, it is believed that even proven reserves are stated very conservatively in some countries[9]. However, if we must consider these figures to be somewhat bleaker than the actual situations that will prevail, our point is made by the table – oil output will gradually diminish everywhere and in some countries much sooner than in others[10].

Change is occurring far more rapidly throughout the region in domestic consumption than it is in the capacity for production – largely as a result of the still very low energy consumption levels in most of these countries. For example, as late as 1975, *per capita* annual consumption of petroleum products in Iraq, Iran and Libya was 4.1, 5.5 and 7.4 barrels respectively; in the United States, it was 28.0 barrels. Projecting both production (*Table 13.9*) and demand (*Table 13.10*) is of course a risky procedure. We have chosen figures that are broadly compatible with several recent studies [11], yet we are aware that the further the projections are made into the future, the more likely that unforeseen events (such as new discoveries or local conservation drives) will result in very different situations in actuality.

Having stated these reservations, we can nonetheless note the rapid rise in the proportion of domestically consumed oil (*Table 13.11*). Since actual production figures are used for 1980 in *Table 13.9*, while potential maximums are indicated for later years, there is a drop shown in the ratios of *Table 13.11* between 1980 and 1985, but in most cases, the rising tendency is clear by 1990.

Table 13.11 *Projected ratios of domestic consumption to production: 1980–2000*

Country	1980	1985	1990	1995	2000
Bahrain	0.286	0.350	0.486	0.656	0.893
Egypt	0.410	0.305	0.423	0.588	0.818
Iran	0.516	0.261	0.437	0.659	1.047
Iraq	0.085	0.085	0.133	0.207	0.323
Kuwait	0.023	0.020	0.031	0.050	0.079
Libya	0.056	0.085	0.156	0.290	0.595
Oman	0.039	0.043	0.061	0.081	0.111
Qatar	0.021	0.028	0.049	0.085	0.155
Saudi Arabia	0.037	0.038	0.070	0.128	0.234
Syria	0.697	0.524	0.724	1.111	1.538
United Arab Emirates	0.026	0.034	0.054	0.094	0.150

Although these results are derived from quite recent studies, in a number of cases changing circumstances already would affect our evaluations. Iraq, for example, may have to wait many years beyond 1985 before production will reach 4 million barrels a day as a result of the disruptions of the war with Iran that began in late 1980. What now seems likely to be a prolonged period of reduced production in Iran, a situation which has prevailed since 1979, will mean that Iran can produce at higher levels in 1990 and beyond than those which are indicated in *Table 13.9*. Furthermore, the obvious differences in economic policy in Iran under the ayatollahs make the projected consumption figures of *Table 13.10*, based on Pahlavi-era growth rates, unbelievably high. The latest exploration reports from Egypt indicate a continued high degree of success and the likelihood that Egypt will be producing far more than 1 million barrels a day in the 1990s. There have also been recent reports from Qatar that are pessimistic about its ability to maintain the production levels shown in *Table 13.9*, but these are not at present confirmed. Obviously, if we are interested in such projections as are shown in these tables, we would have to be revising them continually on the basis of the most recently available data.

The first point to be made in closing this section is to reiterate what was said earlier: some countries may find themselves using half or more of their oil production at home within the next decade. Bahrain and Syria face the most immediate problems, but Iran, Libya and even Qatar may well be in difficulty during the 1990s.

Increasing oil exploration is promising in the medium-term, as a palliative for these problems, perhaps not for the small and already much-probed territories of Bahrain and Qatar, but certainly for Syria, Iran and Libya. It should be pointed out that, at the present time and for the foreseeable future, the major repositories of exploration technology and drilling equipment are the large international oil companies. Given recent government policies, it seems unlikely that these companies will be very interested in exploring in Syria, Iran or Libya during the early or mid-1980s. Syria in particular could be a major gainer if it could succeed in reversing this attitude and in attracting a sizable exploration effort.

The second point concerns the real level of oil prices, which along with production determine oil revenues. Since 1973, the world economy has experienced enough surprises to caution us against going very far out on a limb when talking about prices in the 1980s. Nevertheless, there now does seem to be plenty of evidence that energy in general and petroleum in particular is facing more elastic demand in the early 1980s than a decade earlier. That makes it likely that price increases should be counted upon by exporting countries to maintain the real value of oil revenues only if the decline in the volume of exports is modest, say 2–4 percent annually; any country which, for technical or other reasons, faces a more rapid drop will see lower real oil revenues, barring a repetition of the events of 1973 or 1979.

Thirdly, we should mention briefly the energy-intensive industries being emphasized by development planning ministries throughout the Middle East. At least superficially, these industries would seem to represent the region's comparative advantages, and where they rely on presently un- or under-utilized natural gas resources, it is likely that in fact they do. But crude petroleum is exported at world prices, while in many Middle East countries, it is sold domestically for 10 percent (or even less) of the world price. Much of this petroleum goes as fuel or feedstock to export-oriented industries, which are also generally subjected to very low corporate taxes by world standards as was indicated earlier. Whether these doubly-subsidized industries ever become truly competitive in world markets, only time will tell; in the meantime, their output represents petroleum eventually exported at a much lower fiscal return to the producing country's government. While these industries of course may prove to have net benefits over the long run for Middle Eastern economies, the countries undertaking their development and maintenance should keep in mind that they could be undermining their fiscal systems by diverting increasing proportions of oil output to purportedly domestic uses in order to subsidize, for an indefinite period, inefficient industries.

Of course, as long as diversification of the tax base is resisted, it is unlikely that the domestic beneficiaries[12] of these policies will make up significant amounts of the foregone tax revenue. As was indicated elsewhere, abdication of the fiscal mechanism as a major policy tool for guiding domestic investment may considerably aggravate the situation as regards inefficiently-operated industries which are subsidized with cheap energy. This problem, obviously, is not limited to those countries with more modest hydrocarbon endowments. In fact, it seems likely it will prove to be greater in those countries in which great resource riches allow the pursuit of ambitious industrial development schemes, such as Saudi Arabia, Kuwait and the United Arab Emirates.

Notes

1 The table lists data which includes some non-tax revenues, and thus it is not strictly comparable with *Table 11.22*.

2 These sources, as indicated in *Table 10.14*, include a number of official publications. We have also used several reports from private organizations, including a number of papers by Dr. Odeh Aburdene of the First National Bank of Chicago and a recent study by Ms Susan Bluff of the Bankers' Trust Company (London): OPEC's $350 Billion Balance Sheet, *Euromoney*, (September 1980).

3 Of course, the oil exporters would do themselves great economic and social harm if they tried to diminish their non-citizen populations abruptly through expulsion, but most of them seem to be planning on a gradual diminution of the expatriate element, especially as oil production matures. Some of the sparsely populated countries would eventually decide to moderate their current naturalization laws in favor of at least some non-citizen categories (for example long term residents of Arab and/or Islamic background who have important skills), giving many of these people a stake in national wealth for the long term situations we are discussing in this section.

4 Cf. notes to *Table 11.24* relative to the methods employed in making these estimates.

5 Upper and lower limits used in these calculations wee chosen *before* prime rates of 20 percent began to be quoted in 1980 in the UK and the USA.

6 Which ignore the possibility of drastically disruptive revolutions.

7 One-time items in the Gulf Emirates and Saudi Arabia include such expensive items as land reclamation and broad-based literacy and other adult education programs. Many aspects of industrial development plans should not recur for 15, 25 or even 50 years.

8 For Iran this number is a statistical anomaly. As can be seen in *Table 13.9*, production fell almost 76 percent between 1978 and 1980. If we used the average annual production in the six years before the Iranian revolution to compute this ratio, it would be more like 34 years.

9 Especially in Iraq and Saudi Arabia.

10 We have not discussed in this work natural gas production in the Middle East. Primarily this is because it was a negligible factor for tax considerations during the period we have analyzed. This will undoubtedly not be so, however, during the coming decades. As can be seen from *Table 13.8*, whereas these 11 countries are credited with about 60 percent of the world's discovered proven petroleum reserves, they account for less than 25 percent of natural gas reserves. It should

be remembered that until very recently the most common end for Middle Eastern gas was seen in thousands of wasteful flares, while running a poor second was reinjection of the gas to maintain oil field pressures. Very little was actually used, internally or for export. Thus, there was little interest in exploration for or measurement of gas reserves. In fact, it is quite likely that the region has vast undiscovered reserves, as recent successful exploration in Qatar, for example, has shown. Undoubtedly, as world oil reserves dwindle and as the technology for transporting gas over long distances improves, this hydrocarbon will provide a major source of tax revenue. But again, we are faced with a situation that only prolongs the period where exported fuels can provide most of a country's budget. Also, even with natural gas reserves, some countries (notably Bahrain and Syria) still have to face serious resource depletion before the end of this century.

11 These figures are derived from a number of sources, and represent the conclusions of no specific study. Principally, they are based on: 'Domestic Energy Requirements in OPEC Member Countries', *OPEC Papers*, 1, (1), August 1980; 'Oil Consumption, Production and Trade in Developing Countries', *OPEC Review*, 3, Autumn 1979; and a number of papers presented at the First Arab Energy Conference, sponsored by the Arab Fund for Economic and Social Development and the Organization of Arab Petroleum Exporting Countries, and published in *Energy in the Arab World* (OAPEC, Kuwait 1980). The relevant papers include 'Energy Demand Forecasts for the Arab Countries in 1985, 1990 and 2000' by A. T. Sadik, H. Salek and M. Al-Badrawi, 'Evaluation of the Energy Status in the Arab Countries', by U. Jamali, 'Available Energy Sources in the Arab World vis-a-vis Future Demand', by F. Al-Muwakki, and 'Medium and Long Term Projections of the Demand for and Supply of Energy in the ECWA Region', a preliminary report of the United Nations Economic Commission for Western Asia (National Resources, Science and Technology Division). Also useful were the individual country reports in *Energy in the Arab World*, as well as various articles in *Middle East Economic Digest, Middle East Economic Survey, Oil and Gas Journal, Petroleum Economist,* and *Petroleum Intelligence Weekly.*

12 The real beneficiaries of such subsidies most likely include nationals of the oil-producing countries (such as the owners of these enterprises) and foreigners (such as companies originally building and equipping the plants and the foreign workers that they employ). If the subsidies are adjusted to allow these industries to undersell their competitors in world markets, foreign consumers would also benefit by, in effect, buying oil at less than the world price.

Part VI

Conclusions

Review and recapitulation

At this point we should reiterate the goals we set out for this work and then summarize the major points that have emerged from the analysis undertaken in their pursuit. Our goals were several:

(1) to introduce and define the major categories of taxation as commonly used in economics textbooks, with the purpose of providing a framework for the statistical presentations and discussions of the main body of the study;

(2) to explore and summarize the main points of Islamic teaching on economic considerations, particularly as these impinge on taxation questions, drawing both on scriptural (Quranic) principles and later developments within the Islamic polity;

(3) to present in categorical form the fiscal profiles of each of the 16 Middle Eastern countries included in the study and to discuss the patterns (and major changes therein) of taxation during the post World War II period in each case;

(4) to examine the 16 countries in an overall LDC fiscal context, utilizing various models to try to explain variation in the relative degree of tax effort in terms of relevant economic and social factors;

(5) to analyze these 16 countries specifically, in the light of the results of the econometric analysis, relative to the manner in which they each utilize the fiscal resources available to their societies, the extent to which they adhere to Islamic principles in matters of taxation, and the ways in which the major taxes that they have employed affect their populations; and

(6) to make recommendations, where relevant, about tax policy in coming years.

In this regard we first set out in Part II to derive an analytic framework, discussing the differences between direct and indirect taxation and defining the major types of levies grouped under each heading. In Chapters 2, 3 and 4 we looked at each kind of tax in turn, particularly in the context of their use in developing economies considering such questions as impact on different classes and sectors within the economy and relative ease of administration. Comparative data were presented for most major taxes to present a picture of how much they are used by LDCs across this group's spectrum of national income.

Chapter 5 presented a brief analysis of traditional Islamic economic principles with the intention of relating practical considerations of tax policies to the general theological and ethical ones of equity and justice. We can summarize the relevant points as follows:

(1) the material bounty of the earth is due exclusively to the creative activity of God and it is His gift to His human creatures;

(2) though this gift is to the whole human race, its benefits are not in fact evenly distributed for a variety of reasons;

(3) this uneven distribution is part of the divine plan and allows opportunities for the more economically fortunate among the faithful to show their submission to God's will by unselfishly sharing their riches with the poor of the community;

(4) Islam stresses the obligation of all to work as they can to support themselves and their families, but those who cannot do so are entitled to help from the community;

(5) the community has the right to play a role in overseeing the almsgiving obligations of the faithful;

(6) because the needs of the poor may exceed almsgiving or because the community may have further legitimate requirements, the community may institute other levies;

(7) non-Muslims may be required to bear part of the governmental costs; and

(8) serious transgressions of Quranic requirements carry with them the risk of the wrath of God, in this world or the next.

In addition, it should be kept in mind that despite the unchanging nature of the Quran at its core, Islam has always allowed itself a fair degree of flexibility in adapting to changing circumstances.

Part III was devoted to a case by case analysis of the fiscal profiles of first the oil exporting countries and then the non-oil exporters over approximately the last 30 years. Though this section also presented some cross sectional comparisons, the intention here was to set forth the data on an individual country basis, discussing the particular situations found in each of the 16 countries.

Comparisons among Middle East countries and of the group with other LDCs were central in Part IV, where we undertook an econometric analysis of the relationship of tax capacity (or more properly, tax effort) with a number of variables which reflect aspects of three major economic factors: the general level of economic development, the degree of openness of a national economy to the world at large, and the sectoral composition of the national economy. An examination of the recent literature revealed several problems with existing tax capacity models: lack of statistical significance for many variables with considerable *a priori* importance; lack of stability when they are applied to different samples of LDCs; relatively low degree of explanatory power indicated by regression analysis; strong reliance in the final versions of some models on explanatory variables which may not well reflect the factors they purport to represent. In addition the earlier studies included few Middle Eastern countries. Thus we proceed first to use a previously tested model with a larger sample including all the countries that we are considering in this effort and then to develop another model which we believe meets several of the objections to earlier formulations. This model related a country's tax effort to the size of its agricultural sector, the ratios of mineral exports and total imports to GNP, the demand elasticity for its exports, and the degree of monetization of the economy. When it was applied there was some evidence of structural difference between the Middle Eastern and other developing countries; tests to determine if in fact this difference was between resource rich and resource poor LDCs were inconclusive.

In Part V, we evaluated the tax policies of the Middle Eastern countries from two points of view: first, how they had been used as policy instruments over the period of the study, and second, how they had been used relative to general social principles. In the first case we considered taxes as a means of mobilizing the financial resources of these societies in the service of their common goals of economic development and modernization. In the second case we were concerned with questions of equity and justice, both from general economic and specifically Islamic aspects.

As far as mobilizing financial resources are concerned, the criterion used in cross-section and over time in the earlier chapters was the ratio of tax receipts to GNP – tax effort as an indicator for tax capacity. For the Middle East as a whole, for the two sub-groups of oil and non-oil exporters, and for each of the 16 countries, we saw this ratio rising over the three decades of the studies, with the increases being dramatic in many cases. However, the two sub-groups became increasingly polarized during this time period, though in the late 1970s nearly all countries in the region had tax ratios above 20 percent, a level that was matched or bettered by only a few LDCs in other parts of the world. The dependence of both numerator and denominator on oil prices (and hence on the economic rent that foreign consumers will pay) reduces the usefulness of this ratio as a measure of tax effort for the nine oil exporting countries. In addition, this criterion is essentially static in nature, in a region undergoing a highly dynamic process of economic change.

In the absence of sufficient data to make tax elasticity computations, we analyzed changes in fiscal receipts in terms of tax buoyancy. These calculations were presented for the entire data period and for four sub-periods: the relatively quiescent 1950–1962 interval, the more dynamic 1962–1968 interval, and the post 1968 era of world inflation, punctuated by the 1973 oil price rise. The highest buoyancies were found in the 1950s, which began with very low tax ratios in many countries, with the more recent periods seeing rates of growth for tax receipts and GNP that were more in line with one another. Also over time the gap between the two sub-groups has narrowed, although the oil exporters continue to have higher buoyancies. It was notable that for most countries and sub-periods, calculated buoyancies exceeded unity – that is, tax receipts grew faster than national income.

From the equity point of view, we reviewed what statistics are available on income distribution in the region and then considered the progressive and regressive aspects of the tax burden. Though income distribution data are sparse, which led us to be more cautious against drawing too many conclusions from them, they did present a regional pattern of maldistribution which is similar to that found throughout the developing world. This evidence is supportive of the need for tax policies, if the interests of equity are to be served, that at the very least do not have the effect of increasing the degree of maldistribution.

In Part II we discussed the tendencies of some taxes to be progressive and others regressive. In the more industrialized countries, the fiscal furtherance of income equality has involved reliance on such direct taxes as progressively scheduled personal income, inheritance and business profits levies. However, as we indicated earlier, these types of taxes are often impractical as major sources of revenue in developing countries for administrative and political reasons. On the other hand, fiscal theory textbooks warn against the tendency of many indirect taxes (such as excises, other taxes on imported or domestically produced consumables, or government fees for services) to be regressive. These taxes are also often easier to administer than direct taxes and are thus favored by countries with less sophisticated fiscal bureaucracies.

However, such tendencies and problems do not unalterably decree regressive tax systems for developing countries. Progressive income, inheritance and profits taxes may be difficult to administer; they are not impossible. Furthermore, while an LDC may be able to use these taxes only in a minor fashion at the beginning, as economic and social development proceeds and the degree of monetization advances, they can become increasingly important sources of revenue. So called regressive taxes such as those on consumption, are such insofar as they tend to be general in their application because the marginal propensity to consume is highest at low income levels. But if consumption taxes are discriminatory, with lower rates for necessities, they can actually be progressive in their effect.

Progressive taxes on non-oil income (personal and/or business) are found in nearly all Middle Eastern countries, but they vary widely in their relative use of these levies – the People's Democratic Republic of Yemen, for example, was about 1065 times more dependent on income taxes than Kuwait (22.4 percent of total revenues versus 0.021 percent). The richer oil exporting countries use these taxes far less on average (1.9 percent of total revenues) than do the non-oil exporters (11.9 percent), but even the latter seven countries rely generally less on them than do LDCs in other parts of the world. This is despite the fact that the Middle Eastern countries (oil and non-oil alike) are richer and more urbanized than other LDCs, and have as well economies that are more monetized than most LDCs – all characteristics that should promote greater use of income and profit taxes.

We then suggested that it would be more fitting to discuss these levies within a broader Islamic context. *Zakat*, the traditional Islamic fiscal obligation to the community, was assessed against wealth, yet in modern society the wealth of many individuals is not easy to measure. For example, the 'wealth' of professionally trained people is found in their skills, which generate income, which in turn can be measured and taxed. The wealth of capitalists involves both tangible and intangible assets, which produce taxable profits. Thus we have argued for lumping together a number of modern and traditional levies under the heading 'religiously appropriate' taxes – taxes which either by the letter or the spirit of Islamic teaching have as their *raison d'etre* the redistribution of the fruits of society from the rich to the poor.

But even this enlarged category represents an only slightly larger portion of Middle East tax revenues than do income and profits taxes alone. On a GNP weighted basis, the 16 country average rose only from 5.2 to 6.5 percent; the nine oil exporters received about 4.4 percent, on average, of their revenues from personal income and non-oil profits taxes, and 4.8 percent from the broader 'religiously appropriate' category, while for the seven non-oil exporters, the former grouping accounted for about 10.5 percent of all revenues and the latter for 16.5 percent.

In fact, if we compare the Middle Eastern countries, the 'core of Islam', with other predominantly Muslim countries in Africa and Asia (see *Table 14.1*), we see they rank below most of these 'peripheral' countries as far as use of the so called 'religiously appropriate' taxes are concerned. Among the 16 Middle Eastern and 18 other Islamic fiscal authorities, certainly the richest (regardless of location) do not tax themselves heavily in this way (see *Figure 14.1*). One could make a case that those countries that are 'more sophisticated' as regards political, economic and social systems find it more convenient to use taxes such as those on personal and corporate incomes (generally conceded to be easier to administer in more advanced countries).

Thus in the Middle East, Egypt, Lebanon, Syria and Jordan are leaders in this regard; elsewhere, we see high proportions for Turkey, Algeria, Morocco and Tunisia. But how then do we explain exceptions – such as Bahrain, a major world banking center, with no such taxes[1], or 'primitive' economies like Afghanistan, Mali, and Niger, all of which well outrank Egypt, the Middle Eastern country with the second highest percentage of taxes in the religiously appropriate category?

Actually, the only pattern suggested by a perusal of *Table 14.1* and *Figure 14.1* derives from the recent colonial past of most of these countries: ten of the 11 ex-French territories collect 20 percent or more of their revenues from the various income, profits and wealth taxes that comprise this category – only 5 'non-French' countries (Turkey, Guinea-Bissau, Afghanistan, South Yemen and Egypt) are also above this level – and this pattern strongly suggests that recent colonial era[2] taxing patterns are probably still more important in shaping the fiscal profiles than previous centuries of adherence to Islam.

Table 14.1 *'Religiously appropriate' taxes as a percentage of total revenues, Middle Eastern and other Muslim countries, by per capita GNP*

	A (%)	B ($)		A (%)	B ($)
Middle East					
Bahrain	0.0	4 050	Oman	1.5	2 510
Egypt	21.3	340	Qatar	0.3	11 370
Iran	11.3	2 000[a]	Saudi Arabia	0.5	7 230
Iraq	2.2	1 570	Sudan	11.1	330
Jordan	13.5	940	Syria	15.1	860
Kuwait	0.1	12 690	United Arab Emirates	0.0	14 800
Lebanon	20.0	1 000[a]	Yemen Arab Rep.	7.0	510
Libya	2.7	6 520	Yemen People's Dem. Rep.	22.4	350
Other countries					
Afghanistan	27.0	220	Maldives	10.5	140
Algeria	24.1	1 140	Mali	25.5	120
Bangladesh	5.5	80	Mauritania	20.0	270
Brunei	0.5[a]	9 190	Morocco	24.8	610
Chad	20.0	130	Niger	28.7	190
Comoros	25.6	180	Pakistan	11.5	200
Gambia	13.0	210	Senegal	22.9	380
Guinea	29.3	200	Somalia	9.2	120
Guinea-Bissau	35.4	180	Tunisia	20.6	840
Indonesia	13.0	360	Turkey	50.8	1 110
Malaysia	16.0	970	Upper Volta	14.6	140

Notes: A, 'Religiously appropriate' share of total taxes.
B, Per capita GNP.
[a] Estimated.

If Middle Eastern countries are not notable, either in general or in comparison to other Muslim countries, in the relative position held in their overall fiscal profiles by these taxes that we argue are related to Quranic ideals, there are indicators that at least some of them are in the process of moving to greater conformity with their traditions. As was pointed out above in Chapter 10, among the non-oil exporters, all but two (the twin Yemen republics) have buoyancies for the 'religiously appropriate' grouping that exceed those for all taxes (cf. *Table 10.16*). If this tendency continues in the 1980s, we could expect Jordan, Lebanon and Syria at least, and possibly the Sudan as well, to join those other Islamic states that collect at least a fifth of their revenues from these sources. Even this would not distinguish them particularly from those LDCs which do not have a significant Islamic background, as can be inferred from the comparative statistics on income and profits taxes shown in *Table 10.10*.

On the other hand, the prevailing pattern for the oil exporting countries is one of buoyancies for the 'religiously appropriate' category that are less than for other taxes (mostly oil-based receipts), and thus for a shrinking share for

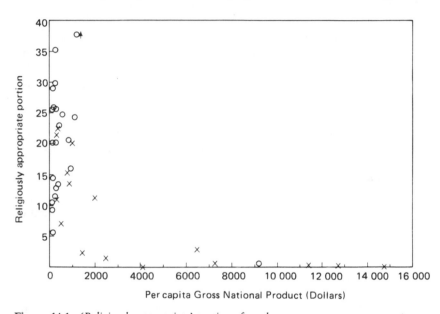

Figure 14.1 *'Religiously appropriate' portion of total tax revenues versus per capita GNP, Middle Eastern and other Muslim countries.* × *Middle Eastern countries;* ○ *other Muslim countries*

the levies that have some claim of kinship to those that Islam has traditionally sanctioned. As the 1980s continue, the richest Muslim countries (and in several cases, paradoxically those that are most conservative in their adherence to religious law) will become even less *specifically* Islamic in their fiscal structures.

The poorer Muslim countries in the Middle East (and especially, apparently, elsewhere) make more serious attempts – whether out of fiscal necessity, colonial legal heritage, or devotion to Islamic ideals is not for us to judge – than do their richer compatriots[3] to assess their richer citizens for the needs of the community. But we must raise one question in possible defense of the wealthier countries: how should we take account of the fact that the oil exporters are engaged in an attempt to convert a nonrenewable natural resource (oil) into renewable resources of various types across a wide spectrum of economic sectors?

Obviously, any revenue derived from the sale of a nonrenewable natural resource to any willing customer (whether domestic or foreign, whether Muslim, *dhimmi* or infidel), which is then devoted to the acquisition of renewable assets (of a type allowed under Islamic law) must be exempted from consideration when calculating that portion of the bounty of a society that must be tendered to the current needs of that society. We are using contemporary (and non-Islamic) economic measures of *current* national income (GNP) to gauge national wealth. This is obviously distorted in the peninsular states, Iraq, and Libya by the high value of the oil sector component, where conventional methods of calculation increase income measures by what is in fact the extent of a transfer of assets from the nonrenewable category to what planners hopefully foresee as renewable resources[4]. What we really need to indicate the degree of faithfulness that Muslim oil exporters actually reflect to Quranic taxation principles is a mechanism that will first, recalculate national income downward in light of this asset transformation; and secondly, estimate that portion of revenues from the oil industry that reflect this asset transformation as opposed to what can be termed its current economic activity.

We propose to tackle neither of these tasks at this point in our efforts. Nevertheless, we can point out that, even if we make very generous estimates for the *directly* oil-generated portions (all that properly should be considered in asset transformation terms) of annual national income measures, a rather small proportion of current private income finds its way into public coffers in the form of income, profits or wealth taxes. For example (cf. *Table 10.15*), even if in extreme cases, such as the smaller Gulf Emirates, we reduced national income by 50, 60 or 70 percent to reflect only non-oil activities, and taxes by 80, 90 or even 95 percent on the same basis we could not ignore the facts presented above in Chapter 7 for most of the oil exporting countries: only tiny fractions of their fiscal revenues are collected from their own citizens, rich or poor – and these fractions are not much higher even if we make allowances for the receipts from their large expatriate colonies, who also derive their incomes from their economies' activities[5].

Although we have steadfastly avoided discussions of the expenditure side of Middle Eastern budgets, we could easily show that current, as opposed to capital budgets of the oil exporters far exceed locally derived receipts, even if we adjust current budgets by subtracting from current expenditures such infrastructural investments as education and health. We cannot avoid concluding that most, if not all, of the Middle Eastern oil exporters have, during the 1970s, avoided taxing their own resident communities (Muslim and otherwise) to anywhere near the degree that is necessary to fulfil traditional Islamic public revenue goals.

Even in the revolutionary atmosphere of post Pahlavi Iran, there has been no notable move to enhance the Islamic aspects of the country's tax structure. Although adjustments were made to income and other taxes to provide some relief to the urban working class, these did not have specifically religious motivations. Of course, this lack of change may be attributable to *Shi'i* Islam's traditional reluctance to grant the state a role in the collection and disbursement of *zakat*[6].

This analysis of the disproportionate role of oil export taxes in nine of the countries that we are discussing takes us to Chapter 11, and thus to several other considerations. First of all, the overreliance on oil taxes results in an almost total abdication of domestic taxes as policy tools in guiding the pre-eminent goals of internal economic development. Secondly, and most immediately consequent on the former, is the failure to prepare for the eventual decline and demise of exported petroleum as a major source of revenue – this problem is more obvious in the immediate future for small, mature oil producers, such as Bahrain, but also must be considered by countries which are vulnerable to unfavorable political and military events, such as Iran and Iraq in early 1981.

Thirdly, there is the entire and very complex question of potentially unwisely rapid exploitation of petroleum resources because a lack of other tax sources to finance perceived capital and current budget needs, leading to a policy of short run maximization of oil revenues. This question deserves an entire volume and can only be alluded to in our closing chapter.

Fourthly, we have pointed out in several sections of Chapter 11 that, when massive oil revenues that are easily collected from foreign consumers obviate immediate needs for domestic taxes, development planners may decide in favor of investments in industrial projects that can survive, in the long run only with the implicit subsidies that low or non-existent domestic taxes provide relative to competitive world markets. The whole political experience of more than a century and a half of movement toward freer world trade proves the intrinsic difficulty in removing, even gradually, any such subsidy once it has been granted.

Finally, there are only two critical factors that will enter into world energy demand equations for the late 1980s and 1990s that we discussed in some detail in Chapter 13 insofar as they affected the major suppliers of the Middle East. First, if the surplus-earning states of the 1970s continue to earn surpluses in the 1980s, what will happen to their incentive to continue to produce petroleum products? They have already reduced domestic taxes to a minimum and increased budgets to a near-maximum by capital absorption standards since the OPEC price action of 1973. As the returns on past overseas investments rise rapidly, this can only press downward on production incentives[7], even without any sizable reduction in the grandiosity of development investment schemes that persists into the 1980s among some of the less populated exporters.

In addition to the implications of these situations for world oil markets, there are also domestic fiscal considerations involved. In the absence of a sizeable tax structure based on their own economies, the oil exporters are dependent on foreign consumers for their operating revenues. When they add foreign investments to oil sales, they merely add another external revenue source. If circumstances interrupt these flows of funds, even a very rich country could quickly find itself in serious fiscal difficulties. Revolutionary Iran first saw its revenues drop when strikes and other internal unrest disrupted oil production in 1978 and 1979. In 1980, the major part of its overseas investments were seized in the aftermath of the American hostages crisis, and then with the outbreak of war with Iraq, oil exports all but ceased. By early 1981, Iran seemed to be close to international bankruptcy, and only the printing presses allowed the government to pay its domestic bills with increasingly worthless *rials*[8].

Secondly, domestic consumption of petroleum products continues to grow rapidly in the exporting countries, as on the one hand, these products are marketed at low subsidized prices and, on the other hand, energy-intensive technologies that figure prominently in regional development plans come into increasing use. While some Middle Eastern countries might increase oil production to meet rising domestic demand (for example, Iraq), most have already reached near maximum production levels. Thus, incremental domestic consumption will eventually be at the expense of exports. As we pointed out above, this problem will affect some countries far more than others over the next few years. Those whose domestic demand will squeeze exports most will need sizeable increases in real oil prices to maintain current oil tax receipts in real terms.

We have indicated, then, a fairly extensive spectrum of fiscal problems affecting a group of countries that most western observers would fairly characterize as among the most fortunate of the developing countries. While these observers might well miss the long run social implications of these oil exporters' policies of minimizing the role of domestic non-oil taxes, they cannot ignore the arguments of the last several paragraphs, nor the overriding conclusion we derive from them: if the fiscal policies of the Middle Eastern oil exporters continue into the 1980s basically unchanged they will eventually result in serious problems for their economies and probably for those of their major customers.

It may seem anticlimatic now to turn to the less dramatic situations of the seven countries that we have grouped together under the heading of non-oil exporters. But while at the end of the 1970s they had only about a sixth of the aggregate GNP of the nine oil-exporting countries, they also had about 55 percent of the region's population, as well as the bulk of the next most important natural resources after oil – farm land, the largest concentrations of skilled labor, and the most industrialized economies.

Although this group is more diverse economically than the oil exporters, there are a number of fiscally related factors that pertain to most of its members. They are generally richer and more diversified than most LDCs, and tend thus to have broader tax bases. They have at least the potential to tap these bases widely, since they also have sizable cadres of trained bureaucrats. Emigrant remittances from nationals working in neighboring oil economies and elsewhere have become increasingly important during the 1970s in almost all the non-oil exporting countries.

They all have theoretically progressive personal income and business profits taxes which in effect are most heavily paid by the urban middle classes, since minimum income exemptions effectively exclude the very poor and administrative difficulties hamper accurate collections from the rich or rural taxpayers. However in most cases, these taxes have been increasing in relative importance over the period we examined. Consumption related taxes are more heavily used, with different degrees of relief from the regressive nature of such taxes provided in various countries. Relief takes the form of low (or even no) tariffs on necessities and the highest tariffs for luxury goods. Again the general effect is probably to hit hardest at the urban middle classes.

It was indicated earlier that consumption taxes are probably the best way that these countries can tap emigrant remittances; taxes directly on the remittances would either discourage them or send them into channels that would avoid official scrutiny, and income taxes on their recipients would be hard to collect. As can be seen from *Table 14.2* the export of labor from these countries has become a major element in their economies; the ratio of

Table 14.2 *Remitted earnings from emigrant workers (1972–1979)* *($ millions)*

	1972	1974	1976	1977	1978	1979
Egypt	104.2	268.2	755.1	896.7	1772.8	2213.2
Jordan	20.7	75.4	411.0	455.3	520.2	600.5
Sudan	NA	NA	12.4	40.0	67.6	117.8
Yemen Arab Rep.	NA	156.9	795.1	1193.3	1313.6	1465.9
Yemen People's Dem Rep.	30.5	43.8	120.8	184.7	257.7	316.7

Source: Balance of Payments Yearbook.

remittances to GNP ranged from 1.25 percent in the Sudan to 44 percent in the Yemen Arab Republic by the late 1970s.

A number of points about individual countries can be mentioned in summary. In the case of Egypt (and to a lesser extent, Syria), the argument was made that the prospects of increased oil revenues are not totally favorable from a fiscal point of view. If such receipts become the occasion of reformulating the current tax structure to relieve domestic taxpayers, then few additional funds may become available for development spending. The danger is particularly acute when oil receipts are diverted to support current budget spending rather than being invested in renewable resources. Syria faces further problems in that while it is now more dependent than Egypt on oil revenues, its production prospects for the 1980s are much bleaker. Thus it may very soon be forced to find major fiscal alternatives within its own economy to what has become in the 1970s an easy tax on foreign consumers.

Jordan has come to rely on a revenue source of a different type that may also begin to decline in importance: economic assistance from foreign governments and international institutions has been about equal to domestic tax receipts for the past 30 years. While Jordan's strategic importance remains high enough to ensure a continued high level of aid from its principal benefactors, it seems likely now that the country's per capita GNP has exceeded $1000 annually, these benefactors may begin to level off their assistance.

Lebanon has already plunged into a fiscal crisis, occasioned by years of civil strife the causes of which, we argued above, were partly reflected in the country's fiscal profile. It is hard to imagine how the elements of economic dissatisfaction in the inter-communal conflict can ever be diminished with fiscal policies like those of the past which favored a small minority of better-off urban Lebanese and ignored the needs of whole portions of the countryside.

In concluding, it can only be pointed out that while there are social, economic and fiscal similarities found across the Middle East, even the oil exporters differ enough one from another to preclude analyzing them and prescribing for them as though they were a single unit. We have indicated a number of problems that are common to several countries, but the urgency of these problems is not the same everywhere, nor are the solutions. Certainly Saudi Arabia with 50 years oil left at current production levels has much longer to construct a diversified domestic tax base than does Libya with 20 years. Iraq, with massive oil reserves and bountiful farmland has more alternatives to explore than one of the Gulf Sheikhdoms where water is almost as rare as petroleum. However, one statement can be made which covers all the Middle Eastern states in our survey: up until now, none have realized the full potential of tax policy as an instrument of long-term economic development.

Notes

1 Obviously, light income and profits taxes help to attract banks, but pre-civil war Lebanon was perhaps the world's preeminent *laissez-faire* economy without abdicating its right to levy taxes in this area.

2 For which data adequate to make comparisons are unfortunately not available.

3 Among which we can certainly include Brunei, the only predominantly Muslim,

non-Middle Eastern oil exporter with a large export value-to-population ratio. Though only approximate figures for Brunei's disaggregated fiscal accounts are available, we are quite safe to rank this British protected East Indian sultanate with its compatriots of similar colonial history along the southern littoral of the Gulf – that is, at the very bottom (one percent or less) in fiscal revenues derived from religiously appropriate sources.

4 They also of course swell the tax side of any tax–GNP proportion as well. Our point here, however, is that massive oil revenues distort whatever tax-to-income measures may be readily available.

5 Nor even if we allow for the fact that the capital-surplus Islamic members of OPEC also have made during the 1970s general annual allowances in the form of economic assistance to the poor outside their borders – that is, to other LDCs both within and without the Muslim world. For further discussion see Cummings, Askari, and Salehizadeh, An Economic Analysis of OPEC Aid, *OPEC Bulletin*, **25** (September, 1978).

6 This problem was encountered during the summer of 1980 when *Shi'i* protestors in neighboring Pakistan forced the government there to grant them exemptions from a new law enforcing *zakat* levies on savings accounts.

7 Assuming that oil prices remain at least constant in real terms.

8 It should be recalled from Chapters 7 and 11 that Iran with at least a modest internal tax structure and relatively low overseas investment per capita was *less* susceptible to these problems than would be several other oil exporters in the Gulf region.

Exchange rates and calendars

Throughout this work we have made use of two convenient simplifications. First we expressed many tables in terms of US dollars to facilitate cross-country comparisons. The exchange rates used, which were annual averages, are shown in *Table A.1*.

Secondly, we have reported data in terms of the Gregorian calendar – that is, in terms of a 365-day (or 366-day) year beginning on 1 January. But in most parts of the Middle East, traditional calendars continue in use, in parallel with the Gregorian calendar. In three countries included in this study, even to this date, fiscal data are only reported in terms of the local calendar.

In the case of Iran this does not present us with much of a problem. The Iranian calendar is based on the solar year and has the same pattern of leap year corrections as the Gregorian calendar. Only the first day of the year is different. Iran still follows the practice, as did Europe until a few centuries ago, of beginning the year at the vernal equinox, 21 March (see *Table A.2*). Iran also dates its calendar from the *Hijra* of the Prophet Muhammed in the year 622 of the Christian era.

For those countries which still use the traditional Arab format enshrined in Islam's religious calendar (here Qatar and Saudi Arabia), the problem is slightly more complex. For this calendar is lunar, not solar, in basis; the ordinary year has only 354 days. As can be seen from *Table A.2*, during the period of our study there was about one more year (1367 to 1400 A.H.) by the Islamic calendar than there was by the Gregorian calendar (1947 to 1979 A.D.).

Wherever these other calendar systems were used in our original sources, we have expressed the data in the closest Gregorian equivalent.

Table A.1 *Annual average exchange rates of Middle Eastern currencies versus the US dollar (US$ per currency unit)*

Year	Bahrain (dinar)	Egypt (pound)	Iran (rial)	Iraq (dinar)	Jordan (dinar)	Kuwait (dinar)	Lebanon (pound)	Libya (dinar)
1950	NA	2.8700	0.0310	2.8000	2.8000	2.8000	0.2907	2.8000
1951	NA	2.8700	0.0310	2.8000	2.8000	2.8000	0.2632	2.8000
1952	NA	2.8700	0.0310	2.8000	2.8000	2.8000	0.2801	2.8000
1953	NA	2.8700	0.0310	2.8000	2.8000	2.8000	0.3135	2.8000
1954	NA	2.8700	0.0310	2.8000	2.8000	2.8000	0.3086	2.8000
1955	NA	2.8700	0.0132	2.8000	2.8000	2.8000	0.3077	2.8000
1956	NA	2.8500	0.0132	2.8000	2.8000	2.8000	0.3125	2.8000
1957	NA	2.8500	0.0132	2.8000	2.8000	2.8000	0.3141	2.8000
1958	NA	2.8500	0.0132	2.8000	2.8000	2.8000	0.3141	2.8000
1959	2.1000	2.8500	0.0132	2.8000	2.8000	2.8000	0.3170	2.8000
1960	2.1000	2.8500	0.0132	2.8000	2.8000	2.8000	0.3155	2.8000
1961	2.1000	2.8500	0.0132	2.8000	2.8000	2.8000	0.3248	2.8000
1962	2.1000	2.4833	0.0132	2.8000	2.8000	2.8000	0.3323	2.8000
1963	2.1000	2.3000	0.0132	2.8000	2.8000	2.8000	0.3229	2.8000
1964	2.1000	2.3000	0.0132	2.8000	2.8000	2.8000	0.3253	2.8000
1965	2.1000	2.3000	0.0132	2.8000	2.8000	2.8000	0.3755	2.8000
1966	2.1000	2.3000	0.0132	2.8000	2.8000	2.8000	0.3194	2.8000
1967	2.1000	2.3000	0.0132	2.8000	2.8000	2.8000	0.3121	2.8000
1968	2.1000	2.3000	0.0133	2.8000	2.8000	2.8000	0.3168	2.8000
1969	2.1000	2.3000	0.0133	2.7942	2.8000	2.8000	0.3073	2.8000
1970	2.1000	2.3000	0.0131	2.7849	2.8000	2.8000	0.3059	2.8000
1971	2.1064	2.3000	0.0131	2.9647	2.8000	2.8200	0.3098	3.0400
1972	2.2800	2.3000	0.0131	2.9792	2.8000	3.0472	0.3278	3.0400
1973	2.5046	2.5343	0.0146	3.3862	3.0390	3.3919	0.3831	3.3778
1974	2.5333	2.5556	0.0148	3.3862	3.1198	3.4104	0.4296	3.3778
1975	2.5284	2.5556	0.0148	3.3862	3.1305	3.4483	0.4330	3.3778
1976	2.5278	2.5556	0.0142	3.3862	3.0115	3.4203	0.3444	3.3778
1977	2.5275	2.5556	0.0142	3.3862	3.0373	3.4898	0.3237	3.3778
1978	2.5809	2.5556	0.0142	3.3862	3.2620	3.6362	0.3384	3.3778
1979	2.6214	1.4286	0.0142	3.3862	3.3270	3.6203	0.3084	3.3778

Note: NA indicates exchange rate not available from quoted source.

Source: *International Financial Statistics*; *Yearbook of International Trade Statistics*.

Table A.1 *(continued)*

Oman (rial)	Qatar (rial)	Saudi Arabia (rial)	Sudan (pound)	Syria (pound)	United Arab Emirates (dirham)	Yemen Arab Rep. (rial)	Yemen PDR (dinar)
NA	NA	NA	2.8716	0.4566	NA	NA	2.8000
NA	NA	NA	2.8716	0.4566	NA	NA	2.8000
NA	NA	0.2667	2.8716	0.4566	NA	NA	2.8000
NA	NA	0.2667	2.8716	0.4566	NA	NA	2.8000
NA	NA	0.2667	2.8716	0.2793	NA	NA	2.8000
NA	NA	0.2667	2.8716	0.2793	NA	NA	2.8000
NA	NA	0.2667	2.8716	0.2793	NA	NA	2.8000
NA	NA	0.2667	2.8716	0.2793	NA	NA	2.8000
NA	NA	0.2667	2.8716	0.2793	NA	NA	2.8000
NA	0.2100	0.2667	2.8716	0.2793	0.2100	NA	2.8000
NA	0.2100	0.2222	2.8716	0.2793	0.2100	NA	2.8000
NA	0.2100	0.2222	2.8716	0.2793	0.2100	NA	2.8000
NA	0.2100	0.2222	2.8716	0.2703	0.2100	NA	2.8000
NA	0.2100	0.2222	2.8716	0.2618	0.2100	NA	2.8000
2.8000	0.2100	0.2222	2.8716	0.2618	0.2100	0.9000	2.8000
2.8000	0.2100	0.2222	2.8716	0.2618	0.2100	0.6840	2.8000
2.8000	0.2100	0.2222	2.8716	0.2618	0.2100	0.4730	2.8000
2.7670	0.2100	0.2222	2.8716	0.2618	0.2100	0.4860	2.7333
2.4000	0.2100	0.2222	2.8716	0.2618	0.2100	0.3250	2.4000
2.4000	0.2100	0.2222	2.8716	0.2618	0.2100	0.2250	2.4000
2.4000	0.2100	0.2222	2.8716	0.2618	0.2100	0.1777	2.4000
2.4075	0.2106	0.2237	2.8716	0.2618	0.2106	0.1841	2.4073
2.6055	0.2280	0.2410	2.8716	0.2618	0.2280	0.2132	2.6057
2.8686	0.2505	0.2710	2.8716	0.2617	0.2502	0.2166	2.8624
2.8952	0.2533	0.2817	2.8716	0.2686	0.2526	0.2186	2.8952
2.8952	0.2544	0.2843	2.8716	0.2703	0.2524	0.2132	2.8952
2.8952	0.2524	0.2833	2.8716	0.2596	0.2530	0.2192	2.8952
2.8952	0.2526	0.2837	2.8716	0.2547	0.2562	0.2192	2.8952
2.8957	0.2580	0.2942	2.6619	0.2547	0.2583	0.2192	2.8952
2.8952	0.2651	0.2975	2.3542	0.2547	0.2621	0.2192	2.8952

Table A.2 *Islamic, Iranian and Gregorian calendar equivalents*

Islamic (Hijral) year	Gregorian date of year's start		Iranian year	Gregorian date of year's start
1367	14 November	1947	1326	21 March 1947
1368	2 November	1948	1327	21 March 1948
1369	23 October	1949	1328	21 March 1949
1370	13 October	1950	1329	21 March 1950
1371	2 October	1951	1330	21 March 1951
1372	21 September	1952	1331	21 March 1952
1373	10 September	1953	1332	21 March 1953
1374	30 August	1954	1333	21 March 1954
1375	20 August	1955	1334	21 March 1955
1376	8 August	1956	1335	21 March 1956
1377	29 July	1957	1336	21 March 1957
1378	18 July	1958	1337	21 March 1958
1379	7 July	1959	1338	21 March 1959
1380	25 June	1960	1339	21 March 1960
1381	14 June	1961	1340	21 March 1961
1382	4 June	1962	1341	21 March 1962
1383	25 May	1963	1342	21 March 1963
1384	13 May	1964	1343	21 March 1964
1385	2 May	1965	1344	21 March 1965
1386	22 April	1966	1345	21 March 1966
1387	11 April	1967	1346	21 March 1967
1388	31 March	1968	1347	21 March 1968
1389	20 March	1969	1348	21 March 1969
1390	9 March	1970	1349	21 March 1970
1391	27 February	1971	1350	21 March 1971
1392	16 February	1972	1351	21 March 1972
1393	4 February	1973	1352	21 March 1973
1394	25 January	1974	1353	21 March 1974
1395	14 January	1975	1354	21 March 1975
1396	3 January	1976	1355	21 March 1976
1397	23 December	1976	1356	21 March 1977
1398	12 December	1977	1357	21 March 1978
1399	2 December	1978	1358	21 March 1979
1400	21 November	1979	1359	21 March 1980

Categorical groupings of taxes

Because of the basically comparative nature of this study, we have striven as far as possible to classify similar taxes under the same headings for the 16 countries discussed above. The general headings used were direct taxes (then broken down into income taxes, royalties and property taxes), indirect taxes (then broken down into customs' receipts, excise, sales, and production taxes, and other indirect taxes), and state enterprises. These were used in similar tables for 15 countries (with the exception of Qatar): *Tables 7.1, 7.3, 7.6, 7.10, 7.13, 7.18, 7.23, 7.28, 8.1, 8.5, 8.8, 8.13, 8.17, 8.20* and *8.23.*

However, statistical reporting differences among these countries did not allow us to use exactly the same categorization in all cases, and thus it would be useful for the reader to consult the listings below. For each country, we have indicated exactly what major taxes are included under the several subcategories.

Direct taxes

(1) Income taxes: Bahrain – none; Egypt – personal income, corporate profits, and inheritance taxes; Iran – personal income, non-oil corporate profits, and inheritance taxes; Iraq – personal income, non-oil corporate profits (exception: includes oil company taxes in 1950/51), inheritance taxes, all income related defense surtaxes; Jordan – personal income and corporate profits taxes; Kuwait – corporate profits taxes; Lebanon – personal income, corporate profits and inheritance taxes; Libya – personal income and non-oil corporate profits taxes; Oman – non-oil corporate profits taxes; Saudi Arabia – personal income and corporate profits taxes (exception: beginning in 1975/76, oil company profits taxes and oil royalties are not separately reported); Sudan – personal income and corporate profits taxes, all income related defense surtaxes; Syria – personal income, corporate profits and inheritance taxes; United Arab Emirates (Abu Dhabi) – oil company profits taxes; Yemen Arab Republic – personal income and corporate profits taxes; Yemen Peoples' Democratic Republic – personal income and corporate profits taxes.

(2) Royalties: Bahrain – all oil revenues; Egypt – (when separately available) mostly non-oil related; Iran – all oil revenues; Iraq – all oil revenues

(exception: 1950/51 when oil company profits taxes were reported with other corporate profits taxes); Jordan – phosphate royalties and oil company payments (for prospecting rights and pipeline transit fees); Kuwait – oil royalties only through 1974/75, thereafter includes sales of state owned oil company; Lebanon – none; Libya – all oil revenues; Oman – all oil revenues; Saudi Arabia – oil royalty data separately available only through 1974/75; Sudan – none; Syria – oil pipeline transit fees; United Arab Emirates (Abu Dhabi) – none; Yemen Arab Republic – none; Yemen People's Democratic Republic – none.

(3) Property taxes: Bahrain – none; Egypt – urban real estate, rural land, and automobile taxes; Iran – urban real estate and rural land taxes; Iraq – urban real estate, rural land, and palm grove taxes, plus land registration fees; Jordan – urban real estate, rural land and livestock taxes; Kuwait – property transfer taxes; Lebanon – urban real estate, rural land and automobile taxes; Libya – urban real estate and rural land taxes; Oman – none; Saudi Arabia – *zakat* levies against individuals and businesses; Sudan – rental property taxes and *zakat* levies; Syria – urban real estate, rural land, automobile and television taxes, plus land registration fees; United Arab Emirates; (Abu Dhabi) – none; Yemen Arab Republic – rental property taxes and *zakat* levies; Yemen People's Democratic Republic (preindependence Aden Colony only) – urban real estate.

Indirect taxes

(1) Customs levies: Bahrain – import duties; Egypt – import duties and trade related fees; Iran – import duties and trade related fees; Iraq – import duties; Jordan – import duties; Kuwait – import duties and levies on reexports; Lebanon – import duties and trade related fees; Libya – import duties; Oman – import duties; Saudi Arabia – import duties and trade related fees; Sudan – import duties and foreign exchange taxes; Syria – import duties and trade related fees; United Arab Emirates (Abu Dhabi) – import duties and trade related fees; Yemen Arab Republic – important duties, defense surtaxes on imports and trade related fees; Yemen People's Democratic Republic – import duties.

(2) Excise, sales, and production taxes (Note: none of the countries under consideration employ sales taxes in the sense of the term in Europe or North America, that is, a levy on a general range of consumer goods and services; however, specific commodities are singled for excise taxes): Bahrain – excise tax on gasoline; Egypt – excise tax on various luxuty goods and services; Iran – excise taxes mostly on fuel, automobiles, alcohol and tobacco; Iraq – excise taxes mostly on fuel, tobacco and alcohol, and production taxes on agricultural output; Jordan – excise taxes mostly on such items as tobacco, matches, and salt; Kuwait – none; Lebanon – excise taxes mostly on fuel and tobacco; Libya – excise

taxes on several locally produced items and returns to the government by state-owned monopolies; Oman – none; Saudi Arabia – excise tax on gasoline; Sudan – excise taxes on several luxury goods, and production taxes on major agricultural commodities cultivated mostly for export (and collected at the point of export), such as cotton, gum Arabic, groundnuts and cottonseed; Syria – excise taxes on tobacco, fuel, cement and sugar, and production taxes on cotton (collected when cotton is exported) (Note: this category also includes export levies on most other agricultural exports, which generally have been both a small fraction of domestic production of the particular commodity and rather small relative to cotton exports; however, during the 1970s, Syrian exports of some fruits and vegetables have increased dramatically and with them it can be assumed, production tax receipts have also grown); United Arab Emirates (Abu Dhabi) – none; Yemen Arab Republic – excise taxes in some cases, in addition to customs' duties, are imposed on several imported goods of a luxury nature and on some local services (including cinema tickets); Yemen People's Democratic Republic – excise taxes mostly on gasoline, alcohol and qat, and post independence production taxes on output in both the fisheries and agricultural sectors.

(3) Other indirect taxes (Note: government agency fees are considered to be user fees or taxes): Bahrain – government agency fees; Egypt – government agency fees, stamp duties and the net returns realized by government owned sales agencies that market several major commodities; Iran – government agency fees and stamp duties; Iraq – government agency fees and stamp duties; Jordan – government agency fees, stamp duties, and several otherwise unidentifiable taxes; Kuwait – government agency fees; Lebanon – government agency fees; Libya – government agency fees; Oman – government agency fees and various otherwise unidentifiable taxes; Saudi Arabia – government agency fees, stamp duties, and a highway tax imposed on salaried Saudi Arabian citizens until 1975 (as a percentage of reported income but generally seen as a tax on major non-business highway users); Sudan – government agency fees; Syria – government agency fees and stamp duties; United Arab Emirates (Abu Dhabi) – government agency fees; Yemen Arab Republic – government agency fees and stamp duties; Yemen People's Democratic Republic – government agency fees and stamp duties.

State enterprises

Bahrain – mostly rental income from government property; Egypt – public utilities, rental income from government properties and net returns from the Suez Canal; Iran – public utilities and net returns from other state owned monopolies (such as tobacco); Iraq – public utilities, ports administration and government owned banks; Jordan – public utilities; Kuwait – public utilities and net profits from non-oil state owned enterprises (Note: excluding returns from overseas investments); Lebanon – mostly profits from gambling casino and oil refinery; Libya – mostly rental income from government property; Oman – public utilities and returns from overseas investments; Saudi Arabia – public utilities, rental income from government property and net returns from transportational facilities (ports, airports, and railroads); Sudan – rental income from government property, net returns from agricultural schemes and net profit of state corporations and banks, including increasingly important sales of oil during the 1970s; Syria – public utilities, net returns from state-owned commercial enterprises, rental income from government property, and (increasingly by the mid 1970s) an unspecified portion of total oil revenues; United Arab Emirates (Abu Dhabi) – public utilities (Note: data not separately available after 1974); Yemen Arab Republic – rental income from government property and net profits of state-owned monopolies; Yemen People's Democratic Republic – rental income from government property, public utilities, and (during the 1970s a quarter share of net profits of state owned corporations (that is, after payment of income taxes).

In Part V, we made use of two further categories – 'religiously appropriate' and consumer related taxes. These groupings were used in similar tables for each of the 16 countries: *Tables 11.1, 11.3, 11.5, 11.8, 11.12, 11.13, 11.14, 11.15, 11.18, 12.1, 12.4, 12.7, 12.10, 12.12, 12.13* and *12.14.*

For each country, we have indicated what major taxes are included under these two categories.

'Religiously appropriate' taxes

Bahrain – none; Egypt – personal income, corporate profits, inheritance, Urban real estate, rural land, and automobile taxes; Iran – personal income, non-oil corporate profits, inheritance, urban real estate and rural land taxes; Iraq – personal income, non-oil corporate profits, inheritance, urban real estate, rural land, palm grove and agricultural production taxes, plus income related defense surtaxes and land registration fees; Jordan – personal income, corporate profits, urban real estate, rural land and livestock taxes; Kuwait – non-oil corporate profits and property transfer taxes; Lebanon – personal income, corporate profits, inheritance, urban real estate and rural land taxes; Libya – personal income, non-oil corporate profits, urban real estate and rural land taxes; Oman – non-oil corporate profits taxes; Qatar – non-oil corporate profits taxes; Saudi Arabia – personal income and non-oil corporate profits taxes and *zakat*; Sudan – personal income, corporate profits, rental property and agricultural production taxes, income related defense surtaxes, and *zakat*, *'ushr* and *jizyah*; Syria – personal income, corporate profits, inheritance, urban real estate, rural land, automobile, television and agricultural production taxes, and land registration fees; United Arab Emirates – none; Yemen Arab Republic – personal income, corporate profits and rental property taxes, and *zakat*; Yemen People's Democratic Republic – personal income, corporate profits, urban real estate and agricultural production taxes.

Consumer related taxes

Bahrain – import duties and gasoline excise tax; Egypt – import duties, trade related fees, and excise taxes on various luxuries; Iran – import duties, trade related fees and excise taxes on various luxuries; Iraq – import duties and excise taxes on various luxuries; Jordan – import duties and excise taxes on various commodities; Kuwait – import duties; Lebanon – import duties, trade related fees and excise taxes on various commodities; Libya – import duties and excise taxes on various commodities; Oman – import duties; Qatar – import duties; Saudi Arabia – import duties, trade related fees, and excise tax on gasoline; Sudan – import duties, foreign exchange fees and excise taxes on various luxuries; Syria – import duties, trade related fees and excise taxes on various commodities; UAE – import duties and trade-related fees; Yemen Arab Republic – import duties, defense surtaxes on imports, trade related fees and excise taxes on various luxuries and services; Yemen People's Democratic Republic – import duties and excise taxes on various commodities.

Index

Abu Dhabi, 110, 128, 129, 258, 259, 261, 262,
    263, 288
  customs duties, 137
  direct and indirect taxes, 137
  income tax, 137
  oil production, 134, 135, 136
  overseas investments, 305
  revenues, 135, 137, 138
Abu Dhabi Investment Authority, 299
Accelerated depreciation, 25, 26
Aden, 174, 175, 291, 293
Aden Protectorate, 174
Ad valorem duties, 45, 48
Africa,
  personal income taxes in, 21
  poll taxes in, 20
Agricultural income,
  taxing of, 19, 30, 159
Agricultural land,
  taxation of, 30, 143
    difficulties of, 31
    income distribution and, 31
Agriculture,
  in Sudan, 159
  tax ratio and, 184
Ajman, 258, 263
  revenues, 135
Alcohol, taxes on, 46, 48
Almsgiving, 5
Automatic stabilizers, 17

Bahrain, 57, 214, 261
  composition of exports, 278
  consumer taxes, 224
    ratio to total revenue, 223
  customs duties, 97, 98
  direct and indirect taxes, 92, 97
  diversification of economy, 96, 98, 226,
    228
  domestically generated tax revenues, 268
  domestic oil consumption, 311, 312, 313
  exchange rates, 334
  excise, sales and production taxes, 97, 98
  GDP, 231
  GNP, 227, 228
  government receipts, 90

Bahrain, *(cont.)*
  growth of oil and non-oil tax, 298
  income tax as percentage of national
    income, 216
    ratio to total taxes, 215
  major taxes in, 98
  official development assistance, 274
  oil production, 88, 96, 227
    future, 310
  oil reserves, 245, 309, 310
  oil revenues, 227, 228
    relative to total revenue, 94, 209
  oil royalties, 96
  per capita tax load, 94
  price indices, 239
  prosperity, 226
  ratio of import duties to total tax, 244
  ratio of tax revenue to GNP, 202
  religiously appropriate taxes, 220, 221, 227
    ratio to total income, 255, 324, 325
  state enterprises, 97, 98
  taxation in, 96–98
  tax buoyancy, 207, 208, 227, 228
  tax policy performance, 226–231
  tax ratio, 227, 228
  tax revenues, 90, 97
  total revenue, 96
  zakat, 229
Banking, in islamic theology, 70
Business profits taxes,
  non-oil exporters, 329
  percentage of tax from, 218

Calendars, 333, 336
Capital budgets, 326
Capital gains tax, 32
Capitalism, compatibility with Islam, 60
Ceylon, export tax on tea, 40
Chelliah model of tax ratio, 183 *et seq.*
  basic hypothesis, 186
  compared with revised model, 191
Chile, export taxes, 40
Chow test, 191
Conspicuous consumption, 14, 16
Consumer taxes, 221
  buoyancy of, 224

Consumer taxes, (*cont.*)
    countries levying, 341
    ratio to total revenue, 223
Consumption,
    conspicuous and essential, 14, 16
    tax on, 44
Contracyclical operations, 41
Corporate income tax, 9, 22–27
    development and, 24
    double taxation agreements and, 26
    excessive, 27
    foreign owned corporations and, 22
    in developing countries, 23, 24
    per capita GNP and, 24
    public revenues and, 22
Customs duties, 221
    countries levying, 338
    evasion of, 41
    exemption of, 44

Death duties, 33
    distribution of wealth and, 34
Defence, taxes for, 146
Developing countries,
    corporate income tax in, 23
    direct taxation in, 10, 11
    excise taxes in, 47
    export taxes, 37, 38
    import duties in, 41, 42
    personal income taxes in, 14
    property taxes in, 28, 29
    ratio of consumer taxes to total revenue,
        223
    ratio of import duties to total taxes, 244
    ratio of income to total taxes, 215
    sales tax in, 47
    tax ratios, 187, 204
    types of taxation in, 9–13
Development,
    corporate income tax and, 24
    excise taxes and, 46
    import duties and, 43, 45
    Islam and, 60
    role of direct and indirect taxation in, 11
    sales taxes and, 49
    tax ratio and, 182, 183, 184, 188, 190
Direct taxation, 9, 14–44, 337
    classification of, 9
    role in economic development, 11
    share of revenue, 91, 92
Diversification, 210, 231, 234, 244, 245, 314
Domestic taxes, 327
Double taxation agreements, 26
Dubai, 258, 259, 260, 261
    customs duties, 136, 138
    oil production, 134, 135, 136
    revenues, 135, 138

Economic development, *see Development*
Economic exploitation in Islamic theology,
    69
Economic surplus, 14
Egypt, 186, 226, 287
    agriculture, 268
    assessment of tax performance, 266–272
    business profits tax, 218, 266
    composition of exports, 278
    consumer related taxes, 222, 224, 267, 270
    customs duties, 144, 145, 146, 147, 270
    defence taxes, 146
    direct and indirect taxes, 92, 143, 144
    domestic oil consumption, 311, 312
    domestic taxes, 267, 268
    exchange rates, 334
    excise, sales, and production taxes, 144,
        145, 147, 270
    GDP by industrial origin, 269
    GNP, 266
    general revenue tax, 146
    government receipts, 90
    income distribution, 210, 212, 213
    income tax, 144, 145, 270, 271
        ratio to total taxes, 215
    industry, 268
    land tax, 143, 145
    local government revenues, 147, 148
    major taxes, 145
    monopolies, 271
    official development assistance, 274
    oil production, 88, 143, 267, 271
        future, 310
    oil reserves, 245, 266, 309, 310, 329
    per capita tax load, 94
    price indices, 239
    profits tax, 143, 146
    property taxes, 144, 271
    ratio of import duties to total tax, 244
    ratio of tax revenue to GNP, 202
    ratio to total revenue, 223
    religiouslyappropriate taxes, 220, 221, 267,
        268
        ratio of to total tax, 255, 324, 325
    royalties, 144, 145
    stamp duties, 145
    taxation in, 143–148
    tax buoyancy, 207, 270
    tax ratio, 204, 266, 267
    tax revenues, 90, 144
    wealth taxes, 145
Emigrant remittances, 289, 293, 294, 329
Entertainment, tax on, 48
Essential consumption, 14
Estimates of revenues, 135
European Economic Community, VAT in,
    52
Exchange controls, 45

Exchange rates, 333, 334, 335
Excise, sales and production taxes, 45–48,
    221
  countries levying, 338
  development and, 46
  in developing countries, 47
Exports,
  composition of, 278
  tax ratio and, 186
Export taxes, 37–40
  distribution of, 39
  in developing countries, 37, 38, 39
  marketing boards and, 40–41
  shifting forward, 40

Fiscal policy,
  for future, 297
  inflation and, 4
  interaction with Islamic theology, 5
  taxation as instrument of, 6
Fiscal profiles, 319
Fujairah, 258, 263
  revenues, 135
Full loss carry forward policy, 24

General Agreement on Tariffs and Trade
    (GATT), 45, 52
Gold, 64
Government expenditure, inflation and, 18
Gross domestic product by industrial origin,
    230, 269
Gross National Product, 201
  corporate income tax and, 24
  direct taxation and, 12
  import duties and, 43
  non-oil exporters, 328
  ratio of taxes to, *see Tax ratio*
  sales taxes and, 49

Ijma', 61, 65
Import duties, 9, 41–45
  ad valorem, 45, 48
  as percentage of total tax, 244
  development and, 43, 45
  exemption of, 26, 44
  GNP and, 43
  importance of, 41
  in developing countries, 42
  inflation and, 45
  tax ratio and, 182, 189
  undesirable features, 45
Import licensing, 45
Import substitution industries, 44
Incentives, income tax and, 17
Incentive goods, 44

Income,
  distribution of, 3, 210–214, 322
    Gini coefficient, 213
    in Islamic theology, 69, 76
    Kunzets index, 213
    Lorentz curves, 213
    modification of, 213
    selected countries, 211
    standardized E index, 213
  equality of, 322
    income tax and, 17
  in Islamic theology, 68
  per capita, tax ratio and, 182, 184, 188
  unequal distribution of, land taxes and, 31
Income tax, 214
  corporate, 9, 22–27
    development and, 24
    double taxation agreements and, 26
    excessive, 27
    foreign owned companies and, 22
    in developing countries, 23, 24
    per capita GNP and, 24
    public revenue and, 22
  deductions, as policy instrument, 18
  exemptions, 19, 24, 25, 26
  from business profits, 218
  incentives and, 17
  income inequalities and, 17
  inflation and, 17
  non-oil exporters, 329
  on agricultural income, 19
  personal, 14–22
    difficulties of, 20
    in African countries, 21
    in developing countries, 15
    in LDCs, 20
  progressive, 17
    development and, 17
    protection and, 17
  proportion of total tax revenue, 18
  public investment and, 16, 17
  ratio to total revenue, 215
  spare time work and, 17
Indirect taxation, 9, 37–56, 338
  classification of, 11
  collection, 222
  inflation and, 18
  role in economic development, 11
  share of revenue, 91, 92
Industrialized countries,
  income tax as percentage of national
    income, 216
  ratio of import taxes to total tax, 244
  ratio of income to total taxes, 215
  ratio of consumer taxes to total revenue,
    223
  tax ratios, 206
Industry, energy-intensive, 313

Inflation, 4, 208
    fiscal policy and, 4
    government expenditure and, 18
    import duties and, 45
    indirect taxation and, 18
    in Iran, 103, 235
    in Yemen, 172
    land taxation and, 30
    protection against, 17
    savings and, 16
Inheritance, in Islamic theology, 71
Interest,
    in Islamic theology, 68
    prohibition of, 70
Investment,
    private, 3
        direction of, 24
        double taxation agreements and, 26
        encouragement of, 24, 25, 26
        tax incentives, 24, 25, 26
    public, income tax and, 16, 17
Iran, 186, 229, 267
    ad valorem duties, 102
    calendar, 336
    composition of exports, 278
    consumer taxes, 224, 232, 233, 234
        ratio to total revenue, 223
    corporate profit taxes, 101, 218
    customs duties, 100, 102, 233
    direct and indirect taxes, 92, 100
    dispute with IPC, 105, 107, 108
    diversification, 231, 231, 234
    domestically generated tax revenues, 268
    domestic oil consumption, 311, 312, 313
    exchange rates, 334
    excise, sales, and production taxes, 100,
        102, 103, 233, 234
    GDP by industrial origin, 230, 231
    GNP, 231, 232
    government receipts, 90
    growth of oil and non-oil tax, 298
    imports, 234
    income distribution in, 210, 213, 235
    income tax, 100, 101, 102, 232, 234
        as percentage of national income, 216
        exemptions, 104
        ratio of to total taxes, 215
    inflation in, 103, 235
    Islamic Republic of, 80
    major taxes, 102
    non-oil taxes, 103
    oil economy, 99
    oil exports, 99, 237
    oil production, 88, 89, 232, 236
        future, 310
    oil reserves, 309, 310
    oil revenues, 99, 231, 232, 236, 237
        relative to total revenue, 94, 209

Iran, (*cont.*)
    overseas investments, 104, 299, 305
        per citizen return, 301, 302, 303, 304
        returns, 104, 299
    per capita tax load, 94
    price indices, 239
    profits tax, 100, 102, 232
    property taxes, 100, 102
    ratio of import duties to total tax, 244
    religiously appropriate taxes, 220, 221, 231,
        232, 235
        ratio to total tax, 255, 324, 325
    revolution, 60, 99, 100, 103, 115, 122, 234,
        326, 327, 328
    stamp duties, 102
    taxation in, 98–105
    tax buoyancy, 207, 208, 232
    tax changes under republic, 236
    tax exemptions, 101, 102
    tax policy performance, 231–237
    tax problems, 237
    tax ratio, 202, 232
    tax relief, 104
    tax revenues, 100
    total government revenue, 99
    war with Iraq, 241, 288, 303, 305, 328
Iraq, 229
    agricultural incomes, 109
    agricultural resources, 238
    assessment of tax performance, 237–241
    balance of payments, 303
    business profits tax, 218
    composition of exports, 278
    consumer related taxes, 224, 238, 240, 241
    customs duties, 106, 108, 109, 110
    Development Board, 105
    direct and indirect taxes, 92, 106, 108
    domestically generated tax revenues, 268
    domestic oil consumption, 311, 312
    excise, sales, and production taxes, 106,
        109, 110
    GDP by industrial origin, 230
    GNP, 237, 238, 240
    government receipts, 90
    growth of oil and non-oil tax, 298
    income distribution in, 210, 212, 213
    income taxes, 106, 108, 240
        as percentage of national income, 216
        ratio to total tax, 215
    inheritance taxes, 102, 109
    land taxes, 109, 110
    licence fees, 109, 110
    major taxes, 109
    oil production, 88, 107, 108, 238, 241
        future, 310
    oil reserves, 245, 309, 310
    oil revenues, 102, 105, 107, 108, 109, 238
        allocations, 107

Iraq, (*cont.*)
  oil revenues, (*cont.*)
    relative to total revenue, 94, 105, 209
  overseas investments and returns, 111, 299
    per citizen return, 301, 302, 304
  per capita tax load, 94
  price indices, 239
  property taxes, 106, 109
  ratio of import duties to total tax, 244
  religiously appropriate taxes, 220, 221, 238, 240
    ratio to total tax, 255, 324, 325
  stamp duties, 109
  state enterprises, 106
  taxation in, 105–112
  tax buoyancy, 207, 208, 239, 240
  tax exemptions, 109
  tax on luxury goods, 240
  tax ratio, 202
  tax revenues, 90, 106
  trade balances, 110, 111
  war with Iran, 241, 288, 303, 305, 328
Islam, 4, 6, 228, 319, 320
  calendar, 336
  compatibility with capitalism, 60
  economic development and, 60
  economic principles, 74
  fiscal revenue in, 68
  income distribution in, 76
  inheritance in, 71
  interaction with fiscal policy, 5
  interest (usury) and, 68
  land taxes, 64
  Marxism and, 60
  poll tax, 66
  potential revenue resources, 73
  private ownership in, 75
  profit in, 74
  property and responsibility in, 74
  rent and, 71
  Sunni teaching, 254, 255
  tawhid, 67
  taxation and, 60–83, 218, 235
    summary of, 67
  taxes on natural resources, 66
  tolerance in, 78
  '*Ushr* and *Kharaj*, 64
  zakat, 61, 67, 68, 72, 74, 75, 77, 79, 80, 219, 229, 323
Islamic Development Bank, 70

Jizyah, 5, 66, 77, 220
Jordan, 267
  assessment of tax performance, 272–276
  business profits tax, 150, 151, 218, 275
  composition of exports, 278
  consumer related taxes, 224, 273, 276
    ratio to total revenue, 223

Jordan, (*cont.*)
  customs duties, 148, 149, 151, 222
  direct and indirect taxes, 92, 148, 149
  domestically generated tax revenues, 268
  Encouragement of Investment Law, 151
  exchange rates, 334
  excise, sales, and production taxes, 149, 151, 222
  export taxes, 151
  foreign aid, 150
  GDP, 272
    by industrial origin, 269
  GNP, 272, 273
  government receipts, 90
  income tax, 148, 149, 150, 151, 275
    ratio to total tax, 215
  land taxes, 151
  major taxes, 151
  official development assistance, 274
  oil related income, 150
  overseas aid to, 273, 330
  per capita tax load, 94
  phosphate mining, 150
  price indices, 239
  property taxes, 151
  ratio of import duties to total tax, 244
  religiously appropriate taxes, 220, 221, 273
    ratio to total revenue, 255, 324, 325
  royalties, 149, 150
  taxation in, 148–151
  tax buoyancy, 207, 272
  tax ratio, 202, 204, 275
  tax revenues, 148, 149, 272

Kharaj, 5, 64, 74, 77
  definition, 65
  parts of, 65
Kuwait, 110, 122, 128, 129, 133, 140, 237, 288
  assessment of tax performance, 242–246
  budget surpluses, 245
  business profits tax, 113, 218, 242, 243
  composition of exports, 278
  consumer taxes, 224, 242, 243
    ratio to total revenue, 223
  customs levies, 113, 114
  direct and indirect taxes, 92, 114
  diversification, 210, 244, 245
  domestically generated tax revenues, 268
  domestic oil consumption, 311, 312
  exchange rates, 334
  excise, sales, and production taxes, 243
  Fund for Tomorrow, 299
  GDP by industrial origin, 230
  GNP, 242
  government enterprise profits, 116
  government receipts, 90
  growth of oil and non-oil tax, 298

Kuwait, *(cont.)*
 import duties, 243, 244
  ratio to total taxes, 244
 income tax, 112, 114, 116, 215
  as percentage of national income, 216
  ratio to total tax, 215
 Industrial Encouragement Law, 113
 major taxes, 116
 oil production, 88, 89, 112, 115, 242, 246
  future, 310
 oil reserves, 245, 309, 310
 oil revenues, 112, 117, 242, 244
  relative to total revenue, 94, 209
 overseas investments, 113, 114, 115, 116,
  117, 242, 305
  budget expenditure and, 306
  non-oil revenues and, 308
  per citizen return, 300, 301, 304, 307
  returns, 299
 per capita tax load, 94
 prices indices, 239
 property tax, 114, 116, 243
 religiously appropriate taxes, 220, 221
  ratio to total revenue, 255, 324, 325
 royalties, 114, 116
 taxation in, 112–117
 tax buoyancy, 207, 208
 tax ratio, 202
 tax revenues, 112, 114, 242
 wealth tax, 113

Land,
 sale of, 32
Land-betterment taxes, 32
Land taxation, 30, 165
 difficulties of assessment, 31
 income distribution and, 31
 inflation and, 30
 in Islam, 64
 presumptive methods of assessment, 31
 special assessments, 32
 urban, 31
  local government and, 32
Lebanon, 57, 186
 assessment of tax performance, 276–280
 business profits tax, 154, 218, 279
 civil war, 157, 158, 276, 279, 330
 composition of exports, 278
 consumer related taxes, 224, 277, 280
 crisis, 330
 customs duties, 152, 153, 154, 155, 156,
  157, 158, 222
 direct and indirect taxes, 92, 153, 157, 158
 domestically generated tax revenues, 268
 domestic oil consumption, 311, 312, 313
 exchange rates, 334
 excise, sales, and production taxes, 153,
  154, 156, 158, 222

Lebanon, *(cont.)*
 exports, 277, 278
 government receipts, 90
 GDP by industrial origin, 269
 GNP, 277, 278
 imports, 156, 277
 income distribution in, 210, 212, 213
 income taxes, 152, 153, 154, 157, 148, 279
  ratio to total tax, 215
 land taxes, 155
 major taxes, 154
 official development assistance, 274
 oil and mineral revenues, 152, 154
 per capita tax load, 94
 property taxes, 153, 154, 157, 158
 ratio of import taxes to total taxes, 244
 religiously appropriate taxes, 220, 221, 277
  ratio to total revenue, 255, 324, 325
 taxation in, 152–158
 tax buoyancy, 207
 tax ratio, 202, 204
 tax revenues, 153
  effect of civil war, 157, 158
 total revenues, 152
 wealth taxes, 280
Less developed countries (LDCs), 3
 collection of tax in, 222
 corporate income tax in, 23, 24
 direct taxes and GNP, 12
 excise taxes in, 46
 export taxes in, 37
 incentives in, 17
 income tax, 216
 land taxes in, 31
 natural resources, 194
 personal income tax in, 20
 property taxes in, 29
 sales taxes in, 49
 tax ratios, 204
Libya, 140, 288
 assessment of tax performance, 246–249
 balance of payments, 303
 banking in, 70
 business profits tax, 218
 consumer taxes, 224
 corporate income tax, 120
 customs duties, 118, 119, 120, 121
 direct and indirect taxes, 92, 118
 domestically generated tax revenues, 268
 exchange rates, 334
 excise, sales, and production taxes, 118,
  119, 123, 247
 exports, 117
 GDP by industrial origin, 230
 GNP, 247
 government enterprises, 123
 government receipts, 91
 ground rents in, 117

Libya, *(cont.)*
  growth of oil and non-oil tax, 298
  import duties, 247, 248
    ratio to total taxes, 244
  income distribution in, 210, 213
  income tax, 118, 119, 120, 121, 123, 247, 248
    as percentage of national income, 216
    ratio to total tax, 215
  local government revenues, 123
  major taxes, 119
  oil production in, 88, 119, 246, 247
    future, 310
  oil reserves, 245, 309, 310
  oil revenues, 121, 122, 123, 247
    relative to total revenue, 94, 121, 209
  overseas investments, 122, 305
    per citizen return, 302, 304
    returns, 299
  per capita tax load, 94
  price indices, 239
  property taxes, 118, 119, 120, 123, 248
  religiously appropriate taxes, 220, 221, 247, 248
    ratio to total tax, 255, 324, 325
    royalties, 118, 119
  taxation, 117–123
  tax buoyancy, 207, 208
  tax ratio, 202
  tax revenues, 118
  trade surpluses, 121
  wealth tax, 120
  zakat in, 120, 248
Licence fees, 54
Local government, urban land tax and, 32
Luxury goods, tax on, 44

Marketing boards, 40–41
Marxism, Islam and, 60
Middle East,
  as commercial centre, 60
  compared with other developing countries, 6
  definition of, 4, 87
Mineral production, tax ratios and, 184, 187, 188, 190, 191, 192, 194
Mines, 102
  taxes on, 66
Muhammad, 60, 75, 76

National income, relation to savings, 16
Natural resources, 194
  taxes on, 66
North Yemen, *see Yemen Arab Republic*

Oil, domestic consumption, 311, 312
Oil companies, nationalization of, 57

Oil depletion, tax revenues and, 308–314
Oil exporting countries, 5
  trade surpluses, 58
Oil generated tax, role of, 88
Oil exports, 327
Oil industry, growth of, 87
Oil prices, 313
Oil production, growth of, 88
Oil reserves, 245
Oil revenues, 87, 327
  dependence on, 297
  ratio to total receipts, 94, 209
  types of, 91
Oman, 267, 288
  assessment of tax performance, 249–251
  business profits tax, 125, 218
  consumer taxes, 224, 250
  customs duties, 124, 125
  direct and indirect taxes, 92, 124
  diversification, 250
  domestically generated tax revenues, 268
  domestic oil consumption, 311, 312
  exchange rates, 335
  GDP by industrial origin, 230
  GNP, 250
  government receipts, 91
  growth of oil and non-oil tax, 298
  import taxes, 250
    ratio to total taxes, 244
  income tax, 124, 125, 215
    as percentage of national income, 216
    ratio to total tax, 215
  official development assistance, 274
  oil production, 88, 249, 250
    future, 310
  oil reserves, 245, 309, 310
  oil revenues, 125, 250
    relative to total revenues, 94, 209
  per capita tax load, 94
  religiously appropriate taxes, 220, 221, 250
    ratio to total tax, 255, 324, 325
  royalties, 124, 125
  state enterprises, 124
  taxation in, 123–126
  tax buoyancy, 207, 208
  tax ratio, 202, 206
  tax revenues, 124
OPEC, 87, 103, 113, 117, 257
Openness of economy, 183, 189
Organization of Arab Petroleum Exporting Countries (OAPEC), 87
Ores, taxes on, 67, 102
Overseas investments, 299, 300
  budget expenditure and, 306
  growth of, 305, 307
  non-oil tax revenues and, 308
  per citizen return, 300
  returns on, 327

Ownership,
  absolute and legal, 75
  in Islamic theology, 74
  private, 75

Phosphate, 150
Poll tax, 5, 220
  in Africa, 20
  in Islam, 66
Population,
  Muslim percentage, 219
  urban, 217
Price indices, 239
Private ownership in Islam, 75
Problems of future, 297
Profit in Islamic theology, 68, 74
Profits tax, 22–27
Property in Islamic theology, 62, 74
Property taxes, 27–35
  countries possessing, 338
  in developing countries, 28, 29

Qatar, 110, 140, 229, 251
  assessment of tax performance, 251
  business profits tax, 218
  consumer taxes, 224, 252
  customs duties, 127, 128
  direct and indirect taxes in, 93
  domestically generated tax revenues, 268
  domestic oil consumption, 311, 312, 313
  exchange rates, 335
  foreign investment, 127
  GNP, 251, 252
  government receipts, 91
  growth of oil and non-oil tax, 298
  income tax, 215
    as percentage of national income, 216
    ratio to total tax, 215
  industrial enterprises, 128
  investment income, 128
  investment policy, 128
  major taxes, 128
  non-oil revenues, 251
  oil exports, 126
  oil production, 88, 89, 108, 252
    future, 310
  oil reserves, 245, 309, 310
  oil revenues, 126, 127, 128, 251
    relative to total revenues, 94, 209
  overseas investments, 128, 299, 300, 304, 305
    budget expenditure and, 306
    non-oil revenue and, 308
    per citizen return, 300, 301, 302, 303, 304, 307
    returns, 299
  per capita tax load, 94
  public utilities fees, 128

Qatar, (*cont.*)
  ratio of import taxes to total taxes, 244
  religiously appropriate taxes, 220, 221, 252
    ratio to total tax, 255, 324, 325
  taxation in, 126–129
  tax buoyancy, 207, 208
  tax ratio, 202
  tax revenues, 90, 127
Qiya, 61
Quran, 61, 63, 73, 77, 78, 120
  on interest, 68, 70
  on material things, 76
  on private ownership, 75
  on taxation, 5, 326
  on *zakat*, 62

Ras al Khaimah, 258
  imports, 138
  revenues, 135
Regional fiscal policy for future, 297
Regression analysis, 6, 182
Religiously appropriate tax, 79, 221, 323, 324, *see also Zakat, etc*
  as ratio of total tax, 220, 255, 324
  countries levying, 340
Rent in Islamic theology, 71
Riba, 69

Sales taxes, 48–51
  contribution of, 49
  development and, 49
  GNP and, 49
  in developing countries, 47
  levying of, 49
  retail, 50, 53
  single-point, 50
  wholesale, 50, 53
Saudi Arabia, 110, 140, 237, 288, 289
  assessment of tax performance, 253–258
  assistance to Bahrain, 227
  banking in, 70
  business profits tax, 218, 256
  consumer taxes, 224, 253, 256
  corporation taxes, 131
  customs revenues, 130, 132
  direct and indirect taxes, 93, 130
  diversification in, 210, 254
  domestically generated tax revenues, 268
  domestic oil consumption, 311, 312
  exchange rates, 335
  excise, sales, and production taxes, 130, 132
  foreign assets, 134
  GDP by industrial origin, 230
  GNP, 253, 254
  government receipts, 91
  growth of oil and non-oil tax, 298

Saudi Arabia, *(cont.)*
  income taxes, 130, 131, 215
    as percentage of national income, 216
    ratio to total tax, 215
  major taxes, 132
  oil production, 88, 89, 108, 129, 133, 253,
    254, 257
    future, 310
  oil reserves, 245, 309, 310, 330
  oil revenues, 129, 131, 253, 254
    relative to total revenue, 94, 209
  overseas investments, 133, 300, 305
    and budget expenditure, 306
    per citizen return, 300, 301, 302, 303,
      304, 307
    returns, 299
  per capita tax load, 94
  pilgrimage taxes, 132
  price indices, 239
  property tax, 130
  ratio of import taxes to total taxes, 244
  religiously appropriate taxes, 79, 220, 221,
    253, 254, 256
    ratio to total tax, 255, 324, 325
  royalties, 129, 130, 132
  taxation in, 129–134
  tax buoyancy, 207, 208, 253
  tax ratio, 202
  tax revenues, 90, 130
  zakat in, 80, 131, 132, 219, 255, 256
Saudi Arabian Monetary Agency, 132
Savings,
  increase in, 14, 16
  inflation and, 16
  ratio to national income, 16
  voluntary, 15
Sharjah, 258
  imports, 138
  oil production, 134, 136
  revenues, 135
Silver, 64
Site valuation and urban land taxes, 31
smuggling, 41, 195, 260
Social security, 62
Social welfare, 214
Society, mobilizing resources of, 201
South Yemen, *see under Yemen, Peoples
    Democratic Republic of*
Stamp duties, 54
State enterprises, 57–59
  contribution to fiscal receipts, 58
  countries possessing, 339
Sudan, 158–163, 186
  agriculture in, 159, 162, 280, 281
  assessment of tax performance, 280–283
  business profits tax, 218
  composition of exports, 278
  consumer related taxes, 224, 281, 282

Sudan, *(cont.)*
  custom duties, 160
  direct and indirect taxes, 93, 159, 160
  domestically generated tax revenues, 268
  exchange rates, 335
  excise, sales, and production taxes, 160,
    161, 162, 163
  GDP by industrial origin, 269
  GNP, 281
  government receipts, 91
  income distribution in, 210, 212, 213
  income taxes, 160, 161, 162, 283
    ratio to total tax, 215
  local government revenue, 162, 163
  major taxes, 162
  natural resources, 158
  official development assistance, 274
  oil exports, 280
  per capita tax load, 94
  price indices, 239
  property taxes, 160, 161, 162, 163
  ratio of import taxes to total taxes, 244
  religiously appropriate taxes, 79, 220, 221,
    281, 282
    ratio to total tax, 255, 324, 325
  stamp duties, 162
  state enterprises, 159
  sugar monopoly, 160, 161, 162, 163, 222
  tax buoyancy, 207, 281, 282
  tax ratio, 202, 204, 281
  tax revenues, 160
  zakat and *'ushr* in, 80, 161, 162, 219, 282
Suez Canal, 147, 154, 172, 174, 277, 292
Sunnah, 61
Syria, 226, 254, 267
  agriculture, 287
  assessment of tax performance, 283–289
  business profits tax, 218, 285, 286
  consumer related taxes, 224, 285, 286
    ratio to total revenue, 223
  customs duties, 164, 165, 166
  direct and indirect taxes, 93, 164, 166
  domestically generated tax revenues, 268
  domestic oil consumption, 311, 312, 313
  exchange rates, 335
  excise, sales, and production taxes, 164,
    165, 166
  GDP by industrial origin, 269
  GNP, 285
  government receipts, 91
  hydrocarbon deposits, 288
  impact of taxes on population, 286
  income taxes, 164, 165, 166, 286
    ratio to total tax, 215
  land taxes, 165
  municipal fiscal revenue, 167
  official development assistance, 274
  oil exports, 284

Syria, (*cont.*)
　oil production, 89, 284
　　future, 310
　oil reserves, 245, 310
　oil revenue, 167, 329
　per capita tax load, 94
　property taxes, 164, 165, 167
　ratio of import taxes to total taxes, 244
　religiously appropriate taxes, 220, 221, 285,
　　287
　　ratio to total tax, 255, 324, 325
　royalties, 164, 165
　stamp duties, 165
　state enterprises, 164, 164, 166, 284
　taxation in, 163–167
　tax buoyancy, 207, 285, 287
　tax ratio, 202, 204, 206
　tax revenues, 90
　total revenues, 163, 164

Tawhid, 67
Taxation, *see also under types*
　as policy instruments, 6
　categorical grouping of, 337
　economic study of, 181–197
　full loss carry forward, 24
　function of, 14
　future problems, 297
　in kind, difficulties of collection, 188
　Islamic teaching, 60–83, 218, 235, 319
　importance of, 3
　on natural resources in Islam, 66
　Quran on, 5
　types of, 9–13
Tax buoyancy, 207, 321
　oil and non-oil, 208, 209
Tax burden, progressive and regressive •
　　aspects, 214
Tax capacity, 320
　differences in, 194
Tax collection, 218
　difficulties, 188
Tax evasion, of VAT, 53
Tax holidays, 25, 26
Tax load, per capita, 94
Tax policy performances, 201–225, 226, 321
　general considerations, 201
　income distribution and, 210
　mobilizing resources of society, 201
　progressive and regressive aspects of tax
　　burden, 214
Tax ratio, 181, 201, 202
　agriculture and, 184
　Chelliah model, 183 *et seq.*
　　compared with revised model, 191
　Chow test, 191
　developing countries, 204
　development and, 182, 183, 184, 188, 190
　exports and, 186, 189

Tax ratio, (*cont.*)
　import ratio and, 182, 189
　in developing countries, 187
　industrialized countries, 206
　mineral production and, 184, 187, 188,
　　190, 191, 192, 194
　per capita income and, 182, 184, 188
　revised models, 189 *et seq.*,195
　　compared with Chelliah model, 191
　specific countries, 202
　usefulness of, 206
Tax relief, foreign owned corporations and, 26
Tax revenues,
　oil depletion and, 308–314
　relation to GNP, *see under Tax ratio*
Tax systems, regressive and progressive, 322
Tithes, 5, 64, 71
Tobacco, taxes on, 46, 48
Towns, population of, 217
Trade surpluses, of oil exporting countries, 58
Trans-Arabian Pipeline, 150, 152
Trucial Coast, 174.
Turnover tax, 51

Umm al-Quwain, 258
　revenues, 135
United Arab Emirates, 134–140, 214
　assessment of tax performance, 258–263
　consumer taxes, 224, 258
　　ratio to total revenue, 223
　customs duties, 136, 138
　direct and indirect taxes, 93
　domestically-generated tax revenues, 268
　domestic oil consumption, 311, 312
　exchange rates, 335
　federal budget allocations, 260
　GNP, 258
　government receipts, 91
　government revenues, 259, 261
　growth of oil and non-oil tax, 298
　imports, 260
　import duties, 261
　　ratio to total taxes, 244
　income taxes, 135
　　as percentage of national income, 216
　　ratio to total tax, 215
　national income per capita, 261
　oil production, 88, 89, 134, 136, 140, 258,
　　262
　　future, 310
　oil reserves, 245, 309, 310
　oil revenues, 258
　　relative to total revenue, 94, 209
　overseas investments, 139, 140, 299
　　budget expenditure and, 306
　　non-oil revenue and, 308
　　per citizen return, 300, 301, 302, 304, 307
　per capita tax load, 94
　postage stamps, 138

United Arab Emirates, *(cont.)*
  religiously appropriate taxes, 220, 221, 258
    ratio to total tax, 255, 324, 325
  tax buoyancy, 207, 208
  tax ratio, 202
United Arab Republic, 165
Urban land tax, 31
User taxes, 54–55
'Ushr, 5, 64, 71, 74, 77, 220, 229, 282
  in Sudan, 161, 162

Value added taxes, 51–53, 216
  administration of, 52
  enforcement of, 53
  evasion of, 53

Wealth,
  distribution of,
    death duties and, 34
    Islam and, 71
Wealth taxes, 27, 34, 35
  applied to corporations, 35
  zakat as, 61
Welfare state, 3

Yemen, *see Yemen Arab Republic and*
  Yemen, Peoples Democratic Republic
Yemen Arab Republic, 281
  agriculture, 290
  assessment of tax performance, 289
  business profits tax, 171, 172, 218
  composition of exports, 278
  consumer related taxes, 224, 290
    ratio to total revenue, 223
  customs duties, 168, 169
  direct and indirect taxes, 93, 168, 169, 170,
    290, 291
  domestically generated tax revenues, 268
  exchange rates, 335
  excise taxes, 168, 169, 170, 291
  foreign aid, 171
  GDP by industrial origin, 269
  GNP, 168, 290
  government receipts, 91
  import duties, 168, 170, 289, 291
    ratio to total taxes, 244
  income taxes, 169, 170, 171, 172
    ratio to total tax, 215
  official development assistance, 274
  per capita tax load, 94
  price indices, 239
  religiously appropriate taxes, 79, 220, 224,
    289, 290
    ratio to total tax, 255, 324, 325

Yemen Arab Republic, *(cont.)*
  remittance boom, 289
  tax avoidance in, 172
  tax buoyancy, 207
  tax ratio, 202, 204, 291
  tax revenues, 169
  taxation, 168–172
  zakat in, 80, 170, 171, 219, 289
Yemen, People's Democratic Republic, 58,
  281, 322
  agriculture in, 176
  assessment of tax performance, 291–295
  business profits tax, 218, 294
  consumer related taxes, 224, 292
    ratio to total revenue, 223
  customs duties, 173, 222, 294
  direct and indirect taxes, 93, 173
  domestically generated tax revenues, 268
  Encouragement of Investment Law, 175
  exchange rates, 335
  excise, sales, and production taxes, 173,
    175, 222, 294
  GNP, 292, 293
  government receipts, 91
  income tax, 173, 175, 176, 294
    ratio to total tax, 215
  inflation in, 172
  official development assistance, 274
  per capita tax load, 94
  price indices, 239
  property taxes, 173
  ratio of import taxes to total taxes, 244
  religiously appropriate taxes, 220, 221, 292
    ratio to total tax, 255, 324, 325
  remittance boom, 293, 294
  state enterprises, 173
  taxation in, 172–176
  tax buoyancy, 207
  tax ratio, 202, 204, 293, 294
  tax revenues in, 173

Zakat, 5, 61, 67, 68, 71, 74, 75, 77, 79, 80,
  201, 219, 323
  collection of, 62, 79, 220
  composition of in Yemen, 171
  in Bahrain, 229
  in Libya, 120, 248
  in Saudi Arabia, 131, 132, 219, 255, 256
  in Sudan, 161, 162, 219, 282
  in Yemen, 170, 219, 289
  levies, 63
  on livestock, 63, 64